JOURNAL FOR THE STUDY OF THE NEW TESTAMENT
SUPPLEMENT SERIES
82

Executive Editor
Stanley E. Porter

JSOT Press
Sheffield

Oral Tradition and the Gospels

The Problem of Mark 4

Barry W. Henaut

Journal for the Study of the New Testament
Supplement Series 82

IN MEMORY
Emile C. Henaut   and   D. Gordon M. Fraser
Jan. 1925–Sept. 1970   April 1934–Nov. 1984

Published by JSOT Press
JSOT Press is an imprint of
Sheffield Academic Press Ltd
343 Fulwood Road
Sheffield S10 3BP
England

Typeset by Sheffield Academic Press
and
Printed on acid-free paper in Great Britain
by Biddles Ltd
Guildford

British Library Cataloguing in Publication Data

Henaut, Barry W.
    Oral Tradition and the Gospels: Problem of
    Mark 4. — (JSNT Supplement Series,
    ISSN 0143-5108; No. 82)
    I. Title II. Series
    226.3

ISBN 1-85075-407-1

CONTENTS

Contents

PREFACE

This book is a revised edition of my doctoral dissertation which was accepted at the University of Toronto in September of 1991. First of all, I wish to express my gratitude to Miss Muna Salloum, formerly the Administrative Assistant of the Centre for Religious Studies, who was of invaluable assistance at numerous times as I charted my path through the myriad of regulations during my programme. I should also thank especially a number of the Centre's community—Michel, Willi, Jackie and Bill—for conversations over coffee, encouragement and friendship during my studies. Their own insights into early Christianity have added significantly to my knowledge.

Secondly, I am particularly fortunate in the advice, encouragement and collective wisdom that I have received from my supervision committee. My association with my supervisor, Professor Heinz O. Guenther, goes back to when I was a first-year MDiv student at Emmanuel College in the fall of 1980. I am extremely grateful for his guidance and support during the current project. Similarly, Professors Peter Richardson and Donald Wiebe have also generously given of their time and made a valuable contribution to the project. I am also extremely grateful for the efforts of Professor David Hill—and all the staff of Sheffield Academic Press—for their work in speedily bringing about this published edition. Thank you one and all.

I should also thank a number of members of the wider 'Mac community'—Professor M.J. Connoly of Boston College was kind enough to forward to me a number of fonts for my computer, as was Jay Treat of the Center for Computer Analysis of Text. Steven C. Muir, of the University of Ottawa, was also kind enough to help with the final proof reading.

My brother and mother deserve particular mention for their heroic endurance during the two years I was busy with the writing and editing. Without their support I doubt that the project could have been completed. I should also mention P.B., Esq., who often kept me company during the otherwise thankless task of writing.

And finally, to Beverley—without whose love and support this project would not have been possible—I owe a special debt of love and gratitude.

ABBREVIATIONS

ALS	*African Language Studies*
ANRW	*Aufstieg und Niedergang der römischen Welt*
BBB	Bonner biblische Beiträge
BETL	Bibliotheca ephemeridum theologicarum lovaniensium
Bib	*Biblica*
BJRL	*Bulletin of the John Rylands University Library of Manchester*
BSO(A)S	*Bulletin of the School of Oriental (and African) Studies*
BTB	*Biblical Theology Bulletin*
BZ	*Biblische Zeitschrift*
BZNW	Beihefte zur *ZNW*
CBQ	*Catholic Biblical Quarterly*
CBQMS	*CBQ*, Monograph Series
ESA	*English Studies in Africa*
ETL	*Ephemerides theologicae lovanienses*
ExpTim	*Expository Times*
HibJ	*Hibbert Journal*
HSCP	*Harvard Studies in Classical Philology*
HTKNT	Herders theologischer Kommentar zum Neuen Testament
HTR	*Harvard Theological Review*
Int	*Interpretation*
JAAR	*Journal of the American Academy of Religion*
JAF	*Journal of American Folklore*
JBL	*Journal of Biblical Literature*
JR	*Journal of Religion*
JRC	*Journal of Religion and Culture*
JSNT	*Journal for the Study of the New Testament*
JSNTSup	*JSNT* Supplement Series
JSOT	*Journal for the Study of the Old Testament*
JSOTSup	*JSOT* Supplement Series
JTS	*Journal of Theological Studies*
NTAbh	Neutestamentliche Abhandlungen
NovT	*Novum Testamentum*
NTS	*New Testament Studies*
PMLA	*Publications of the Modern Language Association*
RB	*Revue biblique*
RST	*Religious Studies and Theology*

SBL	Society of Biblical Literature
SBLDS	SBL Dissertation Series
SBLMS	SBL Monograph Series
SBLSP	SBL Seminar Papers
SBS	Stuttgarter Bibelstudien
SE	*Studia Evangelica* – I, II, III
SJT	*Scottish Journal of Theology*
SNTSMS	Society for New Testament Studies Monograph Series
SR	*Studies in Religion/Sciences Religieuses*
ST	*Studia theologica*
SUNT	Studien zur Umwelt des Neuen Testaments
TAPA	Transactions of the American Philological Association
TJT	*Toronto Journal of Theology*
TU	Texte und Untersuchungen
TZ	*Theologische Zeitschrift*
ZNW	*Zeitschrift für neutestamentliche Wissenschaft*
ZTK	*Zeitschrift für Theologie und Kirche*

INTRODUCTION: THE PROBLEM OF ORAL TRADITION

[A]mong the host of Commandments Jesus singled out two as supreme, Love of God *and of our neighbour*. This pairing of the two ordinances in absolute priority over all other injunctions occurs elsewhere in Jewish thought after the [Hebrew Bible] and may not, therefore, be Jesus' original invention. But the stress he laid on it was unprecedentedly vivid.[1]

What could be more Christ-like than the Golden Rule? The forcefulness of this aphorism, particularly in the Sermon on the Mount, for many captures the essence of Jesus. Michael Grant seems to be engaged, not so much in the historian's craft, but rather in stating the obvious.

But times change. A dozen years later the Jesus Seminar would overwhelmingly deem the Golden Rule an inauthentic saying. In light of the extensive literary parallels from Hinduism, Buddhism, Confucianism, Zoroastrianism and Judaism there is no way of 'knowing' whether Jesus ever uttered this aphorism. The early Christian community had access to a variety of sources for this sentiment and may have ascribed it to Jesus at any time prior to the Gospels. What initially looked self-evident now becomes a victim of what Van A. Harvey calls the morality of historical knowledge.[2] Grant's presentation has become a self-fulfilling prophecy. The vivid presentation of Jesus in the Gospel narrative, which Grant recognizes to be a secondary composition, nevertheless has formed the basis of his reconstruction. Grant has filtered the Gospels through the hermeneutics of C.H. Dodd and J. Jeremias, a method that is now outdated.

This is not simply the problem of the Golden Rule, but a paradigm for the problem of oral tradition. Even allowing that the Golden Rule

1. M. Grant, *Jesus: An Historian's Review of the Gospels* (New York: Charles Scribner's Sons, 1977), p. 27.
2. V.A. Harvey, *The Historian and the Believer: The Morality of Historical Knowledge and Christian Belief* (Philadelphia: Westminster Press, 1966).

was taken over by Jesus, what would this tell us about his teaching? We encounter this saying in Tobit, Isocrates (c. 436–338 BCE), Aristotle (384–322 BCE), Epictetus (1st–2nd century), Thomas Hobbes (1588–1679), Benedict de Spinoza (1632–77), John Locke (1632–1704), Immanuel Kant (1724–1804) and John Stuart Mill (1806–73). What distinctive meaning did Jesus give this proverb, and what does it tell us about him given the vast differences among all those who endorsed this belief? Was Jesus more like a first-century Aristotle, Immanuel Kant or John Stuart Mill?[1]

It is even difficult to find two forms of this saying that are in word-for-word agreement. This is particularly startling given the long history of literary transmission and the place within the Western world of the Gospels. When has 'oral transmission' ceased as the cause for these variations and when have conscious literary motives taken over? Scholars would be hard pressed to come up with a standard measure that could distinguish the verbal differences that result from oral variants and literary redaction.

This study seeks to establish that the oral phase is now lost, hidden behind a series of Gospel texts and pre-Gospel sources that are full-fledged textuality—a textuality that does not intend to preserve an accurate account of the oral tradition but rather to convey a theological response to a new sociological situation. The oral phase is lost because after we employ form and redaction criticism we are left with a tradition that still bears the stamp of the post-resurrectional church and which cannot be traced back through its prior oral transmission. This phase of transmission is murky at best because we lack the critical tools to infer more than the most basic facts of relative dating regarding the material. Orality has too often been assumed to lie behind the observable differences among various traditions, whether between Mark and Q, or the synoptics and Thomas. Closer inspection will reveal that it is impossible to exclude some kind of literary relationship among these various strands of tradition despite the fact

1. Compare: 'Hurt not others in ways that you yourself would find hurtful' (*Udana-Varga*: 5, 18); 'Whatsoever you require that others should do to you, that do ye to them' (T. Hobbes: *Leviathan*, I); 'To do as one would be done by, and to love one's neighbor as one's self, constitute the ideal perfection of utilitarian morality' (John Stuart Mill: *Utilitarianism*). See the extensive list in F.S. Mead (ed.), *The Encyclopedia of Religious Quotations* (Old Tappan, NJ: Fleming H. Revell, 1965), pp. 286-90.

that most scholars believe them to be independent. This literary relationship serves as a barrier to the oral phase—a phase lost to us because, even assuming a prior oral history for a unit, the very communal, anonymous and changeable nature of this medium makes it impossible to trace a tradition's history through this transmission. Without this traceability it is impossible to ascribe any saying to any particular individual, including Jesus. This study will show that ascribing any saying to Jesus is exactly like ascribing to him the Golden Rule. Such reconstructions arise more from the assumptions of the exegete and an uncritical adoption of the post-resurrectional Gospel narratives than from an informed knowledge of the oral medium.

1. *The Universality of Oral Tradition*

Since the four canonical Gospels were written between 35 and 70 years after the crucifixion, one must have some theory of 'oral tradition' to write a history of Jesus. That an extensive oral tradition existed behind the Gospels has been taken for granted. Various factors account for this assumption. First there is the importance of oral speech in everyday life. In conversation we are asked about a mutual friend and we pass along a summary of our last meeting with her. Our retelling of her words amounts to a modern oral tradition. If this is true for our world, why should it have been different for the early Christian communities?

Secondly, there is the extensive oral heritage in which we all share: fairy tales, proverbs and other communal wisdom. The universal existence of orally transmitted folklore, available in such collections as the Brothers Grimm, assures us that every society has an oral heritage. All of us also participate in the communal wisdom of proverbs: 'A stitch in time saves nine'; 'Look before you leap'. Aphorisms—short pithy sayings attributed to a specific speaker—are also well known. 'We have nothing to fear but fear itself'; 'I have nothing to offer but blood, toil, tears and sweat'. Our own 'oral memories' make an extensive oral tradition behind the Gospels seem not only plausible, but indisputable.

2. *Oral Tradition as an Apologetic*

The early Christian sources encourage the assumption. Particularly significant is 1 Cor. 15.3, 'For I handed on to you as of first importance what I in turn had received. . . '[1] Paul presents himself as a link in a chain, and assures his readers of the received tradition's fidelity. This motif of reassurance can become apologetical, linked to such concepts as 'authority', 'fidelity' and 'authenticity'. Such apologetical appeals are implicit in Mark's account of Jesus' habitual teaching practice. At the conclusion to his parable chapter, Mark states, 'With many such parables he spoke the word to them, as they were able to hear it; he did not speak to them except in parables, but he explained everything in private to his disciples' (Mk 4.33-34). This theme of public discourse followed by private instruction is reinforced throughout the Gospel, (cp. 7.14-23; 8.14-21 and ch. 13). Mark's theory of oral tradition involves public discourse in parables in order to mislead the crowds, with private instruction for the disciples, to whom alone is given 'the secret of the reign of God'. This private instruction entrusted to the disciples is presumably the source of Mark's own Gospel. It is a theory of unbroken tradition with but one mediator: Jesus, the disciples, and then Mark. Its view of oral tradition is straightforward: a process of heard—remembered—written. Given the author's own historical proximity to Jesus and his apocalyptic eschatology, it is a thesis that could be readily accepted at face value in its own day.

Luke also has an 'oral tradition' apologetic to reassure his reader of the truthfulness of his account. Luke could not present himself as an eyewitness; instead, his prologue offers the reader reassurance that the tradition has been handed down and delivered 'to us' by 'those who from the beginning were eyewitnesses and servants of the word' (Lk. 1.2). Again the chain of tradition may be summarized in a fashion similar to Mark's, with the addition of but one link: eyewitnesses heard—remembered—delivered—written.[2]

By the second century, we find further links in the chain, and even greater reassurances of fidelity. In a well-known passage, Eusebius

---

1. Translation from the *New Revised Standard Version* (Nashville: Thomas Nelson, 1989).
2. Compare Jn 21.24 on the beloved disciple.

quotes Papias showing that the latter had 'learnt the essentials of the faith' from the pupils of the apostles.[1] There is in this view of tradition the acknowledgement of being removed from Jesus' day by more than one generation, with the apostles, the presbyters, their followers and now Papias in a chain of oral tradition. Here the chain of tradition may be summarized as 1) eyewitnesses heard— remembered—reported—2) presbyters heard—remembered— reported—3) followers heard—remembered—reported—4) Papias heard—remembered—wrote.[2]

The apologetical functions of these reconstructions of 'oral tradition' are clear. The view of an unbroken chain of tradition from the earliest eyewitnesses to the current community guarantees the fidelity of the church's teaching and buttresses the current leadership's authority. Although no longer tenable, this apologetic has had an influence in establishing models of oral tradition.[3] This can be seen by a survey of the early modern understanding of orality.

3. *Early Modern Scholarship and Orality*

With the modern conviction that the Gospels are not eyewitness accounts an understanding of oral tradition became imperative. It was G.E. Lessing's theory (first published in 1784) that the first Gospel was based on apostolic oral tradition and written in Aramaic. This Gospel, now lost, was known variously as the Gospel of the Hebrews or Gospel of the Nazarenes, and served as the source for the various canonical 'translations'. As W.R. Farmer comments, here is the idea that 'the original Gospel was modified during the eye-witness period, which justifies the notion that our canonical Evangelists could all have faithfully reproduced apostolic models. Here is bold interpretation of

1. See Eusebius, *The History of the Church from Christ to Constantine* (trans. G.A. Williamson; Harmondsworth: Penguin, 1965), III, 39, p. 150.

2. Seemingly in contradiction to this emphasis upon the 'living' oral tradition, Papias also maintains the thesis of apostolic origin of the gospels. See Eusebius, *History of the Church*, III, 24; II, 15.

3. Throughout this study I will often be using the term 'orality' in its broadest application: simply to refer to material that has been passed through the oral medium or by 'word of mouth'. I am not necessarily implying a variety of other factors and implications that some theorists ascribe to a predominantly oral/aural milieu prevalent in so-called 'primitive' pre-literate societies.

the Papias testimony. Here is the idea of an Aramaic original'.[1] Since oral variants are normal, verbal differences among the synoptics are evidence of independence. Furthermore, even the most accurate translations will show considerable variation. Lessing's thesis allows for an accurate transmission and translation of the oral tradition and provides a ready explanation for the variations among the synoptic evangelists.

Late in the eighteenth century Johann G. Herder advanced another theory of an oral Gospel. Starting with Peter's preaching in Acts 1.22, Herder theorized that the earliest tradition was structured into an Aramaic oral gospel between 35 and 40 CE. This narrative started with the preaching of John the Baptist and ended with the ascension of Jesus—in similar fashion as Mark's narrative and the summaries in Acts. This Gospel was transmitted orally and then committed into writing by the 'ministers of the word' as mentioned in Lk. 1.2. Mark published this Gospel in Greek, while the Aramaic version was modified and published variously as the Gospel of the Nazarenes and Matthew. The oral tradition in this view in effect, as Farmer notes, is passed on directly from the eyewitnesses to the evangelists.[2] Herder's theory was later incorporated into the work of the historian Gieseler who, in order to explain the agreements among the canonical Gospels in exact wording, advanced the thesis of a complete oral Gospel and its translation into Greek. This thesis was characterized by Bernhard Weiss as 'a supposition which is contradicted by every natural view of the limits within which oral tradition, as regards form or contents, establishes itself'.[3]

The reconstructions of Lessing, Herder and Gieseler may seem quaint in light of the two-source theory. But an examination of the synoptic problem has much to recommend itself for our understanding of oral tradition. For orality and textuality are but two aspects of the same problem. Determining whether the relationship

---

1. W.R. Farmer, *The Synoptic Problem: A Critical Analysis* (New York: Macmillan; London: Colier–Macmillan, 1964), p. 5. See page 4 for summary of Lessing's theory, first published in 1784. Lessing's essay is included in an English translation by H. Chadwick in *Lessing's Theological Writings* (Stanford, 1957).

2. See Farmer, *Synoptic Problem*, pp. 30–32. See J.G. Herder, *Christliche Schriften*, III (Riga, 1797).

3. B. Weiss, *The Life of Christ* (trans. J.W. Hope; Edinburgh: T. & T. Clark, 1883), I, p. 27.

among traditions is a literary or an oral one essentially involves a close examination of the agreements of vocabulary, syntax and order. This is true whether we are examining a passage found in the 'triple tradition' of Matthew, Mark and Luke; the 'double tradition' of Matthew and Luke; or such multiply-attested sayings as are to be found in a number of Mark, Q, 'M', 'L', and the *Gospel of Thomas*. How close must the verbal agreements be to ensure a literary relationship; how great a degree of divergence can be accepted within a literary context; and how great a degree of difference is necessary to ensure independence?

4. *The Synoptic Problem as a Basis for a Model of Orality*

The synoptic problem has a great deal to offer modern-day critics in the development of a model for 'oral tradition'. In particular, the methodological considerations which have proven decisive in eliminating any thesis of a complete 'oral gospel' and which have established the certainty of a literary relationship among the synoptic evangelists need to be borne in mind.

a. *Translation*

One of the first considerations in evaluating claims of independent oral traditions must be that of translation. This is based upon the assumption that the original language of Jesus was Aramaic. Since the Gospels are written in Greek any tradition that goes back to this earliest oral phase would be presumed to have originated in Aramaic and undergone translation. Variations between two written Greek versions of a tradition could, in this view, be accounted for on the basis of independent translations. Translation, furthermore, could have occurred at any number of points in the transmission process, up to and including the evangelists.

But assuming translation variations in wording in the secondary language are no guarantee of literary independence. Translation is often complex and there is rarely only one 'accurate' translation. Moreover, translation style varies in the degree of 'literalness' or 'idiom for idiom'. This phenomenon is no less true of ancient translators than of their modern counterparts. Modern translations of Mark illustrate this well, and this despite the place of the Authorized text among translations. Compare the following two versions of Mk 4.21-23:[1]

Mk 4.21-23

NRSV	NIV
He said to them, 'Is a *lamp brought* in to be *put under* the *bed,* and not on the lamp*stand*? *For* there is nothing *hidden,* except *to be disclosed*; nor *is* anything secret, except to come to light. Let *anyone* with *ears to hear* listen!'	*He said to them,* 'Do you *bring* in a *lamp* to *put* it *under* a bowl or a *bed*? Instead, don't you put it on its *stand*? *For* whatever is *hidden* is meant *to be disclosed,* and whatever *is* concealed is meant to be brought out into the open. If *anyone* has *ears to hear,* let him hear!'

Translation has clear implications for our understanding of orality. At a certain point, extensive agreements in wording make a thesis of independent translation impossible. On the other hand, extensive disagreement in translations need not rule out a direct literary relationship. The above translation variations of the same underlying Greek text demonstrate the care that must be taken before assuming that verbal variations result from independence of oral transmission. This, of course, assumes that the original language of Jesus was Aramaic. But, as Howard Clark Kee points out, there is 'mounting evidence that Jews in Galilee in the first and second centuries CE were bilingual'.[2] This question may be left open; rather we need only be aware of the problem of invoking the explanation of 'translation variants' to account for variations between written traditions.

b. *Direct Literary Dependence*
There are at least two ways in which texts can share a literary relationship. One text can be directly dependent upon another, in a

---

1. This principle can equally be seen in translations of Homer. Compare, for example, passages in W.J. Miller (trans.), *Homer: the Odyssey* (New York: Simon & Schuster, 1969), and E.V. Rieu, (trans.) *Homer: The Odyssey* (Harmondsworth: Penguin, 1946).

2. H.C. Kee, *Good News to the Ends of the Earth* (London: SCM Press; Philadelphia: Trinity, 1990), p. 44. In note 2, page 112 he points to E. Meyers and J. Strange, *Archaeology, the Rabbis and Early Christianity* (Nashville: Abingdon Press; London: SCM Press, 1981), pp. 81-87. Meyers and Strange note that Bar Kochba at one point departs from his usual practice of writing his associates in Aramaic because he is in a hurry and wants to ensure that he is fully understood.

'parent-child' relationship. Matthew and Luke share this relationship to Mark. Direct copying can often lead to extensive agreements, as seen at the Healing of the Leper (Mk 1.44 and Mt. 8.4):

Mt. 8.4	Mk 1.44
καὶ λέγει αὐτῷ ὁ Ἰμσοῦς,	καὶ λέγει αὐτῷ, Ὅρα μηδενὶ
Ὅρα μηδενὶ εἴπης, ἀλλὰ ὕπαγε	εἴπης, ἀλλὰ ὕπαγε σεαυτὸν
σεαυτὸν δεῖξον τῷ ἱερεῖ, καὶ	δεῖξον τῷ ἱερεῖ καὶ προσένεγκε
προσένεγκον τὸ δῶρον	περὶ τοῦ καθαρισμοῦ σου ἃ
ὃ προσέταξεν Μωϋσῆς, εἰς	προσέταξεν Μωϋσῆς, εἰς
μαρτύριον αὐτοῖς.	μαρτύριον αὐτοῖς.

But Matthew and Luke's use of their Markan source should remind us that texts that share a literary relationship are not copied slavishly. The source, for a variety of reasons, is often changed. The modern habit of reading the Gospels in three parallel columns discourages us from recognizing the extent of this redactional reworking of the text. When Mark is compared to both Matthew and Luke simultaneously we have in view the total agreements of both of the secondary texts with Mark. When one alone follows Mark's wording, our eyes follow the appropriate colour underline and we tell ourselves 'Oh, Luke has rewritten the Markan original while Matthew retains it'. A few words later and the opposite case is in view, and we are reassured of Luke's dependence upon Mark and his high estimation of it. As an illustration of this phenomenon I have chosen the infamous introduction to the Healings at Evening, Mk 1.32:

Mt. 8.16	Mk 1.32	Lk. 4.40
Ὀψίας δὲ γενομένης	Ὀψίας δὲ γενομένης	
	ὅτε ἔδυσεν ὁ ἥλιος	Δύνοντος δὲ τοῦ ἡλίου
προσήνεγκαν αὐτῷ	ἔφερον πρὸς αὐτὸν πάντες τούς κακῶς	ἅπαντες ὅσοι εἶχον ἀσθενοῦντας νόσοις ποικίλαις
δαιμονιζομένους πολλούς.	καὶ τοὺς δαιμονιζομένους.	ἤγαγον αὐτοὺς προς αὐτόν.

This reworking of the original occurs not only in the connecting frames, but also in the sayings. A comparison of the conclusion to Christ's Real Family in Mark and Luke reveals how much alteration can occur:

Mk 3.34b-35	Lk. 8.21
ἴδε ἡ <u>μήτηρ μου καὶ</u> οἱ <u>ἀδελφοί</u>	<u>μήτηρ μου καὶ ἀδελφοί μου</u>
<u>μου</u> ὅς ἄν <u>ποιήσῃ</u> τὸ θέλημα	
<u>τοῦ θεοῦ</u>, οὗτος ἀδελφός μου	οὗτοι εἰσιν οἱ τὸν λόγον <u>τοῦ θεοῦ</u>
καὶ ἀδελφὴ καὶ μήτηρ ἐστίν.	ἀκούοντες καὶ <u>ποιοῦντες</u>.

If we did not know from the extensive agreements elsewhere between these two Gospels that we are dealing with a literary relationship, would we postulate such a relationship between these versions of the saying? If, for example, we were dealing with a parallel between Mark and Q, or Luke and Thomas, would not similar verbal differences be seen as proof of the versions' independence?

Such a question becomes less absurd when we remember how 'oral tradition' has regularly been used to explain precisely these redactional changes of the source material. Sir John C. Hawkins is rightly credited with foundational work on the synoptic problem. In particular, his examination of the evidence regarding Mark's Gospel and the parallel traditions in Matthew and Luke still serves as a classic of methodological clarity in presenting the evidence for Markan priority.[1] Yet Hawkins presents a series of texts under the heading 'Words Differently Applied', examining 25 such instances where the same, or closely similar words, are used with different applications in parallel passages of the gospels. Among the examples he cites are Mk 4.19 (ἐπιθυμίαι εἰσπορευόμεναι συμπνίγουσιν τὸν λόγον) // Lk. 8.14 (οὗτοί... πορευόμενοι συμπνίγονται); and Mk 12.20 (οὐκ ἀφῆκεν σπέρμα) // Mt. 22.25 (μὴ ἔχων σπέρμα ἀφῆκεν τὴν γυναῖκα αὐτοῦ). Hawkins' conclusion is instructive:

> Such variant utilizations of the same or similar expressions in parallel passages may seem trifling when regarded separately, and some of them may be accidental; but on the whole, and when taken together with the more important instances on the preceding pages, they convey an impression of having arisen in the course of oral transmission, during which (as often happens) the sound of the words adhered to the speaker's mind more distinctly than the recollection of their original position and significance.[2]

1. J.C. Hawkins, *Horae Synopticae: Contributions to the Study of the Synoptic Problem* (Oxford: Clarendon Press, 2nd edn, 1909), pp. 114-53.
2. Hawkins, *Horae Synopticae*, 77. The texts are given at pp. 68-76. Hawkins applies a similar explanation to examples of transpositions of word order, pp. 77-80.

The hold of 'oral tradition' as an explanation for variations between written texts is so powerful that once planted in the critic's mind, even a scholar such as Hawkins (who is firmly persuaded of the overall literary dependence of Matthew and Luke upon Mark) can be found invoking it as an explanation! The methodological objection is clear: such a procedure undermines the known literary relationship among the texts. If oral tradition is admissible as an explanation in these instances then there is no stopping an infinite postulation of separate 'oral traditions' behind every variation in wording among the three synoptics.

A more recent example of this kind of explanation, albeit in a more sophisticated fashion, is found in J.D. Crossan. He makes the helpful distinction between 'performance' and 'hermeneutical' variations in a tradition. The former refer to synonymous variations in the syntactical formulation of a saying that do not alter the essential meaning of the 'aphoristic core'. It is the difference between 'Ask and you will receive' and 'Whoever asks, receives'. The latter refer to those variations that give an interpretive change to the saying. It is the difference between 'Ask and you will receive immediately' and 'Ask and you will receive eventually'. Crossan argues that:

> Matthew and Luke, looking at a specific aphoristic saying in Mark or in Q might well display oral sensibility and formulate it differently, not only because of theological or grammatical or stylistic reasons, but simply because of residual orality, residual reluctance to be bound finally and irrevocably to one ultimate formulation.[1]

This, of course, might hypothetically be the case. But how can we know in specific instances that this has in fact been the motivating factor behind the change? Crossan can offer few guidelines. Methodologically, such an explanation should only be invoked when all other avenues of approach (in terms of redactional preference) have been tried and failed.

c. *Dependence upon a Common Literary Source*
Secondly, texts can share a common source, and hence be related as siblings to a parent. In the two-source theory Matthew and Luke share this kind of relationship to Q. This kind of textual relationship in a

---

1. J.D. Crossan, *In Fragments: the Aphorisms of Jesus* (San Francisco: Harper & Row, 1983), p. 40. Discussion, pp. 40-41.

sense doubles the possibilities for variation between the two versions. At any point, either or both of the authors might change the original, resulting in a textual disagreement. Nevertheless, extensive agreements even in this kind of relationship are possible, as is known from the famous example at the preaching of John the Baptist (Mt. 3.7-10 // Lk. 3.7-10). Changes do occur, however, and at times the agreement in these so-called 'double tradition' texts is not nearly so extensive. The debate earlier in this century whether or not Q represented a written document or a stream of 'oral tradition' in part revolved around many of these parallel texts that demonstrate greater disagreement. The introduction to the parable of the Great Banquet/Marriage Feast will serve as an illustration of this principle:

Mt. 22.2-3	Lk. 14.16-18
ὡμοιώθη ἡ βασιλεία τῶν	ἄνθρωπός τις ἐποίει δεῖπον μέγα,
οὐρανῶν ἀνθρώπῳ βασιλεῖ,	καὶ ἐκάλεσεν πολλούς,
ὅστις ἐποίησεν γάμους τῷ υἱῷ	καὶ ἀπέστειλεν τὸν δοῦλον
αὐτοῦ. καὶ ἀπέστειλεν τοὺς	αὐτοῦ τῇ ὥρᾳ τοῦ δείπνου εἰπεῖν
δούλους αὐτοῦ καλέσαι τοὺς	τοῖς κεκλημένοις· ἔρχεσθε, ὅτι
κεκλημένους εἰς τοὺς γάμους,	ἤδη ἕτοιμά ἐστιν. καὶ ἤρξαντο
καὶ οὐκ ἤθελον ἐλθεῖν.	ἀπὸ μιᾶς πάντες παραιτεῖσθαι.

Matthew and Luke, likewise, share this same textual relationship in the 'triple tradition' where Mark is their source. We are in the habit of reading Matthew and Luke together with their source in such instances. The 'correct answer' of the underlying original text is immediately obvious. A more useful exercise would be to compare Matthew and Luke directly. As an example, I have chosen the sayings on the Bridegroom, Cloth and Wine:

Mt. 9.15-17	Lk. 5.34-39
καὶ <u>εἶπεν</u> αὐτοῖς <u>ὁ Ἰησοῦς.</u>	<u>ὁ δὲ Ἰησοῦς εἶπεν</u> πρὸς αὐτούς,
<u>Μὴ δύνανται</u> οἱ υἱοὶ <u>τοῦ</u>	<u>Μὴ δύνασθε</u> τοὺς υἱοὺς <u>τοῦ</u>
<u>νυμφῶνος</u> πενθεῖν ἐφ᾽ ὅσον <u>μετ᾽</u>	<u>νυμφῶνος</u> ἐν ᾧ <u>ὁ νυμφίος μετ᾽</u>
<u>αὐτῶν ἐστιν ὁ νυμφίος;</u>	<u>αὐτῶν ἐστιν</u> ποιῆσαι νηστεῦσαι;
<u>ἐλεύσονται δὲ ἡμέραι ὅταν</u>	<u>ἐλεύσονται δὲ ἡμέραι,</u> καὶ <u>ὅταν</u>
<u>ἀπαρθῇ ἀπ᾽ αὐτῶν ὁ νυμφίος,</u>	<u>ἀπαρθῇ ἀπ᾽ αὐτῶν ὁ νυμφίος,</u>
καὶ <u>τότε νηστεύσουσιν.</u>	<u>τότε νηστεύσουσιν</u> ἐν ἐκείναις
	ταῖς ἡμέραις.

οὐδεὶς δὲ ἐπιβάλλει ἐπίβλημα
ῥάκους ἀγνάφου ἐπὶ ἱματίιῳ
παλαιῷ·
αἴρει γὰρ τὸ πλήρωμα αὐτοῦ
ἀπὸ τοῦ ἱματίου,
καὶ χεῖρον σχίσμα γίνεται.
οὐδὲ βάλλουσιν οἶνον νέον εἰς
ἀσκοὺς παλαιούς· εἰ δὲ μή γε,
ῥήγνυνται οἱ ἀσκοί, καὶ ὁ οἶνος
ἐκχεῖται
καὶ οἱ ἀσκοὶ ἀπόλλυνται· ἀλλὰ
βάλλουσιν οἶνον νέον εἰς
ἀσκοὺς καινούς,
καὶ ἀμφότεροι συντηροῦνται.

Ἔλεγεν δὲ καὶ παραβολὴν πρὸς
αὐτοὺς ὅτι Οὐδεὶς ἐπίβλημα ἀπὸ
ἱματίου καινοῦ σχίσας ἐπιβάλλει
ἐπὶ ἱμάτιον παλαιόν· εἰ δὲ μή γε,
καὶ τὸ καινὸν σχίσει καὶ τῷ
παλαιῷ οὐ συμφωνήσει τὸ
ἐπίβλημα τὸ ἀπὸ τοῦ καινοῦ.
καὶ οὐδεὶς βάλλει οἶνον νέον εἰς
ἀσκοὺς παλαιούς· εἰ δὲ μή γε,
ῥήξει ὁ οἶνος ὁ νέος τοὺς
ἀσκούς, καὶ αὐτὸς ἐκχυθήσεται
καὶ οἱ ἀσκοὶ ἀπολοῦνται· ἀλλὰ
οἶνον νέον εἰς ἀσκούς καινούς
βλητέον. καὶ οὐδεὶς πιὼν
παλαιὸν θέλει νέον· λέγει γάρ, Ὁ
παλαιὸς χρηστός ἐστιν.

The following statistics are based on the sayings material only (i.e., beginning with Μὴ δύνανται οἱ υἱοὶ νυμφῶνος·Μὴ δύνανασθε τοὺς υἱοὺς τοῦ νυμφῶνος):

Groom Cloth Wine Statistics

	Matthew	Luke
Total Number of Words	79	112
As Percentage of Other Gospel Text	70.5	141.8
Words in Exact Agreement	48	48
Percentage of Text in Exact Agreement	60.8	42.9
Words in Close Agreement	12	12
Percentage of Text in Close Agreement	15.2	10.7
Total Number of Words in Agreement	60	60
Percentage of Text with Agreements	76	53.6

Only slightly over 50 percent of Luke's text shows close agreement with the Matthean parallel. This text is by no means unusual in this regard. Others could be found where the degree of variations between these Gospels in triple tradition sayings is actually higher. I offer this example merely as a bench-mark. The degree of differences between two parallel traditions in the range of 25 to 50 percent needs not automatically preclude a literary relationship between the two texts. This point is particularly relevant when we come to consider the issue of the independence of such streams of tradition as Mark, Q and Thomas.

Despite such differences, literary dependence can be established between two (or more) documents on the basis of overall agreement of wording, syntax and order. 'Agreement in order' may also occur in word order or in the order of the various sayings or narratives.

5. *Purpose and Assumptions of the Present Study*

The present study seeks to re-evaluate our knowledge of 'oral tradition' in early Christian literature. The ability to infer from written Gospel texts an underlying 'oral' substratum, in particular, will be examined, as will the question of what factors are necessary to demonstrate literary independence between various versions of a saying. Since the oral phase can only be reconstructed from the written texts, direct evidence of this crucial period of pre-Gospel Christian history is lacking. The ability to trace back through this era and the ability to demonstrate a tradition history for various sayings and narratives will also be questioned. The issues of 'authenticity' and 'distinctiveness' as they relate to the historical Jesus will also be highlighted. One need not presume a single authentic saying in the oral tradition to demonstrate the historical significance of understanding this element of gospel origins. Nevertheless, much of the fascination with oral tradition and the scholarly quest for valid methods of recovering this material stems directly from a concern with establishing a core of authentic sayings from Jesus. The present study seeks to re-evaluate the success of such criteria as 'distinctiveness' and 'double attestation' as valid grounds for attributing sayings to the historical Jesus.

The two-source theory of Gospel origins will be my starting point. Q for me represents not simply the 'double tradition' but a written document composed originally in Greek. This document, along with Mark, helped form the basis of Matthew and Luke. I also presume some overlapping between Mark and Q (the 'doubly attested' sayings), but not Mark's direct knowledge of Q as such.

I begin with an examination of the understanding of 'oral tradition' in three representative scholars: R. Bultmann, B. Gerhardsson and W. Kelber. The concept of orality in each needs to be distinguished clearly, and the assumptions inherent in their studies need to be explored. Since Kelber in particular has pointed to the work of M. Parry and A.B. Lord for his model of oral tradition, I next will examine the contribution of folkloric studies for our understanding of oral tradition. Finally, I propose a complete examination of Mk 4.1-

34 to serve as the textual basis for my study. The use of textual, redaction and form criticism as they apply to this passage (and its various literary parallels) will demonstrate the ability (or inability) to reconstruct the previous 'oral history' of this text.

Chapter 1

ORAL TRADITION TAKEN FOR GRANTED

1. *The Beginnings of Form Criticism*

Form criticism originates with the Hebrew scripture scholar Hermann Gunkel, who argued that before J, E, D and P were written the individual stories circulated in oral form. In order to ascertain, therefore, the earliest history of these units they must be viewed individually and apart from their present context.[1] Gunkel believed that these units developed orally over a long period of time in the history of Israel. He classified these units based upon their purpose, using the forms ethnological, etymological, ceremonial and geneological legends.[2]

Gunkel also advanced a principle for separating layers of the tradition that we may term as 'narrative degeneration'. He believed that the art of storytelling degenerated over time, and hence that later additions would show greater care for the thought rather than the form of the story.[3] Even more significant for Gunkel are the omissions that occur in narratives—the tendency to remove objectionable features results in gaps in the narrative.[4]

Gunkel's study had a lasting influence. He shifted the focus from questions of sources to the pre-literary oral phase. Underlying his approach was the conviction that written traditions have oral

1. See E.V. McKnight, *What is Form Criticism?* (Guides to Biblical Scholarship; Philadelphia: Fortress Press, 1969), pp. 10-11.
2. McKnight, *Form Criticism*, p. 12.
3. See McKnight, *Form Criticism*, p. 13. As examples, Gunkel lists the note that Jacob bought a field in Shechem, Gen. 33.18-20 and that Deborah died and was buried at Bethel, Gen. 35.8.
4. McKnight, *Form Criticism*, p. 13. For a more detailed presentation of Gunkel see G.M. Tucker, *Form Criticism of the Old Testament* (Guides to Biblical Scholarship; Philadelphia: Fortress Press, 1971).

antecedents and that the process of writing terminates the oral process. Furthermore, his process of classification based on purpose was the key to form criticism's central insight. And finally, by noting such tendencies as the omission of objectionable features, Gunkel began the process of establishing criteria to develop a history of the oral period itself.

Karl Ludwig Schmidt applied this method to the Gospels for the first time in 1919. He concluded that the Markan framework was not traditional but the evangelist's creation. Hence the separate units had circulated individually in oral form. But Schmidt did not extend his study to an examination of the oral phase itself.[1] We thus have the birth of the fundamental assumption of form criticism: that the tradition consists of individual units joined together by the evangelists.[2]

It is in this context that R. Bultmann and M. Dibelius worked. Bultmann uses an analytic method: he begins with the text instead of the church (although he admits to a provisional picture of the early community and its history).[3] In contrast, Dibelius proceeded constructively: the history of the tradition is reconstructed from a study of the early Christian community.[4] I will focus primarily on Bultmann's view of oral tradition in the following discussion.

2. *R. Bultmann and Oral Tradition*

a. *The Connecting Geographic Links*
Bultmann agrees with Schmidt that the tradition originally comprised separate and brief units, with almost all the connecting references to time and place being redactional. Similarly to Gunkel, Bultmann

1. McKnight, *Form Criticism*, p. 14. K.L. Schmidt, *Der Rahmen der Geschichte Jesu: Literarkritische Untersuchungen zur ältesten Jesusüberlieferung* (Berlin: Trowitzsch & Sohn, 1919), p. v.
2. McKnight, *Form Criticism*, p. 18.
3. R. Bultmann, *History of the Synoptic Tradition* (trans. J. Marsh; New York: Harper & Row, 1963), p. 5; McKnight, *Form Criticism*, p. 19.
4. We will reconstruct Bultmann's view of orality primarily from: R. Bultmann, 'The Study of the Synoptic Gospels', in *Form Criticism: A New Method of New Testament Research* (ed. and trans. F.C. Grant; repr. New York: Harper, 1962 [New York: Willett, Clark & Company, 1934]), pp. 7-75; and *History of the Synoptic Tradition*. For M. Dibelius see *From Tradition to Gospel* (trans. B.L. Woolf; New York: Charles Scribner's Sons, 1935).

begins with two assumptions: first, that before the Gospels were written there was a period of oral tradition; and secondly, that during this oral phase the various traditions circulated as separate units.[1]

But Bultmann also believes that the evangelists relocated a number of the connecting references from their earlier traditional location. Hence he argues that Mark transferred the motive for Jesus' withdrawing into the boat away from the crowd from its original location at 4.1 to 3.9, 'where it stands in a totally unorganic relation'.[2] In this reconstruction Mk 3.9 is not the evangelist's motif; rather, the text is assumed to have had an earlier history in the tradition. This argument is based on the verse's presumed contextual incongruity and creates a view of oral tradition whereby individual verses may be pushed back into an earlier phase of transmission. The whole procedure rests on an assumption of incongruity in Mark's text which can only be solved by relocation. But this does not seriously explore the implications of Mark's motives behind this 'relocation'. The verse's present location shows that Mark needed it at 3.9—might not these same needs have motivated the redactional creation of the verse without any prior tradition?[3] Written traditions do not, necessarily, have oral predecessors.

b. *Fixed Forms and Unliterary Character*
For the form critics, both oral and written tradition are cast in fixed forms. In primitive literature, according to Bultmann, 'literary expression (oral or written) makes use of more or less fixed forms, which have their own laws of style'.[4] This argument has three assumptions. First, both written and oral literature are essentially a single category. Secondly, there is the emphasis on fixed forms (with the implication that literature originates in these 'pure forms'). Finally, there is the emphasis on 'laws of style'.

The first assumption forms an important bridge in the evidence. Because oral tradition leaves no direct evidence of its transmission,

1. See E.B. Redlich, *Form Criticism: Its Value and Limitations* (New York: Charles Scribner's Sons, 1939), pp. 34, 37.

2. Bultmann, 'Study', p. 27. Compare Bultmann's view of Mk. 9.36 ('Study', pp. 27-28).

3. Contrast Bultmann's treatment of Mk 4.10-13, this is the evangelist's insertion due to the incongruity with vv. 33-35. Bultmann, 'Study', p. 28.

4. Bultmann, 'Study', p. 28.

Bultmann proposes to work first with the written traditions and establish 'laws of transmission' which he will infer back into the oral phase. Hence, Bultmann can state that 'it is at this point a matter of indifference whether the tradition were oral or written, because on account of the unliterary character of the material one of the chief differences between oral and written traditions is lacking'.[1]

Bultmann's use of 'unliterary' assumes the essential compatibility of the oral and written media. Implicit is a view of the Gospels as 'unliterary' texts, where the evangelists are compilers rather than authors. Indeed, Bultmann remarks that in general Mark 'refrained from exercising major redactional influences on the transmitted material'.[2] Recent studies do not support these assumptions.[3] Further, as W. Kelber argues, we can no longer equate the hermeneutics of speaking with writing. Noting such theorists as A.B. Lord and W.J. Ong, Kelber states that contemporary 'theorists of orality appear virtually unanimous is emphasizing the linguistic integrity of the difference between spoken versus written words'.[4] Hence, the 'writing performance of Mark is subject to laws different from those that

1. Bultmann, 'Study', p. 28; *History*, p. 6.

2. See Bultmann, *History*, p. 332. Translation, W.H. Kelber, *The Oral and the Written Gospel: The Hermeneutics of Speaking and Writing in the Synoptic Tradition, Mark, Paul, and Q* (Philadelphia: Fortress Press, 1983), p. 5.

3. On Mark's redactional interests see: E. Best, 'Mark's Preservation of the Tradition', in *The Interpretation of Mark* (ed. W. Telford; Philadelphia: Fortress Press; London: SPCK, 1985), pp. 119-33; *idem, The Temptation and the Passion: The Marcan Soteriology* (SNTSMS, 2; Cambridge: Cambridge University Press, 1965); T.A. Burkill, 'Concerning St Mark's Conception of Secrecy', *HibJ* 55 (1956–57), pp. 150-58; *idem*, 'The Cryptology of Parables in St Mark's Gospel', *NovT* 1 (1956): pp. 246-62; *idem, Mysterious Revelation: An Examination of the Philosophy of St Mark's Gospel* (Ithaca, NY: Cornell University Press, 1963); *idem, New Light on the Earliest Gospel: Seven Markan Studies* (Ithaca, NY: Cornell University Press, 1972); W.H. Kelber, (ed.), *The Passion in Mark: Studies on Mark 14–16* (Philadelphia: Fortress Press, 1976); H.-D. Knigge, 'The Meaning of Mark', *Int* 22 (1968), pp. 53-70; W. Marxsen, *Mark the Evangelist: Studies on the Redaction History of the Gospel* (trans. J. Boyece *et al.*; Nashville: Abingdon Press, 1969); R.H. Stein, 'The Proper Methodology for ascertaining a Marcan Redaktionsgeschichte' (ThD dissertation, Princeton University, 1968).

4. Kelber, *Oral*, p. 14. Bultmann admitted the problem of different hermeneutics between oral literature and written texts but bridged the gap by viewing the material as essentially unliterary in nature.

regulate pre-Markan oral drives'.[1] Oral and written traditions thus
operate on different principles.

c. *Stability and Point of Origin*
Oral tradition is also a relatively stable medium for the form critics.
This belief, based on the use of the 'fixed forms', allows Bultmann to
state a bold principle:

> If this be the case, one must recognize and reckon with the fact that the
> tradition possesses a certain solidity, since the form would naturally
> oppose itself to any serious alterations. On the other hand, it will be
> possible to determine in the individual sections whether the appropriate
> form was purely expressed or somewhat revised, and so one should be
> able to determine the age of the section.[2]

This assumption of fundamental stability requires examination. Kelber
notes that a saying that does not speak to an audience's needs will die
out. This he calls 'preventive censorship' and he believes that this
principle has not been adequately taken into account by form
criticism's emphasis upon linear developmental growth. For Kelber,
although oral tradition is capable of growth, it is also susceptible to
abridgement. He points to studies by E.L. Abel, G. Allport and Leo
Postman and states that this 'selective retention of information' is a
datum 'derived from psychological studies of oral transmission'.[3]
Therefore, while a tradition's form or outline remains intact, fewer
words and fewer original details are preserved. Further, the
variations within the tradition do not simply entail expansion or
compression. Rather stock features are combined and interchanged,
the order is varied and shuffled, and motifs are adopted from other
materials.[4]

Form criticism also determines the point of origin for the unit in
the oral phase. Bultmann sees a link between the unit's form and its

1. W.H. Kelber, 'Mark and Oral Tradition', *Semeia* 16 (1979): p. 7. See below:
section 4 and Chapter 2.

2. Bultmann, 'Study', p. 29. Compare M. Dibelius, *Jesus* (trans. C.B. Hendrick
and F.C. Grant; Philadelphia: Westminster, 1949), p. 25.

3. Kelber, 'Mark', p. 31. Citing E.L. Abel, 'The Psychology of Memory and
Rumor Transmission and their Bearing on Theories of Oral Transmission in Early
Christianity', *JR* 51 (1971), pp. 270-81; G. Allport and L. Postman, *The
Psychology of Rumor* (New York: Henry Holt, 1947).

4. Kelber, *Oral*, pp. 30-31. Citing Abel, 'Psychology of Memory', p. 276.

relative age, since it is possible to recognize 'the laws by which the further development of material takes place, i.e. a certain orderliness in change by which a body of tradition is always controlled in its growth'.[1] In order to establish these 'laws of growth' Bultmann believes an examination of how Matthew and Luke deal with their Q and Markan traditions is beneficial. Hence, if we can observe in their editorial practice 'a certain regularity' we 'may certainly assume that the same laws held good even earlier, and we may draw conclusions as to the state of the tradition prior to Mark and Q'.[2] Here again we see Bultmann's principle that the exegete can argue from 'laws' of transmission in the written phase back into the oral transmission. There is also the unargued assumption that redactional techniques seen in Matthew and Luke need not be viewed as individual tendencies nor as written redactional actions: rather, Bultmann proposes to apply the same processes to the oral period.[3]

d. Sitz im Leben *and Orality*

Fundamental to Bultmann's method is the material's *Sitz im Leben*. The literature of any community takes its shape from specific situations out of which grow 'a quite definite style and quite specific forms and categories'. This *Sitz im Leben* is, however, not an individual historical event but rather a typical situation in the community's life. Thus, the literary category by which the material is classified is a sociological concept and not an aesthetic one.[4]

The first form Bultmann identifies is the gospel 'miracle story', noting that these Hellenistic narratives display a close resemblance to those of Lucian of Samosata.[5] A second form is the short narrative setting for a saying. He calls this the apophthegm since its structure is similar to the narratives of Greek literature of this name. This form is also found in Jewish literature, but here the hero's saying is often

---

1. Bultmann, 'Study', p. 29.

2. Bultmann, 'Study', p. 29.

3. See Bultmann, 'Study', p. 32. See Bultmann on the tendency towards greater explicitness (i.e., Lk. 9.38 // Mk 9.17; Lk. 6.6 // Mk 3.1).

4. Bultmann, *History*, p. 4. Compare Dibelius, *Tradition*, pp. 13-14.

5. See Bultmann, 'Study', pp. 36-39. Typical would be the healing of Peter's mother-in-law (Mk 1.29-31). Bultmann's description of the form of the miracle story represents a lasting contribution. Kelber's 'Heroic Tale' is essentially the same, *Oral*, p. 46.

given as a counter-question or as a brief parable.[1] Thus the rabbinic scholastic dialogues find their usual starting point in some particular occasion, for example in the confrontation that results when a pagan philosopher or an emperor attacks a Rabbi on account of some Jewish teaching. The sequence is question and counter-question.[2] The synoptic apophthegms that exhibit this structure (cp. Mk 2.19; 3.24-26) must have an early origin in the tradition. One 'may safely infer that these narratives have almost all been formulated in a Jewish environment and do not belong to the later Hellenistic period of development'.[3] In contrast, the Greek apophthegm is characteristically introduced by some such formula as 'When he was asked by' or 'Once when he observed how'.[4]

Here again we see a model of organic growth. We also see the assumption of material originating in 'pure' forms and degenerating over the transmission process.[5] The thesis of the *Sitz im Leben* encourages the exegete to identify all units in the same form with a similar social setting and point of origin. Thus a paradigm will be held to have originated relatively early in the material's transmission. Bultmann's underlying evolutionary assumption here is no longer tenable. For both forms, parallels that pre-date the synoptic Gospels are abundant in the literature of antiquity. Since both forms were available in the cultural heritage at all points of the oral phase, there is no reason to presume that the earliest church would turn exclusively to the pronouncement story in the origin of Jesus traditions. Nor is this assumption demonstrated by a study of folklore. E.P. Sanders has objected that Bultmann has not demonstrated a tendency in folklore to expand pure forms. 'For the most part, students of folklore do not emphasize the kind of laws of transmission about which Bultmann spoke'.[6] Even the literary phase of gospel transmission fails to prove

1. Bultmann, 'Study', pp. 39-41 with appropriate examples.

2. Bultmann, 'Study', p. 42.

3. Bultmann, 'Study', p. 41. Dibelius' 'paradigm' is the equivalent of Bultmann's apophthegm, while his 'tale' corresponds to Bultmann's 'miracle story'.

4. For example: 'As Diogenes once saw a child drinking out of its hands, he threw away the cup that he had in his wallet and said, "A child has exceeded me in doing without things"', Bultmann, 'Study', p. 42.

5. Similar to Bultmann's thesis that the material developed specificity over time is Dibelius' thesis that the tale owes its existence to the storyteller's artistry.

6. E.P. Sanders, *The Tendencies of the Synoptic Tradition* (SNTSMS, 9; Cambridge: Cambridge University Press, 1969), p. 18 n. 4.

Bultmann's assumption. If we examine Luke's redactional setting for the Banquet parable (14.15-24), and the Good Samaritan (10.29-37), it becomes clear that they are extended pronouncement stories. In each instance the parable comes as Jesus' pronouncement to a question from another actor in the drama. Hence, mere form does not guarantee an oral history.[1]

e. *Double Attestation and Orality*
Bultmann also deals with an especially significant category of sayings: those found in both Mark and Q. Since Bultmann does not postulate Mark's knowledge of Q, his reasoning in these instances is highly significant. We will examine his treatment of two sayings, the controversy over exorcism (Mk 3.22-30; Q 11.14-23) and the confession of faith in Jesus (Mk 8.38; Q 12.8-9).

Regarding the controversy over exorcism, Bultmann believes that the Q tradition may be more original. Basic is the accusation and the image of a divided house and kingdom (Mk 3.22b, 23b-25; Q 11.15-17), which is 'an answer in a form typical in Jewish debates'.[2] To this central core, Bultmann believes the originally unattached saying about plundering (Mk 3.27; Q 11.21-22) has been added. This addition, however, was made after two other originally unattached sayings had also been added (Q 11.19, 20). These sayings are not found in Mark. Thus in this reconstruction we have an early core saying, to which has been added two independently circulating sayings (found only in Q) and then a third. All of this presumably occurred during the oral transmission.[3] This reconstructs a highly active oral phase and encourages the belief that this phase of the tradition can be discovered with a good degree of certainty and detail.

Bultmann proceeds upon the assumption that each sentence amounts to an individual saying with its own prior history of transmission. If this be true, it is strange that none of them can be found in a different context in any of the early Christian sources. The 'added sayings' at Q 11.19, 20 are strangely absent from Mark. If they were added at the pre-literary oral phase, why were they omitted in Mark's form of the tradition? These verses need to be explored in the compositional history of Q, a document many scholars now believe went through a

1. See the critique by Stein, 'The Proper Methodology', p. 52.
2. Bultmann, *History*, p. 13.
3. Bultmann, *History*, pp. 13-14.

number of written editions.[1] These additions may, in fact, be Q's
written redaction. The material in agreement between Mark and Q
(i.e., Mk 3.22b, 23b-25, 26, 27 = Q 11.15-17, 18, 21-22) amounts to
an agreement in sequence of up to five items. Yet there is no logical
necessity for such an order in the material. If Mark and Q truly
inherited separate oral traditions, the agreement in the order of this
core material is remarkable! In other words, this unit's oral history
prior to Mark and Q is far more difficult to ascertain than Bultmann
acknowledges, and the core tradition in Mark and Q may actually
share a literary relationship.

For the saying Confession of Faith, Bultmann reconstructs as the
original 'Whosoever confesses Jesus (and his words), him also will the
Son of Man sometime confess'. He argues that Jesus clearly
distinguishes himself from the Son of Man (cp. Q 17.24, 26, noting
the third person). Since, in the Christian community, Jesus was known
to be the Son of Man, the older form of the saying was not retained.
Hence Matthew's alteration is understandable: 'Whosoever therefore
shall confess me before men, him will *I* confess'.[2] Bultmann's exegesis
is based on a comparison of two independent versions of the saying
(Mark and Q) and on christological considerations.[3]

Bultmann has again overstated his case in assigning this logion to
Jesus. The phrases ἐμοί and ὁ υἱὸς τοῦ ἀνθρώπου need not imply a
distinction of person—they are more likely in synonymous parallelism
with a change of wording. H. Conzelmann has argued for the post-
resurrectional origin of all the Son of Man sayings.[4] The confession of
Jesus is a prime theological concern of the church, as seen at 1 Cor.
12.3. It is difficult to understand 'Whoever confesses Jesus' rather
than 'confesses me' on the lips of Jesus. The inclusion of John the
Baptist's preaching, and the application of Mal. 3.1 to John in both Q

1. See J.S. Kloppenborg, *The Formation of Q: Trajectories in Ancient Wisdom
Collections: Studies in Antiquity and Christianity* (Philadelphia: Fortress Press,
1987), pp. 317-28. It is significant that Bultmann's treatment of these sayings seems
to assume that Q did not have a history of written editions. Hence, any evidence of
additions is pushed back into the oral phase.

2. Bultmann, 'Study', p. 51.

3. In other instances Bultmann argues for the secondary nature of sayings based
on literary form. Compare the treatment of the six antitheses in Mt. 5.21-48 (only 3
originally in this form), Bultmann, 'Study', pp. 51-52.

4. H. Conzelmann, *Jesus* (trans. J.R. Lord; Philadelphia: Fortress Press, 1973),
pp. 43-47.

and Mark, warns that sayings supported by double attestation can be post-resurrectional.

f. *Sayings Based on Hebrew Scriptures or Proverbs*
Bultmann is aware of the vast cultural heritage available to the church and the problem this raises for attributing such sayings to Jesus. He first identifies those sayings that employ an argumentation based on the Hebrew Scriptures. He suspects these sayings of originating in the post-resurrectional theological debates of the primitive community and places them in the early Aramaic phase of the oral period.[1] Yet the Pauline letters also tell of considerable debate regarding Torah in the Hellenistic churches, and Bultmann's assumption is unwarranted. Debate on Torah in early Christian communities cannot be assigned exclusively to the oral phase. These sayings are particularly significant because the Hebrew Bible or Septuagint would be available to the evangelists (or the authors of their written sources). Such material need not have an oral history.

The sayings of other teachers and wisdom figures have also been put on the lips of Jesus during the tradition's transmission. Particularly deserving of mention are proverbs; i.e., words of wisdom which circulated in ancient Israel and the Orient in general.[2] The majority of these sayings have parallels in the Jewish wisdom literature.[3] For example, Bultmann notes the similarity of Mt. 6.24 (Q 16.13) to the saying 'No one can carry two melons in one hand', while Mk 4.21 he compares to 'You don't beat a drum under a rug'.[4]

Bultmann explores a number of possibilities: perhaps Jesus originated some of the Gospels' wisdom sayings; or he may have used proverbs already in circulation; or finally, the church may have put Jewish proverbial material on his lips. These wisdom sayings,

1. Bultmann, 'Study', p. 45.
2. Interestingly, Bultmann limits these sayings to Jewish and Oriental sources. In this category Bultmann places Mt. 6.34b; 12.34b; 24.28; and Lk. 12.2, 3. Bultmann, 'Study', p. 52.
3. 'Study', p. 53, with examples.
4. 'Study', p. 54. Bultmann calls the parallels 'Oriental sayings'. There are so many analogies in the rabbinic literature that one may say 'Not one of the ethical precepts of Jesus was, or needed to be, entirely unique', quoting G. Kittle, *The Problems of Palestinian Judaism and Primitive Christianity* (1926).

Bultmann believes, are least likely to be authentic words of Jesus, and they are also the least significant for historical interpretation.[1]

The sayings in the synoptic Gospels exhibit, according to Bultmann, the same forms as the proverbial wisdom literature of the Hebrew Scriptures and of Jewish literature. As far as Bultmann could determine, all proverbial literature exhibits more or less the same forms.[2]

These proverbial sayings are significant in reconstructing oral tradition in two regards. First, the widespread popularity of such sayings throughout a variety of cultures points to an oral heritage. Such material also forms a background to the early Christian traditions. Secondly, however, the fact of this heritage argues for caution in assuming an oral history behind the inclusion of any such material in the Gospels. The evangelists, and other authors, had access to this material and may have redacted it into their narrative and introduced it into the context for the first time. Bultmann is correct that proverbs have been taken over by the tradition, but he underestimates the number of such instances. The comparisons he has made need to be expanded with a larger literary data base. This vast cultural heritage of proverbs (which circulated in both oral and written form) is a serious barrier to ascertaining a meaningful history of the oral phase. Such sayings may have been taken over during the oral phase of transmission but it cannot be ascertained when this was done or what distinctive meaning they were given during this time. The only clue to their Christian application is derived from the literary texts (i.e., how such material contributes to the meaning of Q, Mark or Thomas). Bultmann's treatment of these sayings assumes too readily that this material was taken over primarily during the oral tradition.

g. *Prophetic and Apocalyptic Sayings*
Another major category of sayings that Bultmann identifies is the prophetic and apocalyptic logia (e.g. Q 6.20-21; 7.22b-23; 10.23-24;

1. Bultmann, 'Study', p. 55.
2. Bultmann gives a detailed exposition of the forms that these aphorisms take, showing extensive examples from Jewish tradition. These include: material formulation; synonymous parallelism; synthetic parallelism; antithetic parallelism with change of figure; figure and material in antithesis; personal formulae; blessings; exhortations; and questions; see 'Study', pp. 70-79.

and 12.8-9). These sayings are distinguished by their brevity and vigour and Bultmann believes that they have their parallel in ancient prophecy rather than in contemporary apocalyptic. This material likely contains authentic Jesus sayings since they 'are obviously not typical products of apocalyptic fancy, but original utterances of a prophetic personality'. Hence, one 'may with perfect right recognize among them authentic words of Jesus'.[1] But not all such sayings are authentic. Rev. 3.20 and 16.15 prove that prophets spoke in Jesus' name. It is probable that some of the prophetic sayings attributed to Jesus in the Gospels originated in this fashion.[2]

By attributing these sayings to Jesus, Bultmann has given them a history as oral tradition. He has also invoked the criterion of dissimilarity by arguing that these sayings are not typical of apocalyptic fancy but rather bear the stamp of an original prophetic personality. The 'uniqueness' of Jesus argument bears closer scrutiny. To what extent is this a theological presupposition of Bultmann which creates as much evidence as it uncovers? Let me examine these sayings in order.[3]

The beatitude form (Q 6.20-21) is not unique to Jesus, nor is concern for the poor and hungry. Both form and content find a home in the theological world of Q, Matthew, Luke and Thomas. Such a broad consensus of agreement undercuts the appeal to 'distinctiveness'. It is difficult therefore to grant much force to Bultmann's argument.[4]

Similarly, the Q sayings at 10.23-24 show signs of a post-resurrectional origin. The eyes that see in the Q context are in direct contrast to those eyes from whom Jesus' sonship is hidden (Q 10.21). What is seen and heard in the ministry of Jesus as a divine proof is also an apocalyptic theme of Q. It is expressly put on the lips of Jesus

1. Bultmann, 'Study', pp. 56-57.
2. Listing Mt. 10.16a; 16.18-19; 18.20; 28.19-20; Lk. 10.19-20; 24.49. See Bultmann, 'Study', p. 57.
3. On the Confession of Faith logion (Q 12.8-9 = Mk 8.38), see above 2 e. See the objection regarding Bultmann's classification here in B.S. Easton, *The Gospel Before the Gospels* (New York: Charles Scribner's Sons, 1928), p. 74.
4. For the beatitude see, Gen. 2.8; 9.26; 14.19-20; 24.27; etc. On the hungry, see Job 24.10; Ps. 146.7; Prov. 25.21; Isa. 58.7; Ezek. 18.7. On the poor, Exod. 22.25; 23.3, 11; Lev. 19.10; Deut. 15.4-12; etc. The beatitude form is found in Q at 10.23-24, which shows an intimate relationship to the theological concerns of Q. For a contrary opinion see, M.E. Boring, 'Criteria of Authenticity: The Lucan Beatitudes as a Test Case', *Foundations & Facets Forum* 1.4 (December, 1985), pp. 3-38.

at Q 7.22, καὶ ἀποκριθεὶς εἶπεν αὐτοῖς, Πορευθέντες ἀπαγγείλατε 'Ιωάννῃ ἃ εἴδετε καὶ ἠκούσατε. The sight beheld (at Q 10.23) is also Jesus' unique sonship, a post-resurrectional concept, and it is difficult to give the saying any other content than this. The solemn λέγω γὰρ ὑμῖν (Q 10.24) bears a post-resurrectional stamp. Finally, the theme of προφῆται καὶ βασιλεῖς is a well-attested Q literary and theological motif (Q 10.13-16; 7.18-35; 13.34-35; 14.16-24).[1]

Regarding Q 7:22b-23, the proofs offered to the disciples of the Baptist are a fulfilment of the prophecy in Isa. 35.5 and 61.1. They are applied as messianic portents of the new age and hence must be seen as post-resurrectional. The proof of Jesus' messiahship offered by this text (i.e., the fulfilment of scripture) makes it difficult to understand why Bultmann did not include the saying in his section of sayings based on the Hebrew Scriptures (see above, section 2, f). Given the christological overtones, the apologetical motif regarding the superiority of Jesus to John, and the double fulfilment of scripture in Jesus' ministry (Q 7.22 = Isa. 35.5; Q 7.27 = Mal. 3.1) it is impossible to ascribe this text to the ministry of Jesus. For both of these texts (Q 7.22b-23; 10.23-24), therefore, Bultmann has not proven an oral tradition. Post-resurrectional, of course, may still be oral; however, these sayings fit so well into Q's literary and theological themes that it is just as easy to see them as Q creations. The post-resurrectional quality of these sayings and their close ties with the theology of Q make it difficult to trace any prior oral history for the units in a meaningful fashion.[2]

h. *Evaluation of Form Criticism*
There can be no doubt that the form critics made a lasting contribution to the understanding of Gospel origins. They acknowledged that tradition is shaped by its context (whether social, theological or literary) and shifted research away from questions of literary sources and on to the process of oral transmission. The first critical tools were advanced to separate secondary layers of tradition from this material in an effort at recovering the earliest tradition. The emphasis on 'forms' also drew attention to the cultural parallels to the

---

1. See R.A. Edwards, *A Theology of Q: Eschatology, Prophecy, and Wisdom* (Philadelphia: Fortress Press), pp. 47-48.

2. See Kloppenborg, *The Formation of Q*, p. 107. On Q 7.22-23; 10.23-24 see Edwards, *A Theology of Q*, pp. 55-56, 65.

synoptic tradition's material and helped establish the appropriate tools for our understanding of these units.

But Bultmann's use of these form critical tools is not without problems. The assumptions of evolutionary growth and continuity between oral and written traditions are inadequately supported. Similarly, the unproven assumption that the mere form of a unit is a precise clue to its point of origin and age can no longer be accepted. Such forms as miracle narratives and pronouncement stories were well known and could equally be employed by the evangelists as redactional techniques. Underlying a great deal of the form critics' analysis has also been a too ready assumption of an oral bed-rock to the traditions. In this regard more recent scholarship on the evangelists as authors in their own rights has outdated Bultmann's view of the Gospel authors as primarily collectors and editors. The concept of the *Sitz im Leben* likewise argues in an evolutionary manner: the social setting of missionary preaching and exhortation, which is believed to underlie a number of the forms, is in turn used to establish the probability of the material having originated in the oral phase. In this regard the argument is circular.

Form criticism also rested too heavily on the evidence of written traditions. Attempts to remedy this deficiency have been made by both B. Gerhardsson (turning to the rabbinic documents) and W. Kelber (who has examined orality as understood in Homer). It is to the first of these critiques that I now turn.

3. *Jesus the Rabbi (H. Riesenfeld and B. Gerhardsson)*

One of the more significant critiques of form criticism is the 'Memory and Manuscript' school of Harold Riesenfeld and his pupils, especially Birger Gerhardsson.[1] This critique is based primarily on a comparison with the process of transmission evident from the rabbinic documents, which is then applied to the oral period of early Christianity.

a. *Kerygma and the Apostles*
Riesenfeld challenges form criticism's emphasis upon a social setting for the tradition in the sermon. This presupposes, he believes, 'an

---

1. H. Riesenfeld, *The Gospel Tradition* (trans. E.M. Rowley and R.A. Kraft; Philadelphia: Fortress Press, 1970).

extraordinary creative capacity in the first Christian generations'.[1]
Instead he turns to Acts for a picture of the earliest Christian
preaching. Luke presents the apostles as having primary responsibility
for the preaching and teaching ministries. The early kerygma, as
presented there, contains an outline of Jesus' life from the preaching
of John the Baptist until his death and resurrection.[2]

This thesis is proved by the countless allusions to the sayings of
Jesus in the Epistles (although there are few express citations). Hence
the early Christian letter-writers were careful to avoid citing Jesus'
words in the context of their original utterance and the sayings were
presumed to be known by the reader.[3] The detailed reconstruction of
the kerygma and the argument that Jesus' sayings were known to
Paul's communities both point to an extensive oral tradition that has
been faithfully preserved by the early church.

Secondly, Riesenfeld points to the first-century milieu of Judaism,
with its extensive tradition—the sayings of the Fathers—which was
carefully handed on from generation to generation. This culminated in
the Mishnah around 200 CE. Since we are well informed on this
material's nature and transmission, we are justified in drawing
conclusions from it regarding the New Testament. The apostles, in
effect, functioned in the same capacity as the Rabbis and oversaw the
transmission of the traditions about Jesus. This procedure is verified
for Riesenfeld by the rabbinic term 'take over' (Παραλαμβάνειν;
קבל). He states:

> The situation as here conceived is not the vague diffusion of narratives,
> sagas, or anecdotes, as we find in folklore, but the rigidly controlled
> transmission of matter from one who has the mastery of it to another who
> has been specially chosen to learn it.[4]

In this process of transmission the Rabbi assumes a supervisory
function and watches over the memorization of both the form and
content of a fixed body of material by approved pupils. The ideal
pupil was one 'who never lost one iota of the tradition'.[5] Since this
tradition was not open to everyone, but transmitted only by approved

---

1. Riesenfeld, *Gospel Tradition*, p. 5.
2. The kerygma's summary, as presented by Riesenfeld, compares closely to the
sermons at Acts 10.37-41; 13.23-31.
3. Riesenfeld, *Gospel Tradition*, p. 12.
4. Riesenfeld, *Gospel Tradition*, p. 16.
5. Riesenfeld, *Gospel Tradition*, p. 16.

pupils under supervision of the Rabbis, it follows that the oral tradition was 'not entrusted to everyone nor was it at everyone's disposal to use as he wished'.[1] Hence the Gospel tradition was not shaped by an unlimited and anonymous multitude, but transmitted by an exactly defined group within the community.[2]

For Riesenfeld, the chief function of the apostles as outlined in Acts 6.2 is preaching. Luke's prologue emphasizes the delivery of tradition by those who were eyewitnesses from the beginning. Traditions relating the words and deeds of Jesus were regarded as holy word, and hence they were not improvised. Rather, 'there was no question of freely narrating or of inventing, even when the speaker was possessed by the Spirit'.[3] The strict laws of transmission would therefore have been in effect from the beginning of the material's transmission.

Even granting the role of eyewitnesses in the formation of the tradition, a problem emerges. Historians emphasize that for eyewitness accounts to be accurate three elements must be present: the witnesses should have been 1) able to see; 2) able to understand what was seen; and 3) not so involved in the action that their own role would have affected what they saw and remembered. Jan Vansina points out that soldiers' reports of battles, for example, are usually deficient in the last two aspects. Hence:

> Eyewitness accounts are only partly reliable. Certainly it is true that complex (battle) or unexpected (accidents) events are perhaps rarer than simple, expected events. Yet even here the account remains imperfect. The expectation of the event itself distorts its observation. People tend to report what they expect to see or hear more than what they actually see or hear. To sum up: mediation of perception by memory and emotional state shapes an account. Memory typically selects certain features from the successive perceptions and interprets them according to expectation, previous knowledge, or the logic of 'what must have happened', and fills the gaps in perception.[4]

In the Gospels there is an intuitive acknowledgement of this problem and an apologetical explanation offered as to why the information is accurate. Often we are told that what Jesus said or did baffled the

1. Riesenfeld, *Gospel Tradition*, p. 16.
2. Riesenfeld, *Gospel Tradition*, pp. 16-17.
3. Riesenfeld, *Gospel Tradition*, p. 20.
4. J. Vansina, *Oral Tradition as History* (Madison, WI: University of Wisconsin, 1985), p. 5.

disciples, thus ensuring recall. Later, when the full significance was revealed, the disciples 'solve' the mystery. The technique is frequent in Mark (cf. 9.9; 11.14, 21) and John (2.17, 22; 15.20). Vansina's evidence suggests that the reverse is far more likely.

There is also the theological overlay in Acts. Riesenfeld's straightforward reading of this evidence is simply no longer possible. Beginning with Hans Conzelmann's *Theology of St. Luke*, Luke the historian has increasingly become known as Luke the theologian. Particularly important in Luke's concept of salvation history is the centrality of 'Jerusalem' and the role of 'the Twelve'.[1] Furthermore, in historical writing in antiquity it was customary to place upon the lips of the central characters speeches that summarized the author's view of what was taking place in the narrative.[2]

b. *Memorization and Transmission*
Riesenfeld places great emphasis upon the process and techniques of memorization to argue for the material's trustworthiness. The material bears this out since some of the sayings are formulated for memorization. The Lord's Prayer (Lk. 11.1-2) states that this was taught by Jesus to his disciples. Similarly, in many sayings we may still hear 'echoes of the Aramaic original'. Thus they were carefully formulated for memorization. The picture at Mk 4.10 of private instruction is accurate enough to allow us to think of the disciples as sitting at Jesus' feet to hear and memorize his words. Jesus taught his

1. H. Conzelmann, *The Theology of St Luke* (trans. G. Buswell; New York: Harper & Row, 1961). Compare E. Haenchen, for whom the account in Acts of the church's growth from Jerusalem to Rome does not represent historical events but rather a theological motif flowing 'entirely from the pen of Luke' (E. Haenchen, *The Acts of the Apostles: A Commentary* [trans. B. Noble and G. Shinn; rev. R.McL. Wilson; Philadelphia: Westminster Press, 1971], pp. 98-110). Compare E.R. Goodenough, 'The Perspective of Acts', in *Studies in Luke–Acts* (ed. L.E. Keck and J.L. Martyn; Nashville: Abingdon Press, 1966), p. 51; H.O. Guenther, 'Greek: Home of Primitive Christianity', *TJT* 5 (1989), pp. 247-79; and C.H. Talbert, *Literary Patterns, Theological Themes, and the Genre of Luke–Acts* (SBLMS, 20; Missoula, MT: Scholars Press, 1974), pp. 15-65.
2. 'Characteristically, these historians created speeches for their heroes in order to give an impression of some of the great ideas of the age', N. Perrin and D.C. Duling, *The New Testament: An Introduction* (New York: Harcourt Brace Jovanovich, 2nd edn, 1982), p. 301. Also W.G. Kümmel, *Introduction to the New Testament* (trans. H.C. Kee; Nashville: Abingdon, rev. edn, 1975), p. 168.

disciples the essential elements of his message and made them learn it by heart.[1]

Riesenfeld's thesis received support from Birger Gerhardsson.[2] He develops a model of transmission for early Christian literature based on the rabbinic materials. As early as the time of Hillel and Shammai there existed a distinction between oral and written Torah.[3] There also developed an organized school system in the land of Israel, in which the written Torah, when studied, was carefully committed to memory. For oral Torah, written notes were also used to facilitate private recitation and memorization. In public contexts, however, this oral Torah had to be cited from memory.[4]

Transmission of the Torah, both written and oral, was deliberate and methodical. Despite the capacity for memorization, Torah was not to be copied out except from a written *Vorlage*.[5] For the oral Torah, Gerhardsson notes the importance of oral tradition in the ancient Near East, particularly in post-exilic Judaism. Traditionalists in this context played an important role in the preservation of the sacred oral tradition, with four centres for its preservation: 1) the home; 2) synagogue and Temple; 3) schools; and 4) high courts. In this milieu children grew up with religious, ethical and social behaviour patterns permeated by Torah, and important passages were learned by heart.[6]

The schools, Gerhardsson emphasizes, transmitted oral tradition methodically. The Rabbis were particularly involved in the transmission, a process not open to 'all and sundry'. This method was so prevalent that he believes it is 'not probable that any such alternative method existed'.[7] He believes that these rabbinic practices were followed within first-century Christian circles since education in antiquity was not characterized by rapid change. Although Rabbi Aqiba was the first to compile a collection of the Mishnah (published orally), older collections still circulated. Thus Rabbi Aqiba's Mishnah was not the first, nor was his method an innovation. These methods

1. Riesenfeld, *Gospel Tradition*, pp. 23-25.
2. See B. Gerhardsson, *Memory and Manuscript: Oral Tradition and Written Transmission in Rabbinic Judaism and Early Christianity* (trans. E.J. Sharpe; Lund: Gleerup, 1961).
3. Gerhardsson, *Memory and Manuscript*, p. 21.
4. Gerhardsson, *Memory and Manuscript*, p. 29.
5. Gerhardsson, *Memory and Manuscript*, p. 46.
6. Gerhardsson, *Memory and Manuscript*, p. 73.
7. Gerhardsson, *Memory and Manuscript*, p. 76.

Gerhardsson thus dates into pre-70 CE Judaism and into the early church.[1]

Repetition of the text was constant. Resh Laqish, for example, repeated his Mishnah paragraph 'forty times' before presenting himself to Rabbi Johanan. The Talmud also gives the impression that the teachers spelled out the oral text at least four times. The pupils had to repeat several times in chorus and individually with the teacher correcting.[2]

But Gerhardsson's backdating of rabbinic techniques to the pre-70 CE era, according to Morton Smith, amounts to 'a gross anachronism'.[3] The Temple's destruction marked a decisive watershed in Jewish history, and it is not clear that the principles of transmission as outlined in the later rabbinic documents were in force in the first century. Smith argues that the earliest sections of the Mishnah were probably fixed soon after the Temple's destruction, and this 'makes it likely that they were not being learned by heart prior to that time'.[4]

The rabbinic documents themselves need to be treated form-critically. As Jacob Neusner has shown, this material has its own complicated history of development before it was committed to writing. In an examination of 'Hillel's Wise Sayings' (including the Golden Rule), Neusner concludes that it is unlikely that such sayings circulated in Hillel's name prior to 200 CE, 'since none is ever quoted, referred to, or attributed to him prior to the third–century masters. This is prima facie evidence that the whole is late'.[5]

Kelber finds it is significant that Gerhardsson has undertaken his investigation of rabbinic transmission with *written* materials. The

---

1. Gerhardsson, *Memory and Manuscript*, p. 77-78.

2. Gerhardsson, *Memory and Manuscript*, p. 105-106, 120.

3. M. Smith, 'A Comparison of Early Christian and Early Rabbinic Traditions', *JBL* 82 (1963), p. 169. See also, J. Neusner, 'The Rabbinic Traditions About the Pharisees Before 70 AD: The Problem of Oral Tradition', *Kairos* 14 (1972), pp. 57-70.

4. Smith, 'A Comparison', pp. 169-70. See also S. Safrai, 'Oral Tora', in *The Literature of the Sages, First Part: Oral Tora, Halakha, Mishna, Tosefta, Talmud, External Tractates* (ed. S. Safrai; Philadelphia: Fortress Press; Assen: Van Gorcum, 1987), p. 36.

5. J. Neusner, *Judaism in the Beginning of Christianity* (Philadelphia: Fortress Press, 1984), p. 69. On related topics see, A.F. Segal, *Two Powers in Heaven: Early Rabbinic Reports about Christianity and Gnosticism* (Leiden: Brill, 1979); and J.N. Lightstone, *Yose the Galilean* (Leiden: Brill, 1979).

chief concern of the 'Scripture specialists', he notes, was the faithful preservation of texts. Similarly, the educational context of the schools and synagogue was focused on written texts.[1] Hence, 'one is inclined to read his [Gerhardsson's] subordination of the oral to the written Torah as a consequence of his methodological and linguistic priorities'.[2] The close linkage of the two media can be seen, Kelber believes, in such terms as 'oral text', 'oral passages of text', 'memory texts' and the like.[3]

Kelber also notes the chirographical basis of Gerhardsson's work—this theory is not based upon a study of the synoptic traditions and their relation to the Gospels.[4] The emphasis on memorization, conservation and the preservation of an author's exact words must be demonstrated by a careful study of the Gospel materials themselves. Recent research into the redactional tendencies of each of the evangelists does not support the emphasis upon rote repetition.

Nor can Gerhardsson's insistence that there was no alternative to the rabbinic method of transmission be supported. Second-Temple Judaism was far more diverse than he imagines. S. Safrai points out, for example, that the 'explicit conception of a tradition to be kept oral and the use of the term Oral Tora itself are advocated only in rabbinic traditions, the earliest of which are attributed to the first Tannaim'. Safrai goes on to argue that even in non-Pharisaic circles, however, the existence of oral traditions could have been an accepted fact. Pointing also to the written literature of the Sadducees, such as their 'Book of Decrees', he argues that

> if we accept the classic division of Second-Temple Judaism into Pharisees, Sadducees and Essenes, it appears that the concept of Oral Tora developed only among the Pharisees. There is no justification in asserting that the literary development of the Sadducees and Essenes proceeded quicker to the stage of written and edited works.[5]

If we look beyond the context of first-century Judaism, it is quite evident from folkloric studies that other material has been transmitted in a context differing from that which Gerhardsson outlines. With

1. Kelber, *Oral*, pp. 8-9.
2. Kelber, *Oral*, p. 10.
3. Kelber, *Oral*, p. 10.
4. This objection must be qualified by Gerhardsson's study of the Sower, which I will examine in Chapter 4.
5. Safrai, 'Oral Tora', pp. 39-40, 45-48. Quotes, pp. 39-40; 48.

such a variety of transmission in existence it is not at all clear that Gerhardsson's thesis is the most appropriate for the Gospels.

Regarding the application of this model to Jesus, Kelber observes that the Gospels do not depict him teaching by memorization. Similarly, Smith notes that Mt. 7.29 states that Jesus did not teach as the scribes.[1] Despite flaws in the formulation of this objection, it carries weight. We must consider the theological motives of the evangelists when we find narratives in which Jesus passes on tradition to the apostles. The portraits framing such traditions as the Lord's prayer (Luke), the Sermon on the Mount (Matthew) or the parable of the Sower (Mark) must be viewed as secondary settings. Mark's private setting for revelation and Luke's emphasis upon the Twelve are two well-documented redactional motifs.

c. *Form and Original Wording*

Authenticity of oral tradition inevitably involves transmissional stability. We have already noted the earliest 'solutions' to nagging doubts about accuracy as advanced by Mark, Luke and Papias. Gerhardsson has a more sophisticated answer. In his model of orality tradition is formulated in a fixed manner and consists of a chain of short passages of text. These are midrashic focal texts assembled on the principle of the continuous scriptural text. He emphasizes the vast extent of this material; the Tannaitic and Amoraic teachers 'have access by memory to enormous quantities of oral traditional material: their teachers' sayings, stories about their teachers and the like, form a body of material which must be classified as oral text material'.[2]

Rabbinic oral tradition attempts to preserve the original wording. The rabbinic texts seldom convey the impression that the Rabbis give an account in their own words of their teacher's positions. The emphasis is usually on quotation from memory of an oral text. The traditions's accuracy is underscored, since even in the Talmud (where there is a need to conserve space) these stories are often given word-

---

1. Smith, 'A Comparison', p. 172. This is somewhat unfair: the motif is a post–resurrectional apologetic designed to assert the superiority of authority and teaching in the Christian community from that in its parent (and rival) Judaism. The verse cannot be used one way or another to ascertain the pre–Easter mode of teaching by Jesus.

2. Gerhardsson, *Memory and Manuscript*, p. 80.

for-word in a number of contexts. Transmission is a process of constant and faithful repetition.[1]

Gerhardsson notes that the ability to relate material in one's own words and to abstract ideas is, in fact, a process developed in the Hellenized West but not practised in ancient Israel; peoples' views were conveyed in their own words. This principle applied in rabbinic Judaism. Although more abstract modes of thought developed, yet 'reverence and care for the *ipissima verba* of each authority remains unaltered'.[2] The pupil's duty is to maintain the teacher's exact wording and the Rabbis formulated rules for this, including fourfold repetition.[3] A saying of Hillel shows this emphasis upon continuous repetition: 'the man who repeats his chapter one hundred times is not to be compared with the man who repeats it one hundred and one times' (*b. Hag.* 9b).

But Gerhardsson is forced into a significant concession. Not all material was transmitted with the same exacting fidelity. The mechanics of memorization do not apply to all texts—it is a well-known fact that some haggadic sayings were transmitted with less attention for their exact wording than halakic statements. Previous study has shown that the wording of certain haggadic traditions can vary from one written version to another except when it comes 'to the decisive catch-word or catch-words'.[4] This admission, however, is limited by his observation that in the talmudic material negative criticism of the received oral text was never advanced by the Amoraic Rabbis and seldom by the later ones. The 'traditionists' text is accepted as being perfectly correct'.[5]

Once again we find the same two essential problems: a view of the rabbinic material no longer tenable and an unproven assumption that these procedures were operative in the Christian community. Safrai, in dealing with the rabbinic prohibition on written notes for the transmission of oral Torah, draws a conclusion that is startling for Gerhardsson's presentation:

> This would imply that the very concept of Oral Tora was generated by the wish of the Sages to preserve the fluidity of their tradition and its

1. Gerhardsson, *Memory and Manuscript*, p. 81.
2. Gerhardsson, *Memory and Manuscript*, pp. 130-31.
3. Gerhardsson, *Memory and Manuscript*, p. 134; cf *b. Erub.* 54b.
4. Gerhardsson, *Memory and Manuscript*, p. 146.
5. Gerhardsson, *Memory and Manuscript*, p. 97.

openness to change and development. Only the words of God spoken to Moses and the prophets, and laid down in the Pentateuch and the prophetic books of the Bible, were considered as fixed texts by the Sages.[1]

d. *Oral Tradition and Mnemonics*

In Gerhardsson's view oral tradition makes extensive use of mnemonics, thus ensuring the material's accuracy. Two aspects of abridgement emerge. The first is the attempt to find summary generalizations. Hillel, for example, calls his Golden Rule the whole of Torah with all else as commentary (*b. Shab.* 31a). Secondly, verbosity is not regarded as praiseworthy. The brief, well-thought-out statement became the rabbinic ideal. Hence, if a Rabbi failed in this respect later pupils would abbreviate. In this sense Gerhardsson admits that the rules of brevity and authenticity at times came into conflict.[2]

As an aid to memorization, texts were often given a name. Other mnemonic techniques such as assonance, *paranomasia* and *parallelismus membrorum* were employed. Material in the Hebrew Scriptures that may reasonably be presumed to be oral tradition is often collected on a catch-word principle, or by association. Gerhardsson points particularly to Isaiah 40–55 where the individual elements are grouped by catch-word association. This principle 'fills its real function in the process of memorization and delivery from memory'.[3] Hence, for Gerhardsson, its use even in written texts shows evidence of continued oral tradition. Thus, if it is used in the editing of written material, 'this is partly a relic of an ancient oral principle of arrangement, but mainly a measure to facilitate memorization and delivery from memory'.[4]

Midrashic association is another mnemonic technique. The biblical text functions as the mnemonic aid and catch-word associations are used to tie traditions to the text. Entire blocks of material can be brought to mind as long as the traditionalist is sure of the catch-words.[5]

1. Safrai, 'Oral Tora', p. 49.
2. Gerhardsson, *Memory and Manuscript*, pp. 142-43.
3. Gerhardsson, *Memory and Manuscript*, p. 149.
4. Gerhardsson, *Memory and Manuscript*, p. 149.
5. Gerhardsson, *Memory and Manuscript*, p. 153.

A related aspect of Gerhardsson's thesis is that writing and written traditions do not have serious consequences for orality and oral tradition. The introduction of writing to a culture implies, at least in the beginning, very little change in the standing of oral tradition. It takes time for a written book to become an independent form of expression rather than an aid to memory. Gerhardsson comments that 'it is only in our own day that the memory has been *effectively* unloaded into books.'[1]

Closer evaluation again reveals problems. Neusner has provided a classification of the mnemonics that appear in the rabbinic materials. He demonstrates that many of the sayings attributed to Hillel and Shammai (and most of the House sayings) display mnemonic patterns, but that sayings attributed to other pre-70 figures tend to lack such features. Neusner even calls into question the widespread assumption that such rabbinic mnemonic techniques were in widespread use prior to the Temple's destruction.[2]

How does this apply to the synoptic tradition? Kloppenborg points out that within the entire Q material such mnemonic devices as elaborated by Neusner 'are almost entirely lacking'. The saying closest to balanced lines with fixed opposites is Q 16.13.[3] This one saying is hardly evidence of widespread Christian use of extensive mnemonic patterning to preserve the exact wording of sayings. Nor can we find material in the Gospels that has been arranged following the order of the Hebrew Bible text. Since this ordering principle served as a mnemonic aid to preserve tradition, its absence in the Christian tradition creates a problem. This absence argues for greater variability in this phase of transmission than Gerhardsson admits.

e. *Literature and Historiography in Antiquity*

Two further aspects of Gerhardsson's study merit examination. He attempts to place the oral transmissional process within the broader historical context of the first century. Literature in antiquity, Gerhardsson argues, is primarily an aural medium. Most ancient literature is intended for the ears as much as for the eyes. Reading was also usually done aloud, and this in a solemn, cultivated and practised

---

1. Gerhardsson, *Memory and Manuscript*, p. 123.
2. See J. Neusner, 'The Rabbinic Traditions About the Pharisees Before 70', in *Early Rabbinic Judaism* (SJLA, 13; Leiden: Brill, 1975), pp. 73-89.
3. Kloppenborg, *The Formation of Q*, p. 46.

cantillation. The Rabbis, in fact, opposed directly any tendencies towards silent reading on the grounds that distinct pronunciation facilitated memorization and guarded against it being distorted. Folklore provides numerous examples where archaic terms have lived on in cantillated texts long after the meaning of the texts themselves has been forgotten.[1]

Ancient historiography provides another argument for Gerhardsson's view that oral tradition was intended to preserve a teacher's life and teachings. Disinterested historiography is a rather late concept. In antiquity there was instead a practical purpose involved in narrating events: that of providing either examples to emulate or warnings. Narrative traditions in rabbinic Judaism were formulated with the basic intention of preserving and spreading 'the many-faceted wisdom of the Torah in the face of all the situations of life'.[2] An eyewitness element is involved in the tradition: the pupils tell what they have seen and heard from the master. This character of the tradition is stressed with such terms as עד, עדות, or העיד.[3]

Taking these arguments in reverse order, it will be quickly seen that Gerhardsson has overstated the evidence with respect to ancient historiography. The evidence presented above (see sections 3, a and b) clearly indicates that Gerhardsson's emphasis upon the role of eyewitnesses and historical fidelity simply cannot be demonstrated in the early Christian documents.

The emphasis upon the oral and 'aural' dimension of literature is a more salient point. Kelber, for example, applauds Gerhardsson's emphasis upon ancient literature as intentionally an aural medium as much as a visual one. But this aspect of ancient literature leaves an unresolved problem. If literature in antiquity was primarily an aural medium, these 'aural emphases' and compositional techniques might appear in the redactional work of the evangelists. If Matthew and Mark, for example, composed their Gospels with an emphasis on the spoken word there is no guarantee that such oral structuring devices as catch-word associations or alliteration reflect a prior tradition. Such devices might simply reflect the 'literary style' appropriate to a Gospel composed with an emphasis upon the spoken word.

---

1. Gerhardsson, *Memory and Manuscript*, pp. 164-67.
2. Gerhardsson, *Memory and Manuscript*, p. 182.
3. Gerhardsson, *Memory and Manuscript*, p. 183.

Positively, the Riesenfeld–Gerhardsson 'memory and manuscript' approach pointed to a number of flaws with previous form-critical studies. Antiquity's emphasis upon literature as an aural medium (rather than a literary and visual one) points to the first awareness that the two media need to be carefully distinguished. The hermeneutics of oral speech and written text cannot, as in Bultmann, so easily be assumed to be fully compatible. Gerhardsson's acknowledgement of antiquity's appreciation of language as sound and its scepticism of the written word (as seen in the Rabbis' opposition to silent reading) are valid points. His detailed exploration of the mechanics and techniques of rabbinic transmission deserves praise. Gerhardsson is acutely aware of the difficulty in ensuring stability in the oral medium, and of the need to explore the details of the transmissional process. Finally, Gerhardsson and Riesenfeld knew that the form-critical emphasis on the *Sitz im Leben* of the Gospel traditions needed further clarity and definition.[1]

4. *Kelber's Program*

a. *Distinguishing the Oral and Written Media*

In developing his own model of orality, Kelber points to a growing body of folklore studies that have vastly enhanced understanding of this medium. Yet biblical scholarship, he maintains, has not profited from this. Kelber believes that this has resulted largely from the tendency of biblical scholars to think predominantly in literary, linear and visual terms.[2] Fundamental to his program is the essential difference between the oral and the written word:

> Contemporary theorists of orality appear virtually unanimous in emphasizing the linguistic integrity of the difference between spoken versus written words. The manner and degree of difference is controversial, ranging from A.B. Lord's proposition that the two media are 'contradictory and mutually exclusive', to R. Finnegan's suggestion of overlaps and interactions, to W.J. Ong's thesis that successive stages both reinforce and transform preceding ones. But there is agreement to the effect that the circumstances of performance, the composition, and the

---

1. On the positive aspects of Gerhardsson's study, see Kelber, *Oral*, p. 13.
2. Kelber, *Oral*, p. 3.

transmission of oral versus written materials are sufficiently distinct so as to postulate separate hermeneutics.[1]

   In oral tradition the speaker addresses the audience, whose presence in turn affects the delivery. Both performer and audience participate in the making of the message. In contrast, an author writes for an absent reader. This 'relative detachment from social context allows the author to exercise controls over his [or her] composition in a manner unknown to the performer of live speech'.[2] In an oral context the social dynamics are totally different, for the speaker must assure the remembrance of information and hence must use such linguistic techniques as formulaic speech and mnemonic patterning. What is transmitted orally 'is never all the information available, but only the kind of data that are orally pliable and retrievable. What lives on in memory, moreover, is what is necessary for present life'.[3] Recognition of these distinct social contexts and their effects upon the tradition raises sharp questions for Kelber regarding both Bultmann and Gerhardsson's understanding of the two media.

   This social dynamic makes survival of oral tradition dependent upon the 'existential intensity' that it shares with the audience. Traditions have the best chance for survival when they focus identification for transmitter and hearer alike. Hence 'oral tradition is controlled by the law of social identification, rather than by the technique of verbatim memorization'.[4]

   This emphasis upon this essential difference between the two media is a welcome contribution. The survival of information through the oral medium, as Kelber rightly emphasizes, is precarious. Like last week's newspaper, oral tradition can quickly become outdated; a fact not sufficiently recognized by Bultmann and Gerhardsson. Jan Vansina emphasizes that traditions about events are maintained only because the events are perceived to be important.

   1. Kelber, *Oral*, p. 14. See also *idem*, 'Mark', p. 20. Noting A.B. Lord, *The Singer of Tales* (HSCL, 24; Cambridge, MA: Harvard University Press, 1960), p. 129; R. Finnegan, *Oral Poetry: Its Nature, Significance and Social Context* (Cambridge: Cambridge University Press, 1977), pp. 24, 160, 169; W.J. Ong, *The Presence of the Word: Some Prolegomena for Cultural and Religious History* (New Haven: Yale University Press, 1967), pp. 104, 239, 282.
   2. Kelber, *Oral*, p. 15.
   3. Kelber, *Oral*, p. 15.
   4. Kelber, 'Mark', p. 25.

As groups and institutions change over time, the notions of 'significance' and of 'interest' also vary and may eventually lead to loss of information. Such losses may also occur because the memory of the event never became part of a tradition in the first place as it did, at that time, not seem to affect society very much. The Kuba remember the first European to come to their country, but not the second one. It was no longer a novelty. Yet the first was only a merchant, while the second was taking over the country on behalf of the Congo Independent State, a fact the Kuba did not know. As a result of such processes of selection, the intentional historical content of traditions becomes closely congruent to social concerns of the past and of the present.[1]

The internal hermeneutics of the two media must be distinguished. The inability of the live audience to 'turn back the page' and review what has gone before when the thread of the narrative is lost has far-reaching consequences. Repetition, recapitulation of the action and other techniques to compensate for this fact of oral life need to be remembered when we examine oral traditions. Yet the obverse may not be true: such techniques may find their proper place in written documents for different hermeneutical reasons. Mark's triple passion predictions and the Lukan triad of Paul's conversion in Acts point to the fact that repetition can live on in first-century literary texts. In explaining such a narrative structure the 'hermeneutics' at work could well be quite different between an orally-performed epic (such as Homer) and a literary text (such as Acts). This problem of how oral hermeneutics may 'live on' in written texts (albeit by fulfilling other hermeneutical functions) has been explored by Kelber, but his presentation fails to draw out appropriate inferences for an understanding of orality.

b. *Oral Patterning and Literary Texts*
If, as Kelber acknowledges, the hermeneutics of oral speech and written text are different, how can we recover material previously transmitted orally from the written text? Do different hermeneutics, and the needs of a literary text at odds with the oral medium, create an unbridgeable chasm between the two media? Kelber notes that the cultivation of literacy in itself will not extinguish orality. Oral forms of thought and expression persist long after the invention of script. The two media, spoken and written word, not only co-existed in the

1. Vansina, *Oral Tradition*, p. 119.

first century but also interacted with each other. Kelber believes that the synoptic tradition linguistically 'is stamped with the hallmarks of oral patterning'.[1]

Kelber points to G. Theissen's sociological analysis that the material reflects a largely rural movement and wandering charismatic prophets. These prophets used orality, not literacy, as their principle medium.[2] Kelber believes it is tempting to trace this early usage of orality to Jesus himself, since he discoursed in the oral medium without ever committing a word to writing.[3]

For Kelber orality and social world co-operate through formulaic communication. He mentions the synoptic sayings that offend against our traditional sense of belonging and that counsel hatred against family and possessions (e.g. Mk 10.29-30; 8.35-38; Q 9.58; 17.33). These sayings demonstrate that the tradition was carried by homeless and itinerant charismatics who considered themselves the loyal followers of Jesus. They adopted Jesus' vagrant mode of life and sayings that supported such a life.[4] Confining these sayings to this one social group, however, may not be realistic. Kelber doubts the form critics' thesis of a *Sitz im Leben* that ties forms of speech into specific social settings. Both the material's effectiveness and its memorability are enhanced in direct proportion to its conformity with rhythmical, acoustic demands. Oral formulae, clichés and commonplaces assure remembering and transmission. Sayings must be articulated in accordance with mnemonic formalities in order to ensure preservation, and Kelber points to a number of studies that have shown the 'extraordinary degree to which sayings of Jesus have kept faith with heavily patterned speech forms, abounding in alliteration, paranomasia, appositional equivalence, proverbial and aphoristic diction, contrasts and antitheses, synonymous, antithetical, synthetic, and tautologic parallelism and the like'.[5] The process also renders the

1. Kelber, 'Mark', p. 22.

2. Kelber, 'Mark', p. 22. See G. Theissen, *Sociology of Early Palestinian Christianity* (trans. J. Bowden; Philadelphia: Fortress Press, 1977).

3. Kelber, 'Mark', p. 23.

4. Kelber, 'Mark', p. 26.

5. Kelber, *Oral*, p. 27. Noting for example studies by: C.F. Burney, *The Poetry of Our Lord: An Examination of the Formal Elements of Hebrew Poetry in the Discourses of Jesus Christ* (Oxford: Clarendon Press, 1925); H. Birkeland, *The Language of Jesus* (Oslo: Jacob Dybwad, 1954); M. Black, *An Aramaic Approach to the Gospels and Acts* (Oxford: Clarendon Press, 1946); R.C. Tannehill, *The*

material changeable and adaptable; indeed Kelber believes that there are 'virtually limitless possibilities for the oral performer to improvise basic patterns of oral compositions'.[1]

Kelber draws two immediate conclusions. The form critics' thesis of the communal nature of the tradition is burdened with eighteenth- and nineteenth-century romantic notions of the mystique of the 'folk'. Instead, one must allow for some role of individuals in the transmission of the tradition. Secondly, as noted above in my discussion of Bultmann, a saying that does not speak to an audience's needs or experience will die out.[2] In addition, variation within the tradition goes beyond compression or expansion and includes interchanging and shuffling of stock motifs. Hence, Kelber asserts, scholars must forgo the notion of the 'original form'. Each oral performance of the text is an irreducible and unique creation, so that the 'concepts of *original form* and variants have no validity in oral life, nor does the one of *ipsissima vox*, if by that one means the authentic version over against secondary ones'.[3]

Kelber's emphasis upon the variability of oral tradition is a sound correction to Bultmann and Gerhardsson. Not only do Parry and Lord emphasize this aspect of orality, but, as Ruth Finnegan notes, '[o]ne of the most significant points to emerge from the study of Yugoslav oral poets is the absence of a fixed text—the primary text or archetype so often sought for in classical studies.'[4] Vansina likewise supports this claim; in oral tradition the 'public likes to hear known tales in new garb'.[5]

This hermeneutical variation does not affect only the oral phase of the tradition. The numerous alterations by Matthew and Luke attest to textuality's need for dressing the old in new garb, the interchanging of stock motifs and other such techniques. This variation at the literary stage needs to be distinguished from that in oral tradition. The

Sword of His Mouth (Semeia Studies, 1; Philadelphia: Fortress Press; Missoula, MT: Scholars Press, 1975); and M. Jousse, SJ, *Études de psychologie linguistique: Le style oral rythmique et mnémotechnique che les verbo-moteurs* (Paris: Beauchesne, 1925) and *idem, Le Parlant, la parole et le souffle* (Paris: Gallimard, 1978).

1. Kelber, *Oral*, p. 27.
2. Kelber, 'Mark', p. 31. Citing Abel, 'The Psychology of Memory and Rumor Transmission', pp. 270-81; Allport and Postman, *The Psychology of Rumor*.
3. Kelber, *Oral*, p. 30. Citing Abel, 'Psychology of Memory', p. 276.
4. Finnegan, *Oral Poetry*, p. 65.
5. Vansina, *Oral Tradition*, p. 26.

techniques of redaction criticism can often provide a hermeneutical explanation for the alteration. Changes to their source material by Matthew and Luke are not simply the substitution of synonymous entities; theological and literary motives are often at work.

Kelber's critique of the form critic's emphasis upon the anonymous 'folk' is valid. Ruth Finnegan examines what she calls 'romantic' and 'evolutionist' theories of oral poetry that depend upon an evolutionist approach, i.e., that societies progress up through set stages with 'survivals' from earlier eras sometimes continuing on into later ones. Emotional expression and natural spontaneity, in this view, are found in 'primitive' language and culture. Examples of such assumptions include J.G. Frazer, who spoke of the survivals of 'the old modes of life and thought', or Lévi-Strauss's opposition of *la pensée sauvage* to *la pensée cultivée et domestiqué.* By setting such assumptions against their historical background Finnegan brings home that they are *assumptions.*[1] Many of the evolutionary assumptions of the form critics, therefore, have been correctly challenged by Kelber. But this is a two-edged sword, for this notion of 'survivals' from one era lingering on into another is distressingly similar to Kelber's thesis that oral linguistic patterns have permeated the written Gospel texts in Mark and Q. Bultmann's evolutionary assumption is still operative!

Similarly, Kelber's insistence that we must allow for some role of 'individuals' in the oral transmission is suspiciously similar to Gerhardsson's 'eyewitnesses'. Vansina has pointed to the model of oral tradition which presupposes an observer witnessing an event and creating an initial message. A second party hears this report and passes it along. This person-to-person process continues until the tradition is written down. Tradition in this model is a chain of individual links. But such a model (as presented in the early Christian documents themselves) is a romanticized view. Most oral tradition is told by many people to many people. Some people hear the account numerous times and fuse various elements of a variety of reports into their own account. Vansina points out that in oral tradition, memory is communal 'since different people hear a single rendering and may or may not render it later themselves. Indeed the earlier performer often is the later listener. This collective character is important also in

---

1. Finnegan, *Poetry*, pp. 30-41. See J.G. Frazer, *Folklore in the Old Testament* (London: Macmillan, 1918).

that it implies a faster pace of remoulding of dormant data in memory.'[1]

Kelber's critique of the form critics and Gerhardsson has substituted one set of assumptions about the *Sitz im Leben* of the oral tradition for another. In rejecting Bultmann's thesis of missionary preaching or Gerhardsson's notion of a rabbinic school, Kelber offers instead a sociological setting largely dependent upon Theissen. The reconstruction of the homeless 'wandering charismatics' in the Q community who lived outside the boundaries of contemporary ethical norms is not without its own problems. The identification with 'homelessness' does not have to have literal fulfilment for the theme to find a welcome in literary texts.[2] Richard A. Horsley has raised strong objections to this aspect of Theissen's project:

> The 'constructive conclusions' that the apostles and others were wandering charismatics. . . are largely arguments from silence (or rather 'absence') or arguments by analogy with apostles such as Barnabas and Paul, who operated outside Palestine. There is apparently no direct 'information' to confirm his inferences by analogy.[3]

In short, Kelber's new set of sociological assumptions cannot guarantee a foolproof method of identifying oral traditions within a written text.

c. *Oral Clustering and Literary Texts*
A second indication of Kelber's oral bed-rock underneath the written text is the clustering of similar form-critical material. He insists that the formulaic quality of oral style be confused neither with mechanized learning nor with literal consistency. Variations on a genre or on clusters of genres are a hallmark of oral style, so it is

1. Vansina, *Oral Tradition*, p. 161. Earlier discussion pp. 29-30.
2. See, Gen. 15.13; 23.4; Exod. 2.22; 20.10; 23.9; Lev. 19.10; 23.22; 24.22. Compare Bultmann's pronouncement story regarding Diogenes, quoted above (p. 34 n. 4). From the third century BCE Buddhist *Dhammapada* (6.87-88), see J. Mascaró (trans.), *The Dhammapada: The Path of Perfection* (Harmondsworth: Penguin Books), p. 47. From Xenophon, *Men*, I, 6, 10.
3. R.A. Horsley, *Sociology and the Jesus Movement* (New York: Crossroad, 1989), p. 43. For my evaluation of Horsley, see my review in *RST* 10.1 (Jan. 1990), pp. 59-61. See also the study by L.E. Vaage, 'Q¹ and the Historical Jesus: Some Peculiar Sayings (7.33-34; 9.57-58, 59-60; 14.26-27)', *Foundations and Facets Forum* 5.2 (June 1989), pp. 159-76.

significant that the material in Mark that is most likely from pre-Markan tradition appears in collections of genres: miracles (2.1–3.6), parables (4.1-34), apophthegmatic controversy stories (11.27–12.37) and *logoi* (13.1-37). Pointing to W.J. Ong, E. Havelock and A.B. Lord, Kelber believes that this clustering technique 'results from the oral habit of analogical or associative thinking'.[1] Hence, when the stories are strung together by thematic association they form a succession of single impressions or 'pluralized instances'.[2] But this logic of like attracting like is ill-equipped to form the Gospel's chronological sequence. Hence, a 'perceptual chasm separates the oral, associative thinking from Mark's causal thinking as it is expressed in his gospel's sequential pattern'.[3]

Kelber believes that Mark as a written text is indebted to the oral heritage. These 'oral deposits' of tradition are more conspicuous in the first 13 chapters of the Gospel and less so in the passion narrative, which he believes constitutes a more densely constructed textuality. The grouping of parables, controversy stories, miracles and *logoi*, in 'cluster-like density' betrays Mark's debt to orality's tendency to link like to like. Other evidence of the oral heritage is to be found in the simple linking of sentences by καί parataxis, the preference for direct speech, the predominance of the historical present, the lack of an 'artistically reflected prose', Jesus' incomplete characterization, the Gospel's 'exposition as a series of events' and the preference for the concrete over the abstract. All of this indicates Mark's 'allegiance to the vitality of the spoken word'.[4]

Admittedly there are problems in recovering originally oral words from the written text. What was once spoken as a living word is now accessible to us only in the printed text. They have, in this sense, 'been silenced', and their original speaking context is forever lost. It may also mean that these 'oral forms have become textualized beyond recognition'.[5] The situation, one suspects, would be quite hopeless except that the written medium can 'freeze' oral forms and preserve

---

1. Kelber, 'Mark', p. 29. Pointing to Ong, *The Presence of the Word*; E.A. Havelock, *Preface to Plato* (Cambridge, MA: Belknap Press, 1963); and Lord, *Singer of Tales*.
2. Kelber, 'Mark', p. 29. The phrase is from Havelock, *Preface*, p. 218.
3. Kelber, 'Mark', p. 30.
4. Kelber, 'Mark', p. 34.
5. Kelber, *Oral*, p. 44.

them in fossilized profiles. Kelber outlines for example the oral form of the 'Heroic Tale', a form similar to Dibelius' tale and Bultmann's miracle story.[1]

A comparison of these stories points to an obvious indebtedness to a recognizable commonplace structure. Stock features or motifs yield a more or less predictable narrative sequence. Even where there are deviations the structure reasserts itself such that the narratives tend to return to formulary stability. Despite, however, this uniformity in structure, Kelber believes that these stories show a remarkable versatility.

Kelber points to a similar basic structure in three Markan 'Polarization Stories'. As with the 'Heroic Tales' the common structure aids transmission while offering inexhaustible narrative licence.[2] He sets out a common pattern for 'Didactic Stories', which is essentially the pronouncement story. There are often, as Kelber notes, two rounds of conversation. He sees an essential tie-in to memorization through the antagonist's question, raising the issue directly and defending the exact opposite of what will be Jesus' position. These opposite positions form a teaching *via negativa* that aids memorization.[3]

Kelber prefers to see these narratives (heroic tales) as not originating primarily in either Hellenistic or Jewish culture, but as products of the oral medium and oral mentality.[4] This represents a strong departure from the procedure of both Dibelius and Bultmann, who used the form to determine the unit's point of origin. For Kelber repetition is both desirable (to ensure preservation) and necessary in oral culture. Knowledge not repeated often enough is lost. He notes that the variability in oral transmissional composition is a feature well documented by Lord. No rendition is exactly the same as the previous

---

1. Kelber, *Oral*, p. 46.
2. The link to orality is strengthened in Kelber's assertion that there is an oral, poetic sense in which Jesus 'demands opposition, a pathological double, and preferably one in personalized form. Evil is not defined as an It, but dramatized as a Thou, endowed with speech and intelligence.' *Oral*, p. 55.
3. Kelber, *Oral*, p. 56.
4. Kelber, *Oral*, p. 50.

one, every performance is a 'true one' and no one performance is the original.[1]

Kelber's thesis is indebted to Bultmann. They share the assumption that certain forms belong to the oral rather than the literary phase of transmission. The names have changed, but essentially the miracle narrative and the pronouncement story belong almost exclusively to the oral tradition. Stock features and motifs may be combined, expanded, substituted or abridged in an endless series of variations during the oral phase, but they all originate there. There is little thought given to the possibility that literary authors aware of these conventions would consciously incorporate, alter or otherwise vary them for theological and literary reasons entirely of their own. When Kelber notes the motif of the exorcist's rebuke as part of the confrontation stage of the heroic tale he overlooks that it has long been recognized—from W. Wrede on—that these elements play a distinctive role in Mark's own theological purposes.[2]

Nor can the clustering technique of like-to-like be ascribed solely to orality. Matthew's redaction of Mark's parable chapter (Matthew 13) displays this technique (cf. the Marriage Feast, Mt. 22.1-14). Clusters of similar form-critical units, rather than being the direct deposit of oral tradition, might indicate a pre-Gospel source. The five controversy stories of Mk 2.1–3.6 and the three parables of Mk 4.3-32 are often thought to result from a written source.[3] John also used a literary signs source, according to Robert Fortna.[4] The clustering technique within these pre-Gospel literary sources might simply result from a textual ordering and not an oral process. While it is true, therefore, that the oral memory is associative in nature and tends to string together like after like, the grouping of similar form-critical units in a written text cannot be assumed to be the direct result of oral transmission. It is possible that the evangelist has inherited a written

1. Kelber, *Oral*, p. 51. Citing W.J. Ong, *Interfaces of the Word: Studies in the Evolution of Consciousness and Culture* (Ithaca, NY: Cornell University Press, 1977), p. 104, and Lord, *Singer*.

2. W. Wrede, *The Messianic Secret* (trans. J.C.G. Grieg; London: James Clarke, 1972 [1901]).

3. The parables will be discussed below. On the controversy stories, see J. Dewey, 'The Literary Structure of the Controversy Stories in Mark 2.1–3.6', *JBL* 92 (1973), pp. 394-401.

4. R.T. Fortna, *The Gospel of Signs: A Reconstruction of the Narrative Underlying The Fourth Gospel* (Cambridge: Cambridge University Press, 1970).

source or grouped the material together himself for his own purposes. We must begin with a careful application of redaction criticism to determine whether any theological and literary considerations of the Gospel author have been at work.

Finally, Kelber's assertion that these stories cannot be ascribed to either a Jewish or Hellenistic environment (but are better understood in terms of the universal phenomenon of oral culture) obscures some significant data. An entire issue of *Semeia* has now been devoted to the pronouncement story, with significant results. Gary Porton's review of this literary unit in the Tannaitic literature demonstrates a significant difference from the synoptic stories, 'for in some of the former the personality of the one who uttered the pronouncement is ignored. In the Gospels, on the other hand, the personality of the one who recited the pronouncements is the central focus.'[1]

The case with Philo and Josephus is equally telling. In 16 out of 17 pronouncement stories, according to L. Greenspoon, Philo 'seems to have taken into his text, with little or no modification, pronouncement stories that were circulating through the Greek world and that were also used by earlier, contemporary, and later writers'. Josephus relates only nine pronouncement stories, none of which are set 'in any period prior to the time of Persian domination'.[2] Hence, the 'biographical interests of Greek writers in philosophers, poets and politicians provide a much better background for the apophthegmatic interests of the early New Testament community in Jesus'.[3] This evidence suggests that the pronouncement stories as we have them in the Gospels are strongly influenced by Hellenistic literary patterns and have their most natural point of origin within this specific milieu.

d. *Parabolic Stories and Orality*

Parabolic stories, according to Kelber, are another easily recognizable component of the Gospels' oral heritage. There are six of these units in Mark: the Sower (4.3-8); the Reaper (4.26-29); the Mustard Seed

1. 'Tannaitic literature is generally unconcerned with the personality of a single individual or of select groups of individuals', G.G. Porton, 'The Pronouncement Story in Tannaitic Literature: A Review of Bultmann's Theory', *Semeia* 20 (1981), pp. 81-99; here p. 94.
2. L. Greenspoon, 'The Pronouncement Story in Philo and Josephus', *Semeia* 20 (1981), p. 76.
3. Guenther, 'Greek: Home of Primitive Christianity', p. 254.

(4.30-32); the Wicked Tenants (12.1-11); the Fig Tree (13.28); and the Doorkeeper (13.34). Parabolic discourse can be found elsewhere in the Gospel (cf. 2.21-22; 3.23-27; 4.21, 22, 24-25; 7.15 and 9.50). Mk 4.33-34, Kelber notes, in fact identifies Jesus, the oral performer, exclusively with parabolic speech.[1] Kelber observes that the oral property of parabolic stories requires little argument: '[s]peaking is the ordinary mode of parabolic discourse, and writing in parables seems almost out of place'.[2]

But parables, despite their incontrovertibly oral nature, are not susceptible to a uniform compositional structure. Individual parables can be mnemonically shaped and groups of parables can be identified by common structures, but there is no single pattern to the form. Nor do they have a formulaic, compositional structure similar to that of the heroic tales, polarization stories or the didactic stories.

Mnemonic patterning has left its imprint on two Markan parables in particular, and on a third to a lesser extent. The Sower has a sharp contrast between triple failure and triple success of the seed; the Mustard Seed contrasts the smallest of the seeds with the largest of plants. These contrasts aid in the memorization and transmission of these parables, since 'the display of opposites appeals to the imagination and holds the attention as few rhetorical devices do'.[3] The third example of this patterning is in the Wicked Tenants: in the *Gospel of Thomas* there is the threefold mission of the owner to the labourers. Trebling, as well as doubling, of narrative features is a common oral strategy. In contrast to Thomas, Mark's version interrupts this structure with the addition of other servants. But, Kelber argues, one has not arrived at the 'original version' by observing that Thomas' version of the story is closer to oral speech and Mark's is more textualized: '[i]n parabolic speech, as in all other acts of speaking, the original form is a phantom of the literate imagination'.[4]

Another aspect of the parables which betrays their oral character is the reversal of everyday expectations. Parables may narrate everyday events, yet frequently this 'everydayness' is put under strain. In the Sower, just as one expects nothing more but inevitable failure, fate is

1. Kelber, *Oral*, p. 58.
2. Kelber, *Oral*, p. 58.
3. Kelber, *Oral*, p. 59.
4. Kelber, *Oral*, p. 59.

1. *Oral Tradition Taken for Granted* 65

turned around through the advent of the good soil. Stark failure is thus contrasted with the abundance of the harvest. In the Mustard Seed there is a paradoxical contrast in the emphasis on the herb's original and concluding state. In parables the impression of realism is deceiving, for the stories contain elements of surprise, hyperbole and paradox. This accords with the growing awareness of the parable's use of shock tactics: it is a story that pretends to be about the ordinary and yet embraces the 'extraordinary within the ordinary'.[1] This hermeneutical extravagance illustrates the mnemonic process of parabolic stories: over and 'above mnemonic patterning, it is the element of excess and irregularity that eases remembering. The trivial facilitates identification, but oddness makes these stories memorable'.[2]

This hermeneutical open-endedness renders parables particularly dependent on the oral context. A parable is not intended to be frozen into textuality; gestures, facial expressions and tone of voice are all crucial aids in conveying the parable's meaning without saying it directly. This implies that no one form can be held as the 'original': every performance is a fresh act, and each social context suggests a different performance. This hermeneutical inexhaustibility is another factor in parables' mnemonic attractiveness. Hence they 'prompt retelling and rehearsing' since they are 'never fully narrated'.[3]

The argument is this: features A, B and C are proper to the oral medium; texts 1, 2 and 3 display characteristics A, B and C; hence texts 1, 2 and 3 were at one point oral. Kelber is correct to emphasize the considerable role that audience and context play in the oral delivery of such an hermeneutically flexible entity as the parable. Tone of voice, gestures, pace and a host of other live delivery techniques affect the parable's 'meaning' in any given performance.[4] All these factors are lost to us in the Gospel text. Yet Kelber has

---

1. Kelber, *Oral*, p. 60, quoting P. Ricoeur, 'Biblical Hermeneutics', *Semeia* 4 (1975), p. 98.
2. Kelber, *Oral*, p. 61.
3. Kelber, *Oral*, p. 62.
4. Compare Vansina's description of oral performance: 'The tale is acted out with body gestures, even when the storyteller is sitting. Sometimes he or she may stand up, move around, and mime parts of the action narrated. In most cases the public is not just watching. The public is active. It interacts with the teller, and the teller provokes this interaction by asking questions, welcoming exclamations, and turning to a song sung by all at appropriate points of the action. The teller and public are creating the tale together.' *Oral Tradition*, p. 34.

overstated the case, I believe, in his assertion that no one form of a parable can be held as more original than another. This is true only of the oral medium, but it certainly is not true of parables incorporated in written Gospels. Redaction considerations must be allowed their proper methodological role. The clearly allegorical features, for example, in Matthew's version of the Marriage Feast as compared with Luke's Great Banquet fit well in the evangelist's textual redactional concerns. These elements are not equally authentic or original details of the oral parabolic story; they are post-resurrectional and secondary alterations. They reflect an historical setting completely out of keeping with that of the historical Jesus. Kelber has not taken account of what specialists of oral tradition have long recognized: the almost total congruence between a society and its traditions. An alteration in the social organization of a society is quickly accompanied by a change in its traditions which bring tale and society back into harmony. As Vansina remarks 'the corpus of traditions constantly changes and cannot correspond to a past reality'.[1] A vast difference exists between the social setting of the historical Jesus and the Gospel authors; scholars must be fully aware of this fact and open to the possibility that the written text of parables (or other units) has been altered in the course of transmission to reflect the new social and institutional situations.

e. *Markan Style and Oral Syntax*

Mark's literary style, according to Kelber, displays the oral heritage behind this Gospel. Included in this evidence are the numerous paratactic devices used to tie the various blocks of tradition together. Kelber notes, for example, the use of ἄρχεσθαι with infinitive verbs (2.23; 6.7); the adverbial εὐθύς and καὶ εὐθύς (1.29; 3.6); iterative πάλιν and καὶ πάλιν (usually with verbs of movement, 2.1; 7.31;

---

1. Vansina, *Oral Tradition*, p. 120. See J. Goody and I. Watt, 'The Consequences of Literacy', in *Literacy in Traditional Societies* (ed. J. Goody; Cambridge: Cambridge University Press, 1968), pp. 27-68. Goody's thesis is of total congruence; Vansina disputes this claim in favour of near perfect congruence. Compare also Vansina's comments on oral society's notion of historical cause and effect: 'Oral societies, however, tend to have a simpler notion of historical causality, one which negates gradual change altogether. They tend to view institutions and techniques as unitary phenomena that came into existence fully fledged as they are in the present. In other words they operate with a notion of change that opposes the present to a single past and not to a variety of pasts', pp. 130-31.

14.40; or speaking, 4.1; 10.1, 10); the ever popular καί (9.2; 11.20) and the formulaic καὶ γίνεται or καὶ ἐγένετο (1.9; 2.15). These connectives, according to Kelber, 'are for the most part derived from the oral repertoire of the gospel's primary building blocks'.[1] They connect the units together into a chronological framework and underscore the narrative's urgency by piling up events one on top of another.

Other stylistic devices contribute to Mark's oral flavour. Kelber points to the deep penetration into the narrative of folkloristic triads, the frequent use of the third person plural instead of the passive (5.14; 8.22) which is in keeping with the popular style of storytelling, and the constant use of the historic present. Further, there is the preference for direct speech, 'or the tendency for indirect discourse to become direct speech' (1.40; 10.32-33) and the use of parenthetical clauses (3.30; 13.14) to enliven the style and serve as *ad hominem* directives.[2] Added to this is the Markan phenomenon of duality, which Kelber notes has been well documented by Frans Neirynck: the vast number of pleonasms, redundancies and repetitions.[3] This massive repetition, so fundamental to Mark's way of thinking and writing, is evidence for Kelber of a concession to oral needs and not a sign of Mark's limitations as writer.[4] This repetition within the text is seldom verbatim: often the first reference is of a general nature while the second adds precision. This narrative repetition serves both speaker and hearer in their narrative and mnemonic needs. Kelber calls this phenomenon 'progressive duplication' and he believes that it fosters recall.[5]

This aspect of Kelber's thesis is supported by Christopher D. Marshall. He believes that in evaluating Mark's skills as a writer allowance must be made for a speaking and not a writing style. 'Indeed', he tells us, 'the written gospel could well be the result of

1. Kelber, *Oral*, p. 65.
2. Kelber, *Oral*, p. 66.
3. Kelber, *Oral*, p. 66. Citing F. Neirynck, *Duality in Mark: Contributions to the Study of the Markan Redaction* (BETL, 31; Leuven: Leuven University Press, 1972), pp. 49-50.
4. Kelber, *Oral* p. 67, here in contrast to V. Taylor, *The Gospel According to St Mark* (London: Macmillan, 2nd edn, 1966), p. 53.
5. Kelber, *Oral*, pp. 67-68.

Mark writing down, more or less verbatim, the story which he had already told several times in oral form'.[1]

An oral flavour to a narrative, however, does not prove an oral tradition. While there is room for debate about the exact scope of Mark's redaction, there is enough consensus to warrant caution in accepting Kelber's argument. The adverbial εὐθύς and καὶ εὐθύς, for example, are not confined to those sections of the Gospel that might be suspected as traditional. These stylistic devices (cf. καί, πάλιν, καὶ γίνεται and καὶ ἐγένετο) are found throughout Mark's narrative, including the connecting geographic links. The folkloristic triads of action to which Kelber points (e.g. three passion predictions) should give us pause. They belong to Mark's overall narrative structure, and are clearly a part of his *literary* technique. By claiming these features as indications of Mark's oral heritage Kelber has not sufficiently questioned the appropriateness of his model of oral tradition. Recognition that these features are part of Mark's literary style should have caused Kelber to modify his view of the deep chasm between orality and textuality.[2]

f. *Jesus the Oral Performer*
Kelber provides us with a reconstruction of Jesus the oral performer. 'It is imperative', he asserts, 'to trace the very phenomenon of early synoptic orality to Jesus himself. Like Socrates, he moved and discoursed in the oral medium, without—as far as is known—ever committing a word to writing'. Jesus' *Sitz im Leben* as an oral performer (partly derived from Parry and Lord's picture of oral bards), represents a different 'Jesus' from that of the canonical Gospels.

> The specifically scribal, Rabbinic model of Jesus the authoritative interpreter of the Torah was clearly shaped by the theological interests of Matthew. All four canonical gospels, however, supply us with the general picture of Jesus as speaker of authoritative and often disturbing words,

---

1. C.D. Marshall, *Faith as a Theme in Mark's Narrative* (SNTSMS, 64; Cambridge: Cambridge University Press, 1989), p. 18.

2. On Markan redactional style, see (for example) H.C. Kee, *Community of the New Age: Studies in Mark's Gospel* (Philadelphia: Westminster Press, 1977); and J. Pryke, *Redactional Style in the Marcan Gospel: A Study of Syntax and Vocabulary as Guides to Redaction in Mark* (Cambridge: Cambridge University Press, 1978).

and not as reader, writer, or head of a school tradition. Insofar as he is featured as a prophetic speaker and eschatological teacher, moving from one place to another, surrounded by listeners and engaged in debate, the gospels will have retained a genuine aspect of the oral performer. His message and his person are inextricably tied to the spoken word, not to texts.[1]

Jesus the oral performer helps Kelber explain the impact Jesus had 'on friends and foes alike'. Spoken words breathe life, 'drawing their strength from sound'. Hearers are addressed directly with an intimacy unattainable by a text. 'One can well imagine Jesus' words interacting with people and their lives, and enacting presence amidst hearers.'[2] Hence, the beginnings of the Christian tradition go back to Jesus himself. 'He sought out people because he had something to say, and part of what he said and did will already have been passed on during his lifetime. For this reason alone, one must disagree with Bultmann's thesis of the post-Easter commencement of the tradition'.[3]

Kelber's portrait is strikingly romantic, given his awareness of the variability within orality and his thesis that no tradition can be claimed as the original. If we are to talk of the historical Jesus in a meaningful way, it is imperative that we first establish a core of authentic material. Kelber has proceeded differently. He notes the general setting for oral performers as set forth by Parry and Lord and applies the model to Jesus. But problems quickly emerge. Jesus the oral performer—if we are to proceed from the evidence of Parry and Lord—must be viewed as no different from any other oral performer. While distinctions are to be made between Moses, Diogenes, Hillel, Honi the Circle Drawer and Avdo Mededović, how are we to make these distinctions in the absence of concrete evidence? All of them performed in the oral medium; Jesus is not distinctive. The vividness of Kelber's account and its ability to 'bring to life' Jesus before the reader's eyes lies in the literary background of the Gospels. Jesus, we are told, moves from one place to another and immediately we see him embark into the boat with the command, 'Let us cross over to the other side' (Mk 4.35). He is 'surrounded by listeners and engaged in debate' and immediately we think of Mark's pressing crowds and hostile scribes and Pharisees. He has a tremendous impact

1. Kelber, *Oral*, p. 18.
2. Kelber, *Oral*, pp. 18-19.
3. Kelber, *Oral*, p. 20.

on friend and foe alike and we hear the wondrous praise 'Where did this man get all this? What is this wisdom given to him?' (Mk 6.2) and remember that 'he taught them as one who had authority, and not as the scribes' (Mk 1.22). Indeed, '[o]ne *can well imagine* Jesus' words interacting with people and their lives, and enacting presence amidst hearers'.[1] And that is precisely the problem, one can draw up a similar such portrait of Paul the oral performer from the narrative in Acts. Contemporary scholarship (and exegesis of Paul's letters) warn us against this assumption.[2]

g. *Kelber's Lasting Contribution*
Kelber's study justly caused a 'scholarly sensation'—if academics can be said to be an excitable lot. He stands in a tradition of Gospel criticism in continuity with Robert Funk, J.D. Crossan and others. The cumulative effect of Crossan's *In Fragments* along with Kelber's text has dramatically altered most Gospel critics' perception of orality. The Parry–Lord insistence on the impossibility of establishing *the* 'authentic' or 'original' form of an oral tradition is much more in evidence. Scholars now habitually speak, like Crossan, of the 'Aphoristic core' or the parable's essential structure. B.B. Scott, for example, can note that 'each extant version of a parable, even if literarily dependent on another version, is a new performance'.[3] Christopher D. Marshall can comment that the 'demands of oral delivery help explain Mark's vernacular Greek and his vivid style.'[4] John R. Donahue remarks that the parables were spoken, and hence 'share in the dynamics of oral, interpersonal dialogue. Things such as the situation that evoked their original utterance, the tone in which they were spoken, and the bodily expression with which they were heard—a shrug, a sigh, or a snarl—all are lost to us'.[5] In all of this we can detect that these scholars have read their Kelber and been suitably impressed and influenced. Almost totally absent is the attempt

---

1. Kelber, *Oral*, p. 19. Emphasis added.
2. See particularly J. Knox, *Chapters in a Life of Paul* (Nashville: Abingdon Press, 1950); G. Bornkamm, *Paul* (trans. D.M.G. Stalke; New York: Harper & Row, 1971).
3. B.B. Scott, *Hear then the Parable: A Commentary on the Parables of Jesus* (Minneapolis: Fortress Press, 1989), p. 5.
4. Marshall, *Faith as a Theme in Mark's Narrative*, pp. 18-19.
5. J.R. Donahue, *The Gospel in Parable: Metaphor, Narrative, and Theology in the Synoptic Gospels* (Philadelphia: Fortress Press, 1988), p. 3.

to recover the original Aramaic wording underlying the synoptic accounts, a quest that occupied much of the time and efforts of an earlier generation of scholars.

Although basing his thesis heavily upon Parry–Lord, Kelber notes an important methodological distinction. In considering the possibility of a full oral Gospel (a thesis developed by J.G. Herder and supported by such scholars in the twentieth century as A.B. Lord and T.E. Boomershine) one cannot appeal to the *Iliad* and the *Odyssey*. Kelber argues that these are oral poems in metrical language. The Gospels, however, are prose narratives with 'a heavy oral substratum, but in themselves something other than transcribed orality'.[1] Kelber notes that Homer and such folksingers as Avdo Mededović were able to draw upon the accumulation of centuries of oral culture whereas Mark's oral heritage had really just gotten underway. The oral substratum for Mark, however, is seen in the full narrative self-sufficiency of the stories.[2]

This distinction needs further exploration. Kelber has pointed to the importance of the fact that Parry and Lord worked with epic poetry, while the Gospels are narrative prose. He has not, however, fully explored the difference this should make in our understanding of orality in the synoptic tradition. This distinction is the focus of Chapter 2. As a prelude to that, it is necessary to draw out the implications of our study of Bultmann, Gerhardsson and Kelber.

5. *Critique of Oral Tradition Taken for Granted*

The above discussion has explored three distinctive approaches to the problem of oral tradition. The early form critics Bultmann and Dibelius represented a profound gain in our understanding of this phase of the tradition. Form criticism allowed scholars to explore that phase of tradition not directly accessible through such tools as source-criticism. The form critics undertook a detailed and careful exegetical study of the Gospel materials. Although a number of their assumptions can no longer be accepted, this aspect of their work is

1. Kelber, *Oral*, p. 78. Noting A.B. Lord, 'The Gospels as Oral Traditional Literature', in *The Relationships Among the Gospels: An Interdisciplinary Dialogue* (ed. W.O. Walker; San Antonio, TX: Trinity University Press, 1978), pp. 33-91 and T.E. Boomershine, 'Oral Tradition and Mark' (unpublished manuscript, 1979).

2. Kelber, *Oral*, p. 79.

particularly commendable. The foundational work of H. Gunkel is important in regard to form criticism's operating assumptions: early form critics took for their model a study of material that was presumed to have circulated orally for generations before finally being set down in documents. It was an unproved assumption of the form critics that the 'laws' of transmission that were thought to have been at work in the materials of the Hebrew Bible were also operative within the transmission of the Gospels' traditions. Fundamental also is the assumption of an active and vigorous stage of oral tradition and transmission, and a view of the Gospels' writers as relators of traditions and not authors in their own rights.

Form criticism was based on an 'evolutionary' assumption. The notion of 'pure forms' is instructive: literary units are conceived as having originated in these pure forms and having degenerated into hybrids during the transmissional phase. The form itself is seen as a sure indication of the unit's point of origin and relative age. The assumption is clear: the Gospel authors would not compose certain forms or units as written units: a paradigm is almost always seen as having originated in the oral phase and not with the evangelist.

Kelber has noted correctly the exclusive emphasis upon a tradition of growth. Bultmann's hypothetical reconstruction of the Q saying regarding a Kingdom Divided is instructive: he has reconstructed a core saying to which were added two other independently circulating sayings and then after that a third, presumably all before the incorporation into Q. Furthermore, Bultmann has tended to assume that the taking over of traditional proverbs and other such cultural materials has been done during the oral phase and not by the evangelists. In his reconstruction of the message of Jesus, he does not place great weight on this material, but he assumes too readily that all such materials had a pre-history during the oral phase.

The memory and manuscript approach to oral tradition also raises questions. The back-dating of the rabbinic techniques to the pre-70 CE era is a key problem, and so is the direct application to the Jesus tradition. Even granting that this method was operative prior to the Temple's destruction does not guarantee that it was employed in the early Christian communities. Gerhardsson has, fortunately, provided a detailed study of the parable of the Sower, and that study will provide a good basis for an evaluation of his thesis regarding the Christian traditions themselves. There is also the problem of reading back into the oral phase the apologetical motifs of the evangelists. Luke's theological concern with the eyewitnesses and the role of the Jerusalem church comes readily to mind.

Kelber's study contributes significantly. Especially relevant is the use of folkloric analysis and the studies of Parry and Lord in his critique of both Bultmann and Gerhardsson. Still, Kelber's analysis leaves a number of important problems unresolved. First, Kelber posits a deep chasm between the two media, but why would Mark freeze and preserve oral forms of speech in his textual medium if the two modes of transmission were so thoroughly incompatible? Like the form critics, Kelber too readily assumes that the form is sufficient guarantee of an oral history. Why is it so impossible that Mark himself might be the first to compose a controversy dialogue or a miracle story, or the first to place onto Jesus' lips an aphorism from the general cultural heritage?

Kelber is quite insistent that in an oral medium the notion of an original form is anachronistic. The form critics' thesis of 'narrative degeneration' allowed them to stratify the synoptic materials on the basis of form. Pronouncement stories, during the course of transmission, evolved successively into miracle narratives, legends and myths. This assumption allowed scholars to trace material back through the oral phase. Each step brought one closer to Jesus. Once it is seen that this assumption is at variance with what specialists of orality emphasize, it is far more difficult to trace material back. After making allowance for the redactional concerns of the author in which one finds a tradition, what principles remain to assist in tracing the unit's history through the oral phase itself?

Even in Kelber there is a fundamental tension regarding this problem. He realizes that the concept of an 'original' or 'authentic' version of an oral unit is meaningless, yet he also wants to postulate a form and context in the ministry of the historical Jesus. Such a notion rests on the assumption that he has established a core of authentic material. Kelber even argues that traditions that are more in accord with oral hermeneutics are not necessarily earlier than those that display a greater degree of textual hermeneutics (as in the parable of the Wicked Tenants).

The compatibility of folkloric studies and the Gospels is still unresolved. Kelber himself notes that the Gospel traditions are not formulaic in nature. Nor were they transmitted as poetry, as were the materials investigated by Parry and Lord. These differences need to be understood fully before the Parry–Lord model of orality can be applied to the Gospel traditions.

Finally, and most importantly, all three approaches suffer from the same flaw: they all start with a reconstruction of the oral phase and follow the tradition through to the written text. This has led to an overwhelming assumption of orality behind the written text. The journey, as it were, is all downstream; Bultmann, Gerhardsson and Kelber alike all get carried along by the current.

What if this assumption is not made? Since the oral phase is no longer available to us any reconstruction of oral tradition must begin with the text. The textual medium itself must be fully analysed in order to establish the limits of a reconstruction of any previous oral tradition. Each author's distinctive literary style and theological concerns need to be established before recourse to 'orality' can be invoked as an explanation. The literary conventions of the first century need to be explored to establish how these various forms functioned in written texts before asking about the oral stage. Miracle narratives, pronouncement stories, chreiae, proverbs, aphorisms, allegories and parables all have their home in the literature of the first century. We cannot assume that a synoptic tradition is guaranteed an oral history. In order to resolve some of these questions I now turn to a detailed examination of Parry and Lord and an assessment of the applicability of their method to Gospel texts.

Chapter 2

ORALITY IN PERSPECTIVE: THE CONTRIBUTION
OF FOLKLORIC ANALYSIS

Life is like a library owned by an author. In it are a few books which he
wrote himself, but most of them were written for him.

Harry Emerson Fosdick

Kelber begins his presentation of orality with a distinction between a
spoken, living word and the written, dead text. It is a difference
acknowledged, he tells us, by virtually every contemporary theorist of
orality. Differences may exist regarding the degree of this distinction,
but agreement exists that one must 'postulate separate hermeneutics'.[1]
But it is significant that Kelber has derived his model of orality
predominantly based on Homer and contemporary Yugoslavian
illiterate bards. Both are formulaic epic, not the Gospels' narrative
prose, and both presuppose a social context of illiteracy. This latter
difference is particularly important given the Gospels' urban
Hellenistic milieu. Hence any oral material in them has passed through
a literate context. Furthermore, the Parry–Lord thesis is not without
controversy; for example, their clear-cut distinctions between the oral
and written word cannot be substantiated. As Vansina remarks, it
'turns out that the only marked difference between oral and written
utterances is that repetition occurs more frequently in oral
communication'.[2] Without Lord's clear distinction, the identification
of the so-called 'oral bedrock' underneath the written Gospel text is
not as easily accomplished as biblical critics have assumed.

1. Kelber, *Oral*, p. 14.
2. Vansina, *Oral Tradition*, p. 69.

1. *The Parry–Lord Thesis*

It is important to recognize the undoubted contribution Parry and Lord have made to our knowledge of orality. Like the Dead Sea Scrolls, their find represents a real breakthrough and it is understandable that the first applications of this insight would be overzealous. Parry's studies, dating from the twenties and thirties, focus on Homer and contemporary Yugoslavian oral poems. Lord began as Parry's student in Yugoslavia and subsequently, after the former's untimely death, continued his studies with a doctoral thesis at Harvard. This work served as the basis of *The Singer of Tales*. H. Levin, referring to Parry as the 'Darwin of oral literature' states that Lord is the one who 'has turned an exciting aperçu into a convincing argument'.[1] Distinctions must be made between these scholars, but there is enough continuity to refer to the Parry–Lord theory of oral tradition.

a. *Performance and Orality*
In setting out to explain the compositional technique of Homer, Parry turned to contemporary epic for his comparison. Lord defines oral epic as 'narrative poetry composed in a manner evolved over many generations by singers of tales who did not know how to write'.[2] For Parry, oral poetry is controlled by the necessities of performance. Performance constricts the poet since there is no time to reflect on the next line. This is different from written poetry—the oral poet must rely on ready-made phrases in composition.[3] Since there is no gap between composition and performance, an 'oral poem is not composed *for* but *in* performance'.[4] Since contemporary Yugoslavian bards can sing 10 to 20 10-syllable lines a minute, Lord argues that these poets

---

1. H. Levin's comments in the preface to *The Singer of Tales*, p. xv.
2. Lord, *Singer*, p. 4.
3. M. Parry, 'Studies in the Epic Technique of Oral Verse-Making, I: Homer and Homeric Style', *HSCP* 41 (1930), p. 77. This study is continued in M. Parry, 'Studies in the Epic Technique of Oral Verse-Making, II: The Homeric Language as the Language of an Oral Poetry', *HSCP* 43 (1932), pp. 1-50. References to this two-part study will be given as, 'Epic I' and 'Epic II' respectively.
4. Lord, *Singer*, p. 13.

must have a 'special technique of composition outside our own field of experience'.[1]

Performance is also constricted by the poem's fixed meter. Poets must thus rely on traditional ready-made formulae that fit this meter, phrases that they have already heard. Since this restricts the poet to those themes or ideas that already have a fixed means of expression, there is an interplay between creativity and restriction. As Parry notes, the poet 'can put his phrases together in an endless number of ways; but still they set bounds and forbid him the search of a style which would be altogether his own'.[2]

Since the Gospels are not transcriptions of performances by illiterate bards, the evangelists were freed from the necessity of rapid composition and could create any number of redactional phrases. Mark's editorial comment at 7.19b is an obvious case. Secondly, the evangelists could dwell on each phrase and change their material as they wished, as seen by Matthew and Luke's rewriting of Mark and Q. This reworking affects both the narrative frames and the sayings of Jesus. No element of the text is immune from alteration. Assuming an 'oral tradition', it is possible that the text would bear no sign of the stylistic expression of orality.

Moving into the oral phase, we must note the effects of the compositional setting. The constraints of rapid epic composition in performance set incredible limitations on the poet, while the Gospel oral tradition might have passed through an entirely different sociological situation which would imply a distinctive technique. These differences in social setting for composition must be borne in mind when we attempt to apply the insights of Parry and Lord to the Gospels.

b. *Orality and a Communal Social Context*
Parry views oral traditional literature as communal. Since the poet relies on a vast number of formulae, the style of the poem is 'the creation of a long line of poets or even of an entire people'.[3] Any one author cannot be responsible for more than the smallest portion of these formulae. After one poet finds a phrase both pleasing and easily used it is taken up by the group and preserved. The first stage in the

1. Lord, *Singer*, p. 17.
2. Parry, 'Epic I', pp. 77-78.
3. Parry, 'Epic I', p. 78.

training of an epic poet is simply listening to older poets performing. 'Even at this early stage the oft-repeated phrases which we call formulas are being absorbed.'[1]

This communal origin of oral epics raises a problem for tracing orality behind the Gospels, particularly for any attribution of material to Jesus. In the parables, for example, scholars have argued that there was a thesaurus of stereotyped traditional elements, such as characterization, plot and phraseology. David Stern suggests that the parablist 'was able to draw upon a kind of ideal thesaurus of stereotyped traditional elements' in order to improvise a parable under spontaneous conditions.[2] But this comparison raises a number of problems for identifying 'oral tradition'. The existence of an extensive thesaurus of common-place plots and characterizations points to a communal origin for such oral tradition and must be regarded as antithetical to attributing the parables to any particular individual. This thesaurus would have been equally available to the evangelists and the authors of any literary sources they inherited. In such instances there is no guarantee that the author has not turned to this thesaurus to provide an appropriate parable for the narrative. If we move back into the oral phase itself, this thesaurus raises a serious barrier to recovery of authentic sayings of Jesus. If we compare the parables to the *Iliad*, it is clear that Jesus cannot be equated with Homer. The latter represents the final textualized performance of an epic that has passed through generations of oral transmission, but Jesus must be viewed as only one in a long tradition of performers. Viewing Jesus as the single source of the parables is simply unhistorical; he stands in the midst of a continually developing tradition. Like the formulae themselves, the parabolic thesaurus must be viewed as a communal composition. No one performer is the author of more than the smallest portion of the whole. To develop Fosdick's illustration, if in the parables we have wandered into Jesus' library we see that he has authored only a few—maybe none!—of the books, but all of them have his name on the title page. Even if Jesus authored a few, how do we tell which ones?

---

1. Lord, *Singer*, p. 21.
2. D. Stern, 'Rhetoric and Midrash: The Case of Mashal', *Prooftexts* 1 (1981), p. 268. See also Scott, *Hear then the Parable*, p. 18: 'Thus the parablist operated like the singers studied by A. Lord and M. Parry or the tellers of Russian fairy tales analyzed by V. Propp'.

c. *Orality and the Formula*

Parry defines the Homeric formula as '*a group of words which is regularly employed under the same metrical conditions to express a given essential idea*' .[1] Thus the essential idea in ἦμος δ' ἠριγένεια φάνη ῥοδοδάκτυλος 'Ηώς is 'when it was morning'.[2] Such formulae are employed regularly without second thought as the natural means of putting an idea into verse. For a formula to be used frequently there must be continual need for it. For example, Homer uses θεὰ γλαυκῶπις 'Αθήνη ('the goddess, flashing-eyed Athene') 50 times in the last half of the verse to express the idea 'Athena'.[3]

The formula must be distinguished from other repeated phrases: without the element of usefulness one does not have a formula but 'a repeated phrase which has been knowingly brought into the verse for some special effect'.[4] As examples Parry gives αἴλινον αἴλινον εἰπέ, τὸ δ' εὖ νικάτω in Aeschylus;[5] and Shakespeare's 'Double, double toil and trouble, / Fire burn and cauldron bubble'.[6] The definition excludes such echoed phrases as χρήισδεις καταθεῖναι ἄεθλον (Theocritus 8, 11-12). Excluded also is the borrowed verse which the poet knows the audience will recall. As Parry emphasizes, 'no distinction counts more for us than this between the real formula and the phrase repeated for the sake of its poetic thought or wording.'[7]

The definition of the formula and its differentiation from other written language, however, is not so straightforward. J.A. Russo points out that Parry's definition was subsequently expanded by scholars who found it too narrow to account for other formulaic

1. Parry, 'Epic I', p. 80.
2. Parry, 'Epic I', p. 80.
3. Parry, 'Epic I', p. 80.
4. Parry, 'Epic I', p. 81.
5. 'Sing the song of woe, the song of woe, but may the good prevail!' Aeschylus, *Agamemnon* 121, 139, 159. Translation by H.W. Smyth, *Aeschylus* (The Loeb Classical Library; Cambridge MA: Harvard University Press, 1926), II. Note also 'Wryneck, wryneck, draw him hither', Theocritus 2, 17; 22; 27; 32; 37; 42; 47; 52; 57; 63; J.M. Edmonds (trans.), *The Greek Bucolic Poets* (The Loeb Classical Library; Cambridge, MA: Harvard University Press, 1912).
6. *Macbeth* IV, i, 10-11; 20-21; 35-36.
7. Parry, 'Epic I', p. 83.

phenomena.[1] J.B. Hainsworth argues that patterns of repetitions of phrase are to be found in all rhetorically organized styles of verbal expression including the Roman orators and the early Greek epic. From this Russo argues that at 'what point such repetition becomes explainable *only* in terms of oral style or oral creation can never be known with certainty'.[2] A further study by W.W. Minton shows that these 'pattern' or structural style formulae are common in later literate poets such as Apollonius Rhodius and thus cannot be treated as distinctively oral characteristics.[3]

Hence, the sharp distinction between oral and written literature disappears when we examine a broader range of written literature. The formulae thus become less certain guides to the recovery of oral antecedents in a written text. The distinction between an oral formula and a repeated phrase is particularly relevant in the study of early Christian literature. Precisely when is a repeated phrase formulaic and hence oral? At Mk 4.9, for example, we find 'Let anyone with ears to hear listen!' Similar injunctions are found at 4.23; Mt. 11.15; 13.43; Lk. 8.8; 14.35. Need we conclude a separate oral performance of the phrase together with its context for every written version? The textual variant adding such a phrase at Mk 7.16 (A, D, K, W) testifies how easily such material can be repeated as redaction. Similarly, Mark relates three passion predictions (8.31; 9.31; 10.33). Is this evidence of three separate oral performances? Considering such ubiquitous Markan phrases as καὶ εὐθύς, καὶ ἔλεγεν αὐτοῖς, or καὶ ἤρξατο διδάσκειν it is clear that Parry's distinction is of fundamental importance. Repetition of a phrase is not proof of an oral tradition behind the written text.

Parry divides the formulae into two classes. First there are those without any likeness to any other, for example the phrase ὀνείαθ' ἑτοῖμα προκείμενα (in the *Iliad* three times and in the *Odyssey* 11

---

1. J.A. Russo, 'Is "Oral" or "Aural" Composition the Cause of Homer's Formulaic Style?', in *Oral Literature and the Formula* (ed. B.A. Stola and R.S. Shannon; Ann Arbor: Center for the Coordination of Ancient and Modern Studies, University of Michigan, 1976), p. 32.

2. Russo, 'Homer's Formulaic Style', p. 33. Noting J.B. Hainsworth, 'Structure and Content in Epic Formulae: The Question of the Unique Expression', *Classical Quarterly* ns 14 (1964), pp. 155-64.

3. W.W. Minton, 'The Fallacy of the Structural Formula', *TAPA* 96 (1965), pp. 241-53.

times).[1] Secondly, there is the formula that forms part of a system used to express similar ideas. Hence ἱερὸν πτολίεθρον ἔπερσε is like ἱερὸν πτολίεθρον ἑλόντες.[2] Parry sets forth an extensive system that expresses the idea 'but when he (we, they) had done so and so'. Variations on this include 'But when I had stayed the wrath of the gods', 'But when they had satisfied their eyes with gazing', and 'But when he had busily performed his tasks'.[3] It is this system, often very extensive, that allows for rapid composition. Parry notes the names/epithets that are fitted into the last half of the verse such as θεὰ γλαυκῶπις Ἀθήνη ('the goddess, flashing-eyed Athene'—50 times). Well over 50 such formulas can be found. Hence, 'the length and the thrift of the system are striking enough to be sure proof that only the very smallest part of it could be the work of one poet.'[4]

The formulaic systems need to be singled out when applying the Parry–Lord thesis to the Gospels. No such systems can be found in this material. Since these systems are based on the necessity of fitting the verse into the poem's meter, they often have to break the normal structures of syntax or keep archaic usages. 'Verbs may be placed in unusual positions, auxiliaries may be omitted, cases may be used strangely.'[5] Archaic forms may also have to be retained to preserve the formula. Hence in μητίετα Ζεύς (19 times in Homer) and Διὸς αἰγιόχοιο (19 times) the Ionic poets had to keep the Aeolic endings or lose the formulae.[6] But since formulaic language is so resistant to change it is impossible to imagine its translation from one language to another. If the oral tradition behind the Gospels originated in formulaic Aramaic, it is impossible to imagine it being translated into formulaic Greek.

The distinctive formula provides its own problems. We have noted the free-floating saying at Mk 4.9 above. Consider the phrase 'relax, eat, drink, be merry!' (Lk. 12.19). This has a close parallel at Isa. 22.12-14; Tobit 7.9; 1 Cor. 15.32; and in an inscription on the tomb

1. Parry, 'Epic I', p. 84.
2. Parry, 'Epic I', p. 85.
3. The system is set forth at 'Epic I', p. 85. See the *Odyssey*, at 4, 47; 4, 583; 8, 276; 8, 282. Translations from A.T. Murray (trans.), *Homer, The Odyssey* (The Loeb Classical Library; Cambridge, MA: Harvard University Press, 1919).
4. Parry, 'Epic I', p. 87.
5. Lord, *Singer*, p. 32.
6. Parry, 'Epic I', p. 136.

of Sardinapalus.[1] The number of literary parallels demonstrates a well-known proverb. But this again puts us in the situation of the Golden Rule and creates a problem in determining an earlier 'oral tradition' behind any single text. The appearance of the motif may in fact be based on the author's conscious use of a known proverb. Paul's use of the saying at 1 Cor. 15.32, for example, is not evidence of an oral tradition behind his discussion of the resurrection, only of the literary citation of a well-known adage. Luke (at 12.19) could be basing himself on the literary text in either Isaiah or Tobit; the phrase itself may not have an 'oral history' as part of an oral parable. It is easier in such instances to assume an oral tradition than to prove it.

d. *Percentage and Volume of Formulae in Oral Epic*
Parry discusses the incredible number of formulaic repetitions in Homer, contrasted to poetry formed when writing is the usual means of composition. In the 1022 verses of Hesiod's *Theogony*, 338 repetitions can be found, most of which are also in Homer. Parry contrasts this to the twenty-five or -six thousand repetitions in Homer's 27,853 verses. Even Hesiod's ratio of repetitions is considerably higher than that found in written poetry. Solon's ratio is close to 21 epic phrases per hundred verses. In Pindar there can be found 52 phrases copied from Homer (48 of only two words), and only 19 of which are word-for-word.[2] This is the result of the special syntax of the formula being inappropriate to the new context of the written poem. Similarly, the number of phrases that Bacchylides could take over from Homer without change is small, only 11 (all of two words each). In Parry's opinion, these repetitions in Pindar and Bacchylides are no longer formulas (as in Homer), they are merely repeated phrases of fine expression kept for their beauty.[3]

There is no internal repetition in Pindar: not one repeated phrase in the 10 pages of the concordance compared to the extensive repetition in Homer.[4] Parry also contrasts the frequency of repetition in Euripides (once in every fortieth iambic verse) to Homer (more than every other verse).[5] There is a qualitative difference between these

1. See Scott, *Hear then the Parable*, pp. 135-36.
2. Parry, 'Epic I', pp. 90-93.
3. Parry, 'Epic I', p. 95.
4. Parry, 'Epic I', p. 99.
5. Parry, 'Epic I', p. 99.

types of repetitions. Most of the repetitions or formulae in Homer do not contain anything in thought or style which would set them apart as particularly effective. For example, Parry finds nothing unusual in ἀλλ' ὅτε δή (Od. 1, 16; 106 times); γαῖαν ἱκέσθαι (Od. 1, 21; 18 times) or οἴκόνδε νέεσθαι [Od. 1, 17; 10 times). This contrasts to Euripides, where the repeated phrases are particularly forceful in expression and rarely used more than once. These phrases are 'not a regular means of expressing the idea but a body of outstanding dramatic artifices'.[1] There is also no indication in them that Euripides was limiting or conforming his thought to the expressions of others.[2] These formulas are inseparable from the thoughts they express. In Euripides, this is different. Parry points to equivalent verses cast in distinctive wording to show that an idea could come to mind without being bound by any one formulaic expression. With formulaic language, thought originates in terms of the formulas and cannot be conceived apart from them.[3]

This aspect of Parry's discussion has clear, and overlooked, implications for the recovery of oral tradition in written Gospel texts. Particularly telling is Parry's observation that the oral formula is not regularly employed by literate poets like Hesiod, Solon, Pindar, Bacchylides and Euripides. He observes that in Pindar and Bacchylides the formula appears merely as a repeated phrase of fine literary expression. The vast majority of oral formulae, in fact, are deemed unsuitable for literary use. The different context is telling. Freed from the necessity of composition in performance, literate authors turned away from the formulaic language of orality to give their thoughts better literary expression. This implies that for the Gospels 'oral tradition' has been translated into the linguistic expression of textuality. Matthew and Luke's rewriting of Mark and Q points to a form of tradition similar to that of Euripides: thoughts may be distilled from their original wording and recast. Mark's introduction to our passage (4.1), καὶ πάλιν ἤρξατο διδάσκειν παρὰ τὴν θάλασσαν· καὶ συνάγεται πρὸς αὐτὸν ὄχλος πλεῖστος... can become for Matthew: Ἐν τῇ ἡμέρᾳ ἐκείνῃ ἐξελθὼν· ὁ Ἰησοῦς τῆς οἰκίας ἐκάθητο παρὰ τὴν θάλασσαν καὶ συνήχθησαν πρὸς αὐτὸν ὄχλοι πολλοί. Even Mark, despite numerous repetitions of

1. Parry, 'Epic I', pp. 104, 122.
2. Parry, 'Epic I', p. 104.
3. Parry, 'Epic I', p. 114.

phrase, is able to vary his wording to a degree impossible in formulaic tradition. Witness the similar themes at 2.13 (cp. 4.1): καὶ ἐξῆλθεν πάλιν παρὰ τὴν θάλασσαν· καὶ πᾶς ὁ ὄχλος ἤρχετο πρὸς αὐτόν, καὶ ἐδίδασκεν αὐτούς.

Formulaic epic poetry, according to Parry, is distinctive in the percentage of the text that has verbal repetitions. Parry quotes the first 25 lines of the *Iliad* and the *Odyssey* with solid underlining beneath phrases found elsewhere in the poems unchanged, and a broken line under phrases that are of the same type as others. I quote here the first five lines of the Odyssey as given by Parry.

The Odyssey

"Ανδρά μοι ἔννεπε Μοῦσα πολύτροπον ὅς μάλα πολλά
πλάγχθη ἐπεὶ Τροίης ἱερὸν πτολίεθρον ἔπερσε
πολλῶν δ' ἀνθρώπων ἴδεν ἄστεα καὶ νόον ἔγνω,
πολλὰ δ' ὅ γ' ἐν πόντωι πάθεν ἄλγεα ὃν κατὰ θυμόν
ἀρνύμενος ἥν τε ψυχὴν καὶ νόστον ἑταίρων.[1]

Parry counts 29 phrases in the first 25 lines of the *Iliad* that are found elsewhere unchanged, and 34 in the *Odyssey*. Over 25 per cent of these occur in at least eight other passages.[2] Lord duplicates these results in his analysis of 15 lines of the 'Song of Bagdad'. Initially confining his comparison to 12,000 lines of other such epics, Lord shows that one quarter of the whole lines and one half of the half-lines are clearly formulaic. No line or portion of a line fails to fit into some formulaic pattern. And had the comparison material been expanded beyond the sample of 12,000 lines, the number of formulae would have increased. Hence Lord states: 'The formulas in oral narrative style are not limited to a comparatively few epic "tags", but are in reality all pervasive. There is nothing in the poem that is not formulaic.'[3]

These results cannot be duplicated for the Gospels. The more numerous repetitions, such as Mark's καὶ ἔλεγεν αὐτοῖς or καὶ ἐξῆλθεν are actually redaction connecting separate units together. The point at which the comparison between Homer and the Gospels seems most promising is in fact at the narrative frames which are

---

1. I have substituted double and single underlines respectively for Parry's conventions. See Parry 'Epic I', pp. 118, 120.
2. Parry, 'Epic I', p. 122.
3. Lord, *Singer*, p. 47.

redactional. The repetition that we encounter most frequently in the Gospels is not the formula, but rather Parry's literary 'repeated phrase'.

e. *Distinguishing Oral from Written Texts*

Lord examines the relationship between oral and written versions of a text. As literacy developed and society sought a permanent text of the song, the singer would be approached to perform the song again. But this would be 'the strangest performance he had ever given', for without the music there would be nothing to aid in keeping the rhythm, while the constant stopping and starting of dictation would also affect delivery. This written version, therefore, would represent but one performance of the text and one moment in the tradition.[1]

Lord raises the problem of 'transitional texts'. Can there be a text that is a transition between oral and written tradition? Lord's thesis is interesting:

> It is worthy of emphasis that the question we have asked ourselves is whether there can be such a thing as a transitional *text*, not a *period* of transition between oral and written style, or between illiteracy and literacy, but a *text*, product of the creative brain of a single individual. When this emphasis is clear, it becomes impossible to turn the question into whether there can be a single individual who in composing an epic would think now in one way and now in another, or, perhaps, in a manner that is a combination of two techniques. I believe that the answer must be in the negative, because the two techniques are, I submit, contradictory and mutually exclusive. Once the oral technique is lost, it is never regained.[2]

The shift to literary compositional technique involves for Lord an acceleration of the breaking of formulaic patterns. This is already observable in the dictated poems, but such instances are felt to be imperfections. When the poet consciously breaks these patterns, and such a break is felt desirable, then we are involved in literary composition.[3]

In differentiating literary from oral texts, Lord offers two main theses. First, there will be a difference in the percentage of formulaic phrases. An oral text will produce a predominance of formula repetitions (with few non-formulaic phrases), while a literary text will

1. Lord, *Singer*, p. 124.
2. Lord, *Singer*, p. 129.
3. Lord, *Singer*, p. 130.

show a predominance of non-formulaic phrases (with few formulaic repetitions). Secondly, an analysis of the different kinds of enjambement is helpful.[1] In oral literature Lord expects we should find that non-periodic enjambement, the 'adding style', is characteristic, while in a literary text there will be periodic enjambement. This test alone is not a reliable guide, since written composition can emphasize composition by line.[2]

Lord's thesis is bold, and the contrast near absolute. The contrast between formulaic epic and non-formulaic literate poetry is so stark it allows for a clear demarcation between the two types of 'literature'. A text that displays a certain volume of formulaic expression and a high degree of adding style non-periodic enjambement is clearly oral. But Lord has not completed the comparisons. He has not questioned whether all oral tradition is formulaic, or whether some literate authors (unlike Pindar, Bacchylides and Euripides) might not choose to write in formulaic language. These questions have been explored by such scholars as Eric Havelock and Ruth Finnegan. Their work shows that Lord's clear-cut distinction between the two media collapses almost entirely. Without these criteria it becomes far more difficult to recover oral antecedents from a written text. I turn first to an examination of Havelock.

2. *Eric Havelock*

a. *Orality and Social Education*
Havelock begins with a different question than that brought by the exegete examining the pre-history of the Gospels. He explores the shape of knowledge when preserved in oral memory and stored for re-use. In Parry's work Havelock detects the reason for the curious speech of Xenophanes, Heraclitus and Parmenides: the 'formulaic style characteristic of oral composition represented not merely certain verbal and metrical habits but also a cast of thought, or a mental condition'.[3] The Pre-Socratics were essentially oral thinkers linked by

---

1. Enjambement may be defined as the 'continuation of sentence beyond end of line, couplet, or stanza'. J.B. Sykes (ed.), *The Concise Oxford Dictionary of Current English* (Oxford: Clarendon Press, 6th edn, 1964), p. 543.
2. Lord, *Singer*, pp. 130-131.
3. Havelock, *Preface to Plato*, p. x.

long habit to the past and 'to forms of expression which were also forms of experience'.[1]

Havelock examines the tenth book of Plato's *Republic*, which treats the poetic experience as 'a kind of psychic poison'.[2] Poetry is attacked because it is educational, and Plato's discussion shows that the performance of poetry was far more central in the Greek civilization than we would at first suspect.[3] Similarly, in any culture the transmission of mores is never left to chance; the tradition is always given some embodiment in a verbal archetype. This is a performative utterance 'which both describes and enforces the overall habit pattern'.[4] In pre-literate societies preservation of this statement is problematic, for the stability of prosaic directives through oral transmission is too unstable. The only 'verbal technology' available for this in a pre-literate society was the rhythmic formula where words are organized 'cunningly in verbal and metrical patterns which were unique enough to retain their shape'.[5]

Havelock then shows that Homer's writings are, in fact, a kind of tribal encyclopaedia that serves an educational function preserving society's mores. Proof of this may be found in Nestor's speech (*Iliad*, 1.277-80), which recapitulates relationships that are basic to the stability of the social structure. Since the authority of a prince is to be maintained because he is a prince (rather than because he is physically more powerful, etc.) Havelock sees here the sanctioning of the 'divine apparatus' behind this social arrangement.[6] An examination of Homer's text shows items of the personal code interwoven with the public. Homer's epic thereby preserves the familiar and proper customs, habits and attitudes of his society. In this system procedures 'have to be observed, and are recorded as operations made up of distinct acts precisely defined, which must follow each other in a certain order'.[7] Even a sea voyage provides a striking example. Comparing the proposal and subsequent narrative description of a voyage 200 lines later Havelock finds that the order of events, of acts

1. Havelock, *Preface to Plato*, p. x.
2. Havelock, *Preface to Plato*, p. 5.
3. Havelock, *Preface to Plato*, p. 37.
4. Havelock, *Preface to Plato*, p. 41.
5. Havelock, *Preface to Plato*, p. 42.
6. Havelock, *Preface to Plato*, p. 68.
7. Havelock, *Preface to Plato*, p. 80.

and of objects is identical. The verbal formulae used, however, to describe this pattern vary considerably. The text is built up of a series of standardized images set in a fixed order. The formulae preserve these images, and the text serves an educational function presenting in a simplified pattern the mechanical operations of a sea voyage. But this oral tradition cannot contain the detailed instructions one would expect of a written text. Numerous specific details of the navigator's skill must be transmitted culturally by example and habitation. Hence, the epic idiom 'is used to preserve techniques only as part of a general education'.[1]

b. *Critique of the Parry–Lord Assumption*

Havelock also stresses oral tradition's need for repetition. Only a written encyclopaedia can separate its material into topics, treating each exhaustively without repetition. Orality demands the opposite procedure. He departs from the Parry–Lord thesis and claims that the comparison with contemporary European oral poetry rests on an unscientific assumption:

> It [the comparison] has lumped together two poetic situations which are entirely different, that of the Balkan peasantry and that of the Homeric governing class. It was of the essence of Homeric poetry that it represented in its epoch the sole vehicle of important and significant communication. It therefore was called upon to memorialise and preserve the social apparatus, the governing mechanism, and the education for leadership and social management, to use Plato's word.[2]

Havelock believes that the different social context means a considerable difference in the nature of oral tradition in the two cultures. The business of government and social leadership in Europe has been conducted by a literate elite for centuries and hence the singer functions primarily as an entertainer. In Homer's case, however, the formulae framed law, history, religion and technology. 'His art therefore was central and functional as never since. It enjoyed a command over education and government, which was lost as soon as alphabetic literacy was placed at the disposal of political power.'[3]

The gulf that exists today between the poetic, 'esoteric', state and everyday culture was not so great in Homer's day. The whole memory

1. Havelock, *Preface to Plato*, p. 83.
2. Havelock, *Preface to Plato*, pp. 93-94.
3. Havelock, *Preface to Plato*, p. 94.

of the civilization was poetized, and this exercised a constant control over the forms of everyday speech. Havelock argues that in an oral culture, permanent communication is represented only in the saga and its affiliate: Homer, far from being special, actually embodies the ruling state of mind. He points to tablets found at Knossos and Pylos which contain communications of the Myceno-Cretan and Mycenaean cultures. Scholars have detected in these directives of the kings a Greek that is rhythmical. If this is so, Havelock argues that 'it is possible to conclude that the directive shaped itself in the ear, not in the vision. It was framed orally for verbal memorization and transmission, and then happened to get written down.'[1] A further example is found in the tablets of Assyria and Ugarit, which also preserve royal correspondence. They repeatedly contain the rhythms of poetic speech and such formulaic devices as the ring form, repetition with speakers changed and other devices that utilize the principle of the echo.[2] The alphabet removed the need for preservation via formulaic composition. After about the fourth century BCE, Havelock believes, one no longer needed to use formulaic language to guarantee a life for what was said.

c. *Significance of Havelock*
Havelock's study is highly significant for the understanding of early Christian literature. First of all, he insists that oral and literate cultures are different in kind. In orality, formulaic language functions as an encyclopaedia for the culture's mores, and the epic becomes a language event.[3] Only with the rise of philosophical analysis, as championed by Plato, could a culture free itself from this tyranny of orality. His study does not provide detailed criteria for separating out material with an oral history within a written text. The closest he comes to this is his emphasis upon such well-known oral devices as rhythm, the ring form, repetition with speakers changed and other forms of echo.

The applicability of evidence from one sociological situation to another is important. In his challenge to Parry and Lord's straightforward application of evidence from modern-day Eastern Europe to

---

1. Havelock, *Preface to Plato*, p. 136.
2. Havelock, *Preface to Plato*, p. 136.
3. See Havelock's description of the process of identification in oral culture, *Preface to Plato*, p. 45.

Homer, Havelock has raised the problem of determining whether either of these two situations is similar enough to that which held in first-century Christianity to be applicable. The Gospels were written in a highly literate urban context of Hellenistic culture. Similar to the situation today, and unlike that found in Homer, the business of government was conducted by a specialized literate bureaucracy, so there was no need for orality to contain the culture's educational encyclopaedia. In Mark we have a literate author (unlike the modern singer of tales) who lives in a culture that is literate enough not to use formulaic language in its everyday life (unlike Havelock's understanding of Homer's situation). In Paul we see a literate author who quotes rhythmic or formulaic language only rarely (cf. 1 Cor. 15.3-5).[1]

Havelock's thesis of the essential incompatibility of the two media (and of a fixed chasm between them) has had an obvious influence on Kelber. Ironically, however, his appeal to Havelock may actually undermine Kelber's thesis. Havelock's insistence that the gulf between poetry as an esoteric state (as in today's culture) and the language of everyday discourse was not as deep in antiquity raises the possibility that language displaying the traits of poetic (or formulaic) language may not have an oral antecedent. The evidence from the court records is instructive: this material points to 'formulaic' language that is generated on the basis of common forms but which does not have a previous oral history. These materials compare well, for example, with the known use by Paul of the Hellenistic literary conventions in his letters.[2] Paul relies on numerous structural and 'formulaic'

---

1. The degree of literacy (in terms of percentage of the population) in the Hellenistic era is not easy to determine. As W.V. Harris points out, although there was a 'vast diffusion of reading and writing ability in the Greek and Roman worlds', previous estimates of majority literacy are probably overly optimistic. 'Even though literacy was always, from early in Greek and Roman history, virtually universal among the men who made up the political and social elite, most people could live out their lives, if they were content to do so, without the use of reading or writing.' See W.V. Harris, *Ancient Literacy* (Cambridge, MA: Harvard University Press, 1989), pp. 13, 29-30. With respect to the transmission of 'tradition' and the composition of the Gospels in early Christianity, it is this literate, elite social culture that predominates, and not one similar to those explored by Havelock and Lord.

2. On this and related issues, see W.G. Doty, *Letters in Primitive Christianity* (Guides to Biblical Scholarship; Philadelphia: Fortress Press, 1973); A.J. Malherbe,

conventions of his day. Similar are modern form letters which sound and look alike, but which lack an oral history.

3. *The Ground Rules of Orality*

The central insight of the Parry–Lord thesis, that it is impossible to establish an original text, remains an influential achievement. As Finnegan notes, it is difficult to overestimate the influence of this approach to oral literature. The theory has been applied to Homer, Hebrew Bible poetry, *Beowulf*, mediaeval European epic and modern Greek ballads.[1] But a number of considerations must be discussed before the Parry–Lord thesis can be applied to Gospels, and before one can state definitively whether there are precise ground rules for oral literature.

a. *Orality and Formulaic Content*
First there is the problem of the sample of material analysed by Parry and Lord in determining the percentage of formulaic text. Finnegan argues that since the Homeric poems were not fully analysed a more rigorous sampling might not support the higher claims for overall level of formularity, and the level might in fact be closer to that in literary texts.[2] Is an 'oral formulaic' style a sign of 'oral composition?' Lord's claim that a pattern of 50 to 60 per cent formulae (with 10 to 25 per cent straight formulae) clearly indicates a written composition has been questioned recently. A study by L.D. Benson shows that a heavily formulaic style is characteristic of some written compositions, specifically Old English translations from Latin originals.[3] A study of the style of traditional Xhosa and Zulu oral poetry in South Africa demonstrates a heavily formulaic content characteristic of the written versions of these poems.[4]

The Cynic Epistles: A Study Edition (SBLSBSD, 12; Atlanta, GA: Scholars Press, 1977).

1. Finnegan, *Poetry*, p. 66.

2. Finnegan, *Poetry*, p. 72.

3. L.D. Benson, 'The Literary Character of Anglo-Saxon Formulaic Poetry', *PMLA* 81 (1966), pp. 334-41, esp. p. 336.

4. J. Opland, ' "Scop" and "Imbongi"—Anglo-Saxon and Bantu Oral Poets', *ESA* 14 (1971), pp. 161-78.

These studies undercut the assertion that formulaic language is a sure sign of oral composition. J.A. Russo supports Finnegan's claim that a more representative analysis of Homer might reveal a smaller percentage of formulae within the *Iliad* and *Odyssey*. Russo compares two other passages from Homer (*Odyssey*, 17, 303-327; and the *Iliad*, 18, 285-309). He points to the striking fact that, in the first passage, close to half of the formulary repeats are used only once elsewhere in the Homeric epics. 'One wonders why', he comments, 'from the earliest analyses of Parry and Lord, no question was ever raised about the propriety of counting together, as equally formulary, phrases repeated many times over, phrases repeated only a few times, and the phrase that is repeated only once.'[1] He believes it possible that some of these repeated phrases may not be formulae at all but merely a 'repeat', a phrase that happens to occur a second time in the poems. Thus in the 25 lines analysed from the *Odyssey*, Russo finds 13 that contain verbatim formulae and surprisingly little formulaic content beyond these straight formulae. Similarly, the analysis of the passage from the *Iliad* reveals a relatively high formulary content, 'but a total formulaic content that again falls far below the 90 per cent we have been led to expect'. Using generous criteria (i.e., allowing single repeats to count as a formula and allowing some single-word formulas) this passage gives a total of 58 per cent formula and 63 per cent formulaic content. Using more stingy criteria (omitting the single repeated phrases) results in 33.5 per cent formula and 38.5 per cent formulaic content.[2] This second set of statistics reduces the formulaic content 'down to where it is comparable to that of literary texts composed by poets who were trying to keep close to an archaic and traditional style, according to the data collected by Professor Lord'.[3] Russo concludes that Homer's formulaic style is not necessarily a sign of oral composition. Since other studies have shown that traditional epithets are common to Irish narrative style, even though these narratives are prose, Russo believes that the epithet systems do not of necessity prove the oral nature of Homer.[4]

1. Russo, 'Homer's Formulaic Style', p. 43.
2. Russo, 'Homer's Formulaic Style', p. 47.
3. Russo, 'Homer's Formulaic Style', p. 47. Citing A.B. Lord, 'Homer as Oral Poet', *HSCP* 72 (1968), pp. 20-21.
4. Russo, 'Homer's Formulaic Style', 48. Citing K. O'Nolan, 'Homer and Irish Heroic Narrative', *Classical Quarterly* 19 (1969), pp. 1-19.

Taken together, this evidence provides abundant justification for the following warning by R. Finnegan:

> A 'formulaic' style is not therefore inevitably a proof of 'oral composition'. Theorists have now to accept that since there can be both an 'oral' and a 'literary' use of formulae one cannot necessarily discriminate between 'oral' and 'written' on the basis of a 'formulaic' style alone.[1]

b. *Composition in Performance*

Composition in performance is not the only model for oral literature. Finnegan argues that there are three ways a poem can be 'oral': in its composition; in its transmission; and/or in its performance.[2] The Parry–Lord thesis focuses upon data derived from oral literature that fall into only the first of these categories. From this Finnegan concludes that 'oral composition' is a useful term to denote a general emphasis upon composition without writing, 'but cannot provide any absolute criterion for definitively differentiating oral poetry as a single category clearly separable from written poetry'.[3]

The emphasis upon composition in performance works well in the Yugoslavian context, but other methods of composition exist. There are, in fact, cases of memorization and near word-for-word reproduction. In Somalia, for example, oral poetry is a highly developed art. B.W. Andrzejewski and I.M. Lewis show that these poets rarely perform their work until composition is completely finished in private: they may spend even days in composition. These poets have repertoires lasting several evenings of recitation, can learn a poem upon only one hearing, and can store poems in their memories sometimes for their lifetime. 'We have met poets who at a ripe age could still remember many poems which they learnt in their early youth'.[4]

1. Finnegan, *Poetry*, p. 70.
2. Finnegan, *Poetry*, p. 17.
3. Finnegan, *Poetry*, p. 19.
4. B.W. Andrzejewski and I.M. Lewis, *Somali Poetry: An Introduction* (Oxford: Clarendon Press, 1964), p. 45. Finnegan, *Oral Poetry*, p. 75, also cites Gordon Innes' research into Mandinka Griots' narrations which found both memorization and fluidity. G. Innes, 'Stability and Change in Griots' Narrations', *ALS* 14 (1973), pp. 105-18, and *Sunjata: Three Mandinka Versions* (London: School of Oriental and African Studies, 1974).

Another fundamental component of the Parry–Lord thesis does not apply equally, therefore, to all oral literature. The relationship between orality and literacy is much more complicated than they imagined, and this makes it far more difficult to apply their model to the Gospels.

c. *Orality and Literacy Incompatible?*

There is also the issue of whether writing is incompatible with oral literature. This position is advocated by Lord and taken up by Kelber.[1] But, as Finnegan points out, writing has been in existence for a much longer period of time and over a wider area than is generally realized. Writing is often used even in societies that use primarily oral channels of communication. 'One would expect', Finnegan writes, 'in fact, that in many such societies written forms would, from time to time, be used in the process of transmitting, composing or memorizing forms of oral literature. This indeed is precisely what one finds.'[2] As evidence of this interaction between the oral and the written she points to many 'traditional' ballads which have much in common with earlier literary romances and which have themselves inspired later literary poems. Likewise, many street ballads have connections with 'traditional songs', while some literary poems are based on earlier street ballads.[3] Finnegan cites evidence that a combination of the two media goes back well into classical Greece and Rome, and can also be found in Europe during the Middle Ages.[4] Hence Finnegan's warning: 'Classifying a poem as, say, "folk" or "oral" or "popular" on the basis of its style, expected audience or origin, gives no *automatic* information about its likely mode of distribution and transmission.'[5]

Finnegan points to evidence from Africa where 'oral and written literature often in practice comprise relative and overlapping rather than mutually exclusive categories'. The Hausa 'Song of Bagauda'

1. See Lord's statement that the two are mutually exclusive, *Singer*, pp. 129, 137.
2. Finnegan, *Poetry*, p. 161.
3. Finnegan, *Poetry*, pp. 161-62.
4. Finnegan, *Poetry*, p. 166. Citing M. Hadas, *Ancilla to Classical Reading* (New York: Columbia University Press, 1954), pp. 50-53; and R. Crosby, 'Oral Delivery in the Middle Ages', *Speculum* 11 (1936), pp. 88-89.
5. Finnegan, *Poetry*, p. 168.

from West Africa appears in both written and oral form, while Swahili poetry often involves an interchange and influence between orally-composed and written verses.[1] Other evidence suggests that literacy and an acquaintance with written literature do not necessarily interfere with oral composition. She notes her own field work among the Limba, where one of the best storytellers was illiterate but was closely followed by a young man in the middle of his teacher's training course.[2]

This evidence shows that Lord's assertion that orality and literacy represent two incompatible media is overdrawn. Scholars would be better served, given the highly literate culture behind the Gospels, in deriving their model of orality from evidence from oral traditional material that circulated in literate cultures.

d. *Oral and Literate Mentalities*
There is also the issue of compatibility between the so-called oral and literate mentality. These two traditions are viewed as essentially incompatible by Parry, Lord and Kelber. This is challenged by Finnegan, who states that oral poetry is not an odd phenomenon within human culture. 'It is found all over the world, past and present, from the meditative personal poetry of recent Inuit or Maori poets, to mediaeval European and Chinese ballads, or the orally composed epics of pre-classical Greek in the first millennium BC.'[3] She points to such well-known carols and hymns such as 'Away in a Manger', which can be regarded as oral poetry; even though they have written versions 'they surely achieve their main impact and active circulation through ever-renewed oral means'.[4] Finnegan notes that a degree of literacy

1. Finnegan, *Poetry*, pp. 137-38. Citing M. Hiskett, 'The "Song of Bagauda": A Hausa King List and Homily in Verse', *BSO(A)S* 27 (1964), pp. 540-67; 28 (1965), pp. 112-35; 363-85; and L. Harries, *Swahili Poetry* (Oxford: Clarendon Press, 1962), pp. 3-5.
2. Finnegan, *Poetry*, p. 138. A study by J.W. Johnson points to Somali poets who rarely perform their work until composition is completely finished in private. J.W. Johnson, 'The Development of the Genre *Heello* in Modern Somali Poetry' (MPhil thesis, University of London, 1971). Similarly, Gordon Innes, while researching Mandinka Griots' narratives, found a fascinating blend of stability and change involving both memorization and fluidity. Innes, 'Stability and Change in Griots' Narrations'. Cited in Finnegan, *Poetry*, pp. 146, 148.
3. Finnegan, *Poetry*, p. 3.
4. Finnegan, *Poetry*, p. 5.

has been a feature of human culture in most parts of the world for millennia. 'This has rarely meant mass literacy (a fact significant for the popular circulation of *oral* literature) but has meant a measure of influence from the written word and literatures even in cultures often dubbed "oral".'[1] Since the two media, literate and non-literate, have co-existed and interacted, it is only natural to find many instances that involve overlap and mixture between them.

> It is not surprising that poetry is propagated sometimes by oral, sometimes by written means, with no great and unsurmountable gulf between the two. Similarly, in the past, when fewer were literate, we should expect 'oral poems' to be influenced by, and interact with, written forms, and indeed sometimes coincide with them.[2]

Oral poetry can exist in a society with partial or even mass literacy, as proven by Yugoslav oral poets (whose epics show constant interaction with printed versions) or modern folk artists such as Larry Gorman, Allmeda Riddle or Woody Guthrie. The 'typical' oral poet is as likely to have some knowledge of writing as to live in a remote and purely oral atmosphere as set forth in the stereotype.[3]

This evidence reinforces the observation that, given the highly literate Hellenistic culture of the first century, scholars would be better served in deriving their model of orality from cultures that display an overlap of literacy and orality. A model of interaction and coexistence better suits the Gospel traditions than a model of a separate era of oral tradition that terminates in a literate phase. This latter model, so often adopted unconsciously by Gospel critics, has its roots in outdated evolutionary assumptions of the nineteenth century.

e. A Distinctive Oral Style?

Finally, there is the problem of defining a distinctive oral style. Finnegan grants that in such matters as the type of society in which oral poetry occurs, the nature of 'oral composition', the mode of transmission or even of the differentiation of oral from written modes, certain patterns may be detectable. But she quickly limits this concession, arguing that the main characteristic is complexity rather than rigidly determined uniformity with constant overlaps, since

---

1. Finnegan, *Poetry*, p. 23.
2. Finnegan, *Poetry*, p. 23.
3. Finnegan, *Poetry*, p. 24.

'there proves to be no definitive and unitary body of poetry which, being "oral", can be clearly differentiated from written and, as it were, "normal" poetry'.[1]

Finnegan notes the criterion of repetition, as expressed by F. Boas: 'The investigation of primitive narrative as well as of poetry proves that repetition, particularly rhythmic repetition, is a fundamental trait.' Boas also includes parallelism, the 'rhythmic repetition of the same or similar elements'.[2] Parallelism is also viewed as a key element by J. Gonda, who regards it as characteristic of 'archaic and "primitive" symmetrical compositions'.[3] Similarly, D. Buchan, in a discussion of Scottish ballads, notes that the habit 'of thinking in balances, antitheses, appositions and parallelisms is intrinsic to the oral mind'.[4]

Here is one of the most important features of oral literature. Finnegan notes that repetition has a real point in an oral context, 'it makes it easier for the audience to grasp what has been said and gives the speaker/singer confidence that it has understood the message he is trying to communicate.'[5]

In Gospel criticism, antithetic parallelism in particular has been advanced as a touchstone of the *ipissima verba* of Jesus by C.F. Burney and J. Jeremias. Jeremias lists 30 occurrences of this literary technique in the Markan sayings of Jesus, 34 in Q, 44 more in Matthew, and another 30 cases in Luke. Although the tradition may occasionally be responsible for this device (cf. Mt. 6.13; 7.13-14), Jeremias argues that only isolated cases are redactional or due to the tradition. Rather, it 'is probable, therefore, that we have to derive the frequency of this usage from Jesus himself'.[6]

---

1. Finnegan, *Poetry*, p. 2.

2. F. Boas, 'Stylistic Aspects of Primitive Literature', *JAF* 38 (1925), pp. 329, 332. Compare the comments by B. Gray, 'Repetition in Oral Literature', *JAF* 84 (1971), p. 290, 'repetition is prevalent in old and primitive literatures because these are both oral literatures and repetition is a direct consequence of their oral nature'.

3. J. Gonda, *Stylistic Repetition in the Veda* (Amsterdam: Noord-Hollandsche Uitgevers-Maatschappij, 1959), p. 49.

4. D. Buchan, *The Ballad and the Folk* (London: Routledge & Kegan Paul, 1972), p. 88.

5. Finnegan, *Poetry*, p. 129. Compare Crosby, 'Oral Delivery in the Middle Ages', p. 107.

6. J. Jeremias, *New Testament Theology. I. The Proclamation of Jesus* (trans. J. Bowden; London: SCM Press, 1971), p. 18, with extensive list.

Despite the fact that orality lends itself to parallelism, it is not clear that a specific proportion of repetition can be used as an unique touchstone of orality. Finnegan objects that the concept of repetition is often too wide for reaching unequivocal conclusions: 'when one considers its many manifestations it turns out often to mean little more than recurrent patterns. If one tries to make it more precise (as in the repetition of incidents only, or *particular* types of stylistic repetition) the theory loses its apparent universality and thus its appeal.'[1] This point applies to parallelism and the paratactic juxtaposition and duplication of incidents. 'There are, after all, clear literary effects in parallelism which apply to written as well as oral verse.' Repetition, she emphasizes, 'has great *literary* and aesthetic effect'.[2] By the same token, Whallon, in his examination of parallelism in Hebrew Bible poetry, refuses to explain it primarily in utilitarian terms (i.e., its use for antiphonal singing or as an aid to memory) but rather sees it as essentially 'for its own impressive elegance'.[3]

Nor should the use of repetition within the oral medium be exaggerated. It is not universal in the sense of being essential to comprehension. Other devices, such as slow delivery or the process of memorization and reflection, can also be used. 'The use of repetition in oral poetry is not just a utilitarian tool, but something which lies at the heart of all poetry. It is one of the main criteria by which we tend to distinguish poetry from prose, in both familiar and unfamiliar cultural traditions.'[4]

Antithetic parallelism deserves special consideration. Jeremias' evidence at first sight is impressive. But a number of the texts displaying this device are now viewed as post-resurrectional. Mk 2.19b-20, with its emphasis on the time after Jesus' death, is a case in point. The explicit awareness of the crucifixion (v. 20) clearly stamps it as secondary.[5] The series of four such parallel statements addressed by Jesus to Simon the Pharisee (Lk. 7.44-47) shows Luke's own

---

1. Finnegan, *Poetry*, p. 130.

2. Finnegan, *Poetry*, pp. 131, 130.

3. W. Whallon, *Formula, Character, and Context: Studies in Homeric, Old English, and Old Testament Poetry* (Cambridge, MA: Harvard University Press, 1969), p. 153.

4. Finnegan, *Poetry*, p. 131.

5. See D.O. Via, Jr, 'Editor's Foreward', in *What is Redaction Criticism?* (ed. N. Perrin; Philadelphia: Fortress Press, 1969), pp. vii-viii.

theological intent, as does the saying addressed to the daughters of Jerusalem (23.28). These instances of antithetic parallelism are entirely literary in origin. The device of polarized contrast within the Gospel narratives is a structurally similar device.[1] Nor is antithetic parallelism exclusively a Semitic structure.[2] Its use can be found in the proverbs and literature of numerous cultures and eras. Far from being a device exclusive to the preaching of Jesus, we are forced to admit that any number of people during the history of transmission would have had access to this literary device.

Hence, sharp distinctions between oral and literate styles are inappropriate. Although repetition and other structures which find their home in oral literature can be identified, they cannot be ascribed exclusively to this medium. These devices also find a natural home in a literary milieu. 'Oral compositional techniques' so often observed in a Gospel text do not, in themselves, guarantee orality.

f. *Epic Laws of Folklore*
Other ground rules for oral literature have been advanced. A classic study is A. Olrik's 'Epic Laws of Folk Narrative', which was originally presented at a 1908 conference in Berlin. Olrik delineates a number of laws of oral folk narrative. As Alan Dundes notes, his 'findings have withstood the criticisms of the passing years and they continue to excite each generation of folklorists'.[3] Fundamental is the concept of the *Sage*, a literary category that includes myths, songs, heroic sagas and local legends. From a comparative analysis of this literature, Olrik argues:

> The common rules for the composition of these *Sage* forms we can then call the epic laws of folk narrative. These laws apply to all European

1. See Mk 1.44-45; 5.18-20; 10.1-2 and Lk. 3.10-14; 4.25-30; 7.29-30; 8.4; 15.1-2; 16.14-15; 19.11.
2. From the Tibetan Doctrine: 'A foolish man proclaimeth his qualifications; A wise man keepeth them secret within himself; A straw floateth on the surface of water, But a precious gem placed upon it sinketh.' In R.O. Ballou (ed.), *The Portable World Bible* (New York: Penguin, 1957), p. 155. 'Call on God, but row away from the rocks' (Indian Proverb); 'Life is given to the peaceful, and death is given to the guilty, the peaceful being "he who does what is loved", and the guilty, "he who does what is hated"' (Document of 3500 BCE). In Mead, *The Encyclopedia of Religious Quotations*, pp. 263, 415.
3. A. Dundes, *The Study of Folklore* (Englewood Cliffs, NJ: Prentice–Hall, 1965), p. 129.

folklore and to some extent even beyond that. Against the background of
the overwhelming uniformity of these laws, national characteristics seem
to be only dialect peculiarities. Even the traditional categories of folk
narrative are all governed by these general principles of *Sage* construction.
We call these principles 'laws' because they limit the freedom of
composition of oral literature in a much different and more rigid way than
in our written literature.[1]

Olrik notes the Laws of Opening and Closing. The *Sage* contains
neither a sudden beginning nor an abrupt ending. It 'begins by moving
from calm to excitement, and after the concluding event, in which a
principal character frequently has a catastrophe, the *Sage* ends by
moving from excitement to calm'.[2] This law is seen in hundreds of
folksongs which end 'not with the death of the lovers, but with the
interweaving of the branches of the two roses which grow up out of
their graves', and in thousands of legends where 'one finds the
revenge of the dead or the punishment of the villain appended to the
principal action.'[3]

Secondly, Olrik notes the Law of Repetition. Written literature has
at its disposal a number of means for emphasis, including degree and
detail of description to depict an object or event's significance. In
contrast, oral narrative lacks the technique of such full-bodied detail
and its spare descriptions are too brief to be an effective tool of
emphasis, so it employs the tool of repetition:

> A youth goes into the giant's field three days in succession and each day
> he kills a giant. A hero tries three times to ride up the glass mountain.
> Three would-be lovers are magically rendered immobile in one night by a
> maiden. Every time that a striking scene occurs in a narrative, and
> continuity permits, the scene is repeated. This is necessary not only to
> build tension, but to fill out the body of the narrative.[4]

This repetition, according to Olrik, is almost always tied to the
number three. But the number three is also a law in and of itself.
Where other numbers such as seven or twelve occur, 'they express
only a totally abstract quantity. Three is the maximum number of men
and objects which occur in traditional narrative. Nothing distinguishes

---

1. A. Olrik, 'Epic Laws of Folk Narrative', in *The Study of Folklore* (ed.
A. Dundes; Englewood Cliffs, NJ: Prentice-Hall, 1965), p. 131.
2. Olrik, 'Epic Laws', p. 132.
3. Olrik, 'Epic Laws', p. 132.
4. Olrik, 'Epic Laws', p. 133.

the great bulk of folk narrative from modern literature and from reality as much as does the number three.'[1]

There is also the Law of Two to a Scene. Two is the maximum number of characters who appear at one time. Three characters each with an individual identity and role would be a violation of this fundamental law of oral narrative. Only in literary drama does one find the interaction of three or more characters.

Important also is the Law of Contrast, for the *Sage* is always polarized. 'A strong Thor requires a wise Odin or a cunning Loki next to him; a rich Peter Krämer, a poor Paul Schmied; near a grieving woman sits a joyful or comforting one. This very basic opposition is a major rule of epic composition: young and old, large and small, man and monster, good and evil.'[2]

The Law of Contrast affects the characterization of the story's actors. The characteristics of protagonist and antagonist are such that they are antithetical. This law even extends itself to some types of plot action: '(1) The hero meets his death through the murderous act of a villain (Roland, Rustem, Rolf Kraki, Siegfried); (2) the great king has an insignificant and short-reigning successor (Hjarward after Rolf, Hjarni after Frodi, 'Shorthair' after Conchobar).'[3]

Olrik also notes the Law of Twins, for example, 'whenever two people appear in the same role, both are depicted as being small and weak'. This rule can apply to real twins (siblings) or simply to two people appearing in the same role. Hence, beings of subordinate rank appear in duplicate: 'two Dioscuri are messengers of Zeus; two ravens or two Valkyries, messengers of Odin'. However, if the twins occupy major roles then the Law of Contrast applies and they are pitted against each other. 'This may be illustrated by the myths of the Dioscuri. One is bright and one is gloomy; one immortal and the other mortal. They fight over the same woman and eventually kill each other.'[4]

There is the importance of placement in oral literature, which Olrik signifies as the Importance of Initial and Final Position. In a series of persons or things the principal one comes first, while the person for whom the narrative arouses sympathy comes last. Olrik designates

1. Olrik, 'Epic Laws', p. 133.
2. Olrik, 'Epic Laws', p. 135.
3. Olrik, 'Epic Laws', p. 135.
4. Olrik, 'Epic Laws', p. 136.

these relationships with nautical expressions: 'the Weight of the bow' (*das Toppgewicht*) and 'the Weight of the Stern' (*das Achtergewicht*). The centre of gravity in folk narrative is always to be found in this latter law. Hence *Achtergewicht*, combined with the Law of Three, is the principal characteristic of folk narrative. Only in a religious context does *Toppgewicht* rule (Odin then being greater than his two attendants); however, when these figures appear in folk narratives then *Achtergewicht* rules and Odin no longer acts as the principal member of the triad. 'Instead the principal member is—as the last of the three gods—Loki.'[1]

Folk literature contrasts with modern narrative by holding fast to the single strand: it does not go back to fill in missing details. Previous necessary background information is given in dialogue, resulting in a strict adherence to patterning. 'Two people and situations of the same sort are not as different as possible, but as similar as possible. Three days in succession the youth goes to an unfamiliar field. Each day he encounters a giant, carries on the same conversation with each one, and kills each one in the same manner.' This rigid stylizing is such that everything that is superfluous is suppressed and 'only the essential stands out salient and striking'.[2]

The *Sage* also has its logic, but this is not commensurable with that of the natural world. 'The tendency toward animism and even more toward miracle and magic constitutes its fundamental law.'[3] The *Sage*'s unity of plot, loose organization and uncertain action in the plot structure are the surest marks of cultivation.[4] He notes what he calls the greatest law of folk tradition: Concentration on a Leading Character.[5]

Olrik's study has rightly stood the test of time in its exposition of the narrative techniques of folk tales. It is not sufficiently recognized that Olrik informed Bultmann's view of orality. Bultmann, in fact, shows a considerable number of these epic laws at work in the parables. The Law of Contrast, for example, can be seen in Luke's parables of the Widow and the Judge (18.1-8), the Pharisee and Publican at Prayer (18.9-14) and the Rich Man and Lazarus (16.19-

---

1. Olrik, 'Epic Laws', p. 137.
2. Olrik, 'Epic Laws', p. 138.
3. Olrik, 'Epic Laws', p. 138.
4. Olrik, 'Epic Laws', p. 138.
5. Olrik, 'Epic Laws', p. 139.

31). In Matthew this contrast is clear in the parables of the Ten Maidens (25.1-13) and the Talents (25.14-30). Triad episodic repetition can be found in the Sower (Mk 4.3-8), Good Samaritan (Lk. 10.29-37), the Great Banquet (Lk. 14.15-24), the Labourers in the Vineyard (Mt. 20.1-16) and the Wicked Tenants (Mk 12.1-12). Two to a scene holds throughout, as seen in the Prodigal Son when the father speaks to each son in turn (Lk. 16.11-32), and in the succession of separate scenes in such narratives as the Great Banquet, the Labourers in the Vineyard, the Pharisee and Publican at Prayer, the Two Sons (Mt. 21.28-32), the Pounds (Lk. 19.11-27) and Matthew's exposition of the Last Judgment (25.31-46). The initial calm in the Law of Opening is especially prevalent in the Prodigal, the Labourers in the Vineyard, and the Maidens. The emphasis upon Final Position also holds throughout, as in the Good Samaritan, the Maidens, the Labourers in the Vineyard, the Pharisee and Publican at Prayer, the Two Sons, and the Rich Man and Lazarus.

Olrik, of course, does not extend his analysis to cover the narrative literature of antiquity, and hence we need to proceed with caution before claiming these narrative techniques as exclusively oral. James M. Dawsey, for example, has detailed a striking number of Olrik's epic laws at work in Acts. Since Pentecost is delayed in the narrative, the book opens in accordance with the Law of Opening and moves from initial calm to excitement. If we count the shipwreck as the final catastrophe, the ending in a period of relative calm in Rome conforms to the Law of Closing. Invariably the interaction is in accordance with the Law of Two to a Scene: Jesus speaking with the disciples (1.6-11); Paul with the leaders of the Roman Jews (28.17-28), Peter with Ananias (5.1-5) and later Sapphira (5.7-10); Philip and the Ethiopian eunuch (8.26-40); Peter with Cornelius (10.1-43); and the angel with Peter in prison (12.6-11). The narrative concentrates on a leading character, first Peter, then Stephen, Philip, Paul, Peter and Paul again in turn. The Law of Twins is found in the numerous combinations of groups and characters which function in the same role: 'men and women' (5.14; 8.3, 12; 9.2); 'women and children' (21.5); 'Jews and Greeks' (14.1, 5; 18.4); 'the people and the city authorities' (17.8); 'Dionysius and Damaris' (17.34); and 'the people and the Gentiles' (26.23). But in spite of these numerous parallels between Acts and folk narratives, Dawsey warns that 'it would be a mistake to return to where earlier form critics were taking us by submerging the creative identity of the author of Acts under a sea of popular stories. I myself do not think for one minute that the writer was only a compiler of sources.'[1]

Many of these 'Epic Laws' can be seen to be at work within the literary presentation of Mark's Gospel as a whole. The narrative focus on Jesus certainly conforms to Orlik's single strand. The Law of Initial and Final Position, and the Law of Opening, can be said to be at work in Mark's presentation of John the Baptist as a prelude to Jesus' advent. Triadic repetition can be found not only in the individual scenes such as the prayer in Gethsamane and Peter's denial, but also in the threefold passion predictions, and the triple entries into Jerusalem (11.7, 27; 14.17). Two to a Scene applies, for example, in the narratives on healing and controversy (2.1-12; 3.1-6), while there are numerous instances of polarized conflict between Jesus and his opponents. Mark, like Acts, frequently uses a double description for what is essentially a single narrative role. 'Simon and his brother Andrew' (1.16); 'James son of Zebedee and his brother John' (1.19); 'all who were sick or possessed with demons' (1.32); 'Simon and his companions' (1.36); 'John's disciples and the Pharisees' (2.18); 'the Pharisees. . . and the Herodians' (3.6); 'those who were around him along with the twelve' (4.10); 'the Pharisees and some of the scribes' (7.1); and 'the Pharisees and. . . Herod' (8.15). The polarization between Jesus and his opponents conforms to the Law of Contrast, a technique seen in Mark's presentation of the anointing and Judas and the 11. These numerous examples from Mark must be seen as part of his literary technique, and warn us that Orlik's epic laws cannot be used in a straightforward manner to identify oral traditions within the Gospel text.

4. *The Application of Folkloric Method to the Gospels*

a. *Lord and the Gospels as Oral Traditional Narratives*
In evaluating the suitability of the folkloric method to the interpretation of Gospel texts it is appropriate to begin with Lord's study, 'The Gospels as Oral Traditional Literature'.[2] He notes that one of the earmarks of an oral traditional narrative is its textual fluidity.

1. J.M. Dawsey, 'Characteristics of Folk–Epic in Acts', in *SBL Seminar Papers 1989* (Atlanta: Scholars Press, 1989), p. 323.
2. Lord, 'Gospels', pp. 33-91.

Full fixed textual stability is possible for Lord in the oral medium only within short forms such as incantations, riddles, proverbs or sayings. In longer narratives an oral fixed text is impossible.[1] Although Lord is aware of the two-source theory of Gospel origins, he offers instead a reconstruction of each Gospel as a performance of a fluid oral text. The Gospels as such are part of a long heritage of life biographies, and 'must belong to a tradition of oral life story or biography. Such a tradition argues the existence of both tellers and audience as well as of stories told.'[2]

The traditional pattern of the hero's life includes: 1) birth, 2) precocious childhood, 3) transition to maturity, 4) marriage, 5) deeds, and 6) death. Fullness of the account in oral traditional literature is not necessarily a sign of a later date, as seen for example in a number of texts in the Parry collection. From this fact, Lord argues that it does not follow that the shortest or least polished text is the oldest, and hence, one cannot assume Markan priority.[3]

In his examination of the parallel sequences and verbal correspondences, Lord notes that oral traditional composers think in terms of blocks and series of blocks of tradition. A pattern emerges in the synoptics wherein a sequence is repeated in two or three Gospels. Hence, for Lord, the fragmentation 'would seem to indicate that the third gospel does not recognize the passage in the other two as a unit but does know the elements of the passage, either separately or as part of a different grouping or passage'.[4] Two factors prevent the conclusion that the relationship is one of written documents: 1) the many cases where a sequence is scattered sporadically in another Gospel and 2) the verbal correspondence, which is less than expected in a manuscript tradition. Lord finds it 'unusual for a writer to choose passages from several documentary sources as if from a buffet. The sporadic nature of the positioning of some of the elements seems more likely to be an indication of an oral traditional relationship among the texts.'[5]

In the account of Jesus' baptism, Lord establishes eight main elements. Following Matthew's order, these are: A: 3.1 (John in the

---

1. Lord, 'Gospels', p. 37.
2. Lord, 'Gospels', p. 38.
3. Lord, 'Gospels', p. 43.
4. Lord, 'Gospels', p. 59.
5. Lord, 'Gospels', pp. 59-60.

Judean wilderness); B: 3.2 (Preaching of repentance); C: 3.3 (quotation from Isaiah the prophet); D: 3.4 (John's dress and diet); E: 3.5-6 (crowds go out to John); F: 3.7-10 (the preaching of John); G: 3.11-12 (Jesus's baptism); and H: Lk. 3.10-14 (John's preaching to special groups). Lord argues that there was a story about John's preaching that contained the seven elements A through G. In Mark, there is to be found a change in order to CABEDG, a change that Lord believes to be 'typical in oral tradition but not easy of explanation in manuscript tradition'.[1]

The baptism itself contains three elements following Matthew: A: 3.13 (Jesus goes out to John); B: 3.14-15 (John tries to dissuade Jesus); and C: 3.16-17 (Jesus' baptism). Since Mark and Luke omit element B, and since Matthew uses the third person, this suggests for Lord that Mark and Luke represent one tradition and Matthew another. Lord argues that as one examines a variety of parallels attempting to establish one account as primary, 'one begins to wonder whether one may be dealing with the kind of oral tradition to which the question of primacy, a question formed in the crucible of manuscript or fixed text tradition, is not applicable in the same way as it is in dealing with literary tradition.'[2]

Lord also examines the verbal parallels among the texts. Interestingly, he chooses the parable of the Sower (Mk 4.1-9). In this instance he believes it clear that Luke was not copied textually from either Matthew or Mark. Matthew and Mark, however, are at times very close, as in 3b, 4, 5, 6 and 7. These verses are almost close enough to justify the conclusion of a written textual relationship; however, the passage is not extensive enough to warrant this. These verses are surrounded by others which are not so close, hence there 'are islands of closeness in lakes (not seas) of divergence rather than the other way around'. Lord is also puzzled by the fact that if the texts were copied then only a few verses were copied consecutively and

---

1. Lord, 'Gospels', p. 61.
2. Lord, 'Gospels', p. 63. Compare his treatment of the sequence of events at Mk 1.16-45 and parallels, which he calls Complex I (which includes the insertion by Matthew of the Sermon on the Mount and the healings of the Centurian's servant and Peter's mother-in-law). This insertion, along with the displacement of order in Luke for the call of the disciples, for Lord, 'is a fundamental principle in oral composition and transmission of non-narrative complexes' and hence further evidence of the oral nature of the Gospels, p. 67.

these not exactly. For example, Lord notes the difference between Mark's singular ('crowd', 4.1) and Matthew's plural ('crowds', 13.2) and Matthew's use of a genitive absolute ('but when the sun rose', 13.6) for Mark's clause ('and when the sun rose', 4.6).[1]

These verses and their surrounding divergences can be explained in another way than copying. In oral traditional literature passages can become reasonably stable verbally in the usage of a single narrator or even a group of narrators. These are frequently used passages which exhibit special stylistic devices that bind them together. As an example Lord gives the beginning of two recordings of 'The Captivity of Djulić Ibrahim', by Salih Ugljanin:

The Captivity of Djulić Ibrahim[2]

Text No. 659	Text No. 667
One morning it had just dawned	One morning it had dawned
In Zadar the cannon are booming,	*In Zadar the cannon are booming,*
Two together, thirty at once.	
	The earth and the mountains tremble.
The governor of Zadar is rejoicing;	*The governor of Zadar is rejoicing;*
He captured the servant Radojica,	He captured the renegade Radovan,
Radojica, the Turkish lackey,	*Radojica, the Turkish lackey,*
And thrown him into the cold prison.	*And thrown him into the cold prison.*
When Rako came into the prison	When Rako came into the dungeon,
There he found thirty Turks,	*There he found thirty Turks,*
And among them Djulić Ibrahim,	*And among them Djulić Ibrahim,*
And next to him Velagic Selim	And by him Velagic Selim.
And his thirty-two comrades.	
Rako gave them greeting,	Rako came in, and gave them greeting,
And the Turks returned it.	And all returned it

Lord's comparison of this text with the Gospels is instructive:

> The textual variations are slight, and whole consecutive lines are verbally exactly the same. In short, verbal closeness and even exactness in frequently used or otherwise important or specially bound passages is not unusual in oral traditional composition. Such passages, therefore, are not necessarily proof of manuscript tradition. Much further investigation of this phenomenon in oral traditional texts is needed before we have a

1. Lord, 'Gospels', p. 86.
2. Based on Lord, 'Gospels', pp. 87-88. In adapting the table I have maintained two columns throughout and *italicized* those portions of text given by Lord in one line that cut across the two columns.

complete comprehension of it, but we have plenty of material, and some research has already been done.[1]

The rest of these poems display a configuration of passages like the one above surrounded by others of considerable divergence; in other words, a pattern not unlike that of the Gospels. Lord is aware that these two versions are from the same singer, unlike the Gospels. Greater divergence exists between versions by different singers, 'except that when a singer has been influenced by a published text without actually memorising the text, the similarities and divergences are more like those that occur between two or more singings of the same song by the same singer'.[2] As an illustration, Lord gives two singers' rendition of the opening of 'Murko Kraljević and Musa the Highwayman', the first published by Vuk Stefanović Karadžić, the second by Parry.[3]

Lord has built a detailed case for the Gospels as oral traditional narrative. He has established an overall narrative structure which conforms to that in oral epics, and he has provided a detailed examination of evidence based on order and the patterns of verbal agreements (and disagreements). He has shown that oral traditional narratives display the same patterns, while excluding the hypothesis of a literary relationship based on the expectation of greater agreement than what can be demonstrated. I turn now to a detailed evaluation of this evidence.

b. *Critique of Lord*

Despite these striking parallels, Lord's essay has failed to gain widespread converts. Gospel criticism continues to be dominated by the two-source theory, or at the very least, some model of literary relationship. But an examination of Lord's comparison is instructive in establishing a model of orality which allows for more sure results in postulating oral antecedents behind the Gospel tradition.

Lord's paper was first presented at an interdisciplinary seminar, and a written response was offered by Charles H. Talbert. He notes a number of problems in the straightforward comparison of oral

---

1. Lord, 'Gospels', p. 88.
2. Lord, 'Gospels', p. 88.
3. See the parallels in Lord, 'Gospels', p. 89.

traditional narratives with the Gospels.[1] First, Talbert examines the Gospels' overall mythic pattern and shows that this structure is not limited to oral literature but is also incorporated into literary biographies, including Suetonius' *Augustus*. Hence, the presence of this pattern in the Gospels is not proof of their oral traditional character.[2]

Secondly, there is Lord's assertion that the Gospels' texts vary as to rule out a literary relationship. But given the conventions of the Hellenistic age, Talbert believes that the textual variations are in fact exactly what we would expect. Josephus' *Antiquities* provides a useful comparison. For books 1-10, Josephus had no other written source than the Jewish Scriptures. An examination of his use of this source shows him to be consistent with the practices of other Hellenistic authors, wherein the source is not copied slavishly.[3] The question of literary dependence in the synoptic tradition cannot be determined on the basis of a few selected passages. Rather, the fact of a literary relationship is determined on the basis of the pattern of agreements based upon the entire Gospels. As B.H. Streeter has shown, of Mark's 661 verses, Matthew reproduces the substance of 600 of these (compressed into about 530 verses employing 51 per cent of Mark's actual words) while Luke, despite his 'Great Omission', reproduces at least 350 verses of Mark (retaining 53 per cent of Mark's actual words). Since Luke reproduces portions of the Markan narrative omitted in Matthew, only about 30 verses of Mark can be said to be unique to his Gospel. In summary, the literary relationship among the synoptics is based upon an extensive evaluation of the pattern of agreements throughout the entire Gospel narratives.[4]

The manuscript tradition within the Gospels provides a useful control. Here we are certainly dealing with a literary relationship among texts. The scribes' willingness to alter their source compares

---

1. C.H. Talbert, 'Oral and Independent or Literary and Interdependent? A Response to A.B. Lord', in *The Relationships Among the Gospels: An Interdisciplinary Dialogue* (ed. W.O. Walker, Jr; San Antonio, TX: Trinity University Press, 1978), pp. 93-102.

2. Talbert, 'Oral and Independent?', p. 95.

3. Talbert, 'Oral and Independent?', p. 96.

4. See B.H. Streeter, *The Four Gospels: A Study of Origins* (London: Macmillan, 1924), pp. 158-81.

well with Matthew and Luke's alterations of Mark and Q in the two-source understanding of Gospel origins.[1]

Thirdly, there is the sequence of episodes and the pattern of omissions and insertions which Lord compares favourably with the pattern found in oral traditional material. The relative order of the three synoptic Gospels has been particularly well studied since it plays a vital role in adjudicating between such competing reconstructions as the Griesbach hypothesis or the two-source theory. Joseph B. Tyson's study shows that the agreement of order among the synoptics is so high that a literary explanation is necessary.[2] Lord has failed to compare extensively the order throughout the entire Gospels and by category, most notably the material common to Mark and one or both other Gospels and within the so-called Q traditions. This kind of extensive analysis not only helps establish the superiority of the two-source theory within a literary relationship but also rules out entirely any thesis of independence. For example, it is well known that within the triple tradition agreements of order between Matthew and Luke do no occur against Mark. Likewise, under the two-source theory, Matthew relocates only seven units from Mark (in two instances two consecutive units are relocated together) while in Luke there are only four relocations of the Markan material. Furthermore, although the Q material has been inserted at different points within the common Markan chronology by Matthew and Luke there is still considerable relative agreement between them on the order of this material (a phenomenon that supports a written source).[3] In other words, if the Gospels are oral performances, how does one explain the relative agreement in order within the so-called Q materials despite their different contexts within the overall chronologies of Matthew and Luke?

Lord's examination of the accounts of the baptism is illustrative. Matthew alone records John's attempt at dissuading Jesus (Mt. 3.14-15) and uses the third person in the address to Jesus by the heavenly voice. From these differences Lord reconstructs two oral traditions,

1. This issue will be examined in greater detail in the next chapter.

2. J.B. Tyson, 'Sequential Parallelism in the Synoptic Gospels', *NTS* 22 (1976), pp. 276-308. As noted by Talbert, 'Oral and Independent?', p. 96.

3. On these and related issues, see Kümmel, *Introduction to the New Testament*, pp. 56-60, and B.W. Henaut, 'Is Q but the Invention of Luke and Mark? Method and Argument in the Griesbach Hypothesis', *RST* 8.3 (Sept. 1988), pp. 15-32.

one represented by Matthew, the other by Mark and Luke. Yet these differences only involve one author changing the Markan source in two respects, hardly an impossibility in a literary relationship. Nor has Lord explored fully the possible theological concerns that might be behind the change. The attempt at dissuading Jesus from baptism subordinates John in the narrative, a change that reinforces Matthew's omission of the Markan motif that John's baptism was for the remission of sins (Mk 1.4 contra Mt. 3.1). Matthew's change to the third person in the voice during Jesus' baptism likewise is highly christological: the voice now is for the reader's benefit (Jesus does not need to be told he is God's son). Lord fails to explore the differences among the texts to determine whether they are part of an extensive redactional pattern.

The comparison of verbal agreements also deserves closer examination. In the synoptics we are not dealing simply with word-for-word agreement between two versions. Rather, this kind of agreement is found extensively throughout all three Gospels. Lord's example of the Sower is unfortunate. The close agreements between Matthew and Mark, he admits, entail verses 3b, 4, 5, 6 and 7. This amounts to almost the entire parable! Lord has to point to disagreements from the wider context to acquire his 'islands' of agreement in 'lakes' of disagreement. But these lakes of disagreement also come from the narrative frames and Matthew's insertion of Q tradition into the context. Lord's examples of word-for-word agreement in oral traditional songs is also inappropriate since he cannot provide examples of the extensive agreement found in the Q traditions.[1] The agreement in wording between Matthew and Luke at times is often well over 70 per cent, a degree of agreement that is often considerably higher than that between these two Gospels in other contexts, especially the narrative sections. This kind of selective areas of agreement, coincidentally in the Q contexts, does not fit well with an oral traditional understanding as advanced by Lord.[2] Lord's perplexity at Matthew's plural ('crowds') compared to Mark's singular as an unlikely and insignificant change in a literary relationship also shows the methodological weakness of comparing the two Gospels

1. See at Q 3.7-9, 16-17; 6.41-42; 7.6b-9, 24-35; 10.13-15, 21-22; 11.9-13, 24-26, 29-32; 12.39-40, 42-46; and 13.34-35.
2. Statistics taken from W. Wilkens, 'Zur Frage der literarischen Beziehung Zwischen Matthäus und Lukas', *NovT* 8 (1966), pp. 48-49.

only one verse at a time. For although Matthew elsewhere is capable
of maintaining Mark's singular 'crowd' (cp. at Mk 4.1b; 8.1, 2, 6;
9.14), there are enough instances of a systematic change to the plural
to view the form as a Matthean tendency (cp. at Mk 3.7, 9; 4.35;
6.33, 39, 45; 7.31-33; 8.6b, 10; 11.9; 12.12). Redaction criticism of
the Gospels has provided abundant evidence that many of these
initially perplexing changes are understandable in the overall
theological and literary context of the Gospels.[1] The change of Mark's
indicative 'and when the sun rose' (4.6) to the genitive absolute in
Matthew, 'but after the sun arose' is not so puzzling. It avoids a
repetitive use of the indicative, particularly in light of Mark's 'and
immediately it withered' just a half-verse earlier. The change,
actually, allows for a smoother literary text and is precisely the sort
of alteration we would expect in a textual relationship. Lord also is
forced to admit that there is a greater degree of divergence between
two different singers' versions of the same song 'except when a singer
has been influenced by a published text without actually memorising
it'.[2] This only pushes the problem back a step: for here Lord really
would need to hypothesize a written published text circulating and
available to the synoptic authors in order to account for the extensive
verbal agreements. How this readily differs from Q or the two-source
theory or better accounts for the data is difficult for me to see.

Lord's analysis also confuses the verbal similarities in the Gospels
with the formulaic language in Homer or Yugoslavian bards. In the
latter case the word-for-word agreement between two performances is
not remarkable. As Parry demonstrates, these phrases are part of an
extensive system of formulae. Each phrase is duplicated in a different
context within the epic. If we remember that Homer uses θεὰ
γλαυκῶπις ᾿Αθήνη ('the goddess, flashing-eyed Athene') 50 times,
we can see the striking difference with the Gospels. Usually the phrase
which appears in two or three Gospels cannot be found in a different
passage. Lord has assumed that the agreements among the synoptics
are comparable to formulae, when in fact they are usually bound to
the immediate context.

Lord's mistake in identifying the pattern of agreement among the
Gospels as independent oral performances warns us against assuming

---

1. See the extensive presentation by Hawkins establishing Markan priority in
Horae Synopticae, pp. 117-53.
2. Lord, 'Gospels', p. 88.

an explanation of 'oral tradition' for variations among texts. The fact that he has identified the textual variations that have resulted from Matthew and Luke's redactional rewriting of their sources shows us that there is almost nothing syntactically that will distinguish oral from redactional variations. A textual relationship between two passages has to be established not on a verse-by-verse basis but by an extensive examination of all the textual data. Two texts which initially look like independent oral variants might actually, upon closer examination, be shown to share a textual relationship once adequate allowance has been made for the redactional and literary concerns of each author. This principle is particularly important for the doubly attested material in Mark and Q, and the synoptic sayings which can be found in the Apostolic Fathers or Thomas.

c. *Oral Patterns in Written Texts*
Any application of the folkloric ground rules of orality must also take into account that oral patterns of expression appear in written texts without a previous oral history. Such often-cited criteria as alliteration, dualities, triads, chiasmus and inclusion are found in written texts. In fact, once a reader starts looking for just these patterns one will be surprised at the frequency they are encountered within written texts. This fact of literacy is important given that some theorists of orality attribute many of the observable features of orality exclusively to that medium.

Consider Shakespeare's *Richard III*. As a play written for live performance it needs to incorporate mnemonics. And the poetic nature of the material lends itself to the rhythms of oral poetry. Since literature in antiquity (and hence the Gospels) was composed as much for the ear as the eye, the parallel is appropriate. I give a number of examples of oral techniques from Act I, scene iii.

> *Richard.* [A] Meantime, [1] God grants that I have need of you.
> [2] Our brother is disgraced, [3] and the nobility
> Held in contempt, [B] while great promotions
> Are daily given to enoble those
> That scarce, some two days since, were worth a noble.
> *[dual contrast, triad, and reversal of image; 76-81].*

> *Queen Elizabeth.* My Lord of Gloucester, I have too long borne
> [1] Your blunt upbraidings [2] and your bitter scoffs.
> By heaven, I will acquaint his Majesty
> Of those gross taunts that oft I have endured.

114 Oral Tradition and the Gospels: The Problem of Mark 4

> I had rather be a country servant maid
> Than a great queen with this condition,
> To be so [1] baited, [2] scorned, and [3] stormed at.
> *[duality; alliteration - b; reversal of image; triad; alliteration - s; 102-108].*

Newspaper articles also rely on 'oral' structuring devices. Consider the following examples from 'Doctor shortage taking toll', by Beverley Spencer:

> Business is booming for [1] McKay and [2] other Regina specialists. They have [1] full appointment books and are in [2] demand for [2a] hospital committees and [2b] medical lectures. *[duality; triad]*. . .

> Getting specialists to come to Regina isn't easy, according to [1] hospital administrators, [2] government officials and [3] physicians who do the recruiting. *[triad]*

> There is a national shortage of specialists, especially in [1] radiology and [2] ophthalmology, which forces the city to compete with [1] Montreal, [2] Toronto and [3] Vancouver for staff. *[duality; triad]*

> And Regina's reputation as a small centre with [1] limited resources, [2] uneasy medical politics and [3] unenviable climate doesn't make it any easier, [1] administrators and [2] specialists say. *[duality; triad]*[1]

The triadic repetition of events, so frequent in Homer and folktales, is not confined to oral tradition. In Mark there is the threefold prediction of the cross and resurrection and the threefold declaration of Jesus' divine sonship, while in Acts there is the story of Paul's conversion (9.1-9; 22.6-16; 26.12-18). The technique is evident in the following passage by David Eddings:

> Belgarath knelt beside the flagstone he'd uncovered and rapped sharply on it three times with the pommel of Barak's heavy sword. The sound seemed to echo hollowly from underneath.

> The old man waited for a moment, then repeated his signal.
> Nothing happened.

> A third time Belgarath hammered his three measured strokes on the echoing flagstone. A slow grinding sound started in one corner of the large chamber.[2]

1. B. Spencer, 'Doctor shortage taking toll', *The Regina Leader Post* (Monday, December 19, 1988).
2. D. Eddings, *Magician's Gambit: Book Three of the Belgariad* (New York: Ballantine, 1983), p. 171.

Such structures also naturally form a part of so-called objective scholarly analysis. Consider the following discussion by James G. Williams:

> [1] However entertaining [1A] a Charles Dickens, [1B] a Theodor Dreiser, [1C] an Erskine Caldwell may be, the reader must respond sharply to the social conditions described. [2] However [a] paradoxical and [b] dreamlike [2A] a Kafka or [2B] a Borges, questions about the human condition must press on the reader if he or she is attentive to the text. [3] However fantastic [3A] Tolkien's world of middle-earth where [a] hobbits and [b] other strange creatures abound, every fan of Tolkien knows that the fantasy is about [a] real faith and [b] real hope in our actual human existence.[1]

Many of the techniques of orality, therefore, find a natural home in literary texts. The oft-mentioned features of orality such as parallelism, triads, polarized contrasts, reversal of image, inclusion, chiasmus, ring structure and echo all can be found in the literary techniques of many authors from a variety of eras and cultures. In orality we find an exciting interplay between the old and the new, with an 'improvisation on an existing stock of images and forms' being 'the hallmark of fictional narrative of all sorts'.[2] But this is equally true of the written text; in literary rhetoric we find an interplay between the old well-known patterns and the new vivid expression of the author.

5. *Orality in Perspective*

a. *Orality and Textuality in Continuity*
The results of the above discussion can now be put into perspective. The recovery of an original oral substratum to the written text is far more complicated than often acknowledged. The relationship between orality and textuality is far more subtle than is usually thought: the great chasm between the two, and the resulting linguistic indicators of orality, presumed by such scholars as Lord and Kelber turn out to collapse entirely upon closer examination.

Further complicating the identification of oral tradition is the fact that the Gospels are textuality and not transcribed orality. Unlike

---

1. J.G. Williams, *Gospel Against Parable: Mark's Language of Mystery* (Sheffield: Almond Press, 1985), p. 24.
2. Vansina, *Oral Tradition*, p. 12.

Homer, where the language of the oral performance has been transcribed to preserve a permanent record of the epic, the Gospels were written with an entirely different purpose. Each of the evangelists took as the starting point the desire to convey a literary and theological text to the reader. As a literary exercise the Gospels now give any prior oral tradition in the language of textuality: a language that has been redacted to conform to the theological and stylistic outlook of the author. At each point in the narrative the evangelist has had the opportunity to reflect upon every last word and conform it to that literary intent. A close evaluation of Matthew and Luke's handling of their sources confirms that no part of the narrative is immune from this process. Geographic frames, miracle narratives, pronouncement stories, aphorisms and parables alike have all been transmitted to us in the stylistic and theological expression of textuality.

Secondly, we have seen the complete absence of distinctive and unique ground rules for orality. Certainly scholars can identify a number of hallmarks of oral expression and catalogue a variety of variations on the theme of repetition. None of these, however, can be ascribed exclusively to the oral medium. Each of the oral techniques identified, which serve a particularly useful function in the oral medium, finds a natural home in textuality. The techniques now serve different hermeneutical functions in the literary text, and this fact must be remembered in an exegesis, but the fact remains that the techniques of orality have been taken over by numerous authors. This is particularly true, we have seen, for the literary techniques of Mark and Luke. Hence the identification of oral patterns in a text does not establish an oral history for the unit. One must, after identifying such patterns, investigate them thoroughly in terms of the theological and stylistic tendencies of the author of the document. These oral patterns might, upon further examination, accord fully with the redactional concerns of the author. The universality of many of the oral techniques also serves as a strong warning against assuming too easily a particular point of origin for a saying. Antithetic parallelism, for example, can be found in the literature of numerous cultures and eras, and cannot be confined to Galilee and Judea.

The assumption of an early and exclusively oral phase of transmission terminating in written documents only after a lengthy passage of time also may not be warranted. The growing awareness of pre-synoptic written sources, a history of redaction within Q, and the inclusion in Paul's letters of some synoptic sayings and other parenesis warns that the literary phase of transmission may have started much earlier than is often thought. The highly literate urban context of the Gospels suggests that Finnegan's evidence of interaction between orality and textuality is a far more appropriate model for the synoptic transmission.

In this regard, the question of establishing either oral independence or a literary relationship among versions of a tradition needs to be handled with care. Lord's identification of the Gospels as independent oral performances serves as a good warning. The question of independence regarding the doubly attested sayings common to Mark and Q, or of various sayings common to the synoptics, Apostolic Fathers and Thomas should not be answered too quickly. If a direct relationship of dependence (parent to child) cannot be established this still does not preclude an underlying textuality. Shared sources may still be at work. Such a relationship needs to be determined, not on the basis of the particular saying in question, but in terms of the overall shared material. The Q traditions serve as an appropriate model in this regard. The variations observable between Matthew and Luke in such texts as the Lord's Prayer, Beatitudes and Great Banquet, viewed only one saying at a time could quite easily support a thesis of independent oral traditions. The Q hypothesis, however, is established on the basis of overall agreement on a much wider basis of material. Is there enough material available to establish or exclude a textual relationship in such outstanding issues as Mark and Q or the synoptics and Thomas?

Finally, there is the problem of the oral phase itself. The quest for the 'original' version of a saying immediately runs into serious problems. Only with respect to shorter units and a transmissional context of memorization can one speak in terms of the 'original' form. There is no evidence, however, that such a transmissional process was ever used during the assumed oral phase of synoptic transmission. Rather, verbal fluidity is the norm. Each performance is a new event and each is as authentic as the last. The adjudication of relative dating can only be accomplished with much difficulty and is particularly dependent upon what is known of the history of early Christianity from other datable literary sources. Here Paul's letters stand in the forefront. Only when a saying displays characteristics clearly dependent upon a certain phase of church history (and thus becomes anachronistic in an earlier era) can a date be established for a unit.

The oral phase must also be viewed in the wider cultural heritage of antiquity. Proverbs, parables, beatitudes and other such traditions, like Homer's formulae, are part of a vast communal effort. Only the least part may be attributed to any individual. This heritage, it must be remembered, was available to the evangelists, the authors of any pre-Gospel sources and any oral performer during the material's transmission. Discovering precisely when a saying entered the tradition and its transmissional history, is incredibly complicated.

This determination is complicated because orality is very much context-bound for its meaning. Performer and audience interact and the context of every performance is ever fresh. Each oral performer during the transmission of the material had his or her own distinctive style. Any saying passed on through the oral transmission will have undergone a process of alteration wherein each performer has fused the tradition with various motifs and variants from the vast cultural heritage. Establishing a trajectory through this process and a continuity of distinctiveness to arrive back at an authentic saying of Jesus is no small task.

b. *Orality and Redaction Criticism*
Redaction criticism must also be allowed its place in determining whether an oral substratum underlies a text. 'Common sense' alone would forbid a reconstruction of an oral history behind most of the literary examples cited above (section 4, c). Indeed, the factor of redactional considerations is implicit even in Parry. His central distinction between the formula and the repeated phrase, drawing upon such examples as *Macbeth* and Marlowe, seems immediately obvious on the grounds of common sense. But a full theoretical justification would necessitate such considerations as context, genre and individual authorial style. Similarly, such repetitions as the Markan phrase καὶ ἔλεγεν αὐτοῖς or the threefold repetition of the passion prediction are most easily accounted for as part of Mark's literary world when redaction criticism is used.

The debate between such scholars as Lord and Finnegan reinforces this procedure. In noting the problems with a straightforward application of the Parry–Lord thesis to the Gospels, it is well to emphasize that other cultural examples of orality noted by Finnegan are not perfectly compatible with the Gospel traditions. The heavy emphasis upon memorization in Somalia cannot be assumed to be the process at work in the synoptic materials.

Even more culturally relevant criteria such as antithetical parallelism need to be examined in the light of redactional considerations. Jeremias's impressive list of synoptic sayings cast in this device can no longer be seen as an adequate basis for claiming this material as authentic. And without Jeremias's assumption that the form belongs primarily to Jesus (and must therefore have had an oral transmission) the recovery of an active oral tradition that cast sayings in antithetic parallelism is in doubt. For this structural technique is equally at home in literary texts and would have been available either to Mark or the author of any of his written sources. The aphorism of the wedding guests at Mk 2.19b-20 is a notable case in point. Dan O. Via examines the variety of sociological situations assumed in the narrative, and in particular the post-resurrectional setting of at least verse 20 (perhaps also 19b).[1]

Redaction criticism is essential in at least two respects. Positively, redactional considerations must first be explored in order to determine the likelihood of a passage being the evangelist's creation. Passages that can be shown to have strong ties to the theological and literary tendencies of the Gospel author are unlikely candidates for an earlier oral history. In such instances there would have to be strong offsetting evidence for the passage to be considered 'oral traditional'. Negatively, redaction criticism has a role to play in isolating those passages that might be deserving of closer scrutiny. Where texts can be shown to have a relative absence of the author's redactional vocabulary, style and theological motifs the possibility of the text being traditional must be given serious consideration. It is the integration of these two methodological considerations, redaction criticism in light of the so-called ground rules of orality, which will concern me in my examination of Mk 4.1-34.

1. Via, in *What is Redaction Criticism?*, pp. vii-viii.

Chapter 3

TEXTUALITY AS A BARRIER TO ORALITY:
THE MARKAN REDACTION OF 4.1-34

One works in a methodological circle—the model of orality undoubtedly influences the exegesis of the text. Yet close inspection of specific passages must inform the very understanding of orality— otherwise the model is constructed in a vacuum. As the long history of critical scholarship has shown, particularly in the radical change in understanding of the evangelists as authors, the text is often the one ugly fact that destroys an otherwise beautiful theory.

Despite this problem, recovery of oral tradition must begin with the text since it is the only access to this phase of early Christianity. One can deal with orality only as it is preserved in the textual medium, and it is here that one encounters the first major obstacle, for this medium does not give directly transcribed orality, but rather a fully textualized tradition. A thorough understanding of the evangelist's theological and literary intentions is necessary before any prior oral tradition can be recovered. Nor can one assume that Mark intended to present an accurate presentation of the contemporary oral tradition. The Gospel narrative is a literary and theological work in its own right, and Mark's purposes have stamped the tradition at virtually every point. He may have so modified any inherited tradition that its earlier form is unrecognizable and hence irrecoverably lost. Matthew and Luke's practices with their sources Mark and Q can serve as a bench-mark in this regard. Their agreements run close to 70 per cent in shared vocabulary in many (but not all) of the Q traditions, while comparison with Mark shows that they preserved about 50 per cent of his actual words.[1] Recovery of the Q source is at least controlled by its preservation in two Gospels, and when disagreements arise (i.e., in

---

1. See above, Chapter 2, section 4, b; Streeter, *The Four Gospels*, pp. 158-81; Wilkens, 'Zur Frage', pp. 48-49.

wording or order) one can see if either or both differences are in harmony with the evangelist's theological concerns as expressed elsewhere. The recovery of the Markan source—oral or written—is not as straightforward as even this difficult task! Mark may not have been as kind to his sources. Since literate poets often turned away from the formulaic language of orality,[1] the textual nature of his Gospel may have led him to alter fundamentally the linguistic expression of any oral sources. The benchmark derived from Matthew and Luke's use of literary sources thus may be a misleading comparison. And if Mark employed a written source one may not have access to another redacted form of this document to inform a reconstruction. Nor may one be able to infer sufficient information about the literary and theological intentions of the source to reconstruct the earlier form of any oral tradition which may have found its way into this pre-Gospel tract!

These issues are vitally important for recovering any oral traditions behind Mk 4.1-34. This perplexing and controversial passage offers the strange theory that Jesus taught in parables in order that outsiders neither comprehended nor be saved. This is, as John Meagher states, 'a curious policy'.[2] The harsh intent of vv. 11-13 has caused great anxiety among scholars, and numerous tradition histories have been advanced that confidently include a variety of sources—both written and oral—and multiple pre-Markan stages. But much of this confidence is misdirected: such reconstructions are based only on Mark's text and fail to take adequate account of the problems of recovering orality. Because of the continued attention the passage has drawn in the secondary literature and its central theme of 'oral tradition' I have chosen it as a test case. The problems inherent in recovering any oral tradition behind this passage will provide abundant proof of the essential inaccessibility of this phase of the tradition.

1. *Text Criticism*

I begin with text criticism for three reasons. First, before I can begin to discuss the passage I must reconstruct, as best I can, Mark's original

1. See above, Chapter 2, section 1, b.
2. J.C. Meagher, *Clumsy Construction in Mark's Gospel: A Critique of Form- and Redaktionsgeschichte* (New York: Edwin Mellen, 1979), p. 85.

wording. There is little sense in isolating signs of orality or redaction if these are based on secondary readings. Secondly, the manuscript tradition shows us how the text was treated at the literary stage—the degree of stability and inviolability—allowing me to test a number of key assertions discussed above. Thirdly, an examination of the alterations to Mark's text provides a good clue to the 'trouble spots' within the passage. The spots at which the scribes felt it necessary to 'improve' Mark often underscore the importance of the phrase in the overall context.

It is not my intent to challenge the text of the UBS 3rd edition. The committee has done an admirable job establishing the most likely form of Mark's autograph. Rather, I highlight the fact that the practice of reading the Gospels in a printed critical edition provides a false sense of security. The reconstructed text looks so solid that one forgets it is just a scholarly reconstruction that exists in no one manuscript. Each witness to Mark is actually different. Were I to compare any two manuscripts of Mark, such as Sinaiticus (א) and Bezae (D), I would find that there are significant differences; if I were unaware of the textual relationship between these manuscripts it might prove tempting to ascribe the differences to some form of 'oral variants'. If the variation between these manuscripts at v. 21, for example (א: Μήτι ἔρχεται ὁ λύχνος ἵνα ὑπὸ τὸν μόδιον τεθῇ ἢ ὑπὸ τὴν κλίνην; οὐχ ἵνα ὑπὸ τὴν λυχνίαν τεθῇ; versus D: Μήτι ἅπτεται ὁ λύχνος ἵνα ὑπὸ τὸν μόδιον τεθῇ ἢ ὑπὸ τὴν κλίνην; καὶ οὐχὶ ἵνα ἐπὶ τὴν λυχνίαν τεθῇ), were found in the context of Mark and Q or Thomas it might quickly give rise to a thesis of independence. At first glance, most of the variants are comparable to those that naturally occur in oral performances as detailed by Lord. Furthermore, the number of variants is considerably larger than is often remembered. The critical apparatus of the Nestlé–Aland edition of Mark's parables sermon shows variants at approximately 40 points. But this does not present all of the variants. A comparison with the critical apparatus of Alford's *Greek New Testament* yields numerous other textual variants.[1] For convenience, I have gathered together the more important of these variants under a number of categories.

---

1. See H. Alford, *Alford's Greek Testament: An Exegetical and Critical Commentary* (repr. Grand Rapids: Guardian, 1976 [1844–77]).

a. *Addition or Deletion of the Article*
Addition or deletion of the article frequently occurs. In an oral
context, since perfect memorization of the text over an extended
passage is impossible, this is an expected kind of near synonymous
change of expression. But in manuscripts which share a textual
relationship, these variations cannot be assumed to be synonymous.
The first such change is found at v. 1. The absence of the article in the
phrase εἰς πλοῖον ἐμβάντα (א, B*, C, L, θ) enjoys considerably
stronger textual support than its inclusion in the Western tradition
(εἰς τό πλοῖον ἐμβάντα—B², D, W, Δ). The scribes probably wish
to make explicit a connection with Jesus' injunction at Mk 3.9 (καὶ
εἶπεν τοῖς μαθηταῖς αὐτοῦ ἵνα πλοιάριον προσκαρτερῇ αὐτῷ
διὰ τὸν ὄχλον). Thus it is likely that a connection exists between
these verses—Jesus embarks into the boat to avoid being pressed in
upon by the crowd, the very boat that the disciples prepared for him
due to his earlier foresight.

Alexandrinus and Sinaiticus (corrected) add the article at v. 3; this
preference for the articular infinitive in the genitive is explicable on
stylistic grounds, the context expressing purpose.[1] Both Matthew and
Luke also make this alteration, and hence one could attribute the
variant to assimilation to their texts. This explanation, in a sense, only
pushes the problem back a step: in such cases we must investigate the
motives of Matthew, Luke and the scribes (in not assimilating the texts
to agree with Mark).

Finally, there is the deletion of the article at v. 11. Although the
manuscript evidence is almost equally divided (τὰ πάντα, A, B, C,
L—πάντα, א, D, K, W, θ) the omission is likely secondary. This
brings the phrase into closer agreement with v. 34, where Jesus
ἐπέλυεν πάντα. In other words, these two verses, 11 and 34, are
intimately connected in the scribe's mind and must be harmonized into
complete conformity.

b. *Change of Word Order*
Mark's word order has been altered at numerous points in the
manuscripts. Since Greek varies word order in near endless
combinations with only minor differences in emphasis, these kinds of

1. The genitive of the articular infinitive is used to express purpose or result (Lk.
9.51 and Acts 5.31). See E. Van Ness Goetchius, *The Language of the New
Testament* (New York: Charles Scribner's Sons, 1965), p. 201.

changes would fit particularly well in the context of orality. Why have the scribes deliberately altered Mark's word order? An important instance is found at v. 1 with εἰς πλοῖον ἐμβάντα (א, B*, C, L, θ) altered to ἐμβάντα εἰς τό πλοῖον in Alexandrinus. This likely reflects the copyist's preference for the word order of verb-object, a trend in Hellenistic Greek.

c. Stylistic Variants

Stylistic variation is an extremely broad category encompassing virtually any alteration. In an oral context subtle distinctions are often lost due to the immediacy of the situation and the necessity for rapid composition. Such variants find a natural explanation in terms of synonymous equivalents chosen unconsciously, or as part of the more natural performance style of the performer. These choices in the oral medium are often unconscious; in a textual situation, however, these variants arise in a conscious effort to improve the literary quality of the work. Particularly with Mark, such temptation must have been strong for the scribes due to the notoriously inelegant Greek.

The first two cases involve Bezae and the addition of ὅτι. At v. 5 the Western text's reading (D, W) of καὶ ὅτι for ὅπου allows for a causal sense, explaining why the seed failed. Mark's simple observation that the rocky ground lacked soil has become the explicit cause of the seed's failure as expressed at 6a. The alteration creates a more intimate relationship between vv. 5 and 6. Similarly, at v. 28 the causal conjunction ὅτι has been added by Bezae (D) to smooth out the abrupt nature of the αὐτομάτη. Both of these changes result from the scribes' desire to produce a more fully integrated text.

At v. 15 the slight difference between εἰς αὐτούς (B, W) and ἐν αὐτοῖς (א, C, L, Δ) is easily explained if the former were the original and the latter were preferred by some scribes as more appropriate with the verb ἐσπαρμένον. The change in prepositions from εἰς το ἐπί (א, C) at v. 18 is also a seemingly minor stylistic variation. Since ἐπί with the accusative has the meaning of 'on' or 'in' some scribes may have felt that this better conveyed the sense of the verse. The ὅτι recitative in Vaticanus (B) at v. 21 was likely added to set off the direct discourse.[1] Similar is the addition of the

---

1. The reading is too poorly attested to be original and non-Markan in style. The omission is very well attested, including manuscripts of the Alexandrian, Byzantine, Western and Caesarean types (א, A, C, D, W, θ).

hortatory exclamation ἴδετε in family 13 in v. 21. The addition offers a neat parallel to the Ἀκούετε of verse 3a. The inclusion of τί at v. 22 has slightly weaker textual support (א, A, C, L, Δ— Alexandrian and Byzantine) than the absence (B, D, K, W, θ— Alexandrian, Western, and Caesarean). It is also easier to see the emphatic enclitic pronoun being added (to create greater emphasis) than omitted.

There is minor dissatisfaction with Mark's plain introduction in the parable of the Seed Growing Secretly (4.26). The simple ὡς ('as, like') is by far the best attested (א, B, D, L, Δ) and the likely cause of the other variants. Attempts at a more precise comparison include ὅταν ('whenever'—W), ὡς ἄν/ἐάν ('when, as soon as'—A, C) and ὥσπερ ('as, just as'—θ). The relatively late date of the manuscripts in question certify the secondary character of these emendations.

d. *Harmonization with Other Contexts*
Alterations often harmonize the verse with another part of the narrative. We have already seen this motive in the addition of the article at v. 1. The variation in wording is often slight and comparable with those expected in an oral situation. But the motivation is thoroughly textual. In an oral performance it is impossible for the bard to integrate fully every part of the narrative to its maximum potential—there are simply too many connections to be made! But in the textual medium, the ability to edit the 'finished product' allows for a degree of integration unattainable in the oral medium.

Two such alterations are found in v. 5 and have been occasioned by the description of the rocky ground. The addition of another καί in Vaticanus may reflect harmonization of the passage with the allegorical explanation at vv. 16-17, allowing the two-part structure to be plain in both texts. Similarly the verb for growth, ἐξανέτειλεν, has been changed to ἀνέτειλεν in the Washington manuscript, perhaps in an effort to parallel fully the actions of the seed and sun.

The final example I wish to examine occurs at v. 8. The difference is between καὶ ἄλλα (B, C, L, W, θ) and καὶ ἄλλο (א*, A, D, f). Both readings are attested in the Alexandrian, Byzantine and Western text types. The former is to be preferred, not only on the grounds of slightly stronger manuscript attestation (B, C, W and θ) but also since the latter reading seems more likely to result from a desire to harmonize the verse to the previous uses of καὶ ἄλλο.

e. *Harmonization with Matthew or Luke*

Harmonization with the text of either Matthew or Luke also affects the textual transmission. The first such instance is found at v. 1 where Koridethi (W) reads ἔν τῷ αἰγιαλῷ and contains the same non-Markan vocabulary found in Matthew. It seems that Mark's penchant for duplicate phrases has again offended; the change allows for a more precise geographic term and avoids the third use of Mark's pet-term θάλασσα within the verse.

Verse 10 includes two disputed readings of this class. Manuscripts of the Western (D, W) and Caesarean (θ) types have had problems with Mark's curious phrase οἱ περὶ αὐτὸν σὺν τοῖς δώδεκα. They have substituted the more natural μαθηταὶ αὐτοῦ—which is similar to the parallel in both Matthew and Luke and the phrase used, interestingly enough, by Luke and Mark in a very similar context at Mk 7.17. These same manuscripts have also altered the object of v. 10 to τίς ἡ παραβολὴ αὕτη. This reading is again influenced by the Lukan parallel. Like the third evangelist, the scribes noticed the tension between the plural object and the allegorical exposition of a single parable. This motive also lies behind the reading of the Byzantine text (A), the singular for 'the parable', a reading also in agreement with Luke's parallel. Verse 10, therefore, has occasioned particular attention from the scribes and is seen to need greater clarity.

Such assimilation lies behind the variant at v. 15. The addition of ἐν ταῖς καρδίας αὐτῶν reflects a desire to explain the allegory fully: the word is sown in the heart. The addition also reflects knowledge of Mk 8.17 and indicates that the two verses are tied together—πεπωρωμένην ἔχετε τὴν καρδίαν ὑμῶν.

Perhaps the most significant is the change of ἔρχεται to ἅπτεται in the Western tradition (D, W, f¹³) at v. 21. This most likely reflects harmonization with Luke's ἅψας: one does not simply bring out a lamp, one lights it.

f. *Addition or Deletion of Phrases*

The addition of phrases that substantially alter the verse's meaning also occur. The first instance is Bezae's (D) addition to v. 9: καὶ ὁ συνιῶν συνιέτω. The influence of v. 12 is plain: hearing and

understanding must go together.[1] At v. 12, the addition of the explicit
τὰ ἁμαρτήματα in Koine, Western and Caesarean manuscripts (A,
D, θ) avoids any ambiguity. Alexandrinus and Koridethi (A, θ) have
an interesting addition at v. 24—τοῖς ἀκούουσιν. The copyists have
made a connection between this law of 'the rich get richer' and the
contrast between the elect and the unbelievers. Only the elect, who
hear, will have more given to them. It is a change similar to
Matthew's redactional addition of 13.16-17 and the insertion by Bezae
at Mk 4.9 (καὶ ὁ συνιῶν συνίετω) noted above.

But the textual medium is not simply one of growth—the copyists
often avoid the duplication of synonymous expressions. We have seen
this at v. 1 in Koridethi's (W) alteration. Bezae's change at the same
spot to πέραν τῆς θαλάσσης likewise avoids the redundancy in
Mark's πρὸς τὴν θάλασσαν ἐπὶ τῆς γῆς. Bezae's (D) deletion of the
infinitive at verse 3 similarly avoids Mark's repetition of the same
root in the noun and verb. Comparable alterations have been made at
v. 4. The Washington manuscript's deletion of the phrase ἐγένετο ἐν
τῷ σπείρειν avoids duplicating the infinitive while Bezae removes
the unnecessary ἐγένετο.

A number of copyists have found the subject in v. 18 redundant.
The problem centres around the phrases ἄλλοι εἰσίν and οὗτοί εἰσιν.
A variety of solutions have been found—essentially manuscripts of the
Koine family (A) have used the latter phrase only, placing it in the
former's place and omitting the subsequent repetition. This also brings
the verse into closer parallelism with the other allegorical
explanations. Similar is the solution in the Western and Caesarean
manuscripts (W, θ) which omit the phrase ἄλλοι εἰσίν entirely.

The triple stumbling block of v. 19 has occasioned dissatisfaction—
an assessment supported by both Matthew and Luke, who alter their
parallels. Western and Caesarean texts (D, W, θ) have omitted
altogether the third of Mark's phrases (καὶ αἱ περὶ τὰ λοιπὰ
ἐπιθυμίαι). They have also substituted βίου for αἰῶνος, while two
of them (D, θ) have altered the remaining phrase to ἀπάτη τοῦ
κόσμου. The resulting 'the cares of life and the delight in the world'
indicates a subtle theological change, more in keeping with dualistic
theology which perceived this world as a place of sin.[2]

1. The change is consistent with the addition at 8.16, where the exhortation to
hearing is repeated in D.
2. The reading in Δ—ἀγάπη τοῦ πλούτου is an interesting case of influence

Finally, mention may be made of v. 24. Bezae (D) has omitted the redundant phrase καὶ προστεθήσεται ὑμῖν, although the deletion transforms a triadic sentence structure into a more formally balanced dual contrast.

g. *Curious Phrases Changed*

Curious expressions also get singled out for alteration. I have already noted the alterations to Mark's unusual designation of audience at v. 10, and the dissatisfaction with his choice of verbs at v. 21. Similar variants can be found. At v. 11 the change of γίνεται to λέγεται in Bezae and Koridethi (D, θ) reflects dissatisfaction with Mark's confusing idiom ἐν παραβολαῖς τὰ πάντα γίνεται. Given the contrast between speaking plainly with explanations to the inner circle and the use of parables as vehicles of disinformation to outsiders, the change to λέγεται produces a more unified text. The curious aorist subjunctive at v. 30 θῶμεν (ℵ, B, C*, L, D) has also been changed either to δῶμεν (W) or παραβάλωμεν (A, C², D, θ). Although τίθημι can be used in the sense of 'to present, describe (by parable)',[1] the scribes probably felt this a sufficiently unusual usage of the word to require a change. This is also reflected in that neither Matthew nor Luke have retained Mark's wording in their parallels (Mt. 13.31; Lk. 13.8).

The change from πάντα to αὐτάς in the Western tradition (D, W, it) harmonizes v. 34 to the allegorical explanation (vv. 13-20) and the antecedent παραβολῆς (v. 34a). πάντα is an exaggeration since Jesus could not have explained literally *everything* privately. The alteration emphasizes that Jesus explained all the parabolic sayings to his disciples.

Two sayings of Semitic idiom have been altered. At v. 12 the change by Bezae of ἀφεθῇ to ἀφεθήσομαι avoids the divine passive. The original has God as the implied subject and the alteration to the first person makes Jesus the explicit subject. This important theological assertion harmonizes the passage to Mk 2.10: Jesus, the Son of Man, has the authority to forgive sins on earth. Since Jesus is the one who speaks in parables, the change keeps the focus throughout on him. The Semitic formulation of vv. 8 and 20 have caused the most

from the Pastorals.

1. See B.M. Newman, Jr, *A Concise Greek–English Dictionary of the New Testament* (London: United Bible Societies, 1971), p. 182.

complicated set of variants. It is best to treat the two textual problems together, and the various readings are given below:

Textual Variants Mark 4.8, 20

	Textual Support	
Reading	*Verse 8:*	*Verse 20:*
1) ἕν. . .ἕν . . . ἕν	A, C², D, θ	L, θ, (א, A, C², D)
2) τὸ ἕν . . . το ἕν . . . το ἕν	W	W
3) εἰς. . . ἐv . . .. ἐv	B²	—
4) εἰς. . . ἕv . . . ἕv	L	—
5) εἰς. . . εἰς. . . εἰς	א, C*, Δ	—
6) ἐv. . . ἐv . . . ἐv	𝔐	𝔐
7) ἐv. . . — . . . —	—	B*
8) ἐv. . . — . . . ἐv	—	C*

The variants are numerous, although the inclusion of the numeral ἕν for v. 9 is supported by the Byzantine and Western types.[1] A number of poorly attested readings can be quickly eliminated: variants 3, 4, 6, 7, 8. Assuming that Mark's text was more likely the same at both verses, reading five is secondary. Reading one is thus most likely the original: particularly in the early unicals this could easily give rise to the preposition ἐv. The idiom with the numeral is cumbersome, and in light of ἔφερεν it is understandable why some scribes would believe a preposition, particularly εἰς, was suitable.

h. *Significance of Text Criticism for Orality*

The above discussion demonstrates that even within a 'scribal' context word-for-word reproduction of the text is not found. Numerous deliberate alterations occur, and this despite the sacred and canonical status of Mark's text after the third century. Most of the changes are quite comparable with those that occur during oral transmission. In other words, linguistically there is nothing to distinguish an oral variant from a textual emendation.

These alterations have a direct bearing on any ability to recover oral tradition. If the textual medium is not fully stable, how much more so the oral phase? This problem is particularly acute since the written text acts as the guide for each subsequent copyist. Orality has fewer guides to stabilize the tradition. Each oral telling is a new performance, highly dependent upon its context. Variation, rather

---

1. I include the variants ἐις . . . ἕv . . . ἕv (L) and the triple τό ἕv in W.

than stability, is the desirable norm.[1] The ability to reconstruct Mark's autograph is also aided by the significant number of witnesses to the text, witnesses that can be dated with some certainty and classified into various traditions. Recovery of any oral tradition is severely limited in this regard. Mark gives us only his redacted witness to any tradition he has incorporated. How could we expect to arrive at Mark's autograph with only Bezae?

Even when Markan traditions appear in Q or Thomas one is dealing with at most three versions—and each as incorporated in a document with its own distinctive theology. This is, it must be admitted, a more narrow basis for establishing the tradition's prior form than the reconstruction of Mark's autograph. Text criticism cautions that texts that are literarily related may display significant variation. The scribe's willingness to change the Markan original suggests that perfect reproduction of a saying need not be present to establish a literary relationship. Mark's Greek is known for its inelegance. If Thomas were dependent upon the Markan tradition is it realistic to expect near-perfect agreement? The doubly attested traditions common to Mark and Q have their own problems. Variation between these two forms of the tradition may be due to redaction of a common source by either or both authors. Mark's inelegant Greek and theological redaction of the tradition should caution us not to demand near-perfect agreement in this material before we consider the possibility of a shared source. Finally, text criticism underscores a distinctive problem with the tradition in Thomas. The manuscript data-base for establishing this text is very narrow. We are dependent upon one fourth-century Coptic translation and some early third-century Greek fragments. This does not bode well for establishing Thomas' autograph, particularly since the translator has at times 'harmonized' the translation to conform with the Coptic translations of the Gospels![2]

---

1. See above, Chapter 1, section 4, a; Chapter 2, section 1, a, b.
2. E.g., see J.M. Robinson. 'On Bridging the Gulf From Q to the Gospel of Thomas (or vice Versa)', in *Nag Hammadi, Gnosticism, and Early Christianity* (ed. C.W. Hedrick and R. Hodgson, Jr; Peabody, MA: Hendrickson, 1986), pp. 152, 161.

2. *Previous Tradition Histories of Mark 4.1-34*

The copyists were among the first to note a number of problems with this passage. In particular, the awkwardness of the audience at v. 10, and the continuity between the question regarding parables (plural) and the response regarding the (single) parable of the Sower has caused problems. Scholars have responded to these issues by a variety of tradition histories of Mk 4.1-34. The tensions in the text, it is often claimed, result from a difference between 'source' and 'redaction'. Mark has inherited a parable tract, which itself has undergone a series of 'editions', and has not fully integrated this material to the wider context.

Implicit in all such reconstructions is a confidence in the ability to trace back through the pre-Markan stages, including the oral phase, with a good degree of precision. A close inspection of many of these tradition histories reveals, however, that they share two fundamental flaws. First, the identification of editorial seams in the narrative are often based on a mistaken understanding of Mark's redactional purpose. What many modern scholars take to be a fundamental contradiction turns out, upon closer examination, to be nothing other than Mark's characteristic manner of expression. Secondly, these studies are over-confident that they can reconstruct the prior shape of Mark's inherited traditions, especially with respect to the oral phase. This error is due to an uncritical adoption of many of Bultmann's form-critical assumptions.

a. *D.W. Riddle and a Pre-Gospel Source (1937)*

Donald W. Riddle was among the first to postulate a pre-Gospel source underlying Mk 4.1-34. Since vv. 33-34 are 'unintelligible' in their present location, their referent must be found in an earlier context:

> It is only when this statement is relieved of the requirement that it agree with its context—a fundamental principle fo[r] form-criticism—that it has rational meaning. Obviously the statement refers to the collection of parables, i.e., to the contents of the source; not to anything which precedes or follows.[1]

---

1. D.W. Riddle, 'Mark 4.1-34; The Evolution of a Gospel Source', *JBL* 56 (1937), p. 77.

The verses, according to Riddle, are inconsistent with 'the plain fact' that Jesus teaches by other than the parabolic form. They find their natural meaning as the conclusion of the parables collection which Mark incorporated into his Gospel. Viewed in this context, 'at once it [the statement] has rational meaning'.[1]

The ultimate materials for this source are the three seed parables. 'Presumably', Riddle tells us, 'the parables were orally circulated for some time before they were written.' They were then collected 'as they were used by early Christian preachers and teachers, because of their identity of theme, the figure of seed'.[2] It is an 'open question' whether the parables 'circulated orally in their aggregate form'.[3] A setting was provided in two steps. First came the introductory formulae: 'And he taught them many things in parables', 'And he said to them in his teaching' (4.2a, b) and 'And he said' (4.26, 30).[4] The concluding formula was probably supplied at this stage (i.e., some form of vv. 33-34). As Riddle explains:

> This is indicated not merely by the fact that it is inconsistent except as a conclusion of the source, but also by its inconsistency with the statement (added later) that parables were used to veil truth which was known to those of an inner circle; the concluding formula in stating that Jesus explained things to his followers cannot be squared with this.[5]

The crucial second stage in the supply of the setting introduced the major structural problems. Here, for the first time, the distinction between the public pronouncement of the parables and their esoteric function for an inner circle was introduced. This is expressed, for Riddle, by the addition of vv. 1 (complete) and 10-12. This latter addition, however, was originally placed not after v. 9 but rather between vv. 32 and 33.[6]

The aphoristic sayings within Mk 4.2-25 represent another problem: did they belong to the source or were they added by Mark? Riddle prefers the second possibility. These are 'perfect examples of sententious logia, which in the primitive stages of the gospel tradition

1. Riddle, 'Gospel Source', p. 77.
2. Riddle, 'Gospel Source', p. 79.
3. Riddle, 'Gospel Source', p. 79.
4. Riddle asserts that the lack of antecedent (v. 2) is not important, 'Gospel Source', p. 79, n. 5.
5. Riddle, 'Gospel Source', pp. 79-80.
6. Riddle, 'Gospel Source', pp. 80, 82.

existed separately and were circulated separately; even after some of the stories and sayings were written these persisted in oral form'. Secondly, since certain of these sayings appear several times in the Gospels 'they were never securely "anchored"'. Thirdly, other such aphoristic clusters in Mark (i.e., 9.40-50; 11.24, 25) indicate that the evangelist has in all cases been responsible for their location, 'unless it can be thought that these, too, had found their resting places before they came to the gospel'. The double occurrence of the saying at Mk 4.9, 23, however, indicates that one of these is to be attributed to the source, the other to Mark. Finally, Riddle points to the different placement of the sayings within the later stages 'of the evolution of the gospel traditions' (i.e., Matthew and Luke–Acts) as further evidence that 'they were not there in the same form which they have in the source as it was incorporated by the writer of the earliest gospel'.[1] Riddle's reconstruction of the source's evolution may be set forth:

Riddle's Pre-Gospel Source

Stage	Verses	Description
Oral A		
	3-8	Sower
	26b-29	Seed Growing Secretly
	30b-32	Mustard Seed
Oral B?	as above	3 Seed Parables in aggregate form
One:		
	as above	Written tract of three Seed parables
Two:		
	2a, b	Introduction: Teaching in Parables
	9	Exhortation to Hear
	26a	'And he said'
	30a	'And he said'
	33-34	Concluding Formula
Three:		
	1	Public Setting: Teaching by the Seaside
	10-12	10-12: Private Instruction (placed after v. 32).

The aphoristic sayings came later, perhaps as late as the evangelist. The allegorical interpretation (vv. 13-20) also represents for Riddle a latter addition to the source. The key question is when the saying on the esoteric teaching was added. Although some scholars see this as the work of the evangelist, Riddle believes this unlikely. Had Mark added

---

1. All quotes in this paragraph are from Riddle, 'Gospel Source', pp. 80-81.

this section, then the present conclusion—a part of the source—'would almost certainly have been edited away'.[1]

These points receive further support in the forms of the source as incorporated by other evangelists. Luke is aware of the difficulties created by the tension between the public setting at vv. 1-9 and the lack of real transition to the private context at v. 10. As Riddle states, 'the source in Luke–Acts lacks the boat and the seaside setting altogether; thus the question (of the disciples only) is more natural'. Matthew, however, incorporates a form of the source 'which keeps the setting, but which makes occasion for the statement about the nature of the teaching by putting the question, "Why do you speak to them in parables?"' Luke's parallel, 'And when his disciples asked him what this parable meant' reflects a similar process, and hence 'suggests the high probability that the central element, the distinction between exoteric and esoteric teaching, was a tertiary attachment to the parable collection and its setting'.[2]

Riddle sees a sharp distinction between the earlier and the tertiary stages in the source. Jesus did not limit his teaching to parables (as in the source's conclusion), nor were the parables designed for the purposes expressed in vv. 10-11; these were distinctions made as the source developed. In the earlier stages, the parables were used because they were effective in the proclamation of the good news: 'They had their rise either as authentic words of Jesus or in so primitive a period in the production of sayings that they reflect only the earliest environment of the emerging Christian movement'. But the tertiary stage of the source which presents the parables as vehicles to hide divine truths from non-believers represents a clearly different atmosphere.[3]

Riddle believes it likely that the author of Luke–Acts encountered a separate and independent version of the source. Luke has modified the introductory setting and the parable of the Seed Growing Secretly is absent. Riddle believes it unlikely that Luke would have omitted this parable (hence it is more likely he had a copy of the source that lacked the parable). Thirdly, Luke has the parable of the Mustard Seed in a different context (there paired with the Leaven); for Riddle, 'this

1. Riddle, 'Gospel Source', p. 83.
2. All quotes in this paragraph are from Riddle, 'Gospel Source', pp. 83-84.
3. Riddle, 'Gospel Source', p. 84.

suggests that both came to him in the form in which they were known to the writer of the Matthean gospel'.[1]

It also seems certain to Riddle that Matthew had a copy of this source, the chief difference is with the wealth of added material. Riddle finds it curious that the source contains the traditional conclusion with only minor modifications, and that it also has a second ending; 'as a final statement there occurs one of the five-fold examples of the formula, "And it occurred that when Jesus had finished. . . " '.[2] Further evidence that Matthew had an independent copy of the source is to be found in the different location of the aphoristic sayings.[3] There are also differences regarding the application of the Isaiah quote, while Matthew omits the motif of private explanations (Mk 4.34).[4]

To be sure, Riddle's reconstruction can no longer be accepted in all its details. Published in 1937, one quickly sees a number of form-critical assumptions common to Bultmann. Riddle's view of the oral stage is nebulous at best; the seed parables because of their similarity of theme are quickly pushed back into the oral tradition—even to the historical Jesus—and there is the assumption of evolutionary growth. The sharp distinction between the early and tertiary stage hinges upon Riddle's reading of vv. 33-34. The use of 'parables' here, he believes, makes little sense and the tension must be resolved through a reconstruction of successive growth. One is unsure what to make of Mark in the whole process: he inherits a tradition about secret teaching and slavishly incorporates it into his Gospel despite the incongruity. How Mark expected the reader to understand the finished parable chapter within the entire Gospel is left rather murky. Evidence for the source is quickly drawn from the differences within Matthew and Luke. Changes in wording of individual verses, and the omission, addition and relocation of materials is believed to evidence independent sources rather than the redactional activities of the evangelists.

This procedure is no longer tenable: it would soon result in countless parallel sources lying behind the double and triple traditions.

1. Riddle, 'Gospel Source', p. 86.
2. Riddle, 'Gospel Source', p. 86.
3. That is, Mk 4.21 = Mt. 5.15; Mk 4.22 = Mt. 10.26; Mk 4.24 = Mt. 7.2; Mk 4.25 = Mt. 25.29.
4. Riddle, 'Gospel Source', p. 87.

The omission of the Seed Growing Secretly is not fully explained: Riddle believes it unlikely that Luke would have chosen to omit this parable. Yet he must have consciously done so even in Riddle's reconstruction: the parable was right there in his copy of Mark if not the parable sermon. Riddle has not shown how Luke's omission in this instance is substantially different from the other known omissions of Markan materials.[1] The problem with this procedure is evident when we note that Matthew's conclusion to the sermon, one of five such occurrences of the phrase within his Gospel, is evidence for Riddle of the parallel source. Riddle's hesitation to attribute all five of these to Matthew is unwarranted.

Despite these problems, Riddle represented a real breakthrough. He noted the problem of vv. 10-12 and 33-34 and their importance within the chapter. At v. 11 the crowds appear to be outsiders, kept from the secret of God's reign, while at v. 33 Jesus instructs them according to their capacity to hear. Furthermore, after the shift to a private setting at v. 10, Jesus is mysteriously back in the boat by v. 33. How are we to make sense of the chapter as it presently stands? Riddle has also correctly identified the key importance of the seed parables and the triple grouping by similarity of figure. They justly can be said to form the nucleus of the chapter: but when exactly they were grouped together (and by whom) is a question in need of further study. Finally, Riddle has drawn attention to the aphoristic sayings and their place in the chapter. He seems to assume, however, that the difference in genre ensures that these sayings were brought into the context at a later stage than the parables. This also is an assumption that will need further scrutiny. In sum, Riddle's study was a true pioneering effort: like all such endeavours, it contained a number of flaws yet set the tone for a considerable number of later exegetes.

1. On the theory of Markan priority Luke omits such other passages as Mk 6.17-29; 6.45–8.26; 9.9-13, etc. A complete redactional study of Luke would be necessary to discern the motives behind these decisions. Riddle would have to demonstrate that the omission of the Seed Growing Secretly would be against Luke's redactional tendencies as seen in other passages. This objection applies equally for Riddle's willingness to see parallel traditions when the wording varies. That Luke omits the Markan motif of seaside teaching (Mk 4.1) is hardly surprising in light of his treatment of Mk 2.13. Similarly, Matthew's failure to include the motif of private explanation is consistent with his parallel treatment of Mk 7.17, 24. These changes are most easily accounted for as part of the overall redactional tendencies of Matthew and Luke.

b. *J. Jeremias and Mark 4.10-13a (1954)*

Building upon Riddle's central insight, Joachim Jeremias developed his own reconstruction of the passage's development. The contradiction between the references to the boat in vv. 1 and 32 and the private setting in v. 10 shows the artificiality of the grouping. Verse 10 thus reveals a join in the narrative. On the basis of linguistic evidence Jeremias assigns vv. 10-20 to a later stream of tradition.[1] Another problem regards the question of v. 10 ('they asked him about the parables') which receives two different answers (vv. 11-12 and 13-20). Verse 10 contains nothing that suggests that Jesus was asked why he usually spoke in parables, and the criticism of v. 13 (connected to the interpretation of the Sower) suggests that v. 10 originally related to vv. 13-20.[2] Mark, therefore, has destroyed this literary connection (vv. 10, 13a) by inserting vv. 11-12 into this older context. Linguistic confirmation of this is found in the introductory phrase καὶ ἔλεγεν αὐτοῖς (one of Mark's typical link-phrases, cf. 2.27; 4.2, 21, 24; 6.10; 7.9; 8.21; 9.1).[3] This also explains the unusual description of the audience at v. 10 (οἱ περὶ αὐτὸν σὺν τοῖς δώδεκα); it represents a Markan conflation of the two traditions' separate audiences. Thus, vv. 11-12 are an 'independent logion' which must be interpreted apart from its present context. Jeremias asserts we 'may assume' it is 'very early'.[4] Evidence of its origins within Galilee

1. J. Jeremias, *The Parables of Jesus* (trans. S.H. Hooke; New York: Charles Scribner's Sons, 2nd rev. edn, 1972 [1954]), p. 13. Subsequent references will employ the short title *Parables*. Evidence of the secondary character of the verses is found in C.H. Dodd, *The Parables of the Kingdom* (London: James Nisbet, rev. edn, 1936 [1935]), p. 15.
2. Compare H. Räisänen, *The 'Messianic Secret' in Mark* (trans. C. Tuckett; Edinburgh: T. & T. Clark, 1990), pp. 116-17. He finds the transition between vv. 11-12 and 13 harsh, since the latter presupposes that the disciples should have understood the parable of the Sower. Verse 13 'can hardly be brought into agreement with v. 11, where it says that the secret of the kingdom of God has been "given" to the disciples, unless one flees into the realm of paradox and dialectic where all cats are equally grey'. As the discussion will show, I believe the impasse is resolved through a literary-critical solution. As Räisänen himself notes elsewhere, 'it should be noted that Mark's "story world" is not completely in order. The only view which helps us forward here is that Mark has projected different viewpoints *of his own Christian community* on to the canvas of the history of Jesus, but without taking account of the logical sequence of his narrative' (p. 112).
3. Jeremias, *Parables*, p. 14.
4. Jeremias, *Parables*, p. 15.

and the Land of Israel includes the antithetic parallelism (v. 11b) and the circumlocution to indicate the divine activity (three times: δέδοται, γίνεται, ἀφεθῇ). Even more decisive are the agreements in Mark's free quotation of Isaiah with the Targum against both the Septuagint and the Hebrew Bible. These include use of the third person;[1] the use of participles for βλέποντες and ἀκούοντες; the verb 'forgive' (ἀφεθῇ; שבק) instead of 'heal' with the plural rather than singular (Hebrew לו); and the avoidance of the divine name through use of the passive. All this evidence for Jeremias 'creates a strong presumption in favour of the authenticity' of the logion.[2]

Jeremias then examines the original meaning of the antithesis in vv. 11-12. There is a sharp contrast between the disciples and outsiders to the faith. The contrasting parallelism (11a versus 11b) requires that μυστήριον correspond to παραβολή, which can only happen if the latter is given the sense of 'riddle'. Thus the contrast is, 'to you the secret is revealed; those outside are confronted with riddles'.[3] The use of γίνεσθαι as an impersonal verb (with a dative) in the sense of 'to happen' is also not idiomatic Greek but a Semitism, (translating the Aramaic ל חוה, 'to belong to someone, to happen to someone, to be assigned to someone').[4] This gives as the proper translation for Mk 4.11b, 'But to those who are without all things are imparted in riddles', or as Jeremias paraphrases, 'they remain obscure for them'.[5] The ἵνα should be regarded as introducing a free quotation of Isa. 6.9-10 which expresses God's purposes, not those of Jesus himself. An adequate translation would be, 'In order that (as it is written)' while the μήποτε translates an original Aramaic דלמא which has a sense of 'unless'. The translation would be:

> To you has God given the secret of the Kingdom of God; but to those who are without everything is obscure, in order that they (as it is written) may 'see and yet not see, may hear and yet not understand, unless they turn and God will forgive them'.[6]

---

1. ἵνα βλέποντες βλέπωσιν against the original second person.
2. Jeremias, *Parables*, p. 15; quoting T.W. Manson, *The Teaching of Jesus* (Cambridge: Cambridge University Press, 2nd edn, 1935), p. 77.
3. Jeremias, *Parables*, p. 16.
4. As an example of the Semitic idiom, Jeremias gives Gen. 15.1, 'The Word of the Lord came unto Abraham in a vision'. Translation, Jeremias, *Parables*, p. 16.
5. Jeremias, *Parables*, pp. 16-17.
6. Jeremias, *Parables*, p. 17.

The passage's present location is due to a Markan misunderstanding. He has incorrectly taken the catchword παραβολή in the sense of 'parable'; in fact the passage does not refer to Jesus' parables, but rather to the perpetual twofold issue of all proclamation: the offer of mercy and the threat of judgement.[1]

At least three stages in the compositional history of Mark's parable chapter result: 1) the gathering together of the three seed parables; 2) then the addition of the allegorical explanation; 3) and finally the Markan addition of an older tradition (vv. 10-12) into its present location. As the subsequent discussion will show, this theory, coupled with Riddle's pre-Gospel parable source, proved extremely influential.

c. *E. Schweizer (1965) and T. Weeden (1971)*

Eduard Schweizer developed his own theory of the parable chapter's history. He believes that Mark inherited the motif of the esoteric explanation of the parables from the tradition. Mark's contribution, however, was to show that this explanation did not work.

Schweizer, taking his lead from Jeremias, believes that prior to Mark the parable of the Sower and its allegorical explanation were linked by an earlier form of vv. 10 and 13a (reproof for failure to understand the parable). Subsequently, v. 10 was modified into closer resemblance to its present form and the theory of esoteric teaching (vv. 11-12) was added. Mark's contribution was to add v. 13b (Jesus' reproof) in order to demonstrate that the disciples, despite their advantages, are also among the blind who do not truly hear. Thus, the problems caused within Mark's Gospel by 4.10-13a and 34 were not of Mark's making; rather these verses were part of his inherited tradition.[2]

1. Jeremias, *Parables*, p. 18.

2. E. Schweizer, 'Zur Frage des Messiasgeheimnisses bei Markus', *ZNW* 56 (1965), pp. 1-8. A summary of Schweizer's position is found in Meagher, *Clumsy Construction*, pp. 99-100. See also T.J. Weeden, Sr, *Mark—Traditions in Conflict* (Philadelphia: Fortress Press, 1971), pp. 141-43. References to this latter work will employ the short title *Traditions*. Similarly, H. Räisänen, *Die Parabeltheorie im Markusevangelium* (Schriften der Finnischen exegetischen Gesellschaft, 26; Helsinki: Lansi-Suomi, 1973), pp. 27-33 finds vv. 11-12 as pre-Markan tradition in conflict with Mark's own theology. He points to the description of Jesus teaching out of compassion at 6.34 as evidence of this tension in Mark with the hardening theory of 4.11-12. The former, he argues, 'spricht entscheidend gegen die Parabeltheorie, indem er zeigt, dass das Lehren Jesu nicht auf Verhüllung seiner Botschaft zielt,'

Schweizer points to the incompatible theologies in 4.11-12 and the rest of Mark's Gospel. The pattern of the elect fully comprehending the secret of God's reign while outsiders remain uncomprehending, so evident in vv. 11-12, actually fails to hold true elsewhere in Mark. The disciples remain blind to the mystery. Hence, immediately after we are told that the disciples have special understanding they are rebuked for an obtuse incomprehension (v. 13b). Thus Mark 4.11-12 and 4.13b, for Schweizer, could not have come from the same author. Rather, 4.11-12 is more in keeping with the perspective of 4.14-20.[1]

Schweizer's theory received enthusiastic support from T. Weeden. He finds it unlikely that v. 34 is Markan redaction; if it were, Mark would be exposed as an inconsistent writer or a feeble-minded thinker. Even a quick reading of the Gospel shows that Jesus did not teach only in parables. There is also non-Markan vocabulary in v. 34; including χωρίς, ἐπιλύειν, τοῖς ἰδίοις μαθηταῖς, and the use of δέ in successive clauses given Mark's usual preference for καί.[2] There is further conflict between 4.11-12, 34 (which assert that Jesus' teachings are always obscure to outsiders) and the rest of the Gospel.[3] The Syrophoenician woman (7.27-29), the rich young man (10.17-22), the Pharisees (12.1-12) and the scribes (12.28-34)—contrary to 4.11-12, 34—all understand Jesus. The disciples, on the other hand, are the most obtuse characters in Mark's christological drama; continually

---

p. 34. Räisänen has subsequently modified his interpretation of the tradition history of Mark 4; see *'Messianic Secret'*, pp. 76-144.

1. Schweizer is not alone is seeing a fundamental difference in perspective between 4.11-12 and 4.13. See Räisänen, *Die Parabeltheorie*, p. 71, 'Wenn Markus is ist, der V. 13b augesetzt, dann kann er nicht gut auch V. 11-12 eingefügt haben'. Also pp. 118-25.

2. Weeden, *Traditions in Conflict,* p. 143. Weeden follows here J. Gnilka, *Die Verstockung Israels* (Munich: Kösel, 1961), pp. 59-61. Gnilka notes that the verb ἐπιλύειν and its substantive in particular are used in the literature of antiquity with reference to the interpretation of riddles, dreams and prophecies; cf. *The Shepherd of Hermas* 5,3,1-2; 5,4,2-3; 5,5,1; 5,6,8; 5,7,1; 8,11,1; 9,10,5; 9,11,9; 9,13,9; 9,16,7.

3. A similar reading of Mark can be found in Räisänen, *'Messianic Secret'*, p. 93. Verses 1-2, he believes, are in conflict with a strong parable theory: 'What kind of a "teaching" would it be if one only spoke unintelligible riddles?' Mk 6.34 also tells against such a theory for Räisänen since 'it shows that Jesus' teaching is not intended to hide his message'. Hence, Mk 4.34, which corresponds to 4.11-12, 'is thus an impossible generalization in the context of Mark's gospel'.

they fail to perceive (cf. 6.52, 8.17). Mark's insertion of 4.21-25 also contradicts the usual interpretation of 4.11-12, 34. The sayings of the Lamp and Measure emphasize that there is no limit to the scope of revelation or its recipients. This contrasts sharply with the secrecy motif, and hence these 'blatant incongruities raise serious questions about the adequacy of the traditional interpretation of Mark 4 and of its place and purpose in the Gospel as a whole'.[1]

The purpose behind Mark's incorporation of 4.11-12, 34 is found in his polemic against his opponents' *theios-aner* theology. The concept of a hidden revelation open only to the elect few is in total keeping with the *theios-aner* attitude, while the use of allegory to extrapolate sacred mysteries from the literal text of scripture is 'a hermeneutical technique employed by those of the *theios-aner* persuasion'.[2] The parable of the Sower (4.3-9), its interpretation (4.14-20), the Growing Seed (4.26-29), the Mustard Seed (4.30-32) and the cluster's concluding statement (4.33-34), Weeden believes, all belonged to Mark's opponents. In 4.11-12, Mark provides the rationale of his opponents; a position to which he was violently opposed but incapable of ignoring.[3] Mark exposes this position as ludicrous since the 12 continually fail to perceive throughout the narrative.[4] A further bombshell falls from Mark at 8.32: καὶ παρρησίᾳ τὸν λόγον ἐλάλει. Since ὁ λόγος (used extensively within the interpretation of the Sower) is the opponents' term for the Gospel, Mark adopts it to underscore his suffering christology of Jesus.[5]

d. *J.C. Meagher (1979)*

John Meagher examines this passage in a thorough critique of many commonly held assumptions of form and redaction critics. He bases his objection, in part, upon a comparison with the contemporary oral tradition of joke-telling. The well-told story is not the 'evolutionary

1. Weeden, *Traditions in Conflict*, p. 141.
2. Weeden, *Traditions in Conflict*, p. 144.
3. On page 149 (n. 17), Weeden explains that this unit was originally a part of the tradition of Mark's opponents. But within that tradition it did not appear in its present location. Weeden believes it possible that it originally appeared after 4.33-34. The hypothetical reconstruction of a different position subsequently relocated by Mark is deeply dependent upon the suggestions by Riddle.
4. Weeden, *Traditions in Conflict*, pp. 147-48.
5. Weeden, *Traditions in Conflict*, pp. 151-52.

product of a logical succession of stages of growth, [and] the triumph of orderly laws' but rather 'a creative rescue operation, effected despite the botched and awkward versions of the joke already in circulation'.[1] He illustrates this principle with four examples, that of 1) Information Improvidence; 2) Inaccurate or Misleading Information; 3) Formal Breakdown; and 4) Massive Misunderstanding.[2]

Meagher finds Schweizer and Weeden's exegesis of Mark 4 unsatisfactory. Weeden does not really explain why Mark has incorporated materials that are diametrically opposed. Even if Schweizer and Weeden are correct in interpreting Mark's motives, Meagher argues that it is unlikely that he would have chosen the words or images that we find in his Gospel.[3]

The interpretation antedated Mark and was together with the parable since its creation.[4] The transition to the interpretation originally required only a simple phrase such as v. 10a. Thus the public setting and the interpretation are both undoubtedly early and pre-Markan. The three seed parables and the allegorical interpretation formed a pre-Markan continuous public discourse without the interruption of vv. 11-12. This public framework included v. 33 and the smaller parables of vv. 21-33. It is v. 34b that offers an 'emphatic thrust' against the spirit of this public discourse.[5]

Verse 10 is composite, and the question about the parable is so apt for the transition into the explanation that it 'must be closely associated with it as an early stage of traditional development'. The shift to a private setting at 10a, however, is out of keeping with the setting of public discourse and must be 'artificially imposed'. Like Jeremias, Meagher sees at least two stages in the description of the audience. 'Those who were with him' is ambiguous and awkward, hence it is more self-conscious than the earliest stage. The addition

1. Meagher, *Clumsy Construction*, p. 4.
2. Meagher, *Clumsy Construction*, pp. 7-12.
3. Meagher, *Clumsy Construction*, p. 103.
4. Meagher, *Clumsy Construction*, p. 106. In note 30, (p. 155) Meagher argues that despite Jeremias there is no reason to separate the two units: this too neatly stratifies the usages of the first century. He sees no reason to deny that both might fit into the time of the earthly Jesus. This controversy will receive a detailed analysis in the next chapter, 'Allegory and Orality'.
5. Meagher, *Clumsy Construction*, pp. 107-108.

'with the twelve' also sounds like special pleading and might be an addition to the earlier general reference to the private audience.[1]

Verse 11 is smoothly fluent and not easily dismembered. Verse 12, being a quote of Isaiah, is also integral. Following Jeremias, Meagher believes the quote out of place since it has nothing to do with private instruction. Hence, 'verse 12 found its place in the tradition as a comment on some relative failure of Jesus' public teaching, the Isaiah quotation thus establishing that this was foreknown or foreordained and not to be attributed to any insufficiency in Jesus' proclamation'. This is unlikely to be Mark's invention since it conflicts with the main thrust of ch. 4 and is understandable in a number of pre-Markan contexts.[2]

Verses 11 and 12 were most likely joined in a pre-Markan phase 'when it was perceived that some inner circle was privy to ultimate salvific secrets that had been present in the teaching of Jesus but somehow hidden within them'.[3] Verse 11 is post-resurrectional: it represents a setting similar to the view of Jesus' public ministry reflected in Matthew's version of the Jonah tradition. As Meagher explains, the term '*Parables* has here evidently lost its previous sense of illuminating illustration and has somehow come to mean *riddles*'.[4] Verse 11 does not say that everything is preached in parables, but rather that all things *happen*. Therefore, the reference is not to the characteristic preaching but rather to the decisive events of Jesus' public career.[5]

Since the Isaiah quote (v. 12) was probably appropriated early in the tradition, its linguistic background is likely not the Greek version. Following Jeremias, Meagher believes a link with the Targum likely given the close agreements (e.g. the key term of forgiveness along with the other evidence). There is also general plausibility since the Targum would have been heard in the synagogues of Galilee and Judea. A theology wherein God intentionally impeded salvation would have ill served Jewish-Christian purposes. It would have been preferable to suggest that people were self-blinded and dull of heart, a reading more in line with the Targum's version of Isaiah 6. This is a

1. Meagher, *Clumsy Construction*, pp. 108-109.
2. Meagher, *Clumsy Construction*, pp. 111-12.
3. Meagher, *Clumsy Construction*, p. 112.
4. Meagher, *Clumsy Construction*, p. 114.
5. Meagher, *Clumsy Construction*, p. 114.

perennial problem and any context from John the Baptist on would fit the passage.[1]

But this is not what Mark gives us! His text accords more with the harsher version of the Hebrew, so that Jesus teaches in a 'strategy of deliberate obfuscation in order to prevent the outsiders from seeing, repenting, and being forgiven'.[2] Verses 11-12 together point to a time when doubts arose as to whether Jesus' parables were illustrations or riddles, and this has to be post-resurrectional.[3] This likely occurred when the community realized that the events in Jesus' life were parables of revelation and that the parables of Jesus' teaching could be read as secret revelations of these events.[4]

Meagher finds in a number of Markan 'duplications' parallel traditions. Some form of 4.33 (arising from the time of Jesus' preaching) and 4.34 (arising originally from post-resurrectional insight) likely came to Mark simultaneously. Unwilling, or unable, to choose he passed along both. The specification of the audience at v. 10 'is undoubtedly a conciliating conflation of two versions, one of which, as in Matthew and Luke, spoke of the disciples, another of which, like Jn 6.67, insisted on specifying the Twelve'.[5]

The ambiguity regarding parables or parable points to a shift in setting at vv. 11-12, with the insertion into a public teaching context being artificial. The tradition at 4.34 that Jesus explained everything to his disciples is probably the cause of the insertion of vv. 10-12. Mark and his predecessors found in the tradition an established representation that Jesus privately explained the parables to his disciples. A

---

1. Meagher, *Clumsy Construction*, pp. 118-19. 'It is not unlikely that in early post-resurrection days, a reflection upon the difference between those to whom it has been given to know the mystery and those who see only riddles where the former see revelation might have remembered in a benevolent spirit the regretful observation of the Isaiah Targum that (through their own fault) most people see but do not understand', p. 119.

2. Meagher, *Clumsy Construction*, p. 120.

3. Meagher, *Clumsy Construction*, p. 124. This 'theological outrage' must be seen as intentional: 'It is not sufficiently credible to propose that Mark 4.11-12 is only an unfortunate misformulation of an essential truth, blissfully unknown to those who passed on the general lore and wretchedly bungled by those who managed to insert it here against the tide of the context. Even the principle of clumsiness has its limits', pp. 123-24.

4. Meagher, *Clumsy Construction*, p. 125.

5. Meagher, *Clumsy Construction*, pp. 130, 126.

striking non-Markan representation of this occurs when the disciples ask for and receive a private explanation of the parable of the Wheat and the Weeds (Mt. 13.36-43). This passage proves that 'the combination of public parable and private explanation was Mark's inheritance, not his invention'. Thus, some form of v. 10 was likely in place before the introduction of vv. 11-12, and the manuscript variant 'parable' may represent the original version of this verse. Verse 13b is the final redactional touch, while v. 10 represents a Markan favourite reflexive response. As at 7.18, Mark likes to concentrate on the disciples' failure to understand, and the tradition allows him to introduce the motif here.[1]

e. *Philip Sellew (1990)*

A more recent author to employ Riddle's thesis of a pre-Markan source is Philip Sellew.[2] He begins with an important assumption: in light of the 'likelihood of multiple paths of transmission for most of this material, and much of that process within an oral mode', we must be wary of claiming too great a precision in any reconstruction of a saying's 'original wording'.[3]

Previous studies have used the introductory formulae (καὶ λέγει αὐτοῖς, or καὶ ἔλεγεν αὐτοῖς) to separate the levels of tradition in the passage. After a thorough review of the evidence, Sellew concludes that we must look beyond these formulae to trace the pre-Markan history of the material.[4] The formal structure of interpretation in vv. 14-20 along with the near quotation of phrases from the parable point to a written source for these latter verses.[5] Verses 33-34 provide for Sellew the needed clue to unravel the text's compositional history. These verses are notoriously difficult to reconcile. Verse 33

---

1. Meagher, *Clumsy Construction*, pp. 131, 133, 138.
2. P. Sellew, 'Oral and Written Sources in Mark 4.1-34', *NTS* 36 (1990), p. 239. See also his more extended study, 'Early Collections of Jesus' Words: The Development of Dominical Discourses' (ThD dissertation, Harvard Divinity School, 1986). Regarding the form of the units, Sellew notes A. Jülicher, *Die Gleichnisreden Jesu* (Leipzig: Mohr [Paul Siebeck], 2nd edn, 1910), I, pp. 93-118.
3. Sellew, 'Oral and Written Sources', p. 239.
4. Sellew, 'Oral and Written Sources', pp. 252-54. Cf. Räisänen, *Die Parabeltheorie*, pp. 93-102; M. Zerwick, *Untersuchungen zum Markus-Stil: Ein Beitrag zur stilistischen Durcharbeitung des Neuen Testaments* (Rome: Pontifical Biblical Institute, 1937), pp. 57-75.
5. Sellew, 'Oral and Written Sources', pp. 257-59.

seems to close out the account of Jesus speaking to the crowd. Yet
v. 34 returns us to the theme of 4.11-12. The effect makes one want
to read the adverbial conjunction καθώς (v. 33) in a more restrictive
sense: the crowd could not understand the parables very well at all.
This tension between vv. 33 and 34 is so pronounced that most com-
mentators acknowledge a seam in Mark's sources, or an inconsistency
in his redaction. Usually v. 33 is viewed as the conclusion of the
source and v. 34 as Mark's redaction. But since several scholars have
shown the non-Markan character of v. 34b, this view is problematic.[1]

This leaves us with the uncomfortable situation where Mark appears
more a slave to his sources than master of them. The verses are
actually, for Sellew, evidence of two different sources. Verse 33
represents the conclusion of a collection of seed parables; v. 34 comes
from the same stream of tradition as 4.11-12. Mark has, in effect,
retained the conclusion of the parable source but revised it through
the addition of v. 34. These sources overlapped in that both included
the Sower. The first of these was a collection of similitudes employing
the image of a growing seed. These similitudes were gathered together
due to their unity of theme and structure, and the collection has 'all
the hallmarks of oral composition and transmission: repetition of key
vocabulary from unit to unit; a compact and shared structure; similar
plot and meaning in each similitude'.[2] Most likely it represents
another example of an early 'dominical discourse'; it is a source which
may have still been in oral form when Mark incorporated it into his
Gospel. It included the three main seed parables and a brief setting of
the scene. Since much of the vocabulary in Mk 4.1-2 is often found in
redactional settings, we cannot be sure of the precise scope of the
source's introduction. Its conclusion probably was very similar to that
of v. 33.[3]

Mark's second source was of an entirely different nature: instead of
a dominical discourse, the words of Jesus were collected in the
technique of apocalyptic dream and vision interpretation. This source
followed the pattern of saying, request for interpretation and struc-

1. Sellew, 'Oral and Written Sources', p. 260. The linguistic evidence is similar
to that presented by Weeden: κατ' ἰδίαν, χωρίς, ἐπιλύειν, τοῖς ἰδίοις μαθηταῖς,
and the use of δέ in successive clauses given Mark's usual preference for καί.
2. Sellew, 'Oral and Written Sources', p. 261.
3. Sellew, 'Oral and Written Sources', pp. 261-62. The reconstruction bears a
striking resemblance to Riddle's source at stage 2.

tured explanation. It is a pattern that 'almost certainly presupposes use of the written medium'.[1] The note of Jesus' exasperation may also have been present, since the motif is formulaic for such scenes. Caution is in order in describing the contents of this source beyond what is evident in Mark 4, but Sellew (taking his cue from W. Marxsen) notes the similarity of such passages as Mk 7.14-23; 8.14-21; and 10.2-12. It is an open question whether any of these texts were also a part of Sellew's second source, although 8.14-21 in particular 'is so clearly expressive of Mark's point of view and recapitulates earlier topics so well that it is almost certainly Mark's own creation after the pattern he found in the traditional material'.[2]

The two sources exhibit a sharp contrast in outlook regarding Jesus' sayings. In the written 'apocalyptic dream interpretation' source Jesus' sayings do not speak for themselves, but are rather in need of interpretation. In the oral parables ('dominical discourse') source the parables are understood as self-evident, and hence, Mk 4.33 likely represents a remnant of this collection. One has to admit, Sellew argues, that 'the seed similitudes could not have seemed very opaque in an agricultural society'. The 'apocalyptic dream interpretation' stream of tradition lies behind Mk 4.9, (10-12), 13-20, 34 and views Jesus' words as riddles in need of special techniques of interpretation.[3] The contents of these two sources may be summarized as below:

Dominical Discourse	*Apocalyptic Dream Interpretation*
(Originally Oral source; perhaps	(Definitely Written source, pre-dating
written prior to Mark)	Mark)
Introduction, ?	Introduction, ?
The Sower, 4.3-8	The Sower, 4.3-8
Seed Growing of Itself, 4.26-29	Exhortation to Hear, 4.9
Mustard Seed, 4.30-32	Sower House Teaching, 4.10-12
Conclusion, 4.33	Sower Interpretation, 4.13-20
	Private Instruction, 4.34
	Purity House Teaching, 7.14-23 (?)

That Mark employed more than one source in ch. 4 (and that both contained a version of the Sower) is not subject to Occam's razor on

1. Sellew, 'Oral and Written Sources', p. 262.
2. Sellew, 'Oral and Written Sources', p. 262. See W. Marxsen, 'Redaktions-geschichtliche Erklärung der sogenannten Parabeltheorie des Markus', *ZTK* 52 (1955), pp. 255-71.
3. Sellew, 'Oral and Written Sources', p. 263.

the following grounds. The breadth of attestation (e.g. Mark, Q, *Gospel of Thomas*, *1 Clement*, Justin) for these similitudes demonstrates that their transmission was not restricted to one narrow group of Jesus' early followers. Since the Mustard Seed is to be found in Mark, Q and Thomas (triple attestation), while the Wheat and Tares is in Matthew and Thomas (double attestation), it should not be surprising that the Sower was included in two pre-Markan sources. Secondly, we know the Sower was transmitted apart from its allegorical interpretation since this interpretation does not affect the parable's meaning for other writers outside the synoptic tradition.[1] Even at the close of the first century one can still find independent oral traditions of the Sower and other sayings of Jesus.[2] Even if this reconstruction is less tidy than is desirable, it represents the evidence more fairly than does an artificially simple one. The unilinear model of the evolutionary growth of one source has too many strains to be credible since the interpretation of vv. 14-20 and the material of 11-12 cannot be made to fit comfortably within such a theory. And since the process of grouping together disparate materials must be presupposed for Mark in the composition of his Gospel, it makes sense to view this stage of the process as Mark's contribution.[3]

f. *Summary of Results*
The above survey is by no means exhaustive of scholarly reconstructions of Mk 4.1-34. It serves instead as an entry point into the text and into the on-going critical discussion that has been devoted to this passage. A number of common themes may fairly be said to have emerged from examination.

First of all, there is the issue of Riddle's thesis of an underlying parable source. To anticipate the subsequent analysis (in Chapters 4 and 5 of this text), this finding in itself need not be in question.[4] Mark

1. Sellew, 'Oral and Written Sources', p. 263. He points to M.F. Wiles, 'Early Exegesis of the Parables', *SJT* 11 (1958), pp. 287-301, here p. 293.
2. Citing H. Koester, *Synoptische Überlieferung bei den Apostolischen Vätern* (TU, 65; Berlin: Akademie Verlag, 1957), pp. 20-21; *idem*, 'Three Thomas Parables', in *The New Testament and Gnosis: Essays in Honour of R. McL. Wilson* (ed. A.H.B. Logan and A.J.M. Wedderburn; Edinburgh: T. & T. Clark, 1983), pp. 195-203.
3. Sellew, 'Oral and Written Sources', p. 265.
4. On this see also H.W. Kuhn, *Ältere Sammlungen im Markusevangelium* (Göttingen: Vandenhoeck & Ruprecht, 1971), pp. 99-146.

most likely inherited a written source containing the three seed parables (and perhaps the allegory). What is at issue is Riddle's assumption that this source represents a direct 'transcribed orality' that would allow immediate access to the oral phase. The confidence in reconstructing an elaborate sequence of development, in Riddle no less than four written stages prior to Mark and two stages of orality, is simply unfounded.[1] Each stage back, by implication, takes us another giant step closer to the historical Jesus and rapidly diminishes the distance from final text to ultimate author. Real-life history is not so straightforward. Even assuming two stages prior to Mark (i.e., the three parables and then the allegorical interpretation) there is simply no way of knowing how long a time span elapsed. To take an arbitrary example, there is no reason why a document that originated in Damascus and was sent on to Antioch could not have an allegorical appendix within a week of arrival. Reconstructing in exact detail the real history of the parable tract is a far more difficult, and inexact, process than the reconstructions of Riddle, Jeremias or Meagher acknowledge.

The dismemberment of the chapter is also an issue. Tensions between vv. 10, 11-12, and 13 require an explanation. Why do the disciples inquire about the 'parables' after hearing only the Sower? Does v. 13a more naturally follow v. 10 or can we read Mark's sequence in a different fashion?[2] These initial tensions require close scrutiny. The chapter also seems to have a conflicting view of parables and revelation. Some verses seem to imply the parables should be understood even by outsiders (9, 13a, 33), while others imply they are intended to veil Jesus' message (11-12). Which of these viewpoints represents Mark's theology, or is his thesis more complicated than is usually presumed?

The subsequent analysis will show that Mark presents a more unified presentation of the parables and revelation than is often thought. The reconstruction of tensions actually results from a form-critical presupposition: that the units are best understood outside of

1. Riddle speaks of the written stages 1 to 3. However, he does not include the allegorical interpretation which he regards as clearly secondary and non-Markan. Hence he is contemplating no less than four written stages prior to Mark.

2. See Räisänen, *Die Parabeltheorie*, 'Der Übergang von V. 11-12 zu V. 13 ist äusserst schroff. . . V. 13 kann nicht mit V. 11 in Einklang gebracht werden', pp. 69-70.

their present Gospel context. This encourages exegetes to find the text's meaning as a self-contained unit. The dismemberment that has resulted is reminiscent of many presentations of the J, E, D, P reconstruction which often separated out single verses by source. But the 'Documentary Hypothesis', it must be remembered, is based on a close literary analysis of a much larger textual base than one chapter in Mark! The vocabulary, theological and syntactical distinctions between J and E, for example, are based on parallels throughout no less than 50 chapters in Genesis alone. These attempts have been to dismember 34 verses of Mark (without other parallels from the source to act as a control)! The assumption that such duplications as at vv. 1-2, 10 (audience), 10-13 (response to question), 33-34 must have their explanation in a poor harmonization of two sources is simply an unsupported methodological assumption. If focus is shifted to the chapter's role in Mark's entire narrative a different result becomes clear. The entirety of vv. 1-2, 10, 13, and 33-34 must be ascribed to Mark, and the tensions noted within this sequence are simply part of Mark's characteristic narrative technique. And without the distinction between a private and public context within the parable source vv. 11-12 cannot be viewed as antithetical to Mark's purposes. Rather, they represent the centre piece of the sermon and an intimate part of his overall secrecy motif. I turn first to an examination of Mark's narrative inclusion vv. 1-2, 33-34.[1]

3. *Mark 4.1-2, 33-34: A Redactional Inclusion*

Since Karl L. Schmidt it has been customary to view the geographical framework as the evangelist's creation.[2] This indicates that 4.1-2 and 33-34 deserve close inspection for redactional vocabulary, syntax and theological themes. The reconstruction of the pre-Gospel source's history, and the role of vv. 11-12 in the chapter, rely in part upon viewing a portion of these verses as traditional. Arguments for such an understanding of these verses are based on supposed contextual incongruity and non-Markan vocabulary and syntax. A close examination of the verses within the context of Mark's Gospel and the evidence advanced for their 'traditional' nature, however, will show

---

1. Inclusion is the patterning device of setting off a section as a unit by means of an a, a´ pattern.

2. Schmidt, *Der Rahmen der Geschichte Jesu*, V.

that the entirety of all four verses are Mark's literary inclusion to his parable sermon.

a. *Mark 4.1.*

καὶ πάλιν ἤρξατο διδάσκειν παρὰ τὴν θάλασσαν. . .

Mark 4.1a introduces a favoured theme and contains a number of vocabulary items often found in redactional settings. καί is a well-known Markan conjunction, while πάλιν has been identified by such scholars as J.C. Hawkins, R. Morgenthaler, Lloyd Gaston, Martin Friedrich and E.J. Pryke as a redactional term.[1] It is pleonastic (again, a well-known Markan stylistic feature). Close to half of its occurrences refer to previous texts, and Mk 4.1 fits this pattern (cp. 2.13 and 3.7). Mark often uses this word with verbs of teaching, argument or dialogue; and within contexts of Jesus' 'house' and his teaching mission.[2]

The phrase ἤρξατο διδάσκειν is thoroughly Markan. Mark often uses ἤρξατο as an auxiliary with an infinitive.[3] Of the 17 occurrences

1. For πάλιν, cp. 2.1, 13; 3.1, 20; 5.21 etc. Mark's redactional vocabulary and style has been closely studied. See, for example: Hawkins, *Horae Synopticae*, pp. 12-15; R. Morgenthaler, *Statistik des neutestamentlichen Wortschatzes* (Zürich–Frankfurt: Gotthelf-Verlag, 1958); L. Gaston, *Horae Synopticae Electronicae: Word Statistics of the Synoptic Gospels* (SBL Sources for Biblical Study, 3; Missoula, MT: Scholars Press, 1973); Pryke, *Redactional,* pp. 136-37. A comparative table has been collected by F. Neirynck, 'The Redactional Text of Mark', *ETL* 57 (1981), pp. 146-49. Neirynck has also provided an updated list adding in more recent work by P. Dschulnigg, *Sprache, Redaktion und Intention des Markus-Evangeliums: Eigentümlichkeiten der Sprache des Markus-Evangeliums und ihre Bedeutung für die Redaktionskritik* (Stuttgarter Biblische Beiträge, 11; Stuttgart: KBW, 1984); and M. Friedrich, 'Tabellen zur markinischen Vorzugsvokabeln', in *Der Dreuzigungsbericht des Markusevangeluums: Mk 15,20b-41* (ed. J. Schreiber; BZNW, 8; Berlin: de Gruyter, 1986), pp. 395-433. See F. Neirynck, 'Words Characteristic of Mark: A New List', *ETL* 63 (1987), pp. 367-74. In order to simplify the notations, references will primarily be based upon Pryke and Neirynck's two comparative tables.
2. Pryke, *Redactional*, p. 97.
3. Pryke notes the following redactional instances of this structure: 1.45; 2.23; 4.1; 6.2, 7, 34, 55; 8.11, 31, 32; 10.28, 32, 41, 47; 11.15; 12.1; 13.5; 14.19, 33, *Redactional*, pp. 79-80. The observation is supported, for example, by H. Koester, 'A Test Case of Synoptic Source Theory (Mk 4.1-34 and Parallels)' (paper presented at SBL Gospels Seminar, SBL Convention, Atlanta, 31 October 1971), pp. 28-31;

of διδάσκειν within Mark, Pryke identifies 15 as redactional, Gaston 11.[1] Even more telling, the phrase ἤρξατο διδάσκειν is used four times in Mark, while in two other instances ἤρξατο is completed with κηρύσσειν.[2]

The seaside locale, especially in the context of teaching, is a Markan redactional motif. We may note the occurrence of the identical παρὰ τὴν θάλασσαν at 1.16; 2.13; 5.21. The redactional character of θάλασσα is recognized by Gaston, Morgenthaler, Friedrich and Pryke.[3] Despite the fact that some scholars see πάλιν as simply resumptive and without connection to any prior passage,[4] the heavy concentration of redactional vocabulary indicates that the verse points back to 3.7-9 and 2.13 (which itself refers to the seaside call stories, 1.16-20). The reference to this theme at 2.13, which seems at first reading to be entirely gratuitous, now receives its fulfilment. Mark has prepared for the reader a connection between the seaside and Jesus' characteristic teaching. This connection, far from being traditional, is completely dependent upon Mark's chronology.[5]

καὶ συνάγεται πρὸς αὐτὸν ὄχλος πλεῖστος...

This next phrase incorporates another common Markan motif, the great crowd gathering around Jesus. Of the five Markan occurrences of the verb συνάγεται, four are located within Gaston's editorial

---

J. Marcus, *The Mystery of the Kingdom of God* (SBLDS, 90; Atlanta: Scholars Press, 1986), p. 13; Kee, *Community of the New Age*, p. 51.

1. See Neirynck, 'Redactional Text of Mark', p. 46; Pryke, *Redactional*, p. 136. Kee also identifies this is 'another favourite Markan term', *Community*, p. 52.

2. For ἤρξατο διδάσκειν, see Mk 4.1; 6.2, 34; 8.31; ἤρξατο + κηρύσσειν, 1.45; 5.20.

3. See Neirynck, 'Redactional Text of Mark', p. 147; 'Words Characteristic of Mark', p. 368; Pryke, *Redactional*, p. 136.

4. E.g. D.E. Nineham, *The Gospel of St Mark* (Harmondsworth: Penguin Books, 1963), p. 134; H. Anderson, *The Gospel of Mark* (New Century Bible; London: Oliphants, 1976), p. 127.

5. Note the comment on πάλιν by L.W. Hurtado: '4.1 puts Jesus in a scene similar to 3.7-12, where Jesus teaches at the shore of Lake Galilee from a fishing boat. As we noted before, a boat is featured often in Mark's narrative, being a kind of symbol for the fellowship of Jesus and the Twelve in the Galilean ministry.' In *Mark: A Good News Commentary* (San Francisco: Harper & Row, 1983), p. 57.

sentences, while Pryke believes that all five are the evangelist's.[1] It is to be found also at 2.2; 5.21; 6.30; and 7.1. Each of these introduces a new episode and is part of the overall geographical and temporal chronology. To this may be added the compound form at 1.33. The similarity in theme, syntax and vocabulary among all six of these examples is strong evidence for the redactional nature of συνάγεται at 4.1. The reference to Jesus, πρὸς αὐτόν, also has close parallels within these examples at 5.21; 6.30; and 7.1. This motif, then, is intimately tied to Mark's overall narrative drama.

The motif of the crowd is a Markan favourite; of the 38 total occurrences of this word, 18 are in Gaston's redactional sentences while Pryke attributes 27 redactional instances of the word.[2] Close parallels in terms of syntax and vocabulary for the phrase can be found at 3.7, 8; 5.21, 24; 8.1; 9.14; and 12.37.[3] The conjunction of such a high number of favourite Markan vocabulary items and literary motifs within these two clauses (4.1a,b) thus provides overwhelming evidence for their redactional character.

ὥστε αὐτὸν εἰς πλοῖον ἐμβάντα καθῆσθαι ἐν τῇ θαλάσσῃ. . .

The explanatory ὥστε clause (with an infinitive) is found 13 times in Mark. Of these, Pryke evaluates at least seven as redactional.[4] Mk 3.20 provides a particularly appropriate parallel for 4.1c since they both occur in a context of the crowd gathering to hear Jesus. The boat, πλοῖον, is accepted as a redactional term by Gaston, Morgenthaler, Friedrich and Pryke.[5] The previously noted addition of the definite article for the boat in Bezae (D) and Washington (W), attests to this verse's relation to Jesus' injunction at Mk 3.9. Concerning the five instances of ἐμβαίνειν in Mark, four are in

1. See Neirynck, 'Redactional Text of Mark', p. 148; Pryke, *Redactional*, p. 137. Supported by Koester, 'Test Case', pp. 28-31 and Marcus, *Mystery of the Kingdom*, p. 13.

2. Neirynck, 'Redactional Text of Mark', p. 148; Pryke, *Redactional*, p. 137.

3. The crowd appears as a literary motif frequently in Mark. Cp. Mk 2.13; 3.9, 20, 32; 4.36; 5.31; 7.33; 8.2; 9.17; 15.8.

4. Redactional: 1.27, 45; 2.2, 12; 3.10, 20; 4.1; possible source, 2.28; 4.32, 37; 9.26; 10.8; 15.5. Pryke, *Redactional*, p. 115.

5. Cp. at 4.36; 5.2, 18, 21; 6.32, 45, 54; 8.10, 14. See Neirynck, 'Redactional Text of Mark', p. 148; *idem*, 'Words Characteristic of Mark', p. 369; Pryke, *Redactional*, p. 137.

Gaston's redactional sentences and all five are viewed as redactional by Pryke.[1] Particularly striking are the usages at 5.18 and 8.10 (cp. 6.45; 8.13). Mark also favours the verb καθῆσθαι. It is found 11 times in his Gospel, of which Pryke evaluates eight to be the work of the evangelist.[2] Appropriate parallels for the verse can be found at 2.6; 3.32; 5.15; 10.46 and 13.3. Finally, I have already noted the redactional character of the term θάλασσα.

καὶ πᾶς ὁ ὄχλος πρὸς τὴν θάλασσαν ἐπὶ τῆς γῆς ἦσαν.

The remaining clause, 4.1d, is so dependent upon its context that it seems impossible to view it as anything but Mark's. Certainly there is little here that I have not already identified as redactional: καί is a Markan favourite; πᾶς ὁ ὄχλος is word-for-word at 2.13; while τὴν θάλασσαν is found at 4.1a. Only the final ἐπὶ τῆς γῆς ἦσαν deserves consideration. The term γῆς occurs nine other times in Mark. If one sets aside the other usages within the parable chapter (4.5, 28, 31) one is left with four other verses (2.10; 9.3; 13.27, 31). Of these, 2.10 suggests Markan redaction, since it is found in a parenthetic digression between vv. 5 and 11. Similarly, the inclusion at 9.3 is likely due to Mark. At 4.1, we find the term set in contrasting parallelism to the locale of Jesus: εἰς πλοῖον ἐμβάντα καθῆσθαι ἐν τῇ θαλάσσῃ. The arrangement is a neat chiastic structure, a, b; b', a'. The contrast fits well with the structure within other so-called Markan summaries. One must consider the parallel at Mk 1.45, with its contrast between entering openly into the city and remaining in secret within the countryside. There is also the Markan contrast between Jesus' injunction to silence and the open proclamation of the word (cp. 7.36). Contrast, or juxtaposition, between clauses is in fact a staple of Markan style. Its inclusion here at 4.1d need not be viewed as due to poor harmonization of source material by the evangelist; rather, it is Mark's own work throughout. Beyond the linguistic evidence, the backward references to similar scenes throughout Mark's chronology so firmly ties the verse to his Gospel's narrative that it is impossible to view it as the work of an earlier redactor of a separate parable source. There is no evidence for Riddle's belief that

1. See Neirynck, 'Redactional Text of Mark', p. 146; Pryke, *Redactional*, p. 136.

2. Pryke, *Redactional*, p. 137.

the verse belongs to a third pre-Markan stage in the development of a separate sayings tract. There is nothing, therefore, within 4.1 on close inspection that is traditional.

b. *Mark 4.2*

καὶ ἐδίδασκεν αὐτοὺς ἐν παραβολαῖς πολλά...

The contrast between public teaching and private explanation is often held to be integral to Mark's source. In this view the public teaching naturally concludes at v. 33. The source, according to its advocates, requires some sort of public setting for teaching as an introduction to the seed parables. In Riddle's original formulation, some form of vv. 2 and 33-34 likely were appended to the three parables early on in the evolution of the source.[1] But this solution becomes questionable when v. 2 is examined closely. There is, first of all, the three clearly Markan vocabulary items καί, ἐδίδασκεν, and πολλά.[2] Nor is this the only time that Mark's Jesus teaches ἐν παραβολαῖς. The verse is suspiciously similar to the introduction to the Beelzebul controversy (3.20, 23), and the (single!) parable of the Vineyard (12.1). 'Parable' as a description of Jesus' teaching also concludes the Vineyard episode (cp. the Markan motif of the authorities fearing the crowd). In both of these instances there can be little doubt about the redactional character of the word. Its use at 13.28 is also striking, if only for the unusual nuance given it by Mark. Aside from its employment at 4.10, 11, 13a,b, 30, 33, 34, it is found at 7.17. The structure and context of 7.17 are remarkably similar to those of 4.10. The clear redactional character of its usage at 3.23; 12.1, 12, and the other indications of Markan syntax and vocabulary within 4.2a leave little doubt about the redactional nature of this latter clause.

καὶ ἔλεγεν αὐτοῖς ἐν τῇ διδαχῇ αὐτοῦ...

The imperfect of λέγω introduced by καί and taking the dative personal pronoun is a well-known Markan connective introducing

---

1. Riddle, 'Gospel Source', p. 79.

2. πὐολύς/πολλά as redactional: Gaston, Morgenthaler, Friedrich, Pryke. See Neirynck, 'Redactional Text of Mark', p. 148; *idem*, 'Words Characteristic of Mark', p. 369; Pryke, *Redactional*, p. 137.

discourse of Jesus.[1] Indeed, the absence of the pronoun (as at 4.26, 30) more likely suggests source material.[2] If we expand the parallels to include λέγω in the aorist (e.g. καὶ εἶπεν αὐτοῖς) or in the historic present (e.g. λέγει) we have an overwhelming number of instances to insure the phrase's redactional character. Furthermore, the redundant structure of 'teaching' followed by καὶ ἔλεγεν αὐτοῖς is to be found at 3.23; 4.2; 9.31; 11.17. Parallels can also be found for the conclusion ἐν τῇ διδαχῇ αὐτοῦ. The term διδαχή is accepted as redactional by Gaston, Hawkins, Friedrich and Pryke.[3] Comparative verses include 1.22, 27; 11.18 and 12.38.[4]

Nothing within vv. 1-2, therefore, would support the thesis of traditional material, either oral or written.[5] The assumption of a

---

1. Exact parallels to this phrase are to be found at 2.27; 4.35; 6.4, 10; 7.9; 8.21; 9.1, 31 and 11.17.

2. Jeremias lists 2.27; 4.2, 21, 24; 6.10; 7.9; 8.21; 9.1 for καὶ ἔλεγεν αὐτοῖς. See *Parables*, p. 14. This attribution of this phrase to source material is controversial, see above in Sellew's discussion, 2, e (second paragraph); Sellew, 'Oral and Written Sources', pp. 252-54.

3. Neirynck, 'Redactional Text of Mark', p. 146; *idem*, 'Words Characteristic of Mark', p. 368; Pryke, *Redactional*, p. 136.

4. On the redactional character of verse 2, see Räisänen, *'Messianic Secret'*, p. 92.

5. Compare the conclusion of W.H. Kelber, *The Kingdom in Mark: A New Place and a New Time* (Philadelphia: Fortress Press, 1974), p. 27. Kelber notes the strong ties to Markan themes and vocabulary and concludes that the two verses are fully explicable as redaction. Similar conclusions are drawn by Koester, 'Test Case', pp. 28-31; Marcus, *Mystery of the Kingdom*, p. 13; Pryke, *Redactional*, p. 136. The heavily editorial tone to the passage is admitted by Taylor, 'This section is a Markan construction. . . that is, a passage put together by Mark himself on the basis of tradition', *The Gospel According to St Mark,* p. 254. Cp. E. Schweizer, these two verses 'are Mark's introduction, even though the detail about Jesus' sitting in the boat comes from the tradition (see 3.9 and 4.35-41)', in *The Good News according to Mark* (trans. D.H. Madvig; Richmond, VA: John Knox, 1970), pp. 89-90. See Bultmann, *History*, p. 341; Best, *The Temptation and the Passion,* p. 71; Burkill, *Mysterious Revelation*, p. 97; Kuhn, *Ältere Sammlungen*, pp. 131, 138. Both verses are part of Gaston's editorial sentences, see Neirynck, 'Redactional Text of Mark', p. 144. J. Lambrecht, 'Redaction and Theology in Mk., IV', in *L'Evangile selon Marc: Tradition et Redaction* (ed. M. Sabbe; BETL, 34; Gembloux: Duculot; Leuven: Leuven University Press, 1974), p. 273, 'The two verses betray the redactional summary character so typical of Mark'. For a contrary view, see R. Pesch, *Das Markusevangelium* (HTKNT, 2; 2 vols.; Freiburg: Herder, 1976), I, p. 230. Pesch assigns v. 1 to a miracle cycle and v. 2 to the parable source.

'public teaching' context in the source entails the total and free redactional rewriting of this introduction by Mark.[1] Such a solution is unduly speculative. Since the material is so manifestly Markan in vocabulary, syntax and outlook it should be ascribed to Mark. I turn now to an examination of vv. 33-34.

c. *Mark 4.33-34*

[33] Καὶ τοιαύταις παραβολαῖς πολλαῖς
ἐλάλει αὐτοῖς τὸν λόγον, καθὼς ἠδύναντο ἀκούειν ˙
[34] χωρὶς δὲ παραβολῆς οὐκ ἐλάλει αὐτοῖς,
κατ' ἰδίαν δὲ τοῖς ἰδίοις μαθηταῖς ἐπέλυεν πάντα.[2]

The dissection of vv. 33-34 is controversial. Scholars find a number of tensions within the verses themselves (e.g. 33c versus 34) and with the view of Jesus' parables in vv. 10-12. As we have seen, Riddle believes these verses are inconsistent with 4.11-12. The latter text views parables as a means of veiling truth except to the inner group. No such veiling seems implied in v. 34.[3] Schweizer and Weeden, on the other hand, regard v. 34 as the original conclusion to the parable source. As Weeden expressed it, v. 34 would reveal Mark as a careless writer if these statements came from his own hand.[4] Sellew, in contrast, sees each verse as the conclusion to a separate source, with v. 34 from the same stream of written tradition as 10-12. The three seed parables, however, circulated for him in oral tradition and have their natural conclusion in v. 33.[5]

---

1. See Gnilka, *Die Verstockung*, pp. 57-58, who concludes that Mark probably created the opening statement of verses 1-2. Even if the pre-Markan source had such an introduction, according to Gnilka, it is now impossible to reconstruct it with certainty, although Mark probably inherited from the tradition the motif of Jesus' habitual teaching by the sea and the location of sitting in a boat. Compare the comment from Marcus, 'if, as there is good reason for thinking, there was a pre-Markan parable source, that source must have had a brief introduction such as "and Jesus said" or "Jesus taught them in parables, saying" ', *Mystery of the Kingdom*, p. 13. The first of these two reconstructions by Marcus (similar to many of the bald introductions in Q or Thomas) need not imply a contrast between public and private discourse. The later reconstruction owes much more to the specifics of Mark's text.
2. The underlined words are those deemed 'non-Markan' by a variety of scholars.
3. Riddle, 'Gospel Source', pp. 79-80.
4. Weeden, *Traditions in Conflict*, p. 140.
5. Sellew,'Oral and Written Sources', pp. 261-62. Räisänen outlined the difficulties in separating diachronic levels of tradition in these two verses. Assuming

Several 'non-Markan' phrases and syntactical structures have been found within the verses: χωρίς (34a), κατ' ἰδίαν, ἐπιλύειν, τοῖς ἰδίοις μαθηταῖς (34b), and the use of δέ in successive clauses given Mark's usual preference for καί.[1] The concluding phrase to v. 33 is also singled out as 'clearly' non-Markan by S. Brown. He believes the phrase is at variance with vv. 11b-12 and a contradiction to v. 34 where the parables require ἐπίλυσις, and thus 'could well come from a collection of Jesus' parables made at a stage when these had not yet been provided with allegorical interpretations'.[2]

Not all of the two verses, however, are viewed as non-Markan. As Brown points out, ἐλάλει αὐτοῖς τὸν λόγον has an exact duplicate at 2.2 which is a part of Mark's redactional framework. Brown disputes the non-Markan character of κατ' ἰδίαν at v. 34. The phrase occurs no less than six other times (6.31, 32; 7.33; 9.2, 28; 13.3). No less than five of these occur in the connecting geographical framework between separate form-critical units. Only the occurrence at 7.33 can make a good case for tradition since it occurs within a miracle story, although even here Mark's hand is likely. Indeed, the withdrawal by Jesus with the disciples alone is a Markan theme that has strong affinities to the secret house teaching. Hence Brown is correct to suggest that κατ' ἰδίαν is redactional.[3]

two strata of traditions, he at first defended the position that the two verses represent two pre-Markan levels of tradition, *Die Parabeltheorie*, pp. 48-64, esp. 58. Subsequently, however, he argued that this 'means that the three stages of Jeremias have to be expanded by a fourth stage. This already looks suspiciously complicated.' He then noted the possible solution of v. 33 being pre-Markan and v. 34 Markan. 'But against that too, there is the question why the pre-Markan v. 33 should be so much more "Markan" linguistically that the Markan v. 34,' *'Messianic Secret'*, pp. 107, 108

1. See Gnilka, *Die Verstockung*, p. 60, and the above discussion on Schweizer and Weeden, 2, c. On κατ' ἰδίαν see Sellew, 'Oral and Written Sources', p. 260; above 2, e.

2. S. Brown, ' "The Secret of the Kingdom of God" (Mark 4.11)', *JBL* 92 (1973), pp. 60-74, here 65. He also points to the Markan hapax legomena from v. 34, χωρίς, ἴδιοι μαθηταί, and ἐπιλύειν, p. 65.

3. A view shared by Pryke, who estimates six of the seven occurrences in the Gospel are redactional. *Redactional*, p. 137. Kee, *Community*, p. 53 notes that this phrase and its synonym, κατὰ μόνας are found eight times in Mark with a context of private instruction or private act. On the Markan character of verse 34b, see also E. Best, 'Mark's Use of the Twelve', *ZNW* 69 (1978), p. 18; Marcus, *Mysterious Kingdom*, p. 88.

Furthermore, evidence for the non-Markan character of v. 33 is not as strong as is usually assumed. The opening clause (33a—Καὶ τοιαύταις παραβολαῖς πολλαῖς) contains three items of Markan vocabulary. The remaining word, τοιαύταις, also has significant parallels. Mark employs it at 9.37 and 10.14 to describe the 'little ones'. There is also the adjective ποικίλαις in the redactional v. 1.34; πλεῖστος at 4.1; and the explanatory gloss καὶ ἄλλα πολλά ἐστιν ἃ παρέλαβον κρατεῖν at 7.4.[1] The middle phrase, ἐλάλει αὐτοῖς τὸν λόγον, as Schweizer points out, has clear parallels at 2.2 and 8.32. The latter in particular seems to be a deliberate editorial contrast to Jesus' previous policy of speaking in 'parables' or enigmatically. The term λόγος is accepted as redactional by Gaston.[2]

The concluding καθὼς ἠδύναντο ἀκούειν likewise has strong credentials as redaction. Pryke evaluates six of the eight usages of καθώς as due to the evangelist.[3] The verb δύναμαι is accepted as redactional vocabulary by Gaston, Morgenthaler and Friedrich.[4] Injunctions to hear are stressed by Mark in the parable chapter and throughout the rest of the Gospel.[5] Indeed, once we question Riddle's assumption that this must be the source's conclusion, it is not at all clear how ἀκούειν would function in such a role. The word owes much of its sense to Mark's wider context, particularly the injunctions at 4.9, 24 and the quote at 4.12. Despite the belief that the phrase is in contradiction to v. 34, it admits implicitly that some people in Jesus' audience were not able to hear (i.e., understand), or that those who did hear did so with only imperfect comprehension. If the clause served as the conclusion to a public teaching source which did not view Jesus' parables as opaque mysteries it is difficult to see the necessity of such a phrase at all. Given Mark's context, however, the

1. Cf. also πολλάκις πέδαις at 5.4; αἱ δυνάμεις τοιαῦται διὰ τῶν χειρῶν αὐτοῦ γινόμεναι at 6.2; ἕν τῶν τοιούτων παιδίων at 9.37; and Jesus' indignant καὶ παρόμοια τοιαῦτα πολλά; ποιεῖτε at 7.13b.
2. That is, in 15 editorial sentences. See Neirynck, 'Redactional Text of Mark', p. 147.
3. Pryke, *Redactional*, p. 137.
4. Neirynck, 'Redactional Text of Mark', p. 146; *idem*, 'Words Characteristic of Mark', p. 368. Cp. at Mk 1.40; 2.7; 6.5; 9.22, 23, 28, 29; 10.26, 38, 39; 15.31, many of which are highly significant contexts. The use in v. 33 is consistent with Mark's practice elsewhere. See C.H. Turner, 'Marcan Usage: Notes, Critical and Exegetical, on the Second Gospel', *JTS* 28 (1926–27), pp. 354-55.
5. Compare at Mk 4.9, 12, 18, 20, 23; 6.11; 7.16, 37; 8.18; 9.7; 12.29; 13.7.

phrase is more understandable. There is, therefore, no significant evidence for tradition within v. 33.[1]

Turning to v. 34, close inspection again reveals little evidence for tradition. In the first half of the verse, setting aside χωρίς, one is left with the very Markan δὲ παραβολῆς οὐκ ἐλάλει αὐτοῖς. It recapitulates v. 33a so well (and forms an 'inclusion' with it), that both must be assigned to the same author. The 'unusual' character of successive clauses beginning with δέ is insignificant when compared Mk 6.15-16a: ἄλλοι **δὲ** ἔλεγον ὅτι 'Ηλίας ἐστίν· ἄλλοι **δὲ** ἔλεγον ὅτι προφήτης ὡς εἷς τῶν προφητῶν. ἀκούσας **δὲ** ὁ 'Ηρῴδης ἔλεγεν...[2] Nor should this be surprising; δέ is in fact a pet Markan term, eclipsed in favour only by καί. The designation τοῖς ἰδίοις μαθηταῖς ιs unusual only in the inclusion of ἰδίοις; 'disciple' is a redactional item.[3] The term fits well with Mark's theme of teaching κατ' ἰδίαν. Within the context of ch. 4, the designation ἰδίοις functions as a reinforcement of the contrast at 11-12. 'To those without' (ἐκείνοις δὲ τοῖς ἔξω—i.e., the crowds who are not Jesus') Jesus teaches only in parables; to those who are on the inside (i.e., his own disciples—δὲ τοῖς ἰδίοις μαθηταῖς) Jesus provides explanatory interpretations. The entire phrase δὲ τοῖς ἰδίοις μαθηταῖς is also accepted as a Markan expression by E. Best and J. Marcus.[4]

Markan vocabulary is found in each clause of the verse: 'parables', 'privately', and 'everything'. What remains is the usage of χωρὶς and ἐπέλυεν, the latter being the only word used less than 10 times throughout the New Testament. Since these words occur infrequently in Mark, can they be assumed to be non-Markan and hence traditional? This assumption must be examined carefully. Might an author not use a word of specialized vocabulary only once or twice in

1. On the Markan character of verse 33, see Schweizer, *Good News According to Mark*, pp. 105-06. 'Mark is writing on his own here, and presents his own theology of Jesus' parables at the conclusion of the section.' In contrast, Räisänen, *Die Parabeltheorie*, pp. 54-55 believes the interpretation of v. 33b in the negative sense of 'according to their ability to hear', is strained and not the original meaning. 'Ein solches Verständnis von V. 33 ist nur moglish, wenn man folgerichtiig von V. 11-12.34 ausgeht und alles andere in ihren Licht deutet. An sich ist es nicht natürlich.'

2. Interestingly, in both instances of successive clauses with δέ we also find the verb λέγω in the imperfect.

3. As per Gaston, Pryke, see Neirynck, 'Redactional Text of Mark', p. 147; Pryke, *Redactional*, p. 137.

4. Best, 'Mark's Use', p. 18; Marcus, *Mystery of the Kingdom*, p. 88.

a document?[1] In fact, infrequent vocabulary is found in other redactional verses within Mark. There is ἀλλαχοῦ and κωμόπολις at 1.38; διαφημίζω, πάντοθεν and φανερῶς at 1.45; ῥαντίζω, ξέστης and χαλκίον at 7.4; and γναφεύς, λευκαίνω and στίλβω at 9.3. A careful examination of Mark's redactional verses reveals a strikingly high number of items that occur fewer than five times in his own Gospel and fewer than ten times within the canon of the New Testament. Other hapax legomena within Mark can also be found.[2] Such a list, of course, does not of itself prove the Markan character of χωρίς and ἐπέλυεν. But it underscores the fact that the most telling arguments for the 'traditional' character of v. 34 involve its supposed theological incompatibility with Mark's interests as expressed elsewhere. I will now examine these arguments more closely in turn.

Weeden believes the non-Markan character of v. 34 is seen clearly in the inconsistent use of 'parables'. If Mark wrote this he reveals himself as a feeble-minded thinker and an inconsistent writer: Jesus in fact does teach using other literary forms than the parable. Likewise, Jesus is understood by others (i.e., beyond the group of the disciples) at other parts of the Gospel. But this outright rejection of the possibility of Markan redaction brings to mind an admonition of R.G. Collingwood: 'Never think you have understood any statement made by a philosopher until you have decided, with the utmost possible accuracy, what the question is to which he means it for an answer'.[3] Weeden essentially objects that if Mark wrote v. 34 he did not do so as Weeden would have expected. Demanding perfect consistency or logic by the canons of twentieth-century expectations is in fact an argument ill-suited to Mark's Gospel. There are, first of all, the numerous logically 'absurd' injunctions to silence or secrecy

1. Kelber, *The Kingdom in Mark*, p. 34, finds that each of the terms τοῖς ἰδίοις μαθηταῖς, χωρίς, and ἐπέλυεν explicable on the basis of the context and in light of v. 33. Each of them also introduces a Markan motif. On the basis of statistical probability alone, every text will likely have a number of infrequently occurring terms. Source material is by no means certain in all such cases.

2. Appendix 1 lists these infrequent vocabulary items within Markan redactional verses. Compare Kee's treatment of κωμοπόλεις and τὰς ἐχομένας, both infrequent in the New Testament as evidence of the evangelist's redaction at 1.38. *Community*, p. 59.

3. R.G. Collingwood, *An Autobiography* (Oxford, Oxford University Press, 1939), p. 74. Quoted by Burkill, 'Concerning St Mark's Conception of Secrecy', p. 158.

(1.44; 3.12; 5.43); the inability to keep hidden (1.44-45; 6.34; 7.24, 36—Jesus in effect becomes incompetent in Mark's narrative drama); the unwarranted harsh treatment of the Leper (1.43); and the repeated disobedience of the demonic spirits (1.24-26, 34; 5.7-9; 9.26). Then there is the question of the disciples: the inner group that repeatedly fails to understand Jesus' teaching or mission (7.18; 8.33-34; 9.5; etc.).

The 'incongruity' involving the 'parables' in v. 34 actually relies on an anachronistic and overly technical definition. In modern literary criticism 'parable' has taken on a technical sense for a story that is metaphorical rather than allegorical. 'Parable' in this sense has become restricted in meaning. It is within this usage that Mk 4.34 becomes nonsensical: for quite clearly Jesus does teach elsewhere in non-parabolic speech forms. But the real question must be: Is the nuance of 'parables' at 4.34 inconsistent with its meaning elsewhere in Mark? The answer must be an emphatic 'No'! Immediately prior to the passage in question, Mark introduces the Beelzebul controversy in the strikingly similar: καὶ προσκαλεσάμενος αὐτοὺς ἐν παραβολαῖς ἔλεγεν αὐτοῖς. What follows are not 'parables' in the technical sense of the word, but rhetorical questions, analogies, aphorisms or similitudes.[1] But for Mark, quite clearly, these sayings are 'parables' in his usage of the word. The parallel at 7.17 is significant since the disciples are not questioning him about a 'parable' in the restricted sense but rather about a legal pronouncement (7.14-15). The Vineyard parable also introduces one parable with the plural (12.1). And, to indulge in an overly literal interpretation, strictly speaking even 12.12 is not a logical contradiction of 4.33-34. Mark does not say that the hostile scribes understood the parable, rather they realized (perhaps only) that the story had been used insultingly against them. There is also the 'unusual' nuance given at 13.28: Ἀπὸ δὲ τῆς συκῆς μάθετε τὴν παραβολήν. Mark here has 'learn the parable' in almost the exact sense that we might say 'learn the lesson'. It is a usage quite at variance with modern scholarly understandings of 'parable' as a literary genre.[2] Quite clearly, for Mark, this was an

1. Mark's introduction at 3.23 almost certainly must be viewed as his redactional setting. The parallel from Q at Lk. 11.17 is singularly lacking in the Markan use of 'parables'.

2. A great deal of recent literature has been devoted to the multi-faceted nature of parables and how, as language events, they differ from simple morals or example

entirely appropriate use of the word within his definition of the term.

The solution to the meaning of 4.33 within Mark's Gospel is quite easily found when we remember that in the first century CE both the Hebrew מׁשל and the Greek παραβολή had acquired a variety of connotations beyond that of 'similitude-parable' and included such sayings as allegories, wisdom-sayings, proverbs, aphorisms, prophetic oracles, and any saying which could be considered a riddle.[1]

The other key to a proper understanding of vv. 33-34 is the function of Mark's language. Mark's narrative is not intended as a logically consistent philosophical treatise. The so-called incongruity between vv. 33-34 is consistent with Mark's writing techniques at numerous other passages. The double statement (negative followed by positive) occurs frequently, most strikingly at 6.5 and 8.14.[2] In the same way that a movie or novel becomes absurd if the viewer (or reader) refuses to 'suspend disbelief', so too Mark's narrative can become inconsistent and evidence of a feeble-minded thinker. Mark's text must be understood in light of the author's engineering language and depth-grammar intents. Just as a soundtrack (or laugh track) helps engineer the appropriate emotional response, Mark has interspersed his narrative with the response of wonder, fear and excitement to Jesus (1.21, 34; 2.12; 12.37). Crowds press in upon him, causing confusion (5.31), danger (3.9) and frustration (2.2; 3.20). Jesus himself is a charismatic and exciting figure, constantly calling to himself the crowds and the disciples (7.14; 8.1, 34; 10.32, 42), being greatly moved emotionally (3.5; 8.2, 12; 10.14) and looking around in dramatic fashion before significant revelations (3.5, 34; 5.32; 10.23, 27). None of these motifs bears up too well under close scrutiny in terms of logic. Indeed, viewed from such a perspective, entire books could be—and have been—written about the shortcomings of Mark's

stories. Mark's exhortation uses 'parable' much like an example story, as has Luke in the wider context of the Good Samaritan.

1. See G.H. Boobyer, 'The Redaction of Mark iv.1-34', *NTS* 8 (1961–62), pp. 59-70, here 61. Boobyer states that παραβολή could be considered a synonym for αἴνιγμα. Also, Scott, *Hear then the Parable*, pp. 10-11, who points out that *mashal* could refer to proverbs, riddles, and is the paradigm for hidden or allusive truth. D. Stern, 'The Rabbinic Parable: From Rhetoric to Poetics', in *SBL Seminar Papers 1986* (Atlanta: Scholars Press, 1986), p. 636 has pointed to rabbinic 'parables' that are used as an indirect expression intended to escape the notice of hostile authorities.

2. See Neirynck, *Duality in Mark*, p. 89.

text.[1] Such an approach is ultimately unsatisfactory for the same reason that a too-quick solution for textual difficulties through the explanation of 'tradition versus redaction' is unconvincing. Both approaches fail to make sense of the text in terms of how the author expected the audience to understand the finished product. Regardless of the source(s) of 4.33-34 and 12.1-12, Mark certainly expected the reader to find 'meaning' within both passages within the context of the Gospel as a whole.[2]

Viewed from the perspective of whether 4.33-34 is consistent with Mark's overall theory of 'Secrecy', and not from the stand-point of whether the modern critic finds such a theory consistent, the verses fit well into the Gospel. Jesus is repeatedly depicted as providing secret teaching to his disciples (cp. 4.10-20; 7.17-23; 8.14-20; 9.27-29; 10.10-12). This theme is reinforced by the repeated withdrawal of Jesus and the disciples, particularly with the inner group of three (5.37; 6.31; 9.2; 14.33). The crowds function ambiguously throughout. Unlike the inner group of disciples, or the caricatures of the openly hostile scribes (who plot to liquidate Jesus), the crowds are 'neither fish nor fowl'. They are the ones who eagerly seek out Jesus (6.34; 9.14) and throng around him (3.9; 5.24), petitioning him for healing miracles (1.32; 6.53-56), and hearing his teaching gladly (12.37). They are the narrative restraint upon the hostile authorities preventing a too-early departure by Jesus from the Gospel (11.18; 14.4). Their position mid-point between the authorities and disciples is perfectly represented structurally at Mk 7.1-23, where we find first public confrontation with the Pharisees and Jerusalem authorities (7.1-13); second, special exhortations to the crowds (7.14-16); and finally, full explanation to the disciples (7.17-23). They are needed to provide a sense of 'drama', 'action', and 'success' around Jesus. They are an additional foil to the authorities—without them, Mark's drama would become uneventful and insipid. Yet at the decisive moment they too are 'manipulated' into calling for Jesus' death (15.11). The theological motivations behind this twist of events are not hard to find: beginning with W. Wrede it has been recognized that Mark finds it necessary to provide an apologetic explaining the 'contradiction' of how Jesus the

---

1. See Meagher, *Clumsy Construction*.

2. On this issue, see B.W. Henaut, 'John 4.43-54 and the Ambivalent Narrator: A Response to Culpepper's *Anatomy of the Fourth Gospel*', *SR* 19 (1990), pp. 287-304.

Messiah (and subsequently his emissaries in the church) failed to make significant inroads into the contemporary Jewish community.[1]

Thematically, therefore, vv. 33-34 fit perfectly within Mark's literary and theological perspectives. Publicly, Jesus speaks the word through many parables, in exact measure with the crowd's ability to perceive and understand; privately, however, he provides secret explanations to the disciples. That the two thoughts seem disjointed is not evidence of the merger of two different sources (tradition and redaction) but rather a fundamental characteristic of Mark's literary technique. Juxtapositions and other forms of 'duality' abound in Mark. Frans Neirynck in particular has demonstrated this essential characteristic of Markan style which is seen, for example, in the numerous duplicate expressions (cf. 1.32: ὀψίας δὲ γενομένης, ὅτε ἔδυσεν ὁ ἥλιος). Regarding this feature Neirynck states:

> Thus, the conclusion may be justifiable (and it has been accepted in many studies on Markan redaction) that we are faced here with one of Mark's most characteristic features of style. If this is so, the double expression might have been conceived as an original unity, typical for Mark's way of thinking and writing. So it is not suitable to assign to different sources each half of such expressions. But it seems to me that the objection we are raising here against the combination theory is also applicable to some sort of mechanical distribution between tradition and redaction as it is found here and there in the literary criticism of our century.[2]

Dissection theories for the two verses need to show a fundamental difference between these verses and the other Markan summaries. They compare favourably, for example, with 1.39, 45; 3.5-6; and 12.12. The verses cohere so well with Mark's redactional concerns that the distinctive vocabulary of χωρίς and ἐπέλυεν do not provide adequate grounds for postulating traditional material. Indeed, when we shave off the clauses that have clear parallels throughout Mark's text so little is left that it is difficult to imagine that 4.33-34 ever was

---

1. The problem of Anti-Judaism in early Christian literature is receiving growing attention. See, for example, P. Richardson with D. Granskou, (eds.), *Anti-Judaism in Early Christianity*. I. *Paul and the Gospels* (Studies in Christianity and Judaism, 2; Waterloo, Ont.: Wilfrid Laurier Press, 1986); S.G. Wilson (ed.), *Anti-Judaism in Early Christianity*. II. *Separation and Polemic* (Studies in Christianity and Judaism, 2; Waterloo, Ont.: Wilfrid Laurier Press, 1986). The narrative role of such characters as the Pharisees, scribes, Sanhedrin and crowds, and the hardening theory of 4.11-12, all need to be read within the context of this polemic.

2. Neirynck, *Duality in Mark*, p. 49.

an adequate conclusion to a parable sermon. Further evidence for their redactional character is found in how closely they parallel the introduction. Verses 2 and 34 are in parallel a,b structure, while v. 34 provides a chiastic a,b,c; c′,b′,a′ parallel to vv. 11-12 (the centre-piece of Mark's parables chapter). Mk 4.1-2; 33-34 are, in essence, the evangelist's inclusion to his parables sermon:[1]

The Markan Inclusion

Mk 4.1-2	Mk 4.33-34
[1] Καὶ πάλιν ἤρξατο διδάσκειν παρὰ τὴν θάλασσαν. καὶ συνάγεται πρὸς αὐτὸν ὄχλος πλεῖστος, ὥστε αὐτὸν εἰς πλοῖον ἐμβάντα καθῆσθαι ἐν τῇ θαλάσσῃ καὶ πᾶς ὁ ὄχλος πρὸς τὴν θάλασσαν ἐπὶ τῆς γῆς ἦσαν. [2] καὶ ἐδίδασκεν αὐτοὺς ἐν παραβολαῖς πολλὰ καὶ ἔλεγεν αὐτοῖς ἐν τῇ διδαχῇ αὐτοῦ	[Cp. v. 35—Jesus and the disciples depart immediately after the sermon on another boating expedition] [33—2a] Καὶ τοιαύταις παραβολαῖς πολλαῖς [2b] ἐλάλει αὐτοῖς τὸν λόγον, [33b—12] καθὼς ἠδύναντο ἀκούειν· [34—11b] χωρὶς δὲ παραβολῆς οὐκ ἐλάλει αὐτοῖς, [11a] κατ᾽ ἰδίαν δὲ τοῖς ἰδίοις μαθηταῖς ἐπέλυεν πάντα.

Verse 34, therefore, must be ascribed to the evangelist.[2] The source's conclusion is forever lost: Mark has omitted it in favour of his own free composition. Textuality, it must be remembered, serves as a barrier to previous tradition, both written and oral.

Since v. 34 recapitulates the themes of 11-12, Mark has highlighted this motif in his conclusion. This centrepiece provides the clue to Mark's intent, and Jesus' secret teaching is a prominent theme. Its

---

1. On vv. 1-2 and 33-34 forming an inclusion, see Lambrecht, 'Redaction and Theology', p. 273. On vv. 33-34 as Markan, see pp. 275-76. On inclusion as a stylistic feature (with an extensive list), see Neirynck, *Duality in Mark*, pp. 131-33.

2. On the redactional character of vv. 33-34: Best, *The Temptation*, p. 74 (n. 2), 65; Bultmann, *History*, p. 341; Kuhn, *Ältere Sammlungen*, p. 134; Neirynck, *Duality in Mark*, p. 131; Pryke, *Redactional*, p. 157. Verses 33-34, redactional for Gaston; v. 34, redactional for W. Schmithals; v. 34a, redactional for J. Gnilka, see Neirynck, 'Redactional Text of Mark', pp. 144, 157-58. On the inclusion between vv. 2 and 33 (with 'parables') see M.A. Tolbert, *Sowing the Gospel: Mark's World in Literary-Historical Perspective* (Minneapolis: Fortress Press, 1989), pp. 148-49.

relationship to previous tradition deserves closer attention, and it is this topic which will concern me now.

4. *Mark 4.10-13: A Redactional Sandwich*

Mk 4.10-12 offers the 'hardening theory' regarding the parables. Its place in Mark's theology is still subject to debate. For scholars such as Riddle, Jeremias, Weeden and Meagher the passage actually represents a non-Markan view of 'parables' and its present location is due to a Markan misunderstanding. Building on this distinction, and the 'tensions' with vv. 1-2, 33-34, they go on to claim a prior history for vv. 11-12 and locate the unit within the very early oral tradition. The above analysis has already shown that all of vv. 1-2, 33-34 must be ascribed to Mark, and hence, the case for prior tradition (and orality) must be made without arguments dependent upon these verses.

For others, the passage contains the evangelist's centrepiece outlining the secret teaching of Jesus. Its redactional nature has been claimed by such critics as R. Bultmann, T. Burkill, F. Neirynck and E.J. Pryke.[1] Its import is underscored, as we have seen, at v. 34 which recapitulates this motif. The following analysis will show that, in fact, this passage is thoroughly Markan in vocabulary, structure and theological outlook. Far from being at odds with the viewpoint of the wider narrative, the unit coheres entirely with Mark's overall purpose.

a. *Mark 4.10*

καὶ ὅτε ἐγένετο κατὰ μόνας, ἠρώτων αὐτὸν
οἱ περὶ αὐτὸν σὺν τοῖς δώδεκα τὰς παραβολαῖς.

Meagher believes that the awkward phrase 'those who were with him' is slightly more self-conscious than the earliest stage. He—and others—find here Markan conflation, one source (similar to Matthew and Luke) spoke of the disciples while the other (similar to Jn 6.67) referred to the Twelve.[2] This strategy of 'divide and conquer' has proven popular; many exegetes believe that the phrase οἱ περὶ αὐτόν

---

1. See Bultmann, *History*, pp. 199, 325 (n. 1), 421; Burkill, *Mysterious Revelation*, p. 98; Neirynck, *Duality in Mark*, p. 53; Pryke, *Redactional*, pp. 13, 156.
2. Meagher, *Clumsy Construction*, pp. 109, 130.

in particular is non-Markan and hence traditional.[1]

The opening phrase, καὶ ὅτε ἐγένετο, is similar to numerous chronological links employing γίνομαι throughout Mark and is therefore redactional.[2] The theme of withdrawal, κατὰ μόνας, occurs frequently, often (as here) associated with secret teaching (cp. 1.35; 6.31; 7.17; 9.2, 8, 28, 33; 10.10; and 13.3).[3] Even more significant is the sequence withdrawal–question. The verb ἠρώτων followed by the personal pronoun is consistently found in these episodes of secret teaching (7.17; 9.28, 33; 10.10). These parallels show the essential Markan character of this portion of the verse.

Turning to the double audience, is οἱ περὶ αὐτὸν σὺν τοῖς δώδεκα non-Markan in vocabulary or style? Although Mark more frequently uses the term 'disciples' (46 times),[4] the specific δώδεκα is no less redactional: it is accepted as redactional by Gaston, Morgenthaler, Friedrich and Pryke.[5] The use of this specific designation is particularly appropriate due to Mk 3.14, Jesus has recently appointed (ἐποίησεν) this group.[6] It is the former phrase, οἱ περὶ αὐτόν, that causes the most difficulty. However, if we note the structural and thematic closeness to the phrase μετ' αὐτοῦ we can find a number of close redactional parallels. The Twelve were specifically appointed at 3.14 for this very purpose. Further parallels are found at

1. A view expressed also by: Bultmann, *History*, p. 67; and Burkill (!) (fudged—'perhaps'), *Mysterious Revelation*, p. 98.

2. Compare Mk 1.4, 9; 2.15, 23; 4.4, 37. In contrast, Best has advanced the thesis that Mark's inherited tradition read 'And when he was alone with the twelve, they asked him about the parables'. Mark would be responsible for the phrase 'those around him'. See 'Mark's Use', pp. 11-35; Marcus, *Mysterious Kingdom*, pp. 80-81.

3. On the association of this term with κατ' ἰδίαν (v. 34), see Kee, *Community*, p. 53. See Lambrecht, 'Redaction and Theology', p. 278 for a 'well known Markan separation' at v. 10.

4. μαθητής as redactional for Gaston, and Pryke. See Neirynck, 'Redactional Text of Mark', pp. 147; Pryke, *Redactional*, p. 137.

5. Neirynck, 'Redactional Text of Mark', p. 146; *idem*, 'Words Characteristic of Mark', p. 368; and Pryke, *Redactional*, p. 136. Pryke evaluates 13 of the 15 occurrences in Mark as due to the evangelist. The Twelve may be found at Mk 3.14, 16; 4.10; 5.25, 42; 6.7, 43; 8.19; 9.35; 10.32; 11.11; 14.10, 17, 20, 43. Lambrecht, 'Redaction and Theology', p. 280, believes οἱ περὶ αὐτόν to be redactional.

6. Cp. redactionally at Mk 6.7; 14.10, 20; note also 10.41.

1.36; 2.19, 25; 4.36; 5.18, 24, 37; 14.18, 20, 33.[1] The redactional description of Jesus' family (οἱ παρ' αὐτοῦ—3.21) provides another structural parallel.[2] But the most telling evidence for the Markan character of οἱ περὶ αὐτόν is found at 3.34. The three clear favourite Markan redactional terms within this phrase (καί, περιβλεψάμενος, and καθημένος), and its close dependence on the context clearly stamps it as redactional. With this verse in mind, the designation at 4.10 is not surprising at all. The last reference in the Gospel to that special group separate from the crowds which followed Jesus (larger than the Twelve) was to τοὺς περὶ αὐτὸν κύκλῳ καθημένος. It is this very same group, Mark insists, that now comes to Jesus for an explanation regarding the public teaching.

Nor can the verse's redundancy be used as evidence of tradition or conflation. I have already noted the parallel at 1.36 (Σίμων καὶ οἱ μετ' αὐτοῦ). The double phrase, particularly the double designation of a group, is characteristic of Markan style.[3] What remains as evidence of 'tradition' in the verse is the 'disjunction' between 'parables' (v. 10) and 'parable' (v. 13). Since Jeremias has championed this inconsistency as evidence of a join in the narrative, I will set aside the issue of vv. 11-12 temporarily in order to examine v. 13.

---

1. At 2.19, the phrase has become a Markan symbol for the fellowship enjoyed by Jesus and the Twelve during his earthly ministry which was broken by the cross. At 2.25 the inclusion is particularly significant. In the Hebrew Bible story David's friends are an imaginary ruse to avoid arousing suspicion. In Mark, these friends who are 'with him' are real and given bread by David and eat. Thematically, these friends 'stand in' for the disciples who are given bread by Jesus.

2. One may note the parallel at 3.6, where the Pharisees take council κατ' αὐτοῦ (referring to Jesus).

3. See Neirynck, *Duality in Mark*, pp. 108-09. Neirynck's entire book provides abundant evidence for this essential feature of Markan style. On the double designation of the questioners, see Räisänen, '*Messianic Secret*', pp. 115-16. He notes the similarity between 8.34 and 3.32, 34: 'Thus the description of the questioners can easily be ascribed wholly to the evangelist, and it is useless to speculate about who might have been mentioned originally at this point'.

b. *Mark 4.13.*

καὶ λέγει αὐτοῖς, Οὐκ οἴδατε τὴν παραβολὴν ταύτην,
καὶ πῶς πάσας τὰς παραβολὰς γνώσεσθε;

Indications of Mark's hand are easily found in v. 13. Since the introduction for discourse καὶ λέγει αὐτοῖς has numerous parallels, its Markan character (as at 10a) need not be in doubt. There is the cluster of Markan vocabulary including καί, πάσας, τὴν παραβολὴν... τὰς παραβολάς and γνώσεσθε. Of the 12 occurrences of this verb, Gaston lists five as editorial, Pryke seven.[1] The conclusion to the Vineyard parable is striking: ἔγνωσαν γὰρ ὅτι πρὸς αὐτοὺς τὴν παραβολὴν εἶπεν. At both 4.13 and 12.12, Mark brings 'parables' and 'know' into proximity. The conjunction of the two motifs at 4.13 is unlikely to be a fortuitous coincidence from the tradition.

Close parallels for the pronoun ταύτην include 4.33a and 6.2.[2] Pryke also evaluates eight of 15 occurrences of πῶς as redactional.[3] πῶς is found frequently enough in Mark that it need not be viewed as strong evidence for tradition; indeed, it is a good indication of possible redaction.[4]

The saying is structured in a chiastic fashion: a) know, b) parable, c) this; c′) all, b′) parables, a′) know. The chiastic structure of 4.1c, d has already been noted, as has the inclusion pattern of 4.1-2, 33-34. Inclusion in particular has been singled out by Neirynck as a stock feature of Markan style.[5] Similarly, the double question occurs no less than 24 other times in the Gospel.[6]

Even more telling are the parallels with other instances of 'secret teaching'. The theme is again found at the conclusion to the Walking on the Water. Mark underscores the disciples' failure: οὐ γὰρ

1. See Neirynck, 'Redactional Text of Mark', p. 146; Pryke, *Redactional*, p. 136.
2. Cf. above regarding the parallels ποικίλαις in the redactional verse 1.34; πλεῖστος at 4.1; and the explanatory gloss καὶ ἄλλα πολλά ἐστιν ἃ παρέλαβον κρατεῖν at 7.4.
3. Pryke, *Redactional*, p. 137.
4. Following Pryke, a redactional πῶς is found at: 4.13; 8.21; 9.12; 10.23, 24; 11.18; 12.35, 41; 14.11. Possible source, 2.26; 3.23; 4.30, 40; 5.16; 12.26, 41; 14.1.
5. Neirynck, *Duality in Mark*, pp. 131-32.
6. Neirynck, *Duality in Mark*, pp. 125-26.

συνῆκαν ἐπὶ τοῖς ἄρτοις, ἀλλ' ἦν αὐτῶν ἡ καρδία πεπωρωμένη. The 'Tradition of the Elders' (7.1-23) also bears a close similarity to this text. After a dispute with the authorities Jesus summons the crowd with the exhortation: Ἀκούσατέ μου πάντες καὶ σύνετε. The command to hear in particular is reminiscent of the injunctions at 4.3, 9, 23, 24. Public teaching is again followed by withdrawal into the house. In near identical language, the disciples question Jesus about the 'parable'. Again, Mark follows with a 'divine' rebuke, set in the form of a double question, and underscores the disciples' inability to comprehend (7.18: Οὕτως καὶ ὑμεῖς ἀσύνετοί ἐστε; οὐ νοεῖτε ὅτι...). The intent at 7.18 is obvious: the disciples have been given the secret of the reign of God, and they have been recipients of special instruction. Thus, they should not be like the crowds who (as at 4.12) ἀκούοντες ἀκούωσιν καὶ μὴ συνιῶσιν. This theme is reinforced at 8.17-18. When the disciples misunderstand Jesus' exhortation regarding the leaven of the Pharisees he chides them Τί διαλογίζεσθε ὅτι ἄρτους οὐκ ἔχετε; οὔπω νοεῖτε οὐδὲ συνίετε; πεπωρωμένην ἔχετε τὴν καρδίαν ὑμῶν. Again, we find the same key vocabulary as at 4.13 with νοεῖτε and συνίετε. The reference to the hardened heart clearly refers back to the Isaiah quote of Mk 4.12. Although not quoted at Mark 4, the Isaiah passage complains that ἐπαχύνθη γὰρ ἡ καρδία τοῦ λαοῦ τούτου.[1] This backward allusion is made plain not only by 6.52 but by the continuation at 8.18 wherein Jesus asks the disciples if they too fall under the crowd's curse: ὀφθαλμοὺς ἔχοντες οὐ βλέπετε καὶ ὦτα ἔχοντες οὐκ ἀκούετε; καὶ οὐ μνημονεύετε. The thematic importance of the disciples' failure to comprehend even after the two loaves miracles is brought home in the unit's conclusion (8.21): οὔπω συνίετε. These three episodes form a triad emphasizing the disciples' inability to comprehend. On the last of these three passages, Sellew has commented that it 'is so clearly expressive of Mark's point of view and recapitulates earlier topics so well that it is almost certainly Mark's own creation after the pattern he found in the traditional material'.[2] But why is it necessary to postulate tradition in 4.13 when one of the parallels so clearly expresses Mark's viewpoint?

There remains the use of the plural in the disciples' question while Jesus' answer elucidates only one parable. The key is found in

1. Isa. 6.10, LXX; also quoted at Mt. 13.15.
2. Sellew, 'Oral and Written Sources', p. 286.

recognizing that we are dealing with a Markan sandwich. It is a technique found often in Mark, most notably at the family/Beelzebul possession episode (3.20-22, 31-35 and 22-30); Jairus' daughter and the woman with the flow of blood (5.21-24, 35-43 and 25-34); the mission of the Twelve and John's death (6.7-13, 30-32 and 14-29); and the cursing of the fig tree, Temple incident (11.12-14, 20-25 and 15-19).[1] There are a number of sandwiches at work in 4.11-13. First of all there is the obvious interlude between the parable of the Sower (4.3-9) and its allegorical interpretation (4.14-20). But this interlude itself is a separate Markan sandwich. The question regarding the parables is interrupted by vv. 11-12 (the secret of the reign of God and the Isaiah curse) and then picked up again at v. 13. The three references to parable are arranged in chiastic fashion by Mark: parables (v. 10); parable (v. 13a); parables (v. 13b). Greg Fay explains well the chiastic structure of vv. 10-13:

A		10		Question (Comprehension)
	B	11a		Positive Results (Disciples)
		C	11b	Parabolic Method
	B′	12		Negative Results (Outsiders)
A′		13		Question (Comprehension)[2]

The question is in the plural because Mark wants to introduce the reason for the parabolic teaching which is designed to mislead the crowds. This theme—that Jesus habitually taught in parables—is prominently featured in the sermon's conclusion. Despite the 'single' parable at vv. 3-8, the plural is appropriate because the disciples were present at 3.23 where Jesus taught 'in parables' while 4.2 emphasizes that Jesus taught ἐν παραβολαῖς πολλά. Given Mark's use of 'parables' (cp. 12.1) this should hardly be surprising.[3] By placing vv. 11-12 as the pivot point around the Sower, Mark has emphasized their

---

1. As per Neirynck, *Duality in Mark*, p. 133. He notes 14.1-2, 10-11 and 3-9; 14.53-54, 66-72 & 55-65; and 15.6-15, 21-32 & 16-20. See J.R. Edwards, 'Markan Sandwiches: the Significance of Interpolations in Markan Narratives', *NovT* 31 (1989), pp. 193-216. Edwards provides further support for the 'sandwich' arrangement of the passage. Also, Kee, *Community*, pp. 54-55. The 'sandwich' arrangement is in fact a form of inclusion, chiasmus in A, B, A′ format.

2. G. Fay, 'Introduction to Incomprehension: The Literary Structure of Mark 4.1-34', *CBQ* 51 (1989), p. 81.

3. The second separate saying at 4.9 may also count in Mark's mind as a 'parable', and hence justify for him the plural.

import. Verse 13 then allows for the continuation of the Sower sequence. Understanding of this single parable is to become programmatic for understanding all the parables. When we remember the standard structure of the controversy dialogue (A, Question of antagonists; B, Counter-question of protagonist; B′, Response to counter-question; A′, Response to question), and compare the sequence at 4.10-13 with that at 7.17-23; 8.15-21; 10.23-31, we will see that Mark characteristically introduces a related second issue into a discussion to heighten the narrative's drama. An immediate response to the first theme (which modern critics find so much more logical) would resolve the tension too quickly. The sequence at 4.10-13, far from evidencing source and redaction, is thoroughly compatible with Mark's compositional techniques and dissection of Mk 4.10, 13 is no more appropriate than it is for numerous redactional passages.[1] There is, in short, no compelling evidence for tradition (oral or written) behind Mk 4.13, and the verse is best understood as redactional.[2]

c. *Mark 4.11*

καὶ ἔλεγεν αὐτοῖς,
Ὑμῖν τὸ μυστήριον δέδοται τῆς βασιλείας τοῦ θεοῦ·
ἐκείνοις δὲ τοῖς ἔξω ἐν παραβολαῖς τὰ πάντα γίνεται...

Since the stock introductory phrase for discourse at 11a and the sandwich arrangement are redactional, has Mark merely placed traditional material at this point in the narrative or are vv. 11-12 throughout redactional?

As Jeremias notes, the antithetic parallelism of v. 11b is a well-known Semitic favourite. My previous discussion of repetition,

---

1. Cp. Mk 1.27-28, 44-45; 3.9; 5.19-20, 43; 6.5-6, 30-34, 53-56; 8.14; 9.9-10.

2. See Lambrecht, 'Redaction and Theology', p. 281 who asserts that v. 13 'completely stems from Mark'. This reading of the text, I believe, is supported by Neirynck's comments quoted above in section 3, c. See *Duality in Mark*, p. 49. Compare his analysis of 4.13, 'the two questions are not unrelated, but the first may be viewed as a conditional clause in connection with the second, or even more exactly, the first stands as a question implying blame on the disciples' lack of insight and forms the non-expressed protasis in καὶ πῶς—γνώσεσθε. Jesus' rebuke of the incomprehension of the disciples is one of the characteristic themes of Markan theology. Mk vii. 18-19 presents a similar context and, again, the explanation of the parable is introduced by the blame on the disciples' lack of understanding in the form of a double question', *Duality in Mark*, p. 57.

parallelism and specifically antithetic parallelism, however, has shown the danger of claiming this form as distinctively oral or Semitic.[1] It is frequently found in Mark's sayings, and most of these verses are usually held to be traditional. But it is also found in the following verses which are possible redaction: 1.8; 7.8, 37; 10.42, 43-44; 13.11; 14.38b; and 14.58.[2] Neirynck gives a detailed examination of the use of antithetic parallelism within Mark, noting the problem of the inability to compare parallel versions of these sayings from other independent sources. It is an open question how often Mark has inherited this form from the tradition and retained it and how often he has redacted the tradition to conform to this linguistic device. Neirynck's comment on the specific form οὐ... ἀλλά and/or οὐ... εἰ μή is perhaps fitting for this entire class of material. The form 'is so well fitting to Mark's proclivity to progressive double phrases, one could raise the question if it is not Mark himself who, by the application of this device, has often reinforced the antithetic character of the sayings of Jesus'.[3] Beyond the precise form of antithetic parallelism Mark exhibits a penchant for other forms of duality and parallelism. The saying at 8.38, which is cast in synonymous parallelism, is an interesting case. Similar to Mark 1.8, a comparison with the Q parallels (Q 3.16; 12.9) shows that the Markan version has a more extensive parallel structure. Such forms as synonymous expressions, the double statement (particularly in negative-positive form), double question, repetition of the antecedent, and the double group of persons can all be extensively documented throughout Mark.[4]

According to Neirynck, Mk 4.11 exhibits the following specific forms of Markan duality: multiplication of cognate verbs, repetition of the antecedent, narrative and discourse, correspondence in discourse, and parallelism in sayings. Multiplication of cognate verbs involves the introduction to discourse at 11a, already noted above. Repetition of the antecedent involves the reference back to 3.31.

1. See above, Chapter 2, section 3, e.
2. Each of these verses is included in Pryke's redactional text of Mark, *Redactional*, pp. 151-76. In the case of 1.8, the Q parallel would suggest that Mark has inherited a traditional saying, and redactionally cast it into antithetic parallelism.
3. Neirynck, *Duality in Mark*, p. 63, discussion pp. 54-63.
4. For synonymous expression, see Neirynck, *Duality in Mark*, pp. 101-106. On the other forms of repetition, see *idem*, pp. 89-94; 125-26; 85-87; 108-10.

There Jesus' earthly family is described as ἔξω στήκοντες and he is informed at v. 32 that his family ἔξω ζητοῦσίν σε. This allusion back to the previous incident accounts for the term τοῖς ἔξω. The thematic tie between the two incidents is clear: Jesus' earthly family are among ἐκείνοις δὲ τοῖς ἔξω to whom ἐν παραβολαῖς τὰ πάντα γίνεται. They contrast with those at 3.34 (τοὺς περὶ αὐτὸν κύκλῳ καθημένος) who do the will of God. It is this latter group that forms the immediate audience of insiders at 4.10-13 (οἱ περὶ αὐτὸν σὺν τοῖς δώδεκα) who are recipients of the secret.[1] This thematic link between 3.31-32 and 4.11 also follows the Markan pattern of narrative and discourse.[2] Correspondence in discourse involves the question-and-answer sequence at 4.10, 11. The repetition of the key phrase τὰς παραβολαῖς... ἐν παραβολαῖς which involves a Markan redactional vocabulary item strongly suggests Mark's hand here.[3] Finally, sayings cast in parallelism are extensively documented by Neirynck.[4]

Jeremias also sees the use of the 'divine passive' within 11-12 as an indication of tradition. It is found three times: δέδοται, γίνεται, and ἀφεθῇ. But since the third of these is found within the Isaiah quote, only the first two are potentially significant. The idiom ἐν παραβολαῖς τὰ πάντα γίνεται (i.e., the use of γίνομαι with the dative as an impersonal) has been held to be unnatural in Greek and the overly-literal translation from a Semitic original.[5] But Elliott C. Maloney argues that the idiom is actually γίνομαι used with a dative of advantage (or disadvantage). He points to parallels from Classical and Hellenistic Greek of this usage including Euripides and Epictetus. He concludes that while the verse in Mark could be the translation of a Semitic original, the idiom is perfectly normal in Greek.[6] In Mark Semitic structures involving γίνομαι are not foolproof evidence of

1. As documented by Neirynck, *Duality in Mark*, pp. 85-87.
2. As documented by Neirynck, *Duality in Mark*, pp. 115-19. That 'those outside' at 4.11 is a reference to the use of the term at 3.31-32 is also seen by W.E. Moore, ' "Outside" and "Inside" A Markan Motif', *ExpTim* 98 (1986–87), pp. 39-43, esp. p. 40.
3. Neirynck, *Duality in Mark*, pp. 126-30.
4. See Neirynck, *Duality in Mark*, pp. 133-34.
5. See above discussion of Jeremias, *Parables*, pp. 16-17.
6. E.C. Maloney, *Semitic Interference in Marcan Syntax* (SBLDS, 51; Chico, CA: Scholars Press, 1981), pp. 182-83. Noting Euripides, *Med.* 755; Epictetus 4.7.20 (note, antithetic parallelism!); 3.24.109; 2.21.17.

tradition, since he is fond of this particular verb. The influence of the Septuagint provides another possible linguistic background of the phrase. There are at least a dozen other Markan uses of 'Semitisms' involving this verb.[1] Even in a more literary author such as Luke, such Semitic phrases are plentiful.[2] The use of this verb in the present (as at 4.11) may be found in Mark at 2.15, 21; 4.37; 6.2; 11.23; and 13.29.

The remaining linguistic evidence for tradition involves τὸ μυστήριον (only here in Mark) and the second divine passive δέδοται. The first of these, similar to the infrequently occurring vocabulary at v. 34, in itself is not definitive evidence of tradition. Likewise, passive constructions are not lacking in Mark (1.2, 9, 14, 15, etc.). Mark also frequently uses δίδωμι (2.26; 5.43; 6.2; etc.). The passive (even the divine passive) and δίδωμι are thus not strong evidence of tradition.

One can now examine the argument of a theological difference in the view of parables and revelation. According to Jeremias and Meagher, the phrase 'all things happen in riddles [= 'parables']' refers to the decisive events of Jesus' mission and not to his preaching. For Meagher this fits a context when the church perceived that the inner circle was privy to salvific secrets that were present but hidden in Jesus' teachings. This interpretation of Jesus' public career being viewed as riddles is attested to especially in Matthew's sign of Jonah (Mt. 12.38-42; cf. Q 11.29-32). 'Parable' has lost its original sense of illuminating illustration and points to an early post-resurrectional setting 'with reference not to the earlier teaching of Jesus but to the matters that most preoccupied his followers in those critical days'.[3]

This reconstruction, however, involves a number of difficulties. The Q narrative regarding the sign of Jonah lacks the key term 'parable'. Likewise, it is questionable whether the passage signifies that the sign of Jesus deliberately intends to mislead or hide the significance of the events in his life. Indeed, the opposite is more likely; Jesus recapitulates previous Hebrew Bible history, including the sign of Jonah, so that all may see its meaning (should they wish).

In this regard Mark's use of ἐν παραβολαῖς is striking and in complete agreement with 'parables' throughout the Gospel. Jesus'

---

1. See Mk 1.4, 9, 11; 2.23; 4.39; 5.16; 6,2, 21, 47; 9.7, 26; 14.17.
2. Cf. at Lk. 1.5, 8, 23, 41, 44, 59, 65, etc.
3. Meagher, *Clumsy Construction,* p. 115; discussion, pp. 112-16.

habitual teaching is ἐν παραβολαῖς, an opaque method to outsiders only fully understood by the elect with subsequent secret explanations. This strategy is expanded at v. 11 to include 'all things', i.e., not just teachings but the totality of reality. The reference is not, strictly speaking, even limited to the events in Jesus' public ministry; rather everything in life comes to outsiders as a mystery or riddle which is not fully comprehended. Mark's hyperbole in τὰ πάντα finds a number of parallels throughout his Gospel. Its closest linguistic kin is the highly favoured redactional πολλά (cf. v. 33). It finds its immediate reinforcement in the sermon's conclusion at 4.34 (ἐπέλυεν πάντα). It is a term that Mark particularly likes to emphasize in contexts of amazement to Jesus' deeds or teachings (1.5, 32, 37; 2.12; etc.).

Beyond the Markan terms 'all' and 'parables' other redactional concerns are present. The phrase ἡ βασιλεία τοῦ θεοῦ occurs two other times in the parable chapter (4.26, 30), providing thematic unity for the saying.[1] The theme of the reign of God is present frequently in Mark (1.15; 9.1, 47; etc.). Its use here, therefore, cannot be held as evidence of tradition. The verb γινώσκω (and its compound forms) is also used often by Mark (2.8, 25; 4.11, 13; etc.). The specific contrast of 'inside' and 'outside' is constantly emphasized by the evangelist. The Gospel is full of verbs of entry and exit (at times within the same verse!) which establish a contrast between Jesus and the world. Demons depart out of (ἐξ) people; Jesus is cast out into the desert; he goes out of the synagogue to enter a house; when his fame spreads he is unable to enter the cities openly but must abide out in the desert; he goes into the region of the Gerasenes and out of the boat; and in the parable chapter, Jesus is in the boat while the crowd abides on the beach.

W.E. Moore places this text within four interwoven themes which relate to the inside/outside motif: (1) the 'failure' of the authorities, people, and kin of Jesus; (2) the failure of the disciples to perceive and understand; (3) the increasing aloneness of Jesus; and (4) glimpses of a pilgrim community 'on the way'.[2]

The place of 4.11 in Mark's theology, particularly as it relates to his 'Secrecy' motif, is to be found in his distinctive use of 'parables'.

1. As seen by the parallel at Q 13.18, the association of 'The Reign of God' and the Mustard Seed parable may be traditional.

2. As at 8.3, 27; 9.33, 34; 10.17, 32, 46, 52. See Moore, '"Outside" and "Inside" A Markan Motif', p. 41.

Mark is not using this term in the modern literary-critical sense but rather as a generic term for any form of mysterious, divine speech including riddles and oracles.[1] Viewed in this light, the cultural background for Mark's thesis is easily found in the theological speculations of apocalyptic literature. *4 Ezra*, for example, contains several different forms of 'parables', all spoken by the divine agent (as opposed to the human seer) and all conveying a divine truth. As P. Patten points out, the 'parable, however, was not always clear in itself but needed a further "interpretation" by the speaker'. This is precisely the pattern we find throughout Mark, particularly at 4.10-20. In *1 Enoch*, similar to Mark, the parables include such literary forms as prophetic discourses, poems and even visions of divine mysteries. The element of authoritative interpretation, as with Mark, is prominent, although the agent of interpretation is an angel. This pattern of interpretation is found at *2 Bar.* 22.1–23.7; hence, as Patten notes, throughout apocalyptic literature parables are not revelatory by themselves, for the 'mystery cannot be immediately understood unless there is an inspired word of interpretation from a divine speaker to point out the intended meaning'.[2]

These dialogues of parable and interpretation share other literary similarities with Mk 4.10-20. Common are the themes of request for interpretation, 'divine rebuke' for stupidity and explanation. We have seen this pattern in a number of Markan scenes. It is also found at *4 Ezra* 10.29-37:

> As I was speaking these words, behold, the angel who had come to me at first came to me, and he looked upon me; and behold, I lay there like a corpse and I was deprived of my understanding. Then he grasped my right hand and strengthened me and set me on my feet, and said to me, 'What is the matter with you? And why are you troubled? And why are your understanding and the thoughts of your mind troubled?'
>
> I said, 'Because you have forsaken me! I did as you directed, and went out into the field, and behold, I saw, and still see, what I am unable to explain'.

---

1. On Mark's use of the term, and the essential agreement of viewpoint between 4.11, 33-34, see Burkill, *Mysterious Revelation*, p. 100.

2. P. Patten, 'The Form and Function of Parable in Select Apocalyptic Literature and their Significance for Parables in the Gospel of Mark', *NTS* 29 (1983), pp. 246-58. For *4 Ezra*, p. 247; noting *4 Ezra* 4.3; 4.13-4; 4.26-43; 4.44-50. On *2 Baruch*, p. 249; final quote at p. 250.

He said to me, 'Stand up like a man, and I will instruct you'.[1]

The pattern is also found at *The Shepherd of Hermas*, 5.1-2:

'Sir', said I, 'I still do not at all understand about the time of deceit and luxury and torture; explain it to me more clearly'. He answered and said to me: 'Your foolishness is lasting, and you do not wish to purify your heart to serve God. See to it', he said, 'lest the time be fulfilled, and you be found still foolish. Listen, then', said he, 'that you may understand it as you wish.'[2]

Common in apocalyptic literature is the theme of the hiddenness of the secrets which are given only to the elect. The Dead Sea scrolls contain the concept of the Messiah who is already born and living unknown on earth until he takes up his messianic office at the end of days.[3] Qumran views the Hebrew Scriptures as a divine book only partially open to outsiders. These divine mysteries were closed to the outside community while understanding was revealed to the Teacher of Righteousness and then conveyed to the entire sect.[4] The Sons of Darkness (the outsiders) were not permitted to know these divine secrets.[5] This apocalyptic 'secrecy' motif is often combined with other themes, as seen in the sense of imminence as the seer Baruch receives a promise of hidden mysteries:

'Go, therefore, and purify yourself for seven days: eat no bread, drink no water, and speak to no one. And afterwards come to this place, and I will reveal myself to you, and tell you hidden truths, and give you instruction about the course of the times for they are coming, and there will be no delay.'[6]

---

1. In M.G. Reddish (ed.), *Apocalyptic Literature: A Reader* (Nashville: Abingdon Press, 1990), p. 86. The translation is from the RSV.

2. Reddish, *Apocalyptic Literature*, p. 264. The translation is from Kirsopp Lake *The Apostolic Fathers* (vol. 2; Loeb Classical Library; Cambridge, MA: Harvard University Press, 1913).

3. As noted by D.E. Aune, 'The Problem of the Messianic Secret', *NovT* 11 (1969), pp. 1-31, here p. 10, citing 1QSa 2.11.

4. Aune, 'Problem of the Messianic Secret', p. 14. Citing 1 QH 2.13-4; CD 20.31-2; 1 QS 5.9.

5. Aune, 'Problem of the Messianic Secret', p. 17. Citing 1 QS 4.6; 9.17; 11.5-6; 1QH 4.7; 5.25-6; 8.12-4; cf. 1QS 5.8, 11; 1QpHab 2.6; 1QH 1.37; 1 QMyst 1.2-4.

6. 2 Bar. 29.5. Reddish, *Apocalyptic Literature*, p. 108. The translation is from L.H. Brockington, in *The Apocryphal Old Testament* (ed. H.F.D. Sparks; Oxford: Clarendon Press, 1984). Cp. 23.6-7, 'And again, you are to be privileged to hear

1 Enoch emphasizes the secret truths revealed to the few and the corollary of the outside community being deceived:

> And now to the Watchers who sent you to petition on their behalf, who were formerly in heaven—and now (say), You were in heaven, but (its) secrets had not yet been revealed to you and a worthless mystery you knew. This you made known to the women in the hardness of your hearts, and through this mystery the women and the men cause evil to increase on the earth. Say to them therefore, You will not have peace.[1]

Enoch holds the hiddenness of the Son of Man to be pre-ordained: 'From the beginning the Son of Man was hidden, and the Most High kept him in the presence of his power, and revealed him (only) to the chosen; and the community of the holy and the chosen will be sown, and all the chosen will stand before him on that day' (*1 En.* 62.7-8).[2]

The theology that outsiders are deliberately misled is present also, for example, at 2 Thess. 2.11: 'For this reason God sends them a powerful delusion, leading them to believe what is false'. Few scholars postulate a direct line of tradition, oral or otherwise, from Mk 4.11 to this text. The Q community's doctrine of call and rejection and its use

what is to come after these times. For my redemption is near and is not as far away as once it was.'

1. *1 En.* 16.2-4 in Reddish, *Apocalyptic Literature*, p. 154. The translation is from M.A. Knibb, in Sparks (ed.), *The Apocryphal Old Testament*. Cp. also *1 En.* 46.2 on the secrets concerning the Son of Man; 64.2, 'And I heard the voice of the angel saying, These are the angels who came down from heaven onto the earth, and revealed what is secret to the sons of men, and led astray the sons of men so that they committed sin.'

2. Reddish, *Apocalyptic Literature*, p. 180. We can even find Mark's specific motif of command to silence and deliberate disobedience in post-biblical apocalyptic literature (and in a passage that is probably not subject to dismemberment theories): 'And a voice came to them [Mary and Joseph], "Do not tell this vision to anyone". But the story about the infant was spread abroad in Bethlehem. Some said, "The virgin Mary has given birth before she has been married two months". But many said, "She did not give birth; the midwife did not go up (to her), and we did not hear (any) cries of pain". And they were blinded concerning him; they all knew about him, but they did not know from where he was.' The text also shows a curious reliance upon Luke's technique of contrasting the response of two groups of people. The *Ascension of Isaiah*, 11.11-4 in Reddish, *Apocalyptic Literature*, p. 289. The translation is from M.A. Knibb in *The Old Testament Pseudepigrapha* (vol. 2; ed. J.H. Charlesworth; Garden City, NY: Doubleday, 1985). Cp. *The Ascension of Isaiah* 11.39; *The Apocalypse of Paul*, 14; 21; 48; conclusion to 51 in C (cf. Reddish, p. 323); 51 (Syriac—Reddish, p. 325).

of the Deuteronomistic tradition against Judaism is also a case in point.[1] These parallels abundantly prove that the theology and literary structure of Mk 4.11 fit in well with contemporary apocalyptic speculations. Verse 11 thus coheres well with Mark's apocalyptic theology and his emphasis on the 'Secrecy' motif.

The model for Mark's shaping of v. 11 is found in the aphorisms, particularly vv. 22 and 25. By placing these three sayings together, vv. 22 and 25 find their perfect realization in v. 11 as applied to the disciples and crowd. Mark appropriates the reversal of hiddenness into revelation for Jesus' identity (v. 22). Jesus' hidden identity often threatens to get out; the demons constantly try to reveal the secret. At 1.34 Mark tells us that as a matter of policy Jesus had to silence the spirits to prevent any premature revelation. The theme is reinforced at the conflict in the Markan summary 3.11-12. When fame of Jesus spreads he could no longer 'openly' enter the cities (1.45). Both the confession of Jesus as Messiah (8.30) and the transfiguration (9.9) are to remain secret until after the resurrection. It is Wrede who perhaps first saw this latter verse as the key behind Mark's secrecy motif. The resurrection is the turning point; what was once secret is now openly revealed. Jesus, the lamp, can now be prominently displayed.[2] That Mark intended vv. 10-13 to be read in the context of vv. 21-25 is underscored by the chiastic pattern he has given the parable sermon. I have already noted the inclusion with vv. 1-2, 33-34. Based upon the presentation by Fay, the following chiastic pattern emerges:

A		1-2	Introduction
B		3-9	Teaching in Parables
C		10-13	Parabolic Method
	D	14-20	Interpretation of the Sower
C'		21-25	Parabolic Method
B'		26-32	Teaching in Parables
A'		33-34	Conclusion[3]

1. Seen in part in Q 10.22. Among others, see on this A.D. Jacobson, 'Wisdom Christology in Q' (dissertation, Claremont Graduate School, 1978).
2. The objection that 4.11 is in conflict theologically with 4.21-22 is well answered by Burkill, 'when verse 21 is read in conjunction with verse 22, the implication seems to be that the lamp *is* hidden, though only for a limited period. It is concealed in order that it should be made manifest on some future occasion', *Mysterious Revelation*, p. 111.
3. See Fay, 'Introduction to Incomprehension', p. 69. Fay subdivides at vv. 1-

The theology of Mk 4.10-11, 13, therefore, is perfectly consistent with the evangelist's 'Secrecy' motif. The passage coheres fully with its immediate context (4.1-34) and with episodes where special teaching or the disciples' failures are featured.[1] There is no need to postulate tradition, oral or otherwise, behind the text, or to resort to ingenious reconstructions of a tradition being 'misunderstood' due to an unfortunate insertion into an inappropriate context. The structure, vocabulary and theological intent argue strongly for redaction at 4.11. I will now proceed to an examination of the Isaiah quote at 4.12.

d. *Mark 4.12*

> ἵνα βλέποντες βλέπωσιν καὶ μὴ ἴδωσιν,
> καὶ ἀκούοντες ἀκούωσιν καὶ μὴ συνιῶσιν,
> μήποτε ἐπιστερέψωσιν καί ἀφεθῇ αὐτοῖς

The Targum is often held as the source of v. 12. The saying, in this reconstruction, was joined to the 'mystery/riddles' logion (v. 11) early in the oral phase. Disagreement in the view of 'parables' and Jesus' public ministry provides further evidence of the logion's traditional character. A thorough investigation of the evidence, however, will show that the verse must be ascribed to Mark.

Agreement between these two sources (against the Septuagint) include: the third person (rather than the second); the use of participles for βλέποντες and ἀκούοντες; the verb 'forgive' instead of 'heal' with the plural (rather than the singular Hebrew לו); and the avoidance of the divine name through the passive. This allows Jeremias to reconstruct an original form of the saying that softens the intent of Isaiah, the ἵνα meaning 'in order that (as it is written)' and the μήποτε translating an original Aramaic דלמא which has a sense of 'unless'. The Aramaic Targum (Jonathan) for Isa. 6.9-10 reads:

2a, 2b-9, but otherwise the presentation follows his arrangement. On the unity of vv. 11-12, 21-25 see Hurtado, *Mark*, p. 61.

1. On the redactional character of v. 11, see Lambrecht, 'Redaction and Theology', p. 284, 'In our view it would be rather hazardous to hold that its actual wording and form are traditional, pre-Markan.'

וֹאמר אייל ותימר לעמא הדין   And he said, 'Go, and speak to this people
רֹשעין מֹשמצ ולא ממתכלין   who hear indeed but do not comprehend
וחזן מחוא ולא ידעין...   and see indeed but do not understand . . .
ויתובון וישתביק להון   and turn again, and it be forgiven them'.[1]

But Jeremias' case collapses when one examines the passage in the wider context. The essential harmony of v. 11 with 4.21-25, 33-34 and the Gospel as a whole regarding Jesus' secret teaching cautions against finding v. 12's meaning in a hypothetical reconstruction. Jeremias' translation of ἵνα is unconvincing: this usage is unparalleled anywhere else in Mark (in every other instance this term expresses purpose—many such clauses having reference to Mark's Secrecy motif). Perhaps the most significant parallel is 11.25. The telic force of ἵνα in its present context is well recognized by scholars.[2] This coheres totally with Mark's apocalyptic view of history: God's will, as revealed in scripture, has predetermined the proper time for all things. When the appropriate time arrives, events unfold in accord with this predestined plan (cf. Mk 1.35; 7.6-7; 9.11-13; 13.1-37; 14.49; 15.28). That the μήποτε should be given a sense of 'unless' rather than 'lest' is unlikely; the term agrees completely with the Septuagint (which gives the latter sense). 'Lest' is in complete harmony with Mark's use of ἵνα.

The use of the Isaiah quote has intimate ties to Mark's narrative as a whole. This text is echoed throughout Mark's Gospel and tied to the theme of the disciples' misunderstanding. A proper evaluation of Jeremias' evidence must situate these agreements with the Targum in the context of Mark's handling of the Isaiah theme elsewhere. In essence, Jeremias' linguistic evidence would hold more weight if Mark's use of the Isaiah quote here did not cohere with his use of

1. As quoted, and translated by C.A. Evans, *To See and not Perceive: Isaiah 6.9-10 in Early Jewish and Christian Interpretation* (JSOTSup, 64; Sheffield: JSOT Press, 1989), p. 70.

2. See Taylor, *Gospel According to St Mark*, p. 257. Also, Meagher, *Clumsy Construction*, p. 120, who admits that the Targum's softening view of Isaiah 'is not what Mark gives us . . . What Mark presents is bent back toward the darker meaning of the original Hebrew.' Nineham, *The Gospel of St Mark*, who acknowledges that while Jeremias' reconstruction of the original sense of ἵνα is possible, it is not what Mark meant by the term, p. 138. J.R. Kirkland calls Jeremias' speculation, 'only that, a speculation', 'The Earliest Understanding of Jesus' Use of Parables: Mark IV 10-12 in Context', *NovT* 19 (1977), p. 6.

Isaiah elsewhere. But Mark has a redactional concern with Isaiah which is not limited to this specific text. The theme of the events of Jesus' career as the fulfilment of Isaiah's prophecy starts at Mk 1.2, καθὼς γέγραπται ἐν τῷ Ἡσαΐᾳ τῷ προφήτῃ. The theme is reinforced by further citations of Isaiah, and hence this text should be seen as part of this overall pattern (cf. Mk 4.12; 7.6-7; 8.17-18; 11.17; 12.32). A comparison of the other Isaiah quotes shows an overall consistency in theme and handling of the original compared with Mk 4.12.

Isaiah Quotes in Mark[1]

Isa. 40.3 LXX	Mk 1.3
φωνὴ βοῶντος ἐν τῇ ἐρήμῳ	φωνὴ βοῶντος ἐν τῇ ἐπήμῳ,
Ἐτοιμάσατε τὴν ὁδόν κυρίου,	Ἐτοιμάσατε τὴν ὁδόν κυρίου,
εὐθέιας ποεῖτε	εὐθέιας ποιεῖτε
τὰς τρίβους <u>τοῦ θεοῦ ἡμῶν</u>.	τὰς τρίβους <u>αὐτους</u>.

Isa. 29.13 LXX	Mk 7.6-7
Ἐγγίζει μοι <u>ὁ λαὸς οὗτος</u> τοῖς χείλεσιν	<u>οὗτος ὁ λαὸς</u> τοῖς χείλεσίν
<u>αὐτῶν τιμῶσίν με</u>, ἡ δὲ καρδία αὐτῶν	<u>με τιμᾷ</u>, ἡ δέ καρδία αὐτῶν
πόρρω ἀπέχει ἀπ' ἐμοῦ, μάτην δὲ σέβονταί	πόρρω ἀπέχει ἀπ' ἐμοῦ· μάτην δὲ σέβονταί
με <u>διδάσκοντες ἐντάλματα</u> <u>ἀνθρώπων</u> <u>καὶ διδασκαλίας</u>.	με <u>διδάσκοντες διδασκαλίας</u> <u>ἐντάλματα</u> <u>ἀνθρώπων.</u>

Isa. 56.7 LXX	Mk 11.17
ὁ <u>γὰρ</u> οἰκός μου οἰκος	Ὁ οἰκός μου οἰκος
προσευχῆς κληθήσεται	προσευχῆς κληθήσεται
πᾶσιν τοῖς ἔθνεσιν.	πᾶσιν τοῖς ἔθνεσιν.

Isa. 45.21 LXX	Mk 12.32
<u>Ἐγὼ ὁ θεός</u>, καὶ οὐκ ἔστιν	<u>εἷς ἐστιν</u> καὶ οὐκ ἔστιν
ἄλλος πλὴν <u>ἐμοῦ</u>.	ἄλλος πλὴν <u>αὐτοῦ</u>.

Mark consistently does not quote the Septuagint in word-for-word agreement. Such changes as word order, shift in person (first to third, etc.) and substitution of terms occur consistently in these quotes. The

---

1. I have underlined the texts to draw attention to differences between the two versions as appropriate.

passage at 7.6-7 is striking because Mark applies this condemnation of a false heart to Jesus' contemporaries. In other words, it is part and parcel of the theme expressed at 4.12. Likewise, Mk 12.32 takes a positive prophecy of Gentile inclusion into the covenant of Yahweh and turns it into a denunciation of corrupt religion. These passages all cohere with the viewpoint expressed at 4.11-12, and Mark's application of these texts has often caused the very kind of linguistic alterations to the Septuagint as we find at 4.12. Could the changes we find in this latter case, therefore, be explicable in terms of Mark's appropriation of the verse?

The use of the third person is hardly surprising. At Mk 6.52 we find the editorial comment οὐ γὰρ συνῆκαν ἐπὶ τοῖς ἄρτοις, ἀλλ᾽ ἦν αὐτῶν ἡ καρδία πεπωρωμένη. The rebukes in the second person plural at 7.18 and 8.17 actually explain the third person at 4.12. Mark has applied the Isaiah oracle to his own generation. In other words, shifting the passage into the first century CE entailed certain alterations. The most natural is the 'externalization' inherent in the change to the third person. The plural becomes a natural change reflecting the crowds (as opposed to 'this people', a collective singular). The curse emphatically does not apply to Mark's Messianic community, and it would be unthinkable that Jesus would direct such an admonition against it. The application to the disciples is part of Mark's overall Secrecy chronology; full realization of Jesus' identity occurs only after the resurrection, and until then they too are under the curse of Isaiah.

Since Isaiah's curse figures prominently in these four passages (4.12; 6.52; 7.18 and 8.17), the text is a key for Mark's theology. This raises the strong possibility that it is used redactionally throughout. Mark's theological intent becomes clearer when the three texts are compared together:

Isa. 6.9-10, LXX

[καὶ εἶπε Πορεύθητι καὶ εἰπὸν τῷ λαῷ τούτῳ] ᾽Ακοῇ ἀκούσετε καὶ οὐ μὴ συνῆτε καὶ βλέποντες βλέψετε καὶ οὐ μὴ ἴδητε [ἐπαχύνθη γὰρ ἡ καρδία τοῦ λαου᾽ τούτου, καὶ τοῖς ὠσὶν αὐτῶν βαρέως ἤκουσαν καὶ τοὺς ὀφθαλμοὺς αὐτῶν ἐκάμμυσαν,] μήποτε [ἴδωσιν τοῖς ὀφθαλμοῖς καὶ τοῖς ὠσὶν ἀκούσωσιν καὶ τῇ καρδίᾳ συνῶσιν καὶ] ἐπιστρέψωσιν καὶ ἰάσομαι αὐτούς.

Mk 4.12

[ἵνα] βλέποντες βλέπωσιν καὶ μὴ ἴδωσιν, καὶ ἀκούοντες
ἀκούωσιν καὶ μὴ συνιῶσιν, μήποτε ἐπιστρέψωσιν καὶ ἀφεθῇ
αὐτοῖς.

Mk 8.17-18

οὔπω νοεῖτε οὐδὲ συνίετε; πεπωρωμένην ἔχετε τὴν καρδίαν ὑμῶν;
ὀφθαλμοὺς ἔχοντες οὐ βλέπετε καὶ ὦτα ἔχοντες οὐκ ἀκούετε.

In both instances Mark's application has 'written out' the same portion
of the text. Both times he reverses the order of 'hearing' and 'seeing',
an agreement against both the Septuagint and the Targum! The order
is in harmony with the injunction at 4.24: βλέπετε τί ἀκούετε. This
is possibly reflected again at 8.17, οὔπω νοεῖτε οὐδὲ συνίετε, since
it is the second element that is specifically tied linguistically in Isaiah
with 'hearing'. The use of participles at 4.12 (βλέποντες,
ἀκούοντες) is also not very telling. The former is present in the
Septuagint and forms the model for the latter. The change in the main
verbs to the subjunctive represents a natural harmonization expressing
purpose with a ἵνα clause.

Mk 11.25 provides a clue to the change of 'heal' to 'forgive'. In an
application of Isaiah to contemporary life this change is natural and
likely to occur independently to a variety of authors.[1] Jesus is our
'spiritual healer' who has authority 'on the earth' to forgive sins.
Mark emphasizes precisely this theme at 2.5b-10. These verses
interrupt the flow of an otherwise complete miracle story and have
good credentials as redaction.[2] In between this text and 4.12 Mark has
placed the tradition about blasphemy and forgiveness of sins.

The place of 4.12 within Mark's Messianic Secret makes Jeremias'
theory of a specific link to the Targum unlikely. His thesis is actually
improbable in a context of 'oral tradition'. First of all there is the
problem of the textual witness to the Targum: we do not possess a

---

1. See Evans' observation that 'forgive' conveys the literal (metaphorical?) intent
of Isaiah's original 'heal'. *To See and not Perceive*, p. 71. A careful study of the
synoptic problem will yield a number of 'minor agreements' of Matthew and Luke
against Mark. While some of these can be due to the common influence of Q, the
two-source theory still must postulate the independent and similar change of Mark by
both authors. On this issue, see B.W. Henaut, 'Is Q but the Invention of Luke and
Mark?', pp. 15-32.

2. See Dewey, 'The Controversy Stories in Mark 2.1–3.6', pp. 109-111;
F.C. Synge, 'Intruded Middles', *ExpTim* 92 (1980–81), pp. 329-33.

first-century copy of this document and cannot be certain that the linguistic parallels actually existed in the text in the time of Jesus. Secondly, the Targum is a written text available to any number of authors: if Mark has not based his tradition upon the Septuagint there is still the possibility of a literary relationship between Mk 4.12 and the written Targum without oral tradition as an intermediary. Jeremias' theory also relies upon precise linguistic agreement between Mark and the Targum in a number of areas. But this kind of precise literal agreement (and stability) most naturally points to a textual medium. The detailed analysis of the oral medium built up over the first two chapters of the present study shows that in oral tradition there can be no 'original form'. Each performance is ever new, and contextually bound to the audience's expectations and reactions. Aside from very limited proverbial sayings, exact reproduction is not the norm. Precise stability in vocabulary, tense and person cannot be expected: these are precisely the details of a tradition that are most subject to alteration during the oral phase. Jeremias' study would also have to show that the Isaiah quote's variation with the Septuagint at 4.12 is significantly different than Mark's use of this source elsewhere. The above examination of the parallels shows the contrary: Mark's use of Isaiah elsewhere leads us to expect precisely the kinds of changes from the Septuagint that we see at 4.12. As Matthew and Luke's redaction of their two sources demonstrate, verbal differences between texts do not necessarily indicate independent traditions.

The same objections, it seems to me, hold regarding the theory that the minor agreements between Matthew and Luke against Mark evidence an independent oral tradition. This theory is advanced by W. Kümmel, who classifies the passage among 'a small number of agreements which can scarcely be depicted as accidental'.[1] But these minor agreements amount to οἱ μαθηταί against Mark 4.10, which is the most natural change for the curious designation of the group; the minor stylistic introduction ὁ δέ (the latter of which is often added by both Matthew and Luke to Mark); the plural τὰ μυστήρια for Mark's singular; and insertion of the infinitive γνῶναι. The plural is a likely change since it implies knowledge of more than one mystery and emphasizes the all-encompassing nature of revelation in Jesus. The insertion of γνῶναι seems most likely due to influence from Mk 4.13,

1. Kümmel, *Introduction*, p. 63. A thesis affirmed by Marcus, *Mysterious Kingdom*, pp. 84-85.

καὶ πῶς πάσας τὰς παραβολὰς <u>γνώσεσθε</u>. Strictly speaking, mysteries and knowledge are known, rather than possessed directly. A theory of oral traditional influence to account for these minor agreements again brings us into a model based upon a fixed memorized text. As the above discussion has made abundantly clear, this kind of fixed text does not even exist in the manuscript traditions of the Gospels, let alone the oral phase of transmission. There is therefore no compelling grounds to support a reconstruction of oral tradition at v. 12, and the verse is best assigned to the evangelist.[1]

5. *Other Editorial Links*

The above discussion has established Mk 4.10-13, 33-34 as redactional. Before proceeding to a discussion of the viability of oral tradition behind the remaining texts it is useful to establish Mark's other editorial links. This will allow me to isolate the chapter's component parts for analysis for tradition.

a. *καὶ ἔλεγεν [αὐτοῖς]*

The Markan connecting link introducing discourse καὶ ἔλεγεν αὐτοῖς has been noted at vv. 11a and 13a. Its duplication within the parable chapter at vv. 21a, 24a, and its use to start the next form-critical unit at v. 35 proves that the placement of 21b-23, 24b-25 are Mark's.[2] Whatever the origins of these aphorisms, they have been placed in their present location by Mark and not the tradition. They now serve as commentary upon the secrecy theme presenting the essential flip-side of vv. 10-12. Just as the commands to silence by Jesus have as their counterpart repeated disobedience and the proclamation of his fame far and wide, so too the secret of Jesus' identity cannot forever be hidden. In conjunction with the transfiguration, Mark's chronology is apparent. Only after the resurrection will Jesus' true identity be openly proclaimed by the Markan community. The sayings, then, in their present locale, are thoroughly christological in intent.

The remaining word link with the absence of the pronoun, καὶ ἔλεγεν, at vv. 9, 26 and 30 is more controversial. Mark's habitual practice is to include the pronoun when introducing a new unit of

---

1. As originally recognized by Bultmann, *History*, pp. 199, 325 (n. 1), 421.

2. Best, 'Mark's Preservation', p. 126 believes that v. 24a possibly belongs to Mark's redaction.

discourse. Its absence is rare, although parallels are to be found elsewhere in the Gospel. At 5.7, the demoniac's speech is introduced without a pronoun (καὶ κράξας φωνῇ μεγάλῃ λέγει); while Jesus' question to the disciples concerning being touched is similarly introduced (ἔλεγεν, Τίς μου ἥψατο—5.30). Other instances can also be found (5.31; 6.24, 35; 7.20; 8.5, 12, 24, 33; 9.21, 24, 39; 10.4, 27, 29, 49; 12.24, 38; 14.6, 18, 62, 67; 15.35). Perhaps the most significant is 7.20. Jesus is again in the house and has been asked by the disciples for an explanation of his public teaching (7.17). Mark introduces his reply at v. 18 with the standard καὶ λέγει αὐτοῖς. Verse 20 continues Jesus' discourse, introducing a 'new' saying with the phrase ἔλεγεν δὲ ὅτι. The introduction, as at 4.26, 30, is totally superfluous. The reader already knows that Jesus is speaking. What makes the instances in ch. 4 significant is the fact that twice the phrase introduces a narrative parable, while Mark has broken the string of three with his more habitual introduction at vv. 11, 13, 21, and 24. The use of this phrase three times within such a short space is unparalleled, and the symmetry of use particularly at vv. 26 and 30 raises the possibility of Mark having copied a prior tradition. If so, this tradition would have to be considered a *written* source: an oral tradition would lend itself to habitual expression more easily than a written text, although even the latter could easily be altered to include the pronoun. This leaves two possibilities: either the verses testify to written tradition, or Mark, for whatever reason, has altered his usual style in an unprecedented manner in accord with the parallel at 7.20.

b. *ἀκούετε, 4.3a, 24*
The prominence given the theme of hearing in the Isaiah quote at v. 13 and the sermon's conclusion at v. 33 testify to the centrality of this motif in Mark's formulation of the parable chapter. The imperative at v. 3a, ἀκούετε, which introduces the parable of the Sower can be reasonably established as Mark's. The verb is regarded as redactional vocabulary by Pryke, who believes 30 of the 43 occurrences are the evangelist's.[1] When we compare the similarity of this injunction to those involving βλέπω we can also establish verse 24b βλέπετε τί ἀκούετε as Mark's.[2]

1. Pryke, *Redactional*, p. 136.
2. Pesch, *Markusevangelium*, I, p. 252 sees βλέπετε and ἀκούετε as Markan, noting 13.5, 9, 23, 33. See also Mk 4.24; 8.15; 12.38; cp. at 5.31; 8.18, 24; 12.14;

This leaves the injunction ὃς ἔχει ὦτα ἀκούειν ἀκουέτω at v. 9 and its parallel εἴ τις ἔχει ὦτα ἀκούειν ἀκουέτω at v. 23. The saying is a popular one, found also at Mt. 11.15; 13.9, 43; Lk. 8.8; 14.35; and Rev. 2.7, 11, 29; 3.6, 13, 22. Of these, Mt. 11.15 comes in the middle of a Q passage without a parallel in Luke, hence it is likely Matthew's redaction underscoring the identification of John and Elijah. Mt. 13.9 is the direct parallel of Mk 4.9, while 13.43 is after the interpretation of the Wheat and the Weeds parable; hence it too is likely a redactional addition based on the model of Mk 4.9, 23. Lk. 8.8 is parallel to Mk 4.9. Lk. 14.35 occurs in a Q context and hence may represent a Q conclusion to the salt saying. The instances in Revelation are used systematically to add dramatic effect to the letters to the various churches. The addition of the same verse in some manuscripts at Mk 7.16 testifies to its popularity as a tool for dramatic emphasis. Given Mark's redactional concern with hearing in the chapter it is likely that at least the inclusion at 4.23 is his.[1] Verse 9 is another matter. The introduction there is one of the three without the pronoun. It is possible that Mark found this saying in a written source after the Sower and before the parables of the Seed Growing Secretly and the Mustard Seed.

This establishes as possibly traditional the following units for further investigation: the parables of the Sower (4.3-8); the Seed Growing Secretly (4.26-29), the Mustard Seed (4.30-32), the allegorical interpretation of the Sower (4.14-20), the four aphorisms (4.21-22, 24-25) and the injunction on hearing (4.9). I will examine claims for the orality of these sayings in the next three chapters.

6. Conclusion: Textuality as a Barrier to Orality

This discussion has not only revealed all of Mk 4.1-2, 10-13, 33-34, to be the work of the evangelist, it has shown how intimately each of these verses are integrated into the Gospel's overall structure. Far from revealing an inconsistent redaction easily dismembered and stratified into component parts, Mark has stamped the chapter as his

13.2.

1. Best, 'Mark's Preservation', p. 126 believes v. 23 to be 'probably' Markan. Pesch, *Markusevangelium*, I, p. 250 argues that the construction of v. 23 is more elegent Greek, while v. 9 betrays more Semitic influence. He is followed by Marcus, *Mystery*, p. 137 who concludes that v. 23 is Mark's.

own throughout. Mark's hand is present not only in the literary expression of key vocabulary and syntax, but also in the theological unity of the passage. Far from being a disconnected section, the parable sermon is intimately bound up with almost every other major section of the Gospel. Mark has not confined his redaction to a few connecting phrases in between inherited blocks of tradition that he has left relatively untouched. Rather, Mark has not hesitated at every point to make his influence felt upon the tradition.

This fact of textuality serves as the first barrier to recovery of any oral tradition. As Kelber has noted, the possibility exists that an oral unit could become so textualized as to be unrecognizable. Kelber, following Bultmann, thought that we had been spared this unpleasantness, although he advanced a different explanation for this fortuitous turn. Mark's oral syntax, he asserted, shows that this has not happened. However, as my examination proves, Mark's oral syntax upon closer inspection turns out to be his habitual mode of textual expression and cannot serve as a direct route to the recovery of previous oral units.

This layer of textuality serves as a serious barrier to recovery of the oral tradition because the critical tools are often lacking to guide us in its 'removal'. The 'original' form of Mark in Matthew and Luke can be recovered because a copy exists to verify the redaction. With Q, one can at least compare and contrast the two versions, and attempt to adjudicate (where differences exist) which text is more likely due to redactional tendencies as seen elsewhere.

But what to do when the source is lost and one has not got two independent textual incorporations of the tradition? With what kind of certainty could one reconstruct the original Markan or Q text if one only had Matthew or Luke to work with? Or again, without Mark, what is to be made of all the common traditions found in Matthew and Luke? These questions are more than interesting exercises of the imagination: they are at the heart of the ability to recover orality. One is often precisely in this situation: any source at Mk 4.1-34 for prior tradition is now lost. One has Mark's text, and can discern his redactional shaping of the material, but there is very little to go on to indicate the prior redactional tendencies of his immediate sources, oral or written. These issues will be explored further in my examination of the three Seed parables, the Interpretation of the Sower, and the Markan aphorisms.

Chapter 4

ALLEGORY AND ORALITY: THE PARABLE OF THE SOWER
AND ITS INTERPRETATION

The interpretation of the Sower (Mk 4.14-20) and its relationship to
the parable is hotly debated. Beginning with Jülicher's distinction
between 'parable' and 'allegory', the verses became suspect as historical Jesus tradition. This distinction was simple but profound. Only
with an interpretive key do the various elements in the allegorical
narrative make sense. In contrast, a parable is a vivid and simple
picture with a self-evident meaning.[1] Despite controversy Jülicher's
fundamental insight has held up. Few contemporary critics accept
anything cast in an allegorical form as an authentic saying of Jesus.

We have already seen the distinction at work in the previous
discussion. Mark's presentation of the 'parabolic teaching' as 'riddles'
could not be accepted by most scholars as representing the *Sitz im
Leben* of Jesus. Basing themselves on Jülicher, the consensus of scholars is summed up well by Perrin:

> [H]istorically speaking, Jesus seems to have been one who was heard
> gladly and understood readily; the idea that his parables are esoteric and

1. Jülicher, *Die Gleichnisreden Jesu*. See the discussion by N. Perrin, *Jesus and
the Language of the Kingdom: Symbol and Metaphor in New Testament
Interpretation* (Philadelphia: Fortress Press, 1976), p. 92. I have always found an
interesting parallel in the comments of J.R.R. Tolkien. In responding to interpreters
who saw in *The Lord of the Rings* an intricate allegory for the Second World War,
Tolkien asserted that the work was 'neither allegorical nor topical'. 'I cordially
dislike allegory in all its manifestations, and always have done so since I grew old
and wary enough to detect its presence. I much prefer history, true or feigned, with
its varied applicability to the thought and experience of readers. I think that many
confuse "applicability" with "allegory"; but the one resides in the freedom of the
reader, and the other in the purposed domination of the author.' *The Fellowship of
the Ring, Being the First Part of The Lord of the Rings* (London: Methuen, 2nd edn,
1966), pp. 2-3 of 'Foreword'.

mysterious, needing a key to be understood, is foreign to everything we know about him. His parables are vivid, simple pictures, taken from real life.[1]

Jülicher's clear-cut distinction soon came to 'wear thin', but Gospel critics have always maintained a distinction between the two forms. The 'New Heremeneutic' as represented by Ernst Fuchs, Eta Linnemann and Eberhard Jüngel soon interpreted parable as a 'language event'. Robert Funk and Amos Wilder afterwards linked parable more closely with metaphor, and Dominic Crossan went on to propound parable as an 'anti-myth' that shatters the hearer's normal myth-established expectations.[2] Throughout the discussion there has been a constant confidence that the distinction between the two forms allows for recovery of the original and authentic parable. As set forth by Jeremias, and subsequently adopted by others, the oral transmission of the parables followed rules that one can reconstruct. Allegorization was the first process of interpretation, either in a separate narrative (cp. Mk 4.14-20) or in the details of the parable itself (cp. Mt. 22.2-13). Moralizing conclusions could also be added (cp. the Unjust Steward, Lk. 16.1-9), or the parable could be provided with a secondary context (cp. the Good Samaritan, Lk. 10.25-37).[3] Despite this process of reinterpretation, scholars have remained confident in reconstructing the original oral form of the parable. As Perrin expresses it, the parables are so distinctive —

> that in broad structural outline they have survived the subsequent process of transmission very well, while, at the same time, the process of reinter-pretation was so obvious and so much at variance with the original thrust of the parables themselves, that the original form and thrust of the para-bles have not proven difficult to reconstruct.[4]

Distinction of literary form was expanded to conform with the criterion of authenticity, that of the 'distinctiveness' of Jesus' use of the parable with that of both contemporary Judaism and the early church. As Jeremias expresses it, 'Jesus' parables are something

1. Perrin, *Jesus and the Language of the Kingdom*, p. 93.
2. See the discussion in Perrin, *Jesus and the Language of the Kingdom*, pp. 107-68. J.D. Crossan, *The Dark Interval: Towards a Theology of Story* (Niles, IL: Argus Communications, 1975), pp. 49-62.
3. See Perrin, *Jesus and the Language of the Kingdom*, pp. 101-02; Jeremias, *Parables*, pp. 11-22.
4. Perrin, *Jesus and the Language of the Kingdom*, p. 3.

entirely new. In all the rabbinic literature, not one single parable has come down to us from the period before Jesus.'[1] The rabbinic parables, it is well known, are usually set in an exegetical context. As David Stern expresses it, the 'Rabbis themselves believed that the mashal had been created for the purposes of exegesis, the study of Torah'. This connection to scriptural exegesis is so clear, Stern continues, that in 'the case of virtually every mashal, it is not difficult to see that the exegesis the mashal supposedly was created to convey must actually have preceded the composition of the mashal'.[2] A contrast is often claimed with the parables of Jesus. Scott, for one, points out that they lack a direct referent to Scripture. Building on Crossan's hermeneutical understanding of parable, Scott notes that most 'common metaphors are epiphoric: the associations are bearers of the implied symbolic meaning. But in the Jesus tradition, the relation is frequently diaphoric: Jesus' discourse changes or challenges the implied structural network of associations.'[3] The implication of this is plain: the rabbinic parables function in a mythic way to establish and reinforce the common shared assumptions of the biblical tradition. Jesus' parables are an 'anti-myth' which shatters the hearer's expectations that have been derived from the biblical myth. Scott also plays off the distinction between collective voice (e.g. proverb) and individual voice (e.g. aphorism) to assert the distinctiveness of the Jesus tradition:

> The most important characteristic of this distinctive voice is[,] to borrow a musical metaphor, a tendency to play in minor keys. Employing traditional stories and plots and stereotyped characterizations, the parables invoke not the major themes of the tradition but its minor ones. The most obvious example of a minor key, although not usually noticed as one, is found in the fact that the presiding symbol of Jesus' language is the kingdom of God, a relatively infrequent term in the first century. The more dominant themes such as those of the day of the Lord, or of God as king, or even of the Torah, are virtually suppressed in the Jesus parables.[4]

This methodology allows scholars to ascribe tradition to Jesus. The non-allegorical form of the parable, coupled with distinctiveness, meets the 'burden of proof' that orality establishes against

---

1. Jeremias, *Parables*, p. 12.
2. Stern, 'The Rabbinic Parable', pp. 632-33, 634.
3. Scott, *Hear then the Parable*, pp. 48, 54, 61.
4. Scott, *Hear then the Parable*, p. 66.

authenticity. This set of assumptions will primarily concern me over
the next two chapters. In contrast to the confidence exhibited by most
scholars, the subsequent examination will establish that recovery of
the oral form of parables is a hopelessly difficult task. The ability to
remove secondary allegorical features gives a false sense of security.
It is by no means clear that the 'process of reinterpretation' subjected
to the parables was confined to the elements enumerated by Jeremias.
'Distinctiveness', on the other hand, like beauty, is almost always in
the eye of the exegete.

I begin an examination of these issues with the allegorical interpretation of the Sower (Mk 4.14-20). It serves as the entry point into the
problem of allegory and orality. Dodd and Jeremias have provided the
linguistic evidence that establishes the unit's origin in the missionary
preaching of the Hellenistic church. Although this thesis is generally
held today, it was not universally accepted earlier. Two dissenting
opinions warrant attention: those of B. Gerhardsson and C.F.D.
Moule. I will examine these studies in turn, paying particular attention
to Gerhardsson's attempt to situate the traditions in his 'Memory and
Manuscript' theory. This analysis will help clarify the model of
orality in early Christianity.

It is helpful first to outline the 'proof' of the interpretation's secondary character. Within vv. 11-20, Dodd notes the following terms
which occur nowhere else within the synoptics: οἱ ἔξω; τὸ μυστήριον
(both in v. 11); πρόσκαιρος (v. 17); and ἀπάτη (v. 19). The term
ἐπιθυμίαι (v. 19) occurs within the synoptics only at Lk. 22.15
where it is used in a different sense. Since this verse is Luke's unique
introduction to the Lord's supper, it is likely redactional. Likewise,
θλίψεως and διωγμοῦ (v. 17) occur only at Mk 10.30 and within the
synoptic apocalypse. These passages likely do not reflect authentic
material about Jesus' life. A similar theme can be found, for example,
in *4 Ezra* 8.41.[1]

Jeremias adds ῥίζαν (v. 17); πρόσκαιρος (v. 17); ἡ ἀπάτη τοῦ
πλούτου (v. 19); αἱ μέριμναι (v. 19); and καρποφοροῦσιν
(v. 20). There is also ὁ λόγος used as an absolute to refer to 'the
Gospel', a usage incompatible with Jesus. Jeremias objects that the
interpretation of 'sowing' as preaching is not characteristic of Jesus,
who prefers to compare preaching with the gathering of the harvest.

1. Dodd, *The Parables of the Kingdom*, p. 15.

The interpretation misses the eschatological point of the parable and transfers the emphasis to a psychological exhortation to converts to examine themselves and test their sincerity. Finally, the lack of the allegorical interpretation in Thomas confirms its secondary character.[1]

1. *Birger Gerhardsson*

Gerhardsson finds in the Sower and its interpretation confirmation of his 'Memory and Manuscript' theory. He is aware that most exegetes, on the basis of language and form, regard vv. 13-20 as inauthentic. But the objection that the interpretation allegorizes the parable has lost much of its force since Jülicher's thesis of one point to a parable has become untenable. He finds its essential unity with the parable in the *Shema'*. Jesus, in rabbinic fashion, created both parable and interpretation as a commentary on this prayer. The unit's pedagogical form and mnemonic patterning assure us that both originated with Jesus and have been faithfully transmitted by the oral tradition. Its form is most clearly preserved in Matthew's Gospel, and differences in the Markan form are due to the evangelist's 'misunderstanding'. Its widespread dissemination, furthermore, is shown by its preservation in Q, and this latter witness to the unit helps in the reconstruction of the original.[2] I will examine these points in detail.

a. *Matthew and the* Shema'
The Sower's fundamental importance and link with the secret of Jesus' proclamation of the reign of God is shown for Gerhardsson by the phrase 'If you do not understand this parable'. That all three evangelists report Jesus narrating and expounding this parable deserves attention. Significant also is their agreement that all four parts of the

---

1. Jeremias, *Parables*, pp. 77-79. The shift in emphasis between parable and interpretation is noted by Kuhn, *Ältere Sammlungen*, p. 114. He notes that there is almost twice as many words in the interpretation compared to the parable dealing with the failure of the seed, while parable and interpretation are about equal in the number of words devoted to the successful seed. See also H.-J. Klauck, *Allegorie und Allegoresse in synoptischen Gleichnistexten* (NTAbh, 13; Münster: Aschendorff, 1978), pp. 186-87, who notes the Semitisms in the parable that contrast to the fact that some idioms in the interpretation are possible only in Greek.

2. B. Gerhardsson, 'The Parable of the Sower and Its Interpretation', *NTS* 14 (1967–68), pp. 165-66.

parable are about hearing; these 'twelve ἀκούειν, like twelve signals, must be accorded the attention they deserve'.[1] The interpretation's emphasis upon the duty to listen takes us to the centre of covenant ideology, since these obligations emphatically involve the duty to hear God's word. Although Matthew wrote after Mark, his interpretation of the parable most clearly preserves the original.[2]

Fundamental to the text is the *Shema'*—which emphasizes the duty to hear, learn and live according God's word.[3] That Jesus regarded the *Shema'* as the first and greatest of all the commandments is shown by Mk 12.28-34.[4] Its basic form may be set forth:

> Hear O Israel: the Lord our God, the Lord is one; you shall love the Lord your God with all your heart, and with all your soul and with all your might.[5]

According to the scribes the phrase 'your whole heart' commanded rule over every evil inclination (including the lust for food, drink, reproduction and sensual pleasures); 'your whole soul' included the duty of martyrdom (the forfeiture of one's soul); while 'your whole might' included all one's mammon (i.e., the longing for property and riches must not replace or reduce one's love for God).

For Gerhardsson, the context makes clear the connection between the Sower (and its interpretation) and the scribal exegesis of the *Shema'*. Although Matthew's omission of Mark's κατὰ μόνας (Mt. 13.10) could be an editorial lapse, it possibly corresponds to reality. Jesus may have taught the disciples in a lowered voice according to the practice of rabbinic literature.[6] This establishes a contrast between the spiritually inert crowds and the inquiring disciples. Jesus speaks to the crowds only in parables (as per vv. 10-17) since it has not been given to them to have an insight into the secrets of God's reign. This is an

1. Gerhardsson, 'Parable', p. 166.
2. Gerhardsson, 'Parable', p. 166.
3. The *Shema'* consists of Deut. 6.4-9; 11.13-21; and Num. 15.37-41.
4. Gerhardsson, 'Parable', p. 169. Mk 12.28-34 does not allow us to see whether each element of the *Shema'* has been carefully considered and interpreted, according to Gerhardsson. The Temptation narrative in Q, however, follows the pattern: 1) evil inclination of heart; 2) place self in danger and test God to save one's soul; 3) offer of all the mammon in the world. 'Parable', pp. 170-71.
5. I have adapted the translation from Mk 12.28-34.
6. In rabbinic literature there is a rule that secrets be taught in a whisper, Gerhardsson, 'Parable', p. 173

application of 'To whom has, more is given', a motif in the Jewish wisdom tradition and the Rabbis (e.g. Prov. 1.5; 9.9; Mek. Vayassa I. 148-85).[1]

Matthew particularly has a pedagogical tone to the Sower: the parable is treated as a familiar pericope with a name. 'The interpretation has a tendency to define and a uniformity of style with symmetrical and repetitive phrases: all of which formal characteristics are typical of rabbinic pedagogics'.[2] Hence Matthew is describing four individual cases which are types, a point reinforced by the fourfold use of the same aorist participle (ὁ σπαρείς).[3] This conforms with the rabbinic tendency to exact repetition.[4]

The interpretation presents *the* four types of listeners. Only with regard to those on the path does Matthew mention the heart. This first type of hearer is linked with the crowd since the fate of the seed depends on whether the heart fulfils its spiritual role. The reference is to a people whose heart is hardened and who do not understand. This 'seed' represents people who disobey the *Shema'* which commands love of God with all of one's heart.[5]

Similarly, the seed on stony ground represents hearers who will not undergo suffering or martyrdom. The most revealing phrase is θλίψεως ἢ διωγμοῦ διὰ τὸν λόγον, while the term πρόσκαιρος has connections with Jewish and early Christian martyrdom texts.[6] This motif, then, parallels the rabbinic interpretation of the *Shema'* to love the Lord 'even if he takes your soul'.

The seed sown among thorns is linked to πλοῦτος, paralleling the scribes' interpretation that might equals mammon. These hearers have failed to love the Lord with all their 'might' or 'mammon'.[7]

The successful sowing again shows the importance of understanding. Mark's vague expression 'receive the word' has been sharpened in

1. Gerhardsson, 'Parable', pp. 173-74.
2. Gerhardsson, 'Parable', p. 175.
3. Gerhardsson is pointing to the strict uniformity of Matthew's introductions within his interpretation of the Sower. This uniformity contrasts to the Markan parallels.
4. Gerhardsson, 'Parable', p. 175.
5. Gerhardsson, 'Parable', pp. 175-76.
6. That is, the choice between τὰ πρόσκαιρα and τὰ αἰώνια. See *4 Macc.* 15.2, 8, 23; 2 Cor. 4.17-18; Heb. 11.25; Diogn.10.8.
7. Gerhardsson, 'Parable', pp. 176-77. Gerhardsson provides an impressive list of parallels for the interpretation's imagery. See 'Parable', p. 177, n. 1.

Matthew to 'understand'. Hearing and understanding become an event. The phrase 'to bear fruit' is a traditional image for an active loyalty to the covenant, a righteousness shown in life and deed. It is a manner of speech found in the words of Jesus.[1] Similarly, the hundredfold yield is a traditional formula. Isaac had just such a yield because Yahweh blessed him (Gen. 26.12). Thus the parallel to the *Shema'* is clear:

> There is no doubt that the man of the good ground is here depicted as the one who fulfils the covenant obligations, living wholly according to the words of the first and greatest command of the law, '*Hear* O Israel, JHWH our God, JHWH is one. And you shall *love* JHWH your God with you whole *heart* and with your whole *soul* and with your whole *might* (riches, property).'[2]

For Matthew the good ground represents the disciples. In Matthew's parable chapter there are two direct quotations from the prophets (Isa. 6.9-10) and the writings (Ps. 78.2). But a far more important role is played by the crucial passage from 'the Law'.[3] This balancing and fullness of sources strengthens for Gerhardsson the connection of the parable with the *Shema'*.

b. *The Parable in Mark and Luke*
Gerhardsson's examination of the parable in Mark and Luke shows the primacy of Matthew's tradition and establishes its inclusion in Q. Despite the two-source theory the Markan form is secondary. It is an important component of Gerhardsson's study since it reverses the expectation that one begin with Mark.

Mark's introduction καὶ ἔλεγεν αὐτοῖς suggests a collection of logia similar to Thomas.[4] The setting presupposes a concrete historical situation. Even in the parable itself the theme of hearing is emphasized as seen in the opening injunction 'Hear', (v. 3a) and the concluding exhortation (v. 9).[5]

Mark, Gerhardsson argues, has not understood the finer points of the unsuccessful sowing, nor has he seen what distinguishes the three

---

1. In Matthew: To make fruit (of trees) at 3.10; 7.17-19; 12.33. Of seeds, 13.26. Of persons, 3.8; 13.23; 21.43. Of fruit/words, 7.16, 20. To do Father's will, Jesus' will, 7.21; 12.50; 21.31. Gerhardsson, 'Parable', p. 178.
2. Gerhardsson, 'Parable', p. 178.
3. Gerhardsson, 'Parable', p. 179.
4. At Mk 4.2, 9, 11, (13), 21, 24, 26, and 30.
5. Gerhardsson, 'Parable', p. 180.

groups. He lacks the key term 'heart' which is found in Matthew and
Luke. The failure of the sowing is not due to human deficiency but the
result of the devil's activity. Hence 'Mark has lost one of the important moments of the parable, that the seed fell *on the path*' and 'it must
be evident that this is only a secondary distortion of an interpretation
that was originally more adequate (cf. Matthew)'.[1] Further evidence
of Mark's 'misunderstanding' is seen in his use of the formula αἱ
περί... ἐπιθυμίαι with respect to lust or desire when it is usually
associated with the heart. 'The fact that Mark has not hesitated to use
this formula can be taken as a further indication that he had not
understood the scribal pattern lying behind the division into three
groups of hearers.'[2]

Gerhardsson notes that Luke agrees with Matthew in linking the
heart with the path, but Luke's interpretation ignores this. The agreements between Matthew and Luke (cp. Mark) proves the parable's
inclusion in Q.[3]

Gerhardsson rejects Jeremias' contention that the interpretation
misses the point of the parable. He argues that the successful sowing
does not concern the hour of the harvest but rather emphasizes seed
that bears abundant fruit. Nor have the details of unsuccessful sowing
been freely selected: the motif of rain, for example, is missing. The
factors in the parable affecting the fate of the seed have been chosen
according to a system, while the birds, sun and thorns have only a
destructive effect. The type of ground is primary. Since it is
uncommon for a field in Galilee to contain so many different types of
soil, Gerhardsson concludes that the parable 'does not offer a purely
natural and unforced agricultural illustration'.[4] He even argues that
the failures could be placed in a different order, mathematics alone
arguing that five other orders are possible! Thus, '[w]e must take
seriously the fact that the parable and the interpretation fit each other
as hand to glove' and that the order has been determined by the scribal
interpretation of the *Shema*'.[5] The primary entity is not the parable,
but the fourfold interpretation. It teaches that when God's word is

1. Gerhardsson, 'Parable', p. 181.
2. Gerhardsson, 'Parable', pp. 181-82.
3. Gerhardsson, 'Parable', pp. 184-85. These minor agreements will be
discussed below, section 3, c.
4. Gerhardsson, 'Parable', p. 187.
5. Gerhardsson, 'Parable', p. 187.

spoken it comes in vain to those who do not love God with their whole
heart, soul and might. This is expressed openly in the interpretation,
but in a veiled manner within the parable. Thus the parable does not
instruct openly; rather its theme is presented in a veiled form. The
parable intends not one point but a complex and concentrated didache.
The parable, Gerhardsson insists, was 'created to be *memorized* and
meditated upon' by an author who '*repeated* it for his hearers many
times'.[1]

c. *The Section's Unity*
In this view, the entire section of the Gospel is more consistent and
interdependent than is usually thought. The general theme is that the
secrets of the reign of God are given to those who have, but not to
those who have not. Jesus' use of imagery should have been readily
understandable to those with 'open ears' in the synagogue. *4 Ezra*
9.29-33 speaks of God sowing his law, bring forth fruit in Israel. The
metaphor of 'sow' as 'teaching' is very common for the time.[2]

Only in Mark is the intent to prevent salvation. Mark and Luke also
present two metaphors that suggest that the intentional mystification is
temporary: a light cannot remain under a bushel, and nothing is
hidden forever. Thus interpreted, 'this whole section of the gospel
appears to be more consistent and interdependent than it is usually
thought to be'. This is true—despite formal unevenness—Gerhardsson
asserts, even in the Markan version.[3]

Why then do the parable and interpretation differ so greatly
linguistically? Because they have been handed down in different ways,
'the former as a fixed text to be learnt by heart, the latter as a
commentary whose actual verbal formulation was more fluid'.
Furthermore, the interpretation must employ a technical terminology
since it is an exposition. It teaches about teaching, and the subject
involves a certain terminology and a definite set of concepts. Even in
Deuteronomy the term 'the word' (הדבר) is used absolutely to desig-
nate the covenant instruction. Since the Hebrew Scriptures and late
Jewish literature employ a didactic tradition upon which the early

1. Gerhardsson, 'Parable', p. 188.
2. Gerhardsson, 'Parable', p. 189 points to Cave's observation that the Hiph'il
form of ירה 'cast', 'shoot' was used both of sowing and teaching. C.H. Cave, 'The
Parables and the Scriptures' *NTS* 11 (1964–65), pp. 374-87.
3. Gerhardsson, 'Parable', p. 190.

church could draw, Gerhardsson sees no reason why Jesus could not have done the same.[1]

2. *C.F.D. Moule*

Setting out to attack a deeply entrenched exegesis of Mk 4.1-20, C.F.D. Moule enthusiastically supported Gerhardsson's thesis. Moule provides further argumentation against the Dodd–Jeremias position, and attempts to demonstrate the unity of parable and interpretation. Both deserve consideration as authentic life of Jesus material. This study, then, complements and enhances the other, and both contain an implicit view of orality that warrants our attention.

The usual distinction between parable and allegory lacks validity for Moule. He likens a parable to a modern political cartoon which presents an interpretive analogy that the viewer must decipher. The usual harsh predestinarian reading of Mark is unwarranted since v. 10 refers not to a determinate number (i.e., his disciples as in v. 34) but to a chance gathering.[2] 'Parable' does not refer to an esoteric utterance designed to conceal secret truths, but rather to a provocative teaching form. Mark does not keep the two groups permanently separate; at 8.17, 21 he applies the Isaiah curse to the Twelve, and it may transpire that those who were at first unresponsive might next time understand.[3]

The verbal tense ὅτε ἐγένετο (v. 10) deserves attention. Although there is no evidence within Mark for the usage 'whenever he was', the phrase could be combined with true imperfects at 'they used to ask. . . and he used to say'. This would give an iterative sense for the verse as a whole.[4]

Moule questions the assumed secondary character of allegory. The description of the various soils in the parable must serve some purpose. If, as v. 13 suggests, this parable is about how parables are received, then the interpretation can be seen as 'extremely natural and unstrained'. Rejecting the insistence upon 'one point', Moule calls the

---

1. Gerhardsson, 'Parable', p. 191.
2. C.F.D. Moule, 'Mark 4.1-20 Yet Once More', in *Neotestamentica et Semitica: Studies in Honour of Matthew Black* (ed. E.E. Ellis and M. Wilcox; Edinburgh: T. & T. Clark, 1969), pp. 95-98.
3. Moule, 'Mark 4.1-20 Yet Once More', p. 99.
4. Moule, 'Mark 4.1-20 Yet Once More', p. 102.

Sower a 'multiple parable' that describes the natural hazards of the seed. The interpretation only makes explicit what the parable implicitly suggests.[1]

Moule also asserts that the parable is not about the harvest but the various receptions for the seed. Regarding the vocabulary, Moule believes that we should examine not only where else these words occur but whether they are out of keeping with Jesus' historical situation. Even in vv. 10-20 every word can be translated into Aramaic and represents an idea contemporary with the time of Jesus. These words occur only here within the synoptics because this is the only appropriate context. The themes 'mystery', 'outsiders', 'time-servers', 'deceit', 'lust', 'persecution' and 'distress' are all found in the Hebrew Bible. Regarding the confusion between the seed and soil, Moule points to Col. 1.6, 10 which shares this imprecision.[2] Since Moule dates Colossians earlier than Mark, the interpretation could very well stem from Jesus as far as substance. Thus, if vv.10-12 are seen as a generalizing statement, then the entire section (Mk 4.1-20) 'becomes an intelligible whole, composed by the Evangelist but with a historically sensitive use of genuinely traditional material'.[3]

Linguistically and form-critically, therefore, Moule finds no evidence for the secondary character of Mk 4.13-20. Like Gerhardsson, he sees in the section a unified whole that has strong credentials as authentic life of Jesus material.

3. *Critique of Gerhardsson and Moule*

The errors in these reconstructions show how one's model of orality generates self-fulfilling evidence. Examination of their failings reveals a number of principles necessary to construct a more reliable model. And without a proper framework, it is impossible to recover oral antecedents to the written Gospel text.

a. *Origin in Pure Forms*
Similar to Bultmann, Gerhardsson believes that tradition originates in 'pure' forms and degenerates during transmission. A text that fails to display this 'pure' archetype must be secondary. This lies behind the

1. Moule, 'Mark.4.1-20 Yet Once More', p. 109.
2. Col. 1.6 refers to the Gospel, while 1.10 refers to believers.
3. Moule, 'Mark 4.1-20 Yet Once More', pp. 111-13.

reversal of Markan priority for the Sower and its interpretation: Mark's failure to parallel the schema (path = heart; rocks = martyrdom/soul; thorns = mammon/might) shows that he has 'misunderstood' and 'corrupted' a more original version. But only textuality allows for ever-greater complexity and fullness of structural integration. Far from being a sign of orality, Gerhardsson's schema needs to be examined in the context of Matthew's redaction![1]

Gerhardsson's linkage of the parable to the *Shema'* likewise requires examination. He justifies this linkage, in part, on the basis of texts such as Mk 12.28-34. The argument is circular because it assumes the authenticity of this latter text. Commentary on the Hebrew Bible is pushed back through the oral phase into Jesus' life even though this material was available to the early church.[2]

Even in Matthew the neat paralleling of the *Shema'* contains problems. There is not, for example, explicit mention of death or martyrdom within the rocky soil. Rather, in the face of affliction and persecution, these hearers are 'scandalized' and fall away. More significant is the equation of the hearers from the 'thorny' ground with those who fail to love God with all their mammon. According to Matthew, in this case ἡ μέριμνα τοῦ αἰῶνος καὶ ἡ ἀπάτη τοῦ πλούτου συμπνίγει τὸν λόγον (Mt. 13.22). Gerhardsson reads this phrase in synonymous parallelism and treats the two halves as interchangeable. There is no reason why the two entities might not be similar but slightly distinct groups, each a half of the same genus of people distinct from those scandalized by persecution at v. 21. The cares of the world might not simply be 'love of money'. Gluttony, drink, lust, power, ambition, vanity, fame or any number of failings might equally be in view, even in Matthew. More importantly, Gerhardsson's link to the *Shema'* is dealt a severe blow when Mark is taken as the primary text. Mark not only lacks the key term 'heart' at the critical spot, but also has misplaced 'desires'. At best, Gerhardsson's thesis might provide a key to Matthew's treatment of the tradition, but it does not get us closer to the 'historical Jesus'.

---

1. Matthew in particular presents Jesus as a teacher of the new law. Gerhardsson has failed to examine the passage within the wider context and in light of redaction criticism.

2. The problems in this out-dated approach have been discussed above, see Chapter 1, section 2, d, f; 1, section 3.

Gerhardsson's conclusion that the fourfold interpretation is primary and his emphasis that these details have not been freely selected is instructive. Certainly five other orders of failure are possible, but the structure implies synchronic ordering. The seed progressively lasts longer but only the good seed survives long enough to come to harvest. Nor need we be surprised at the absence of other 'natural' motifs in the parable to explain the failure of the seed. Gerhardsson notes the lack of rain; but one could just as easily point to similar 'omissions' within any of the parables.[1] Similar is his observation that it is not common for a field in Galilee to contain so many different soils, and Moule's objection that they must serve some purpose.[2] Of course the multiplicity of soils must have some purpose, but this need not be the allegorical interpretation. The 'law of three' pattern in folk tales and written literature has any number of uses. Repetition might simply deepen the sense of disappointment and 'failure' in order to prepare better for the reversal in the harvest. It also 'stretches out' the tale, preventing a too-quick resolution of the dramatic tension.

That interpretation and parable fit together so well need not evidence unitary origin. It simply implies a particularly well-crafted secondary allegory. As we shall see, parable and interpretation fit together so well because the parable itself has been redacted to accommodate its interpretation (note vv. 5b, 6a, 7c, 8b). Although Jülicher's insistence on one-point-per-parable has broken down, the distinction between the two genres of parable (Mk 4.3-8) and allegory (Mk 4.14-20) has held in Gospel criticism.

'Purity of form' is no guarantee of orality, nor is it a sure guide to the earliest version. In each instance the tradition must be extensively evaluated in terms of the literary and redactional characteristics of the document in which we find it. This holds true whether it be for Mark, Q, Thomas or another author.

1. Gerhardsson has failed to mention killing frost, hail, floodwater, flash-fire, meteor storm, earthquake, tornado, marauding army or locust plague. A comprehensive listing of reasons why seed might fail to come to harvest belongs in an encyclopaedia article, not a parable constructed in accord with the 'law of three'.

2. Gerhardsson concludes that the parable 'does not offer a purely natural and unforced agricultural illustration', 'Parable', p. 187.

b. *The Two-source Theory*

Secondly, the implications of the two-source theory have not been applied. I have touched upon this in Gerhardsson's too-quick rejection of Markan priority. A curious form of this appears in Gerhardsson's insistence that we respect the fact that all three evangelists relate Jesus narrating parable and interpretation.[1] Since Matthew and Luke derive the setting from Mark we have only one 'independent' tradition. The argument that the 'twelve ἀκούειν, like twelve signals, must be accorded the attention they deserve'[2] is the same mistake. Although it is possible that Matthew (and Luke) might be drawing upon an independent source, good method demands that the 'differences' in Matthew and Luke be investigated first in terms of their redactional tendencies as demonstrable elsewhere. Implicit throughout this whole procedure is a view of 'biblical authority' which places the text above the reverential and obedient interpreter. Such an assumption, as Collingwood notes, cannot be the basis of critical history.

Equally problematic is Gerhardsson's observation that the prophets and the writings are present in Matthew's parable chapter and the implication that a thematic tie to the 'Law' is more likely in the parable. The Psalms quotation is found in Matthew's rewrite of the sermon's conclusion. It is one of a number of redactional Matthean formular quotations.[3] The quotation from Isaiah, of course, is the meat in Mark's 'sandwich' arrangement. Gerhardsson has, in effect, not seriously questioned whether these three examples of the Law, prophets and writings were brought together redactionally or originated together as a unit.

Gerhardsson's failure to consider the overall structure of the Gospels is seen in his belief that Mk 4.13 indicates that the Sower is fundamental to Jesus' proclamation of the reign of God. The verse's location as the narrative link between two units should suggest a

---

1. Gerhardsson's point seems to be a mechanistic way of determining emphasis within the Gospels. A triply attested unit is to be given greater weight, he implies, than a unit unique to one Gospel.

2. Gerhardsson, 'Parable', p. 166.

3. ὅπως πληρωθῇ τὸ ῥηθὲν διὰ τοῦ προφήτου λέγοντος Mt. 13.35; cp. 2.15, 17; 3.3; 4.14; 8.17; 12.17; 21.4; 27.9. The error is similar to Riddle's belief that Matthew's formular conclusion to the sermon came to him from an independent copy of the parable tract.

Markan gloss here.[1] His observation that the Rabbis sometimes spoke in a lowered voice fits this pattern. He has not considered to what extent the rabbinic texts present a literary motif. But even granting that such was rabbinic practice, Gerhardsson too quickly assumes that this history must be behind the Gospel text.[2]

The argument of the essential harmony of Mk 4.1-34 displays this error. Gerhardsson sees the parable as an application of the motif 'To whom has, more is given', which is known from the Jewish Wisdom tradition and the Rabbis.[3] This compatibility with a Jewish matrix is evidence of 'authenticity' and 'orality'. My previous discussion has already shown that the connection between vv. 10-13 and 21-25 is due to Mark. The hiddenness of the lamp shows the post-resurrectional character of Mark's use of these sayings. Gerhardsson has missed these connotations, one suspects, because he has not looked for them.[4] Moule's attempt to turn the imperfect of Mk 4.10 into a true iterative[5] likewise fails to give priority to the evangelist for a literary motif found consistently within his Gospel; instead Moule attempts to push the material back into the oral phase. This procedure does not account for the numerous parallels to this verse throughout Mark's entire narrative.[6]

Essentially, Gerhardsson and Moule have failed to apply the implications of the two-source theory. Rather than beginning with the redactional concerns of the evangelist as a clue to the text, they have begun with a form-critical assumption of the unit's essential independence from its context. Such an approach, as we have seen, cannot get

1. On the Markan character of this verse, see above, Chapter 3, section 4, a.
2. Gerhardsson has not considered whether the Matthean parallel is consistent with the evangelist's handling of Mark's secrecy theme, nor the possibility of other literary parallels (Hellenistic or otherwise) as a source for Matthew's text.
3. Compare Prov. 1.5; 9.9; Mek. Vayassa I. 148-85; Gerhardsson, 'Parable', pp. 173-74.
4. The above discussion has established Mark's redactional arrangement of the material, and his intent with the Isaiah curse and the crowds. The essential harmony of Mk 4.1-34 is not due to the authenticity of all the material, but rather Mark's redaction.
5. Moule, 'Mark 4.1-20 Yet Once More', p. 102.
6. The problem with Moule's argument becomes clear when we consider the passion predictions. The consistency with which all three synoptic evangelists present Jesus as predicting his own death and resurrection is not sufficient evidence for the historical accuracy of this motif.

us back directly into the oral phase. Neither the evangelists nor their sources present a directly transcribed orality. At each written stage of the tradition the literary concerns of the author must be examined before proceeding to a reconstruction of the inherited 'oral tradition'.

c. *The Invocation of Q*

The invocation of a Q parallel presents another problem. Access to the inherited 'oral form' of a tradition is usually dependent upon the number of independent witnesses. Even if one can 'discount' Mark's redaction, it is not clear what the earlier form of the saying looked like. An independent witness would help, but independent witnesses, at least in this instance, are hard to come by.

Some overlap of Mark and Q is necessary to explain a number of the minor agreements of Matthew and Luke. But as the debate over the Griesbach hypothesis has shown, this overlap should not be invoked too easily lest Q become so expanded that it contain almost all of Mark! 'Minor agreements' against Mark can be found in many contexts. In such instances scholars have to balance carefully the case for a Q parallel against the possibility of coincidental independent redactional change by Matthew and Luke. Hence, a minor agreement in itself might not be sufficient grounds to postulate a Q version of the unit.[1] Caution is in order, and it is provided in that further evidence for a Q version is often found in the non-Markan location of material within Luke. Thus for example, the relocation of the Mustard Seed (Lk. 13.18-19); the Beelzebul controversy (11.14-23); and the Light aphorism (11.33) can best be explained if Luke followed the order of Q in these instances.

But the minor agreements of Matthew and Luke in the parable and the interpretation are not extensive. The infinitive σπεῖραι at Mk 4.3 is paralleled by the articular τοῦ σπείρειν in Matthew and τοῦ σπεῖραι in Luke. As an examination of the manuscript traditions shows, Mark's syntax has also displeased the scribes, some of whom have shown a preference for the articular infinitive.[2] The fact that Mark and Luke agree in tense against Matthew adds credibility to the possibility that the minor agreement of the article is due to independent redaction.

---

1. As argued above, Chapter 3, section 4, d.
2. Cf. Alexandrius and Sinaticus (corrected).

Secondly, there is the deletion of ἐγένετο and the addition of the pronoun αὐτόν to Mk 4.4a The three parallels read as follows:

Mt. 13.4a.	Mk 4.4a	Lk. 8.5b
καὶ ἐν τῷ σπείρειν <u>αὐτὸν</u> ἃ μὲν ἔπεσεν παρὰ τὴν ὁδόν	καὶ ἐγένετο ἐν τῷ σπείρειν <u>ὃ</u> μὲν ἔπεσεν παρὰ τὴν ὁδόν	καὶ ἐν τῷ σπείρειν <u>αὐτὸν ὃ</u> μὲν ἔπεσεν παρὰ τὴν ὁδόν

The deletion of the unnecessary ἐγένετο is understandable; indeed, Bezae has likewise made this change.[1] Is the addition of the pronoun significant enough to suggest a Q version? Since the 'Sower' is representative of the Christian preacher, the clarifying addition is understandable. The minor agreement of Luke and Mark (ὃ) against Matthew (ἃ) provides counterbalancing evidence of independent alteration of the Markan original in this instance.

There is also the preference for ὁ ἔχων over Ὃς ἔχει at Mk 4.9:

Mt. 13.9 & 11.15	Mk 4.9	Lk. 8.8c & 14.35
ὁ ἔχων ὦτα ἀκουέτω.	Ὃς ἔχει ὦτα <u>ἀκούειν</u> ἀκουέτω.	ὁ ἔχων ὦτα <u>ἀκούειν</u> ἀκουέτω.

In this instance, we are dealing with a separate aphorism. It is by no means clear when this saying was joined to the Sower. It is duplicated within Matthew at 11.15 (John's question from prison), and Luke at 14.35 (tasteless salt), both of which are 'Q' contexts. The two versions in Matthew are word-for-word, as are Luke's two versions. Gerhardsson may be correct that the agreement ὁ ἔχων can be ascertained as due to Q. But this proves only that this aphorism was in Q and provides no evidence that the Sower was present as well. Matthew and Luke have harmonized the wording of the logion throughout their Gospels, and their agreement is due to their redactional activity.

Finally, there is the inclusion of 'heart' in the allegorical interpretation:

---

1. One could argue the motive is simply harmonization to Matthew and Luke; nevertheless it is significant that the copyist harmonizes at this instance while leaving Mark as he found it elsewhere when readings from another Gospel could have been employed. Similarly, why not harmonize by changing Matthew and/or Luke to agree with Mark?

Mt. 13.19b	Mk 4.15b	Lk. 8.12b
ἔρχεται ὁ πονηρὸς	εὐθὺς ἔρχεται ὁ	εἶτα ἔρχεται ὁ
καὶ ἁρπάζει τὸ	Σατανᾶς καὶ **αἴρει**	διάβολος καὶ **αἴρει**
<u>ἐσπαρμένον</u> ἐν <u>τῇ</u>	**τὸν λόγον** τὸν	**τὸν λόγον** ἀπὸ <u>τῆς</u>
<u>καρδίᾳ</u> αὐτοῦ.	<u>ἐσπαρμένον</u> εἰς	<u>καρδίας</u> αὐτῶν, ἵνα
	αὐτούς.	μὴ πιστεύσαντες
		σωθῶσιν.

Again, the exact wording of Matthew and Luke differs, while agreement between Luke and Mark (αἴρει τὸν λόγον) exists against Matthew, and Matthew and Mark (ἐσπαρμένον) against Luke. Luke's concluding phrase is telling: it is a clue to his theological intent and supplies the motive for his addition of τῆς καρδίας αὐτῶν.

Given the amount of text (over 200 words) and the nature of these minor agreements, I believe it is far more likely that we are dealing with coincidence of redactional change rather than conflation from Q. And without a Q parallel, it is impossible to escape Markan priority. Mark's version of the Sower must be held as the source of both Matthew and Luke. Any reconstruction of prior tradition, oral or written, must begin with the Markan text.

d. *Linguistic Evidence and Orality*

Finally, and most significantly, Gerhardsson and Moule have not explained the interpretation's extensive linguistic ties to the post-resurrectional proclamation of the Hellenistic church. The argument that the words can be translated into Aramaic, for example, fails to account for the technical sense given a number of these terms. Especially the distinctive use of 'the word' cannot be traced back to oral tradition. Moule's invocation of the Colossians parallel is self-defeating since the context of this epistle is Hellenistic. Even granting Pauline authorship, we are still 30 years after Jesus.[1] Gerhardsson's theory that only the explanation is 'technical' and hence in need of specialized vocabulary cannot explain away the linguistic evidence. Moreover, his belief that parable and interpretation would be transmitted in different fashions is highly artificial. Both, he believes, are transmitted together in the oral tradition yet treated in markedly

---

1. Likewise the 'imprecision' in Colossians regarding who or what 'bears fruit' does not assure the authenticity of the interpretation. The two uses of the image in Colossians are quite separate and show only that the image was quite flexible in its application.

different fashion. Given the flexibility inherent in the oral process and the unconscious forces at work within each performer (which tend towards a uniformity of vocabulary and syntax within the entire performance), Gerhardsson's thesis is impossible. The linguistic differences between parable and allegory are sufficiently great as to require different literary authors. As M. Black notes, the parable exhibits a number of Semitisms, while the interpretation is in ordinary Greek.[1] The allegorical interpretation must be held to have originated in the post-resurrectional Hellenistic community, as Dodd and Jeremias noted.[2]

Given these considerations, Gerhardsson has clearly overstated his case in stating that the parable was 'created to be *memorized* and *meditated upon*' by an author who '*repeated* it for his hearers many times'.[3] His rabbinic model of 'Memory and Manuscript' for the oral transmission of synoptic tradition does not properly explain the data and rests on unfounded assumptions. Since the interpretation must be held to be post-resurrectional, I now turn to the distinctive problem of whether this milieu could possibly have been oral.

4. *The Allegorical Interpretation and Textuality*

A secondary text is by no means necessarily a literary one. Allegory, theoretically, could arise during the oral transmission. In light of Riddle's pre-Gospel source there are three(!) main possibilities for the interpretation's origin: (1) Mark, (2) the author of his written source, or (3) an anonymous performer during the oral phase. We have already seen that many (if not all) of the structural patterns of oral literature apply equally to written texts. A close examination of this allegorical interpretation will reveal that this overlap is not total. Especially viewed from the reverse side of the equation, it will become clear that certain forms of structure and literary form can

1. Black, *An Aramaic Approach*, p. 63. Black believes that these Semitisms result from translation into Greek from an Aramaic original. Semitisms, however, need not evidence an Aramaic original. Also, Koester, 'A Test Case of Synoptic Source Theory'.

2. If parable and interpretation originated together we would be left with an Hellenistic, post-resurrectional origin for both. Their argument of 'unity of origin' cuts both ways!

3. Gerhardsson, 'Parable', p. 188.

only point to a textual medium. To this category of material belongs the interpretation of the Sower.

a. *Indications of Expansion in the Parable*
The interpretation of the Sower is an extremely well-crafted text. As Gerhardsson notes, it fits the parable like hand and glove. But this precision is not evidence that both parable and interpretation originated together. Rather, the parable itself has been redacted to accommodate the interpretation.

Dominic Crossan's analysis of the Sower will serve as my starting point. He divides the parable into five elements: the opening (v. 3); the path (v. 4); the rocky soil (vv. 5-6); the thorns (v. 7); and the good soil (v. 8). Attention is quickly drawn to the rocky soil since it is significantly longer than even the final climactic section. The theme of the lack of ground is stated three times: οὐκ εἶχεν γῆν πολλήν... διὰ τὸ μὴ ἔχειν βάθος γῆς... διὰ τὸ μὴ ἔχειν ῥίζαν. There is also a contrast in image. Verses 5b, 6b depict the seed growing for a while, but vv. 5a, 6a have the seed failing to survive the first morning's hot sun. All of this suggests an expansion at vv. 5-6. Further evidence of expansion is seen at v. 8, where ἀναβαίνοντα καὶ αὐξανόμενα is a 'strange and somewhat belated way of specifying the already noted ἐδίδου καρπόν'.[1]

The expansion of the parable at vv. 5-6 is clearly seen in the exact verbal repetition: καὶ ἄλλο ἔπεσεν ἐπὶ τὸ πετρῶδες ὅπου οὐκ εἶχεν <u>γῆν πολλήν</u>, καὶ εὐθὺς ἐξανέτειλεν <u>διὰ τὸ μὴ ἔχειν βάθος γῆς</u>· [6] καὶ ὅτε ἀνέτειλεν ὁ ἥλιος ἐκαυματίσθη καὶ <u>διὰ τὸ μὴ ἔχειν</u> ῥίζαν ἐξηράνθη. Although one cannot be sure of the exact wording of the source, Mark's known insertion technique argues that much of the material between the two occurrences of διὰ τὸ μὴ ἔχειν is secondary. The interpretation at vv. 13-20 provides the best explanation for these additions to the parable. The allegory 'reads out' the parable, often in very close linguistic parallel to the original. For example, the parable's motif that ὅτε ἀνέτειλεν ὁ ἥλιος ἐκαυματίσθη is paralleled in the interpretation with the observation that γενομένης θλίψεως ἢ διωγμοῦ διὰ τὸν λόγον εὐθὺς σκανδαλίζονται. Crossan argues εὐθὺς ἐξανέτειλεν (v. 5b) corresponds to εὐθὺς μετὰ χαρᾶς λαμβάνουσιν αὐτόν (v. 16);

---

1. J.D. Crossan, 'The Seed Parables of Jesus', *JBL* 92 (1973), p. 246. Discussion, pp. 245-46.

while διὰ τὸ μὴ ἔχειν ῥίζαν (v. 6b) prepares for οὐκ ἔχουσιν ῥίζαν (v. 17).[1] These parallels do not exhaust the close symmetry between parable and interpretation. At times, the parable is almost quoted verbatim in the interpretation. Such elements as the advent of the birds, eating of the seed, lack of root, rising of the sun, growing and increasing, and choking are all given their allegorical counterpart. These parallels can be shown as follows:

The Sower and its Interpretation[2]

3 ἰδοὺ ἐξῆθεν <u>ὁ σπείρων σπεῖραι</u>.	14 <u>ὁ σπείρων</u> τόν λόγον <u>σπείρει</u>.
4 καὶ ἐγένετο ἐν τῷ σπείρειν <u>ὃ μὲν</u> ἔπεσεν <u>παρὰ τὴν ὁδὸν</u>,	15 <u>οὗτοι δέ</u> εἰσιν <u>οἱ παρὰ τὴν ὁδὸν</u> ὅπου σπείρεται ὁ λόγος, καὶ ὅταν ἀκούσωσιν
καὶ <u>ἦλθεν τὰ πετεινὰ</u> <u>καὶ κατέφαγεν αὐτὸ</u>.	εὐθὺς <u>ἔρχεται ὁ Σατανᾶς</u> <u>καὶ αἴρει τὸν λόγον τὸν ἐσπαρμένον εἰς αὐτούς</u>.
5 <u>καὶ ἄλλο ἔπεσεν ἐπὶ τὸ πετρῶδες</u>	16 <u>καὶ οὗτοι εἰσιν οἱ ἐπὶ τ ὰ πετρώδη</u> σπειρόμενοι, οἳ ὅταν ἀκούσωσιν τὸν λόγον
ὅπου <u>οὐκ εἶχεν γῆν πολλήν</u>,	<u>εὐθὺς μετὰ χαρᾶς λαμβάνουσιν αὐτόν</u>,
καὶ <u>εὐθὺς ἐχανέτειλεν</u>	17 καὶ <u>οὐκ ἔχουσιν ῥίζαν ἐν ἑαυτοῖς</u>
<u>διὰ τὸ μὴ ἔχειν βάθος γῆς</u>. 6 <u>καὶ ὅτε ἀνέτειλεν ὁ ἥλιος ἐκαυματίσθη</u>, καὶ <u>διὰ τὸ μὴ ἔχειν ῥίζαν ἐξηράνθη</u>.	<u>ἄλλα πρόσκαιροί εἰσιν</u>· <u>εἶτα γενομένης θλίψεως ἢ διωγμοῦ διὰ τὸν λόγον</u> εὐθὺς <u>σκανδαλίζονται</u>.

1. Crossan, 'Seed Parables', p. 246. Crossan seems to have changed his mind regarding which elements are original and which secondary. He divides the image into two pairs; vv. 5a, 6a against vv. 5b, 6b. In the article 'Seed Parables', he views 5b, 6b and 8b as secondary expansions, arguing that the picture of seed that falls on rocky ground and grows up until the next day's sun is not suited for believers who are fruitful until persecution. We may contrast his book *In Parables: The Challenge of the Historical Jesus* (New York: Harper & Row, 1973). There he argues that the secondary image of the scorching sun (v. 6a) was inserted to underline most forcibly what the advent of tribulation or persecution (vv. 16-17) is really like: not a slow withering but instant scorching (p. 42).

2. Underlined elements in the parable are closely 'read out' by the interpretation.

7 καὶ ἄλλο ἔπεσεν εἰς τὰς ἀκάνθας,	18 καὶ ἄλλοι εἰσὶν οἱ εἰς τὰς ἀκάνθας σπειρόμενοι· οὗτοί εἰσιν οἱ τὸν λόγον ἀκούσαντες,
	19 καὶ αἱ μέριμναι τοῦ αἰῶνος
καὶ ἀνέβησαν αἱ ἄκανθαι	καὶ ἡ ἀπάτη τοῦ πλούτου καὶ αἱ περὶ τὰ λοιπὰ ἐπιθυμίαι εἰσπορευόμεναι συμπνίγουσιν τὸν λόγον
καὶ συνέπνιξαν αὐτό, καὶ καρπὸν οὐκ ἔδωκεν.	καὶ ἄκαρπος γίνεται.
8 καὶ ἄλλα ἔπεσεν εἰς τὴν γῆν	20 καὶ ἐκεῖνοί εἰσιν οἱ ἐπὶ τὴν γῆν τὴν καλὴν σπαρέντες, οἵτινες
τὴν καλήν	ἀκούουσιν τὸν λόγον
καὶ ἐδίδου καρπὸν	καὶ παραδέχονται
ἀναβαίνοντα καὶ αὐξανόμενα	καὶ καρποφοροῦσιν
καὶ ἔφερεν ἓν τριάκοντα	ἓν τριάκοντα
καὶ ἓν ἑξήκοντα καὶ ἓν ἑκατόν.	καὶ ἓν ἑξήκοντα καὶ ἓν ἑκατόν.

The interpretation also exhibits a strong uniformity in the exposition of the various soils. The introduction to the three final soils in particular is regularized.[1] This fact, along with the exactness of the parallels to the parable (which constitute so great a proportion of the interpretation), insure that the allegory must be considered the product of a textual medium.[2] Two possibilities exist: either Mark composed the interpretation (and redacted the parable to fit this text) or both parable and allegory came to him in written form.

Crossan inclines to the second possibility, with a preference for the interpretation being added subsequent to the collecting of the three parables.[3] He believes that the additions within the parable share a similarity of theme with additions to the other seed parables at vv. 28

1. Marcus, *Mystery*, p. 25, notes that the identification is in the form x = y. Pesch, *Markusevangelium*, I, p. 242, has noted a similarity in structure wtih the pesher formula of Qumran in 1QpHab.

2. Confirmed by Sellew, 'Oral and Written Sources', pp. 257-59. The density of literary integration insures the unit's origin in the textual medium. Just as an insurance policy or modern novel has its natural origin in textuality, so too the allegorical interpretation of the Sower. Klauck, *Allegorie*, p. 201, sees the interpretation as similar to the dream interpretations of the Hebrew Bible, in other words, a secondary revelatory step used to unlock the mystery of the parable.

3. This would give the following stages in transmission: 1) Individual Oral Parables; 2) Collection of Three Written Parables; 3) Parables and Allegory; 4) Mark.

and 31-32.[1] The insertions all stress a growth process during the passage of time, presumably with the intention of 'inculcating patience and perseverance and of warning against complacency and laziness'. Since the additions all have a common function, and given that Mark must have effected one of the additions himself, Crossan argues that Mark therefore made all the additions. This represents a shift in emphasis to that of the allegorical interpretation. The source explains why some Christians are defecting and warns against such failures. In contrast, Mark's additions admonish the community on the necessity of growth through time. The bearing fruit of v. 20 is a 'matter of persistent and sustained growth and not an immediate blossoming'.[2]

b. *The Interpretation and Mark's Narrative Drama*
The non-Markan character of the allegorical interpretation, however, is often overstated. It is appropriate to examine this unit within the context of Mark's Gospel to ascertain whether or not he might have composed it himself.

A number of Markan concerns quickly emerge. As Kelber notes, one can detect Mark's own voice in the absolute use of 'The Word'.[3] Secondly, there is the emphasis on 'hearing', a theme not only emphasized redactionally in the parable chapter, but throughout the entire Gospel.[4] The Markan favourites καί (14 times in the interpretation!) and εὐθύς (three times) are prominently featured.

Mark has subtly integrated the allegory into the entire narrative. Each of the soil types prefigures characters and events elsewhere in the Gospel. A number of scholars have noted the parallel between the seed sown on the path and the hostile scribes.[5] But an even closer

1. See Crossan, 'Seed Parables', pp. 251-52; 254-57. This issue will be examined in the respective sections on these two other parables below.
2. All quotes are from Crossan, 'Seed Parables', pp. 257-58.
3. Kelber, *The Kingdom in Mark*, p. 37. Cp. Mk 4.33-4; 8.32; 7.29. See Chapter 3, section 3, c.
4. See for example at the transfiguration, 9.7. Cp. 4.9, 12, 18, 20, 23; 6.11, 14, 20, 29; 7.16, 25, 37; 8.18; 9.7; 12.29; 13.7. One must ask whether an allegory emphasizing perseverance and attempting to explain why some fall away would need such a strong emphasis on 'hearing the word'. Is this a fortuitous coincidence (for Mark), redactional alteration or redactional composition?
5. 'Only one group of characters in the Gospel has been portrayed as utterly opposed to Jesus from the beginning. Indeed, already in the early stages of his ministry they have hardened their hearts and begun to plot together to destroy him.

parallel, I believe, exists between this immediate failure to hear and the reaction of the disciples to Jesus' message of suffering discipleship. This reading out of the birds devouring seed on the path foreshadows events at the first passion prediction. As Mark begins Peter's confession and the first passion prediction, Jesus and the disciples are 'on the way' (καὶ ἐν τῇ ὁδῷ ἐπηρώτα—8.27). After the confession and as a bridge into the passion prediction, Mark carefully emphasizes that Jesus was παρρησίᾳ τὸν λόγον ἐλάλει (8.32). When Peter attempts to dissuade Jesus from a suffering messiahship, the reaction is blunt and swift: Ὕπαγε ὀπίσω μου, Σατανᾶ, ὅτι οὐ φρονεῖς τὰ τοῦ θεοῦ ἀλλὰ τὰ τῶν ἀνθρώπων (8.33).[1] Since the disciples were recently chastised for their inability to hear (8.18), the meaning is plain: Satan has come quickly and devoured the word sown on the path.

'The path' is featured after the second passion prediction (9.33) where failure to hear Jesus' message of suffering discipleship is stressed. The disciples have been discussing who is the greatest. At 10.17, Mark introduces the rich man with Jesus along the 'path/way'. Again, there is a failure to hear, and the man departs. At the third passion prediction Jesus is 'on the way/path' and there is a failure by the disciples to hear. The request of James and John for seats of authority quickly follows (10.25-45). Finally, the path is featured in the healing of Bartimaeus. He is sitting 'on the road/path' as Jesus passes by; 'hearing of' Jesus he calls out and is brought to him. He 'hears' Jesus' question well and asks for healing. The passage ends with the healed Bartimaeus following 'on the way/path' (10.52). The themes of 'hearing' and 'suffering discipleship' are prominent throughout Mk 8.27-10.52, which is foreshadowed particularly by the fate of the first seed.

The stony ground introduces the concept of 'receiving the word'. Unlike the seed on the path, this seed germinates for a time.

These, the ones along the way, are the scribes, the Pharisees, the Herodians, and the Jerusalem Jews', Tolbert, *Sowing the Gospel*, pp. 153-54. Also, Marcus believes this seed represents 'Jesus' determined enemies, the scribes and Pharisees, who from the start of the gospel oppose him with blind fury', *Mystery of the Kingdom*, p. 65. The narrative identifications are limited. As Kuhn, *Ältere Sammlungen*, p. 116 points out, εὐθύς precludes any testing.

1. The redactional character of this verse is seen in two or more participles before the main verb; and the οὐ... ἀλλά construction. See Pryke, *Redactional*, p. 119. Neirynck, *Duality in Mark*, pp. 90-94.

Implicitly, both the seed sown on the rocky soil and among the thorns comprise this category since they both 'receive the word'. A contrast develops, however, between this reception of the word and that exemplified by the seed sown in the good soil. Interestingly, Mark varies the verb between λαμβάνω (v. 16) and παραδέχομαι (v. 20). Perhaps the terms are used synonymously. It is also possible, however, that Mark intentionally uses two verbs to contrast superficial reception and true belief.[1] The latter term (δέξηται... δέχεται) is featured again at 9.37 in a positive sense, where whoever receives a child in Jesus' name, receives Jesus and the one who sent him.

This contrast between initial joyful reception and eventual rejection of 'the word' is played out at number of points in Mark. Herod, for example, ἀκούσας αὐτοῦ ['Ιωάννην] πολλὰ ἠπόρει, καὶ ἡδέως αὐτοῦ ἤκουεν (6.20). Eventually, however, Herod agrees to behead John. The theme is also prominently displayed in the account of the the rich man. His enthusiastic response at 10.20 'Teacher, I have kept all these since my youth' quickly shatters into an appalled sense of disbelief. Finally, we may note the crowd during the fateful events of passion week. After Jesus' verbal 'triumph' in the question about David's son, Mark tells us that ὁ πολὺς ὄχλος ἤκουεν αὐτοῦ ἡδέως (12.37). This phrase in particular has all the signs of Markan redaction. But this initial joyful reception quickly disappears, and soon in the trial scene before Pilate the crowd will demand Jesus' death. The concept of receiving Jesus' word, and the contrast between initial reception and ultimate perseverance, therefore, appear prominently throughout Mark's narrative.

Verse 17 contains other Markan traits. Beyond the well-known οὐκ... ἀλλά construction,[2] we have καί, εὐθύς, τὸν λόγον, and the verb σκανδαλίζονται. This verb receives considerable emphasis at Mk 9.43-48 ('Temptations to Sin'). The cause of failure for the seed sown on rocky ground is significant: θλίψεως ἢ διωγμοῦ διὰ τὸν λόγον. The first of these figures at Mk 10.30 is a phrase that has strong credentials as a redactional gloss—μετὰ διωγμῶν. The latter is

---

1. There is a similar contrast between the two terms in John at 4.43 and 13.20 (= Mk 9.37; Q 10.16). Interestingly, John has chosen the opposite meaning for the terms. Cf. R. Schnackenburg, *The Gospel According to St John*. I. *Introduction and Commentary on Chapters 1–4* (trans. K. Smyth; New York: Herder & Herder; London: Burns & Oates, 1968), p. 464.

2. See Neirynck, *Duality in Mark*, pp. 90-94.

found twice within Mark's mini-apocalypse (13.19, 24). This latter verse includes such redactional indications as ἀλλά, and μετά. More decisive is the account of the disciples' defection from Jesus at the arrest. Jesus' emphatic prediction, πάντες σκανδαλισθήσεσθε receives from Peter an even more emphatic denial, εἰ καὶ πάντες σκανδαλισθήσονται, ἀλλ᾽ οὐκ ἐγώ (14.27, 29). But the fear of persecution and tribulation proves overwhelming, and at the decisive moment the disciples abandon Jesus.[1] The seed sown on the rocky soil, therefore, foreshadows Mark's apocalyptic eschatology particularly well. The themes of persecution, afflictions and apostasy from the community are prime concerns of Mark.

The seed among the thorns also displays signs of Markan composition. The verb συνέπνιξαν (4.7), συμπνίγουσιν (4.19) is echoed in the drowning of the pigs, ἐπνίγοντο (5.13). The cause of 'unfruitfulness' for the seed sown among thorns is given in triadic form, αἱ μέριμναι τοῦ αἰῶνος καὶ ἡ ἀπάτη τοῦ πλούτου καὶ αἱ περὶ τὰ λοιπὰ ἐπιθυμίαι (4.19). Narrative parallels for these concerns are easily found. Marcus points to the Gerasenes, 'whose plea to Jesus to leave their borders may be based at least partly on an economic consideration'.[2] Tolbert links Herod with this soil. 'Herod is prevented from acting on his better instincts by his concern for other things—in this case, his reputation and word before his guests.'[3] Judas too falls into this category—he betrays Jesus for 'a fistful of dollars'.[4] But perhaps the closest parallel is the rich man. As Tolbert observes, the 'episode is remarkable for the degree to which it matches the parabolic type'.[5] The cause of failure is the same—love of money— and the contrast between initial joyful reception and eventual rejection

1. On this theme, see Tolbert, *Sowing the Gospel*, pp. 154-55; Marcus, *Mystery of the Kingdom*, pp. 65-66; Weeden, *Traditions in Conflict*; and Kelber, *The Kingdom in Mark*.

2. Marcus, *Mystery of the Kingdom*, p. 68, n. 197.

3. Tolbert, *Sowing the Gospel*, p. 158. See also Marcus, *Mystery of the Kingdom*, p. 68, n. 197.

4. Mk 14.11. Noted by Marcus, *Mystery of the Kingdom*, p. 68, n. 197.

5. Tolbert, *Sowing the Gospel*, p. 157. The thematic link between the two passages has also been noted by C.E.B. Cranfield, 'St. Mark 4.1-34 Part I', *SJT* 4 (1951), pp. 398-414. 'But did the weeds require such a long time? Mark 10.17-22 gives an example of the choking of the seed by weeds—very quickly, and in the presence of Jesus', p. 408. See also Marcus, *Mystery of the Kingdom*, p. 68, n. 197, 'Already *Herm. Sim. 9.20.2* links Mark 4.18-19 with Mark 10.23'.

of the word is in complete agreement with the allegory. The subsequent dramatic teaching of Jesus on the difficulty, particularly for the rich, of entering the reign of God shows that this is a prominent Markan concern. These echoes of 4.16-17 throughout the rest of Mark's narrative demonstrate that the evangelist has closely linked the passage with what follows.

Finally there remains the good soil. There is a nice formal balance in the phrasing between the triad 'hearing-receiving-bearing fruit' and the increasing yield 'thirtyfold, sixtyfold and one hundredfold'. The climax of the interpretation provides reinforcement for the true relatives of Jesus. At Mk 3.35 Jesus tells the reader that ὃς γὰρ ἂν ποιήσῃ τὸ θέλημα τοῦ θεοῦ, οὗτος ἀδελφός μου καὶ ἀδελφὴ καὶ μήτηρ ἐστίν. The hundredfold yield is also consistent with Mark's promise of reward for the true believer at 10.30 (λάβῃ ἑκατονταπλασίονα).

The indications of free composition by Mark are certainly not as clear within this section of the Gospel as in some of the so-called Markan summaries (cf. 1.28, 39, 45; 3.7-12). Caution is also in order since the perceived connections between the allegory and other narratives might be due in part to the flexibility of the interpretive process. Like allegory itself, these parallels might result from a secondary interpretive process in the mind of the exegete. Nevertheless, the above discussion has shown that the interpretation has been well integrated into Mark's narrative. Mark's own distinctive concerns shine through at various places. Distinctions in sociological context and theological intent between this passage and Mark's Gospel as a whole are not as compelling as is sometimes believed.

Regardless of its ultimate authorship, the passage has no claim to an oral antecedent. It owes its origin to the textual medium. Since the allegory belongs clearly to a textual medium and must be considered a secondary commentary on the parable, the possibility of an oral history can be limited to the parable itself. Since many scholars postulate a written parable tract containing the three seed parables of Mark 4, I will examine the three parables together for signs of an oral history in the next chapter.

Chapter 5

PARABLES AND ORALITY

The parables are widely regarded as the primary form of Jesus' teaching. Indeed, if a non-allegorical interpretation of a parable can be given, the unit is usually claimed as historical Jesus material.[1] The three seed parables, therefore, represent prime candidates for oral tradition. Particularly in light of the parallels in other sources (i.e., Q, *1 Clement* and *Gospel of Thomas*) the possibilities seem initially strong.

The parables are significant in terms of orality because of the markedly different hermeneutical approaches taken to them during the last 50 years. The fundamental insistence of Dodd and Jeremias regarding the secondary character of allegory has held firm. Their eschatological interpretations and reconstructions within concrete settings in Jesus' ministry, however, have not fared as well. The understanding of parable as metaphor and 'performative utterance' has drastically changed the approach of such scholars as Robert Funk, Dan O. Via and Dominic Crossan. This changing understanding of parable needs to be examined in order to determine how effective a control it gives in establishing orality.

Before proceeding to the seed parables a word on the relationship between Thomas and the synoptics is in order. Greek fragments of this Gospel were found in Egypt in 1897 and published under the name Papyrus Oxrhynchus 1 (*Gospel of Thomas* 26-33, 77a). Two

---

1. This general principle can be confirmed by a close examination of the results of the Jesus Seminar on the parables. A comparison of the authentic and inauthentic parables will show that the Seminar has regarded as historical Jesus material units that can be reconstructed in a non-allegorical form. Inauthentic 'parables' are almost always viewed as 'allegories' or secondary stories constructed out of the plot-line of an authentic parable. In this latter category I would include Thomas' parables of the Assassin and the Woman with the Jar.

further fragments, P. Oxy. 654 (*Gospel of Thomas* prologue, 1-7) and
P. Oxy. 655 (*Gospel of Thomas* 24, 36-39) were published a few
years later. These fragments were originally dated by Bernard P.
Grenfell and Arthur S. Hunt with a terminus ad quem (finishing date)
of about 140 CE.[1] A complete version of the Coptic translation of this
Gospel was discovered in Nag Hammadi. Its relation to the synoptic
tradition is controversial. Some scholars see in Thomas a gnostic
document dependent upon the synoptic Gospels.[2] In this view Thomas
does not represent an independent witness to the oral tradition. More
recently a consensus within North American scholarship has formed
which regards Thomas as an early and independent tradition. The
decisive arguments for this position are Thomas' lack of synoptic
redactional and allegorical features (especially with respect to the
parables) and its difference of order from the synoptics.[3] The question
of Thomas' relationship to the synoptics will concern me over the next
two chapters. I have chosen, in the following analysis, to highlight the
latter approach. I propose to leave this complex question 'open' for
the moment. The three seed parables and the five aphorisms of Mark 4
will be used in an inductive fashion as a test case for this problem. It
is my intent to demonstrate that the difficulties in these instances in
using Thomas as an independent tradition shows the elusive character
of this phase of the tradition. Regardless of the ultimate origins of
Thomas, its relationship with the synoptics is highly complex, and
hence it is exceedingly difficult to use Thomas as an independent
testimony to the oral tradition.

I will examine, therefore, each of Mark's three seed parables in an
effort to determine the ability to recover a clear oral history of the
units. The examination will show that even the pre-synoptic form of
these parables represents textuality, not a directly transcribed orality.
This investigation will then allow me to make a number of

1. See Robinson, 'On Bridging the Gulf from Q to the Gospel of Thomas',
pp. 142-43; Scott, *Hear then the Parable*, p. 32.
2. See, for example, R. Grant and D. Freedman, *The Secret Sayings of Jesus
according to the Gospel of Thomas* (Garden City, NY: Doubleday, 1960);
H. Montefiore and H. Turner, *Thomas and the Evangelists* (Studies in Biblical
Theology, 35; Naperville, IL: Allenson, 1962); W. Schoedel, 'Parables in the
Gospel of Thomas: Oral Tradition or Gnostic Exegesis?' *Concordia Theological
Monthly* 43 (1972), pp. 548-60; J.E. Ménard, *L'évangile selon Thomas* (Nag
Hammadi Studies 5; Leiden: Brill, 1975).
3. See Scott, *Hear then the Parable*, pp. 32-33.

methodological observations on the criterion of 'distinctiveness' and its use in establishing authenticity for parables in general.

1. *The Sower (Mark 4.3-8; Gospel of Thomas 9; 1 Clement 24.4-5)*

a. *The Original Form*

Three versions of the 'Sower' warrant attention in an investigation of this unit's 'original' form: Mark, Thomas and 1 Clement. These traditions need to be fully examined in order to establish the earliest recoverable version of this parable. The Markan and Thomas forms are as follows:[1]

Mk 4.3-8	Gospel of Thomas 9
Listen! A sower went out to sow. And as he sowed, some seed fell on the path, and the birds came and ate it up. Other seed fell on rocky ground, where it did not have much soil, and it sprang up quickly, since it had no depth of soil. And when the sun rose, it was scorched; and since it had no root, it withered away. Other seed fell among thorns, and the thorns grew up and choked it, and it yielded no grain. Other seed fell into good soil and brought forth grain, growing up and increasing and yielding thirty and sixty and a hundredfold.	Behold, the sower went out; he filled his hand he threw. Some fell on the road. The birds came; they gathered them up. Others fell on the rock, and did not send roots into the earth and did not send ears up to heaven. Others fell among thorns. They choked the seed and the worm ate them. And others fell on good earth, and it raised up good fruit to heaven. It bore sixty measures and one hundred-twenty measures.

In reconstructing the original form, Crossan excludes the apparent Markan expansions as noted above.[2] Originally, Crossan held vv. 5b (εὐθὺς ἐξανέτειλεν), 6b (διὰ τὸ μὴ ἔχειν ῥίζαν) and 8b (ἀναβαίνοντα καὶ αὐξανόμενα) as secondary. He subsequently came to declare that the image of the scorching sun (v. 6a) was

---

1. Translation of Mark is from the NRSV; from Thomas by D.R. Cartlige, as found in S. Davies, *The Gospels of Thomas and Christian Wisdom* (New York: Seabury, 1983), p. 159. Unless otherwise noted, translations of *Gospel of Thomas*. are from this version.

2. See Chapter 4, section 4, a.

secondary.[1] His comparison with the version in Thomas, particularly with respect to the verbs, establishes a common underlying structure:[2]

Mark	*Gospel of Thomas*
σπείρων/σπεῖραι/σπείρειν	went out/filled/threw
ἔπεσεν/ἦλθεν/κατέφαγεν	fell/came/gathered
ἔπεσεν/ἀνέτειλεν/ἐκαυματίσθη	fell/strike root/produce
ἔπεσεν/ἀνέβησαν/συνέπιξαν	fell/choked/ate
καὶ καρπὸν οὐκ ἔδωκεν	
ἔπεσεν/ἐδίδου/ἔφερεν	fell/brought forth/bore
τριάκοντα	
ἑξήκοντα	sixty
ἑκατόν	one hundred and twenty

Crossan finds the symmetry between the structures striking. Two points, however, are in order. Crossan's initial triad in Mark omits the verbs ἐξῆθεν and ἐγένετο. Thomas' initial triad is based on the inclusion of the phrase 'filled his hand' which Crossan must assign to the underlying oral triadic structure. Thomas' addition to the saying on having (logion 41),[3] and his version of the reaper (logion 21),[4] however, provide strong evidence that this phrase is part of the literary style of the final author. Crossan's omission of ἐξῆθεν also seems unwarranted given Thomas' parallel 'the sower *went out*'.

Even more important is the question of the double image in the rocky soil. Crossan's reconstruction is based on the argument that the image of the scorching sun is original and that the references to the lack of soil are Markan redaction. By the time he published *In Parables*, however, he had had a change of heart. In this latter study he argued that the image of the scorching sun was a secondary insertion which brought the parable into closer parallelism with the allegorical interpretation.[5] Since Thomas also lacks the image of the scorching sun and has in its place a reference to the seed which 'did not take root in the soil', this would bring the two versions of the parable into closer agreement. If one assumes that Crossan's

1. Crossan, 'Seed Parables', pp. 245-46; contra, *In Parables*, p. 42.
2. Crossan, 'Seed Parables', p. 249.
3. Logion 41, 'He who has *in his hand*, it shall be given to him; and he who does not have, even the little he has shall be taken away from him'.
4. Logion 21, 'When the fruit ripened, he came quickly, his sickle *in his hand*'.
5. Crossan, *In Parables*, p. 42. This represents a change from 'Seed Parables', pp. 245-46.

reformulated position is correct, an interesting fact becomes clear when one brackets this phrase and underlines two phrases that are in close parallelism before and after this secondary insertion. The verses are: 5 καὶ ἄλλο ἔπεσεν ἐπὶ τὸ πετρῶδες ὅπου οὐκ εἶχεν γῆν πολλήν, καὶ εὐθὺς <u>ἐξανέτειλεν</u> <u>διὰ τὸ μὴ ἐξειν βάθος γῆς</u>· 6 [καὶ ὅτε ἀνέτειλεν ὁ ἥλιος ἐκαυματίσθη,] καὶ <u>διὰ τὸ μὴ ἐξειν ῥίζαν</u> <u>ἐξηράνθη</u>. The chiastic [a,b; b′, a′] structure and the repetition of the phrase after an insertion (cf. Mk 2.5, 10b) are well-documented Markan redactional techniques. The key terms εὐθύς and διὰ τὸ μή are also Markan favourites. Absolute certainty in this instance is impossible, but the evidence seems to point to καὶ ἄλλο ἔπεσεν ἐπὶ τὸ πετρῶδες ὅπου οὐκ εἶχεν γῆν πολλήν καὶ ἐξηράνθη as the original.[1] The removal of the scorching sun and the duplication regarding the lack of soil still allows for a complete story line. What would be lacking is Crossan's triad of verbs (i.e., ἔπεσεν/ ἀνέτειλεν/ἐκαυματίσθη, fell/strike root/produce becomes ἔπεσεν/ ἐξηράνθη/. . . , fell/strike root/produce).

Theodore Weeden has also reconstructed the original form of the parable. He argues for the secondary character of ὅπου οὐκ εἶχεν γῆν πολλήν (5b); καὶ διὰ τὸ μὴ ἔχειν ῥίζαν ἐξηράνθη (6b); καὶ καρπὸν οὐκ ἔδωκεν (7c); and the phrase ἀναβαίνοντα καὶ αὐξανόμενα (v. 8). Weeden's version can be set forth as follows:

Look:
A sower went out to sow, and while sowing it happened:

Some seed fell along the path	and the birds came	and devoured it.
Other seed fell on rocky ground,	and when the sun came up	it was scorched.
Other seed fell among thorns,	and the thorns grew up	and choked it.
Other seed fell into good earth	and it gave fruit	and yielded
thirtyfold	sixtyfold	one hundredfold[2]

---

1. A different approach is taken by Marcus, *Mystery of the Kingdom*, p. 32. In agreement with Crossan's first reconstruction, Marcus holds vv. 5a, 6a as original while the reference at 5c to the seed springing up immediately on account of not having enough soil and the reference at 6b to withering on account of not having root as secondary. See Scott, *Hear then the Parable*, p. 351. Scott holds that the image of the scorching sun, v. 6a, is a secondary Markan insertion. On Mark's insertion technique, see Kee, *Community of the New Age*, pp. 54-56.

2. T.J. Weeden, Sr, 'Recovering the Parabolic Intent in the Parable of the Sower', *JAAR* 47 (1979), pp. 97-120.

As Burton Mack argues, Weeden's reconstruction shows complete balance in its members, with the 'law of three' applying throughout. There are three episodes of failed seed contrasted with a triple harvest for the successful sowing. Each line is composed triadically (i.e., fall of seed; entrance of agent; action). Vivid verbs are used to describe the actions. The triple geometric progression of the harvest is brought to termination by the 'hundredfold'.[1]

If one follows Crossan and accept the image of the scorching sun as a secondary expansion one need only substitute the phrase ὅπου οὐκ εἶχεν γῆν πολλήν for 'and when the sun came up' and καὶ ἐξηράνθη for 'it was scorched'. To facilitate discussion, I have set out Weeden's proposed original (with the above substitutions) with Thomas' version:

Mark's Source	*Gospel of Thomas 9*
Look:	Behold,
A sower went out	The sower went out;
to sow,	he filled his hand;
and while sowing it happened	he threw.
Some seed fell along the path,	Some fell on the road.
and the birds came and devoured it.	The birds came; they gathered them up.
Other seed fell on rocky ground,	Others fell on the rock,
where it had little soil,	and did not send roots into the soil,
and they withered.	and did not send ears up to heaven.
Other seed fell among thorns,	Others fell among thorns.
and the thorns grew up	They choked the seed
and choked it.	and the worm ate them.
Other seed fell into good earth,	And others fell on good earth,
and it gave fruit	and it raised up good fruit to heaven
and yielded	It bore
thirtyfold,	
sixtyfold,	sixty measures and
one hundredfold.	one hundred-twenty measures.

Can we detect in Thomas an independent version and hence postulate an oral history for the parable? As Crossan notes, there is a parallel of triadic structure between the two introductions. But Thomas avoids the Semitic repetition of the infinitive and has in its place 'took a handful (of seeds)'. As I have argued above, in light of

---

1. See B.L. Mack, *A Myth of Innocence* (Philadelphia: Fortress Press, 1988), pp. 153-54. Also Klauck, *Allegorie*, p. 187, who believes the references to shallow earth, seed springing up and the rootlessness are all secondary.

the identical theme in logions 21, 41, this phrase results from Thomas' literary style and cannot be ascribed to the 'oral form'.

More significant is the rocky ground. Thomas lacks any mention of the scorching sun (Mk 4.6a); instead we find the failure to take root which closely parallels the reconstructed original ὅπου οὐκ εἶχεν γῆν πολλήν καὶ ἐξηράνθη. This is particularly significant if the image of the scorching sun is a secondary element inserted to bring the parable into line with the interpretation.[1] Thomas' rocky soil section also mentions that the seed 'did not produce ears'. A contrast, similar to Mk 4.7b (καὶ καρπὸν οὐκ ἔδωκεν), is clearly drawn with the seed sown on the good soil which does produce ears and yield a crop. Mark includes this as the conclusion to the thorny ground, however, and Thomas has there instead his distinctive 'and worms ate them (the seeds)'. The question of location is significant. Given that the good soil does produce a harvest it is natural to parallel this earlier in the parable. The change of location could therefore be either a literary change or an oral variation.[2] The antithetic parallelism in Thomas at this point can also be translated 'did not send root deep into the earth, nor ear high up to heaven'. This particular phrase has been interpreted by H.E.W. Turner and H. Montefiore as a presentation of true gnosis: '[this seed] seems to be a reference to the heavenward ascent of the soul of the true gnostic'.[3]

The sections regarding the thorns are quite similar. Both Mark and Thomas have the key action of choking out the seed. In place of the thorns growing up Thomas notes that the worms ate the seed. This is a strange motif given that the choking thistles have already killed off the sprouting plants. The rationale for the image is found in such texts as Isa. 66.24 and Mk 9.48. Thomas uses this image at the conclusion to the parable of the Pearl (logion 76).[4] In other words, mention of the

1. See Crossan, *In Parables,* p. 42. This represents a change from 'Seed Parables', pp. 245-46.

2. For a literary parallel for the motif of taking root and producing fruit see 2 Kgs 19.30 = Isa. 37.31; 'The surviving remnant of the house of Judah shall again take root downward, and bear fruit upward'. Thomas' variation, therefore, might be a literary formulation at this point.

3. Montefiore and Turner, *Thomas and the Evangelists,* p. 53. Cited with approval in Marcus, *Mystery of the Kingdom,* pp. 33-34.

4. Logion 76, 'You also must seek for the treasure which does not perish, which abides where no moth comes near to eat, nor worm destroys'. The Q parallel On

worm seems 'forced and unnatural'. While there is no reason to suppose that such mention could not occur during the oral phase (especially since every telling is a new one), still, the lack of direct logical necessity in the image would tend towards its omission in the oral transmission. It seems best to ascribe this phrase to Thomas' literary textualization of the parable.

The conclusion in Thomas is significant: it lacks the ascending progression in triadic form. Indeed, although literary critics make much of this triad, Mark is the only version with this feature. Matthew, Luke and Thomas all differ at this point. The exact triadic parallel between unfruitful and fruitful seed, therefore, is attested by only one version of the parable. This is slim evidence for the exact structure of the oral version! Thomas also has the ground rather than the seed itself produce the harvest. According to Marcus, this could represent an instance of gnostic exegesis, since 'the ground is probably the kingdom within the gnostic, while the seed is the spark of divine light'.[1]

The argument from silence, that Thomas' independence is shown by its omission of the allegorical interpretation, is also not decisive.[2] As Marcus argues, it is possible that Thomas found the allegorical interpretation too 'prosaic', and hence omitted it. The 'Markan interpretation would have represented a premature attempt to decipher the parable's secret, which in actuality could only be grasped through a flash of insight'.[3]

In W. Schrage's analysis, Thomas is both an abbreviated and expanded version of the synoptic parallels, although this in itself does not prove dependence. However, the Coptic translation also shows agreements with the Sahidic versions of Mark and Matthew. Most striking is the agreement to Mk 4.6 of MOYXE NOYNE (μὴ βάλλειν ῥίζαν—compare Mark's μὴ ἔχειν).[4] John Sieber correctly

---

Treasures (Q 12.33-34 = Mt. 6.19-21) appears to lack Thomas' worm. The image in both Thomas' texts would appear to be a consistent literary and redactional theme.

1. Marcus, *Mystery of the Kingdom*, p. 34. See Klauck, *Allegorie*, pp. 199-200.

2. See for example, Koester, 'Three Thomas Parables', pp. 195-97.

3. Marcus, *Mystery of the Kingdom*, p. 34.

4. W. Schrage, *Das Verhältnis des Thomas-Evangeliums zur synoptischen Tradition und zu den koptischen Evangelienübersetzungen: zugleich ein Beitrag zur gnostischen Synoptikerdeutung* (BZNW, 29; Berlin: Töpelmann, 1964), pp. 43-48.

objects that this is evidence only of 'influence on the text of Thomas by the Sahidic version rather than in Thomas' sources themselves'.[1] Instead, he argues that Thomas' failure to reproduce important redactional features of the synoptic versions indicates that his text 'comes from a late stage of the oral tradition, one influenced perhaps either by the written Gospels or by an early harmony of the Gospels'.[2] This hypothesis indicates the complicated history of the Thomas tradition and still does not prove oral independence even at the earliest level of Thomas; indeed Sieber's hypothetical reconstruction invokes 'oral tradition' and immediately has to admit the possibility of influence from other written traditions. This is an ingenious solution if not unduly complicated.

John Horman compares Thomas' version with that found in the synoptics. He argues that just as the extensive agreements among these latter texts prove a literary relationship, so too the agreements between Thomas and the synoptics necessitate a literary relationship. Over half of Thomas' parable translates the synoptic version as closely as can be imagined, with the agreements even following word order. These include 28 words in the Coptic with exact equivalents in Greek in the same word order. Seven other words suggest a common base, while 22 words in Thomas have no synoptic equivalent. Significantly, in Horman's comparison, most of the redactional additions in Mark are left without parallel in Thomas (i.e., the expansions at vv. 5-6, 8b). Thus Horman concludes that the 'close correspondence between the four versions in question seems to me to rule out the possibility that Thomas' version of the parable goes back to an independent translation of the parable from Aramaic'.[3]

An abbreviated version of the parable is also found in *1 Clement*. H. Koester notes that this parallel is often disregarded and asserts that

---

1. J.H. Sieber, 'A Redactional Analysis of the Synoptic Gospels with Regard to the Question of the Sources of the Gospel According to Thomas' (PhD dissertation, Claremont Graduate School, 1966), p. 159.

2. Sieber, 'A Redactional Analysis', p. 160.

3. J. Horman, 'The Source of the Version of the Parable of the Sower in the Gospel of Thomas', *NovT* 21 (1979), p. 335. Compare the conclusion of Marcus, '*both* the Markan parable and its *Gos. Thom.* counterpart have redactional features. The possibility that the *Gos. Thomas* parable represents a reworking of the Markan version cannot be excluded, but the reverse is quite unlikely', p. 34.

any 'literary dependence would be difficult to prove'.[1] Clement's version of this text reads:

1 Clement 24.4-5[2]

Let us take the crops: how and in what way does the sowing take place? 'The sower went forth' and cast each of the seeds into the ground, and they fall on to the ground and they fall on to the ground parched and bare, and suffer decay; then from their decay the greatness of the providence of the Master raises them up, and from one grain more grow and bring forth fruit.	λάβωμεν τοὺς καρπούς· ὁ σπόρος πῶς καὶ τίνα τρόπον γίνεται; Ἐξῆλθεν ὁ σπείρων καὶ ἔβαλεν εἰς τὴν γῆν ἕκαστον τῶν σπερμάτων, ἅτινα πεσόντα εἰς τὴν γῆν ξηρὰ καὶ γυμνὰ διαλύεται· εἶτ' ἐκ τῆς διαλύσεως ἡ μεγαλειότης προνοίας τοῦ δεσπότου ἀνίστησιν αὐτά, καὶ ἐκ τοῦ ἑνὸς πλείονα αὔξει καὶ ἐκφέρει καρπόν.

The version shows considerable variation from the synoptics and Thomas. The triple enumeration of inhospitable soil is missing. The context of comparison has had a considerable effect, however. The motif of the ground, 'parched and bare' and the death or 'decay' of the seed seem particularly tied to the ancient analogy with the resurrection.[3] Implicit is the ancient belief that a seed 'died' before its rebirth as a plant (cf. Jn 12.24; 1 Cor. 15.36-37). Similarly, the motif of 'the greatness of the providence of the Master' is probably dependent upon the context and redactional with Clement. Of the other distinctive elements within Clement's version of this parable, the phrase εἰς τὴν γῆν is natural and can be found in Jn 12.24. The action of casting seed, found in Thomas and Clement, likewise is a natural verb (cp. Mk 4.26). In neither instance need one postulate 'oral tradition' or memorization for the vocabulary in question. Given the context, the particular word is perfectly understandable as part of the textual expression of the metaphor. The verb for producing a harvest

1. Koester, 'Three Thomas Parables', p. 196.
2. Translation and Greek text from Lake (trans.), *The Apostolic Fathers*, I, pp. 50-53.
3. Compare Paul's analogy at 1 Cor. 15.35-38; the tradition regarding Rabbi Meir, *b. Sanh.* 90b and Rabbi Hiyy ben Joseph, *b. Ket.* 111b. See the parallels cited below in section 1, b.

φέρω can be found in Clement, Mark and John, as can the term καρπός. Where Clement seems particularly closely tied to the Markan form of the parable is in the following items, Ἐξῆλθεν ὁ σπείρων (word-for-word); αὔξει (compare Mark's αὐξανόμενα) and the yield based upon τοῦ ἑνός. Clement also includes allusions to Paul. Clement's practice in these parallels—particularly in regard to the degree of verbal agreement—provides a useful control. There is in fact little sense in demanding exact repetition from Clement in the Sower since he does not reproduce these passages in word-for-word fidelity. The parallel *1 Clem* 33.1 and Rom. 6.1-2 is instructive:[1]

Rom. 6.1-2	*1 Clem*. 33.1
Τί οὖν ἐροῦμεν; ἐπιμένωμεν τῇ ἁμαρτίᾳ, ἵνα ἡ χάρις πλεονάσῃ; μὴ γένοιτο· οἵτινες ἀπεθάνομεν τῇ ἁμαρτίᾳ, πῶς ἔτι ζήσομεν ἐν αὐτῇ;	Τί οὖν ποιήσωμεν, ἀδελφοί; ἀργήσωμεν ἀπὸ τῆς ἀγαθοποιίας καὶ ἐγκαταλίπωμεν τὴν ἀγάπην; μηθαμῶς τοῦτο ἐάσαι ὁ δεσπότης ἐφ᾿ ἡμῖν γε γενηθῆναι, ἀλλά σπεύσωμεν μετὰ ἐκτενείας καὶ προθυμίας πᾶν ἔργον ἀγαθὸν ἐπιτελεῖν.

Two other instances again demonstrate allusion without word-for-word fidelity.

Rom. 1.32	*1 Clem*. 35.6
οἵτινες τὸ δικαίωμα τοῦ θεοῦ ἐπιγνόντες, ὅτι οἱ τὰ τοιαῦτα πράσσοντες ἄξιοι θανάτου εἰσίν, οὐ μόνον αὐτὰ	ταῦτα γὰρ οἱ πράσσοντες στυγητοὶ τῷ θεῷ ὑπάρχουσιν· οὐ μόνον δὲ

---

1. Translation and Greek text from Lake, *Apostolic Fathers*, I, pp. 62-63. *1 Clement*, 'What shall we do then, brethren? Shall we be slothful in well-doing and cease from love? May the Master forbid that this should happen, at least to us, but let us be zealous to accomplish every good deed with energy and readiness.'

ποιοῦσιν ἀλλὰ καὶ
συνευδοκοῦσιν τοῖς
πράσσουσιν.

οἱ πράσσοντες αὐτά, ἀλλὰ καὶ
οἱ συνευδοκοῦντες
αὐτοῖς.[1]

1 Cor. 2.9

1 Clem. 34.8

Ἅ ὀφθαλμὸς οὐκ εἶδεν
καὶ οὖς οὐκ ἤκουσεν
καὶ ἐπὶ καρδίαν ἀνθρώπου οὐκ
ἀνέβη,
ἃ ἡτοίμασεν ὁ θεὸς
τοῖς ἀγαπῶσιν αὐτόν.

ὀφθαλμὸς οὐκ εἶδεν,
καὶ οὖς οὐκ ἤκουσεν,
καὶ ἐπὶ καρδίαν ἀνθρώπου οὐκ
ἀνέβη,
ὅσα ἡτοίμασεν κύριος
τοῖς ὑπομένουσιν αὐτόν.[2]

In light of these texts, it is precarious to assume an independent tradition behind Clement's use of the Sower. If we date Clement to 95–96 CE in Rome,[3] we are faced with a situation where the author clearly has in his library a copy of Romans, 1 Corinthians and Hebrews and invokes these texts at numerous points without word-for-word fidelity.[4] Since Mark was published around 70–75 CE and was

1. Translation and Greek text for *1 Clement* from Lake, *Apostolic Fathers*, I, pp. 68-69. 'For those who do these things are hateful to God, and "not only those who do them, but also those who take pleasure in them."'
2. Translation and Greek text for *1 Clement* is taken from Lake, *Apostolic Fathers* 1:66-67. Clement, 'Eye has not seen, nor ear heard, nor the human heart conceived what things the Lord hath prepared for those who wait for him.' I have modified Lake's translation of *1 Clem.* 34.8 to conform with the NSRV where the Greek warrants. This scriptural quote is a striking agreement since it represents a typical Pauline amalgamation of biblical texts. The 'quote' does not appear in the canonical text of the Hebrew Bible. Paul has perhaps run together Isa. 64.3 (LXX), 52.15 and Sir. 1.10. The quote may also represent a now 'lost' apocryphal source (*Testament of Jacob*, or an Elijah apocalypse). See, for example, H. Conzelmann, *1 Corinthians* (Hermeneia; trans. G.W. MacRae; Philadelphia: Fortress Press, 1975), pp. 63-64; E. von Nordheim, 'Das Zitat des Paulus in 1 Kor 2:9 und seine Beziehung zum koptischen Testament Jakobs', *ZNW* 65 (1974), pp. 112-20; H. Koester, 'Apocryphal and Canonical Gospels', *HTR* 73 (1980), p. 115. Similarly, *1 Clem.* 37.3-5 draws upon 1 Cor. 12.21; 15.23 but again paraphrases and adapts Paul's original.
3. See J.B. Tyson, *The New Testament and Early Christianity* (New York: Macmillan, 1984), p. 422. Perrin and Duling, *The New Testament: an Introduction*, p. 227.
4. Regarding Hebrews, compare at 1 Clem. 36.1 (Heb. 2.18; 3.1); 36.2 (Heb. 1.3-4); 17.1 (Heb. 11.37). For a contrasting view on Clement's knowledge of Mark, see Koester, '1. Clem. weist nie auf ein schriftliches Evangelium hin. . . Es läßt

distributed widely enough by the ninth decade to have reached both Matthew and Luke, a copy had likely arrived in Rome by this time. The context alone demands certain modifications to the parable. Clement does not want to dwell on the failed seed: he wants to convince the reader that the resurrection follows death as surely as day follows night. The failed seed suggests that not all are raised! This redactional concern, and his application of the image, also explain Clement's 'failure' to give the allegorical interpretation. Clement's usual practice with early Christian texts suggests that word-for-word reproduction is unlikely.[1] His version of the parable, therefore, is not an independent oral tradition.

The above discussion demonstrates that neither Clement nor Thomas represent an independent version of the parable. Regardless of Thomas' original relationship with the synoptics, in this instance, the Coptic translation displays a textual relationship with the Markan tradition. Either Thomas had access to Mark's pre-Gospel source, or the translation has been harmonized to Mark.

b. *Literary and Thematic Parallels*

Literary parallels for the parable are not lacking. An examination of these parallels is necessary, given the likelihood of a pre-Gospel tract, to determine the possibility that the parable actually originated as a literary unit. The motif of birds eating the seed before it is ploughed into the earth is found in *Jub.* 11.11:

> And Prince Mastema sent crows and birds so that they might eat the seed which was being sown in the earth in order to spoil the earth so that they might rob mankind of their labors. Before they plowed in the seed, the crows picked it off the surface of the earth.[2]

The motif of barren rocky soil is found at Sir. 40.15, ἔκγονα ἀσεβῶν οὐ πληθυνεῖ κλάδους, καὶ ῥίζαι ἀκάθαρτοι ἐπ ἀκροτόμου πέτρας ('The children of the ungodly put out few branches; they are unhealthy roots on sheer rock'). Scott notes that thorns are a common metaphor for the wicked in the Hebrew Bible

---

sich also mit ziemlicher Sicherheit sagen, daß der Verfasser des 1. Clem. keines unserer synoptischen Evangelien benutzte', *Synoptische Überlieferung*, p. 23.

1. For a similar conclusion see H. Koester, *Ancient Christian Gospels: Their History and Development* (Philadelphia: Trinity; London: SCM Press; 1990), p. 70.

2. Translation from Charlesworth, (ed.), *The Old Testament Pseudepigrapha*, II, p. 78.

and rabbinic literature. The motif is found at Jer. 4.3 'Break up your fallow ground, and do not sow among thorns' and in a comment on Exod. 27.8 in the Midrash, 'When at Sinai they were like lilies and roses, now [i.e., after the incident of the golden calf] they have become like rubble, like thorn-bushes'.[1] Jeremias has pointed to Gen. 26.12 as an example of an eschatological text promising an overabundant harvest.[2] Isa. 27.6 also contains the eschatological expectation that the Day of the Lord would produce a fantastic harvest.[3] The triple enumeration (thirtyfold, sixtyfold, one hundredfold) is similar to Sir. 41.4 'Whether life lasts for ten years or a hundred or a thousand, there are no questions asked in Hades'.

C.H. Cave points to a number of scriptural parallels for the parable's imagery.[4] Isa. 55.10 speaks of the rain that waters the earth and brings forth seed to sow and bread to eat. He believes that Mk 4.6 may contain an allusion to Jer. 17.8. Verse 7 has parallels at Jer. 4.3 (see above); Gen. 26.12 (see above); and Hos. 10.12. This latter text commands one to sow in justice and promises to reap what loyalty deserves. Isa. 37.30-31 contains an interesting exhortation and promise:

> And this shall be the sign for you: This year eat what grows of itself, and in the second year what springs from that; then in the third year sow, reap, plant vineyards, and eat their fruit. The surviving remnant of the house of Judah shall again take root downward, and bear fruit upward.

Cave also notes the eschatological promise in Ezek. 36.29-30. Since most of these texts were read in the synagogue on the first three

1. Scott, *Hear then the Parable*, p. 134. The reference is to Rabbah Midrashim Exodus 42.7. Scott lists as a reference A. Feldman, *The Parables and Similes of the Rabbis* (Cambridge: Cambridge University Press, 1927), pp. 186-87.

2. J. Jeremias, 'Palästinakundliches zum Gleichnis vom Säsemann, Mark IV.3-8 par', *NTS* 13 (1966–67), p. 53. ἔσπειρεν δὲ Ἰσαακ ἐν τῇ γῇ ἐκείνῃ καὶ εὗρεν ἐν τῷ ἐνιαυτῷ ἐκείνῃ ἑκατοστεύουσαν κριθήν· εὐλόγησεν δὲ αὐτὸν κύριος LXX 'Isaac sowed seed in that land, and in the same year reaped a hundredfold. The LORD blessed him and the man became rich.'

3. 'In the days to come Jacob shall take root, Israel shall blossom and put forth shoots, and fill the whole world with fruit.' As noted by Scott, *Hear then the Parable*, p. 356. He also points to *b. Ket.* 111b which promises each grape shall yield at least 30 kegs of wine. Compare also Papias' tradition of a saying of Jesus promising a yield of 25 measures of wine per grape, Irenaeus, *Adversus Haereses*, 5.33.3-4. The saying has a close parallel at *2 Bar.* 29.5-6.

4. Cave, 'Parables and the Scriptures', pp. 380-82.

sabbaths of the month of Ab during the three-year cycle of readings, Cave believes it reasonable that the Sower was part of a sermon on repentance near or on the ninth of Ab.[1]

In proverbial wisdom the adage 'You reap what you sow' may be noted. Paul uses the image at Gal. 6.7, while the *Testament of Levi* 13.6 states 'Sow good things in your souls and you will find them in your lives. If you sow evil, you will reap every trouble and tribulation.'[2] Apocalyptic applications of this proverbial image are common. *2 Bar.* 8.9 contains the exhortation 'Sow not again, you farmers; And why, earth, should you yield crops at harvest? Keep to yourself your goodly fruits.'[3]

The image of seed and crop was common in eschatological contexts as a symbol of the resurrection. Paul's use of the metaphor at 1 Cor. 15.35-38 is well known. Rabbinic parallels have been attributed to both Rabbi Meir (ca. 200 CE—*b. Sanh.* 90b) and Rabbi Hiyy ben Joseph (*b. Ket.* 111b). Compare also *4 Ezra* 8.41:

> For just as the farmer sows many seeds upon the ground and plants a multitude of seedlings, and yet not all that have been sown will come up in due season, and not all that were planted will take root; so also those who have been sown in the world will not all be saved.[4]

The image of agricultural endeavour, especially sowing seed, was the standard analogy for *paideia*—i.e., both teaching and culture—in Hellenistic thought. Burton Mack notes a number of ancient texts that use this metaphor:

> The views of our teachers are as it were the seeds. Learning from childhood is analogous to the seeds falling betimes upon the prepared ground (Hippocrates, *Law* III).

> As is the seed that is ploughed into the ground, so must one expect the harvest to be, and similarly when good education is ploughed into your persons, its effect lives and burgeons throughout their lives, and neither rain nor drought can destroy it (Antiphon, fr. 60 in Diels, *Vorsokratiker*).

1. Cave, 'Parables and the Scriptures', p. 382.
2. Charlesworth, *The Old Testament Pseudepigrapha*, I, p. 793. Scott, *Hear then the Parable* also lists Prov. 22.8; Job 4.8; Sir. 7.3; p. 359 n. 66.
3. Reddish, *Apocalyptic Literature*, p. 103. The translation is from Sparks, *The Apocryphal Old Testament*. Compare also *4 Ezra* 4.31; 9.17-19; 9.31; *2 Bar.* 22.5-6; 32.1; *1 En.* 3; 5; 62.7-8; *6 Ezra* 15.13; 16.32, 43, 77.
4. Quoted in Reddish, *Apocalyptic Literature*, p. 81. The translation is from the RSV. Compare *2 Bar.* 70.2, and *The Apocalypse of Peter*, section 4.

Words should be scattered like seed; no matter how small the seed may be, if it once has found favourable ground, it unfolds its strength and from an insignificant thing spreads to its greatest growth (Seneca, *Epistles* 38.2).

If you wish to argue that the mind requires cultivation, you would use a comparison from the soil, which if neglected produced thorns and thickets, but if cultivated will bear fruit (Quintilian, *Institutio oratoria* 5.11.24).[1]

These literary parallels provide a serious barrier to postulating oral tradition for the parable. Virtually every element of the parable's imagery was in place within the literary cultural heritage of the first century. Far from requiring an origin in the oral preaching of Galilee, the 'parable' could have been composed as a literary unit by anyone with access to any of the above texts. To take a modern analogy: when most mystery novels are analysed there is little that is 'new' or 'original'. Characterizations, scenes, plot twists and other such components are so well known as to be stock elements of the genre. So too with the Sower, the component parts are all well attested in the literature of antiquity.

This problem becomes more acute when we recognize that Mark must have had a written source. The literary nature of his tradition is virtually guaranteed since the parable and its allegorical interpretation differ considerably stylistically. M. Black has advanced the case that the parable displays the traits of so-called 'translation Greek' from a Semitic (i.e., Aramaic) original. He notes that in most of the parables of the synoptic tradition we find the aorist participle describing events anterior to the action of the main verb in a frequency that is comparable to idiomatic Greek. The Sower is an exception, and hence Black believes that the absence of the hypotactic aorist participle is evidence of a fairly literal translation of an Aramaic original.[2]

1. As quoted in Mack, *A Myth of Innocence*, pp. 159-60. Mack also notes the chreia of Isocrates quoted by Hermogenes in his handbook on rhetoric, 'the root of *paideia* is bitter, but the fruit is sweet'; and the following analogy from Hermogenes, 'Just as farmers must work the soil before reaping its fruits, so also must those who work with words.' See pp. 160-61, n. 18. The Antiphon quote is taken from H. Diels (ed.), *Die Fragmente der Vorsokratiker* (ed. W. Kranz; vol. 2; Berlin: Weidmann, 9th edn, 1959).

2. Black, *Aramaic Approach*, p. 63. Black admits, however, that this idiom is missing throughout Mark's Gospel as a whole, p. 64.

Secondly, Black points to the enumeration of the seed's harvest at v. 8. The fact that there is no known Greek parallel for the enumeration with ἕν and the corrections in Matthew, Luke and the various manuscript alterations testify just how foreign this construction was felt to be in Greek.[1] To this may be added the Semitic constructions ὁ σπείρων σπεῖραι and ἐγένετο ἐν τῷ σπείρειν. There is also the Semitic preference for the word order verb–subject at ἐξῆλθεν ὁ σπείρων, ἦλθεν τὰ πετεινά, and ἀνέβησαν αἱ ἄκανθαι. Jeremias has also pointed to the use of the definite article which is used in what we usually translate as an indefinite sense at vv. 3, 4, 5, 7, 8.[2]

The Greek style is sufficiently distinctive from Mark's normal syntax as to demand a written source. In a context of non-formulaic oral tradition, Mark's normal syntax could be expected to assert itself to a much greater degree. A written source, on the other hand, acts as a 'skeletal guide' to the author's expression. If we take Matthew and Luke's use of their sources as a guide, even allowing for redaction, we could expect 50 per cent or more of the source to be retained. This would account for the noted Semitisms. But the greater Semitic style of writing may not evidence an original Aramaic oral tradition. Semitisms in Greek may have any number of origins, including simply an author well versed in the literary style of the Septuagint. The case for oral tradition for the unit must be based on more than simply Semitisms or other structural elements. It is time to examine the case for authenticity as it has been advanced previously.

c. *Authenticity and the Ministry of Jesus*
Attempts to locate the saying in the ministry of Jesus are not lacking. For Dodd the parable shows that 'in spite of all, the harvest is plentiful: it is only the labourers that are lacking'.[3] For Jeremias the

1. Black, *Aramaic Approach*, p. 124.
2. Jeremias, *Parables*, p. 11, n. 2: 'The usage is characteristic of Semitic imagery. Already we find in the OT the use of the definite article with an indefinite meaning often in parables and pictorial narratives. In such cases the Semite thinks pictorially and has an image in his mind of a concrete instance, though he may be speaking of a general phenomenon.'
3. Dodd, *Parables*, p. 147. Dodd's interpretation is taken up by Taylor. He too sees a link with the reign of God; by this parable, Jesus illustrates his belief that 'despite unresponsive hearers, the field is white unto harvest (cf. Jn iv. 35)', *The Gospel According to St Mark*, p. 251. Nineham, in contrast, notes the suggested connection with the reign of God but remains uncertain. 'However, we cannot be

story acts as an encouragement during what to human eyes appears as unfruitful labour. Jesus remains confident and joyful, 'he knows that God has made a beginning, bringing with it a harvest of reward beyond all asking or conceiving. In spite of every failure and opposition, from hopeless beginnings, God brings forth the triumphant end which he had promised.'[1] It is even easy for Jeremias to visualize the situation in which Jesus uttered the parable: like the Mustard Seed and Leaven it came during a time of doubt. These latter parables resulted from doubt regarding the meagreness of Jesus' following; the Sower, however, responded to disappointment over 'the apparently ineffectual preaching (Mk 6.5f), the bitter hostility (Mk 3.6), and the increasing desertions (Jn 6.60)'.[2]

Such early attempts to reconstruct a concrete setting in the ministry of Jesus cannot withstand critical scrutiny. References to settings in the Gospel narratives and other sayings are circular arguments assuming the historicity of these other texts—an assumption particularly indefensible in light of the findings of redaction critics. Jeremias' attempt to differentiate even the specific disappointments occasioning such similar parables as the Mustard Seed and the Sower is particularly ingenious. It gives the illusion of the critic's ability to 'push back' through the oral stage to reconstruct a detailed chronology of Jesus' life. Specifically how this is done (i.e., just what details in the stories show they relate specifically only to the narratives Jeremias enumerates for them) is not explained. Jeremias' methodology is intuitive at this point: he senses one story as more appropriate than another as a response for a particular Gospel narrative and postulates a chronological connection. To give an illustration, he traces the Sower back to an earlier date than the Mustard Seed despite the fact that both have been linked together chronologically by Mark.

---

dogmatic about the reference to the Kingdom; it is just possible that the original intention was simply to give encouragement to the disciples in face of the many disappointments and set-backs their sowing of the seed was bound to meet, or even that it was to bring home to the hearers the great responsibility that lay upon them', *The Gospel of St Mark*, p. 135. Again, the interpretation is guided by the overall Markan context.

1. Jeremias, *Parables*, p. 150.
2. Jeremias, *Parables*, p. 151. Jeremias' triple enumeration of the failures corresponds well to the structure of the parable!

More recent reconstructions are more modest in scope. Attempts at linking the passage to a particular time in Jesus' ministry are a matter of the past. What we find instead is an emphasis upon interpreting the story according to the new hermeneutics of 'parable'.[1] This change can be noted in Charles E. Carlston, who is uncertain whether the parable goes back to Jesus. Rather, at the earliest, pre-allegorical stage, the parable 'served in the church as an answer to the problem of the mixed reception given Christian preaching: such reception no more calls into question the full coming of the Kingdom than the loss of some seed creates doubts about the probability of the harvest'.[2] But this interpretation must surely be rejected. It is under the direct influence of the secondary allegory, relating parable solely to the missionary preaching of the early church!

With the emphasis upon parable as metaphor a change can be detected. Illustrative of this approach is the exposition of John R. Donahue. In the story's conclusion, he says, the 'expectation of the hearer is shattered' in the 'contrast between a 75 per cent failure and an extraordinary harvest'. This contrast suggests that 'there is no comparison between the expectation of the kingdom and its effect'.[3] Donahue has interpreted the fourfold structure mechanically: since four types of seed are enumerated they each must represent 25 per cent of the sowing! This is an unnatural—and unnecessary—reading. The harvest is also not given in relation to the total amount of seed sown but in relation to each particular seed: one yields thirtyfold, another sixtyfold, and a third one hundredfold.

A different approach is taken by Scott. He finds it unusual that the parable draws attention to the inevitable failure that accompanies sowing. Since the first three scenes are all accidents, the hearer is left with a kingdom in which failure, miracle and normality are the coordinates. Since a number of first-century texts indicate that a harvest of up to one hundredfold is common, Scott contrasts the expectation of an abundant harvest (encouraged by the story's structure) with the anti-climax of an everyday and ordinary harvest.

---

1. One of the best surveys on the changing understanding of 'parable' in modern scholarship is given by Perrin in *Jesus and the Language of the Kingdom*, pp. 89-93.

2. C.E. Carlston, *The Parables of the Triple Tradition* (Philadelphia: Fortress Press, 1975), p. 148

3. Donahue, *The Gospel in Parable*, p. 34.

Thus, in 'failure and everydayness lies the miracle of God's activity. . .The hearer who navigates within this triangle can experience God's ruling activity under the most unfamiliar guises, even among prostitutes and tax collectors—in the everyday.'[1] In an application of the criterion of distinctiveness, Scott points out that in the Sower, the reign of God 'does not need the moral perfection of Torah nor the apocalyptic solution of overwhelming harvest'.[2] But Scott's thesis relies upon the 'distinctiveness' of Jesus' attitude towards tax collectors and sinners, a distinctive attitude in particular to that of the Pharisees. The interpretation therefore relies upon Jeremias' conclusion that it was the *am ha-aretz* (the 'people of the land') who predominantly figured among Jesus' followers. These people were 'the uneducated, the ignorant, whose religious ignorance and moral behaviour stood in the way of their access to salvation, according to the convictions of the time'.[3] Implicit is a view of these people as 'unwashed masses' held in disdain by the 'morally smug' Pharisees and shown compassion by Jesus. But according to E.P. Sanders, after surveying the appropriate rabbinic literature, 'there is absolutely no passage in the entirety of that literature. . .which in any way supports the assertion that the scrupulous and learned regarded the ordinary people as "the wicked", those who flagrantly and persistently disobeyed the law.'[4] Distinctiveness in this instance does not provide an adequate basis for postulating a setting in the life of Jesus for the parable. Despite Scott's attempt, the story remains 'commonplace' in

---

1. Scott, *Hear then the Parable*, p. 362. Donahue above has followed Jeremias in interpreting a 7- to 10-fold harvest as average. In contrast, in light of Pliny, *Natural History* 18.21.95, Scott interprets a hundredfold harvest as merely a good one. See Scott, *Hear then the Parable*, p. 357.

2. Scott, *Hear then the Parable*, p. 362.

3. Jeremias, *New Testament Theology I*, p. 112.

4. E.P. Sanders, *Jesus and Judaism* (London: SCM Press, 1985), p. 180. Telling also is his observation regarding Lk. 18.9-14 where the note in the *New Oxford Annotated Bible* describes the implied faults as ritual failures: 'This indicates very well how deeply committed New Testament scholarship is to the view that the Pharisees were interested only in ritual and trivia'. Compare I. Zeitlin, 'Many of the earliest rabbis were drawn from the people, working with their hands by day, and studying, discussing and teaching in the evenings and on the sabbaths and festivals. Any antagonism between them and the multitude is out of the question.' *Jesus and the Judaism of his Time* (New York: Polity Press, 1988), p. 102.

its intent.[1] It remains essentially an encouragement to hope despite temporary setbacks. Its appeal and imagery are so common as to be available to literally anyone in the first century prior to Mark.

d. *The Parable and Orality*

The oral history of the Sower remains, therefore, murky at best. *1 Clement* provides no independent support for the oral circulation of the unit. The version in the Coptic *Gospel of Thomas* as we have it shows considerable agreement in word order and vocabulary with the synoptics. Some literary relationship with the synoptic tradition is highly likely. The extent to which its 'independently attested' triadic structures (e.g., 'went out; filled his hands; scattered;' 'fell on rock; took no root; produced no ears;' and 'fell among thorns; choked the seed; worms ate it') are the direct residue of oral tradition rather than simply literary balance written in at the textual level also is not clear. To assume that such structures must result from orality is an unwarranted procedure.

Mark's version provides other problems in retracing the oral history of the story. Most exegetes are agreed that redactional expansion has taken place, and there is also partial agreement as to where these expansions occur (especially with respect to vv. 5-6). But Crossan's inability at first to identify the scorching sun as secondary should remind us that redaction criticism can become an 'intuitive' evaluation which owes much to the literary sensibilities of the critic. Both Weeden and Crossan's reconstructions at times appear to operate on the assumption that the oral original must have been 'triadic', 'paratactic' and 'balanced' in form in accord with the laws of orality. As we have seen above in Chapter 2, these features of style cannot be reserved exclusively for the oral medium. What is perhaps even more telling is that the Markan parable has stylistic characteristics that are significantly distinctive from Mark's redactional practice. This in turn argues for a written source behind Mark's Gospel. Composition from an oral original by Mark would have followed the parable's structure; such features as the Semitic enumeration of the harvest most likely would have been changed to a more idiomatic Greek expression. The story was thus committed to writing prior to Mark by an author

---

1. The same objection applies equally to the interpretation offered by Crossan. Since Crossan interprets the Sower in similar fashion as the Mustard Seed, I have reserved discussion of his view for this latter section of the book.

whose literary style was more Semitic than Mark's. Only this hypothesis can best explain the stylistic features of the text as we have it. However, in view of the extensive biblical, pseudepigraphic and Greco-Roman literary parallels for the text, it is impossible with any certainty to read back beyond this earlier literary stage into any previous oral history. The author of this pre-synoptic tract would certainly have had access to the cultural heritage examined above and it is unclear just how much of the story represents the author's literary crafting or setting down of oral traditions.

Finally, there is the problem of Crossan and Weeden's reconstructed 'original form'. The procedure of identifying 'expansions' relies upon a perfectly balanced triadic structure set in dualistic opposition. But this reconstruction must be viewed as a figment of the critic's literate imagination! As my discussion has shown, there is no 'original' oral form—each performance is a new rendition of the tradition. Olrik's 'law of three' has been misunderstood. As Olrik defined this law, 'Every time that a striking scene occurs in a narrative, and continuity permits, the scene is repeated'.[1] This law refers to the triadic repetition of events, it does not guarantee that these events are narrated in the same number of words. In an oral performance of the Sower there is no reason to assume that the amount of time spent on each of the failed seeds would be equal. Performance interacts with audience reaction. If the performer senses boredom the narrative is abbreviated and brought swiftly to its conclusion. A responsive audience, on the other hand, encourages the bard to 'spin out the tale'. This precisely balanced form would never survive the oral transmissional process! At every telling pressure would be put upon this 'original form' such that it would soon be irrecoverably lost. The identification of expansions within Mark are not, strictly speaking, made on the basis of breaking the oral form. Rather, Mark's redactional insertion technique can be seen, and the expansions are tied to the interpretation.[2]

The oral phase of this parable, if it ever existed, is lost. One can reconstruct, to some degree, the literary form of Mark's inherited

1. Olrik, 'Epic Law', p. 133. See above, Chapter 2, section 3, f.
2. A point noted by Marcus, *Mystery of the Kingdom*, p. 32. 'By themselves, such features do not necessarily indicate editorial expansion, since they are characteristic not only of redacted texts but also of oral narrative.' See also Gnilka, *Evangelium*, I, p. 157.

tradition. One cannot, from this, reconstruct the exact form of an original 'oral tradition'. Nor can one trace back through the oral phase to successively 'earlier' forms of the parable. Its imagery and intent remain so commonplace as to be incapable of sustaining a credible case for 'distinctiveness'. And given that Mark has inherited a written form of the parable one is at an immediate impasse. All critical tools are lacking to reconstruct the redactional tendencies of this earlier author. The act of writing implies a purpose: a written version of the story must have been viewed as an appropriate response to some community need. How this sociological situation directly affected the shaping of the tradition cannot be determined. Hence, without more detailed knowledge of Mark's immediate sources we are at an impasse for accessing the oral phase. In fact, in light of the extensive literary parallels, there is simply no guarantee that the story ever circulated orally in the Christian communities. The literary needs behind the pre-Gospel tract might equally have caused an author to invent the parable from the elements already in place within the literature of antiquity.

2. *The Seed Growing Secretly (Mark 4.26-29; Gospel of Thomas 21c)*

The parable of the Seed Growing Secretly, or the Patient Farmer, presents its own distinctive problems. It is the orphan of Mark's parable sermon, abandoned by Matthew and Luke and much abbreviated by Thomas. Its fate at the hands of modern scholars is no less ignominious. A quick glance through tables of contents, indexes and guides to periodicals will reveal the overwhelming attention that the Sower and Mustard Seed parables have received at the expense of the Seed Growing Secretly. Typical is the treatment of Burton Mack:

> It is neither very provocative as a parable, nor apt as an image of the kingdom of God. Its point is appropriate within its present context, as will become clear, but probably only there. It is best therefore to regard it as a construction composed for that context.[1]

Nevertheless, as a parable it deserves consideration as potential oral tradition.

---

1. Mack, *Myth of Innocence*, p. 153.

a. *The Parable's Omission by Matthew and Luke*

The first problem is the parable's omission in Matthew and Luke. This fact has occasioned surprise and even recourse to an Ur-Marcus hypothesis (i.e., Matthew and Luke did not find the parable in their copies of Mark) or the Griesbach model of synoptic relations.[1] The fact that all extant manuscripts of Mark include the parable renders the first hypothesis extremely speculative. The reason for the agreement of redactional deletion of this parable is not hard to find. Given the limits of space inherent in ancient scrolls and the fact that Matthew and Luke represent the outer limits for a comfortable book length, certain abbreviations in Mark by Matthew and Luke are to be expected. B.H. Streeter has noted the regular compression of Mark's prose by both Matthew and Luke and the latter's 'Great Omission' as space-saving techniques.[2]

The interpretation of the Sower also creates contextual problems for the parable. The allegory leads to an expectation of a similar exposition for the Seed Growing Secretly. Matthew solves the problem by omitting this parable and providing in its place the Wheat and the Tares (complete with allegorical interpretation). The interpretation at Mt. 13.49-50 provides a similar function for the triple parables of the Treasure, Pearl, Fishnet. Luke handles the problem differently. His parable sermon is much more abbreviated and he includes the Mustard Seed with its Q partner the Leaven in a different context (Lk. 13.18-21). But not only is the lack of allegory disturbing, so are the implications of the interpretation of the Sower for the Seed Growing Secretly. If we apply the former as a model to this parable a curious result becomes apparent. If the Sower is Jesus or the early Christian preacher, what would it mean for him to remain idle while the seed grows on its own? If the soil is the various converts and bearing fruit is faithful commitment, what does it mean that the seed grows to harvest automatically? While the allegory of the seeds lends itself naturally to exhortations to faithful perseverance and hope, the most natural allegorical reading of the Seed Growing Secretly undermines this message. This is likely a major factor in the omission of this story by Matthew and Luke.

---

1. See Farmer, *The Synoptic Problem*, pp. 212-13
2. Streeter, *The Four Gospels*, pp. 158-81.

b. *The Parable's Original Form*

Crossan argues that vv. 27 ὁ σπόρος βλαστᾷ καὶ μηκύνηται and 28 αὐτομάτη ἡ γῆ καρποφορεῖ, πρῶτον χόρτον εἶτα στάχυν εἶτα πλήρης σῖτον ἐν τῷ στάχυϊ are redundant and in conflict. The former focuses on the farmer and is capable of 'carrying the contents' of the latter (cp. Mt. 13.26; Heb. 9.4; Jas 5.18), which focuses on the seed's growth. The problem is similar to that at 4.5-6, and Crossan again believes the solution lies in viewing v. 28 as a Markan insertion. The similarity of verbs at 4.20 καρποφοροῦσιν and 4.28 καρποφ-ορεῖ, which differ significantly from the Semitic ἐδίδου καρπόν of 4.8 likewise argues that v. 28 is secondary. Crossan suggests that v. 28 is an addition partially under the influence of v. 20.[1]

Crossan turns to a comparison with Thomas to reconstruct the earliest version. The saying is included with the parable of the Children in the Field and that of the Householder. The inclusion of the exhortation 'Whoever has ears to hear let him hear' suggests that the saying was considered parabolic in Thomas.[2] Thomas focuses upon the moment of the harvest and thus parallels only v. 29 of Mark. The introductions vary, and hence represent for Crossan the separate interests of the two texts' use of the parable. The parable itself in each represents a 'paratactic and threefold structure similar to that noted in the sower'. The Markan version has the double triad of βάλῃ/καθεύδῃ καὶ ἐγείρηται/βλαστᾷ καὶ μηκύνηται and then παραδοῖ/ἀποστέλλει/παρέστηκεν. In Thomas there is a single triad of 'ripened/came quickly/reaped'. 'The former', Crossan concludes, 'may be considered fuller and more original.'[3]

Crossan examines the allusion to Joel 4.13 at the parable's conclusion (Mk 4.29). Joel's prophecy is a reference to God's eschatological judgment 'and is thus an image of punishment as divine vengeance'.[4] But since the reaper in Joel is God, Crossan asks what the meaning of 4.27 would be with its concluding ὡς οὐκ οἶδεν αὐτός. Secondly, Crossan asks whether 'an eschatological judgment of vengeance [is] in keeping with the positive image of the rest of the

---

1. Crossan, 'Seed Parables', pp. 251-52. The addition intends to exhort to patience, much in the manner as do the additions in the Sower parable.

2. The aphorism in Thomas occurs elsewhere only with parables. Cf. Crossan, 'Seed Parables', p. 252.

3. Crossan, 'Seed Parables', p. 253.

4. Crossan, 'Seed Parables', p. 253.

parable and of παραδοῖ ὁ καρπός in particular'.[1] In view of this tension between the image of God (v. 27 against v. 29), and since Thomas does not contain the allusion to Joel, Crossan believes that the quotation is a sharpening of the original image which was something like that found in Thomas with the threefold rhythm of ripening, coming and harvesting.[2]

While Crossan has provided a plausible reconstruction it remains unproven at best. Assigning v. 28 to Markan redaction creates a problem: the verse is a perfect triad, πρῶτον χόρτον εἶτα στάχυν εἶτα πλήρης σῖτον ἐν τῷ στάχυϊ.[3] Precisely why this triad should be assigned to the written level of transmission while the other triads are clear signs of orality is not really clear. For although v. 27 entirely able to carry the contents of v. 28, there is still the problem of orality's need for repetition. On formal grounds, therefore, the filling out of v. 27 by the triad of v. 28 must be held to fit into either a literary or oral context. The linguistic similarity of καρποφοροῦσιν (4.20) and καρποφορεῖ (4.28) which differ from the Semitic ἐδίδου καρπόν (4.8) is more significant. But the Septuagint uses καρποφορήσει to translate Hab. 3.17.[4] This linguistic evidence therefore is not decisive since at least two other possibilities remain. If the allegorical interpretation came to Mark in a written source, harmonization of these two verses (4.20, 28) may have occurred either by the author of the allegory or by Mark himself. The mere inclusion of καρποφορεῖ at v. 28 in itself is not sufficient evidence for the secondary character of the entire verse.[5]

Crossan's argument that the version in Mark is 'fuller' and thus 'more original' merits examination. Implicit is a view of orality where units originate in 'pure' and 'complete' forms and degenerate during transmission into corrupted 'incomplete' scions. This simply is not the case—fullness of performance in oral tradition is usually

1. Crossan, 'Seed Parables', p. 253.

2. Crossan, 'Seed Parables', p. 253.

3. Marcus, *Mystery*, p. 164, notes that the stages of growth in v. 28 are described in 'an emphatically linear manner'. See also Pesch, *Markusevangelium*, I, p 255.

4. As noted by Black, *Aramaic Approach*, p. 163. Black also provides a discussion on the unusual use of παραδοῖ at v. 29; pp. 163-64.

5. Compare Marcus, *Mystery of the Kingdom*, p. 169. 'Such expansion is by no means certain.'

determined by the audience's response. Over the course of oral transmission the length and fullness of a story will vary greatly. Fullness is also no less a literary characteristic. What is more telling in the present instance is the literary context within Thomas. Saying 21 contains three parables which are joined by the theme and word link 'coming'. Children play in a field that is not theirs; when the owners 'come' and say 'Give us our field' the children undress. If a householder knows when the thief is 'coming', the goods will be well guarded. And when the fruit in a field ripens, the harvester 'comes' sickle in hand and reaps. This accounts for the abbreviated nature of the parable in Thomas. With the focus on the moment of action, the previous aspects of the parable become an intrusion to the author's theme. The context thus strongly suggests that had Thomas known the fuller version of the story abbreviation would have still been likely.

On formal grounds alone, therefore, there is no reason to postulate that either Mark or Thomas' version of the parable is closer to the 'oral original'. Redactional considerations within Thomas suggest that the present pithy form of the parable is due to abbreviation. Since Mark inherited a written form of the tradition, and given Thomas' redactional concerns, there is simply no way of proving either independence or dependence in the present case alone.

c. *Literary and Linguistic Background*

A closer inspection of the cultural background of vv. 28-29 is in order to determine their place in the 'original' form of the parable. Scott shows that the key word of v. 28, αὐτομάτη, is found in a number of contexts in the Septuagint. It is used at Josh. 6.5 to describe the mysterious divine activity in the destruction of Jericho, 'And when they shall have shouted, the walls of the city shall fall of themselves [*automata*]'. It is used at Wisdom of Solomon 17.6 to describe the plague of darkness on the Egyptians, 'Nothing was shining through to them except a dreadful, self-kindled [αὐτομάτη] fire'. Or again, Job 24.24 describes the fall of an evil person as an ear of corn that falls from its stalk by itself.[1]

The word is used to translate the Hebrew ספיח, that which springs up of itself in the second year and served as food when no grain could be

---

1. Scott, *Hear then the Parable*, p. 368. The translations of the LXX are by Scott.

sown.[1] The sapiyah (that which grows of itself) is also the free growth of the sabbatical year (see Lev. 25.25; Exod. 23.10-11). 2 Kgs 19.29 uses the term to signify God's grace and concern for Israel.

The Hebrew Bible parallels for v. 28 argue strongly for a similar point of origin for it and the allusion to Joel in v. 29. Although some scholars have suggested that Mark has composed the parable (using the Sower as a model), the linguistic and thematic indications are inconclusive.[2] Unlike such passages as 4.1-2, 33-34; the parable of the Seed Growing Secretly does not exhibit strong characteristics of Markan syntax and vocabulary. Since both the Sower and Mustard Seed also have extensive parallels in biblical and post-biblical Judaism, the most likely time for this would be at the pre-Markan literary stage. This is indicated not only by the biblical parallels but by the Semitic word order of verb–subject (ἐστὶν ἡ βασιλεία τοῦ θεοῦ; παραδοῖ ὁ καρπός; and παρέστηκεν ὁ θερισμός) and the Semitic order of καθεύδῃ καὶ ἐγείρηται νύκτα καὶ ἡμέραν.

1 Clem. 23.3-5 also stresses gradual growth and the certainty of harvest:

> Let this Scripture be far from us in which he says 'Wretched are the double-minded, who doubt in their soul and say "We have heard these things even in the days of our fathers, and behold we have grown old, and none of these things has happened to us". Oh, foolish men, compare yourself to a tree: take a vine, first it sheds its leaves, then there comes a bud, then a leaf, then a flower, and after this the unripe grape, then the full bunch.' See how in a little time the fruit of the tree comes to ripeness. Truly his will shall be quickly and suddenly accomplished. . .[3]

As Marcus concludes, this passage 'is not based on Mark'.[4] But the similarity of theme (and perhaps application) shows the problem in attributing an oral history for the Markan parable. Little scholarly effort has been exerted in reconstructing the oral original of Clement, and even less in situating it in the ministry of Jesus! I turn now to

1. See F. Brown, S.R. Driver and C.A. Briggs, *Hebrew and English Lexicon of the Old Testament* (Oxford: Clarendon Press, 1907), p. 705
2. See for example Lambrecht, 'Redaction and Theology', p. 296; and *idem*, *Once More Astonished: The Parables of Jesus* (New York: Crossroad, 1981), p. 101. See also the discussion in Scott, *Hear then the Parable*, pp. 364-65.
3. Marcus, *Mystery of the Kingdom*, p. 165. Translation is from Lake, *Apostolic Fathers*, I, p. 51. The quote is also found at *2 Clem.* 11. 2.
4. Marcus, *Mystery of the Kingdom*, p. 166.

examine the reconstructions of the Seed Growing Secretly's situation within the ministry of Jesus.

d. *Authenticity and the Ministry of Jesus*

For Jeremias, this parable belongs with the Sower and the Mustard Seed as parables of contrast that provide 'The Great Assurance'. Noting the oft-repeated conjecture that this parable was delivered as a contrast to the Zealots' efforts to throw off the Roman yoke by violence, Jeremias sees the story as Jesus' answer to why he refused to act when the hour demanded it. The parable again responds to doubts regarding Jesus' mission and to frustrated hopes. Just as the farmer patiently awaits the harvest, so too 'God's hour comes irresistibly'.[1]

Again we see an unjustified confidence to relate the story to a concrete historical setting. The specific question that 'provoked' the parable has even been inferred, and the story is interpreted to demonstrate a political philosophy drastically different from that of the Zealots. Jeremias' interpretation is particularly congenial to middle-class, middle-of-the-road sensibilities on the role of violence in resistance to the state, and one wonders whether Jeremias has read his Schweitzer! The ability to situate the story in such a precise historical context goes far beyond orality's ability to preserve context and setting.

C.E.B. Cranfield interprets the parable in harmony with the Lamp aphorism (Mk 4.21). It is a parable of contrast. The narrative reversal between sowing and harvest parallels the fate of the reign of God. 'As seedtime is followed in due time by harvest, so will the present hiddenness and ambiguousness of the kingdom of God be succeeded by its glorious manifestation.'[2] But this interpretation owes too much to the secondary Markan context and especially Mark's secrecy motif. Implicit seems to be a christological assumption of Jesus' awareness of a unique commission from God. This assumption is perhaps more clearly seen in the interpretation of E. Schweizer. He sees in the

---

1. Jeremias, *Parables*, p. 152. This line of interpretation is taken up by Nineham, *The Gospel of St Mark*, p. 143. 'Perhaps originally it answered important remarks from over-zealous disciples and expressed Jesus' conviction that it would be God's act and not human activity like that of the Zealots which would bring about the kingdom'.

2. C.E.B. Cranfield, *The Gospel According to Saint Mark* (Cambridge: Cambridge University Press, 1959), p. 168.

parable a message similar to that of the Sower. He finds it surprising that there is no mention of plowing, harrowing or cultivating. Nor is there mention of drought or storm. The clue to the meaning is in the emphasis upon the harvest. 'Therefore', Schweizer confidently tells us, 'the message of this parable is similar to that of vs. 8: The harvest is sure to come. Jesus has not been commissioned to do more than the sowing. Everything else is God's concern.'[1] But Schweizer's interpretation is still remarkably christological! The sower is Jesus who has a certain knowledge of his unique commissioning from God. Sowing is also essentially Jesus' preaching in accord with the allegorical interpretation of the Sower.

Crossan attempts an exposition of the three seed parables based on his understanding of 'parable' as a unique genre. He believes that the parables represent 'the primary and immediate expression of his [Jesus'] own experience of God'. He rejects an interpretation that sees the parables as primarily ethical or didactic. The parables are not the referent of Jesus' actions, controversies and eventual death (as in Dodd–Jeremias). Instead, they represent the cause of these events.[2] As language events, they bring into being a new experience (and reality) of God, rather than serving as an intellectual apology for a 'message'. For Crossan, both the Seed Growing Secretly and the Wheat and the Tares 'are images of resolute and prudent action, of the farmer who knows how and when to move. They are parables of the response demanded by the kingdom's advent.'[3] What is perhaps most remarkable about Crossan's reading is how similar it is in essence to Jeremias'! The centrality of such concepts as 'resolute response', 'eschatological crisis', 'in breaking of the kingdom', and 'advent inaugurated by the special emissary Jesus' all have their prominent place in both interpretations. Crossan's promises of a new understanding of the parables as language event, and a shift away from 'intellectual message' to anti-myth and mediated reality, remain disappointingly unfulfilled.

Scott also attempts an interpretation of the parable that would pass the criterion of 'distinctiveness'. The man's action in 'sleeping night and day, [and] of not knowing how the seed grows, runs contrary to

1. Schweizer, *The Good News According to Mark*, p. 102.
2. In other words, these events are the effect (and not the cause) of the images in the parables. Crossan, 'Seed Parables', p. 266.
3. Crossan, 'Seed Parables', p. 266.

the injunctions of the wisdom tradition'. Scott points to such injunctions as Prov. 10.5; 20.5; Ps. 126.5-6 and Isa. 28.24. The numerous steps between sowing and harvest from Isaiah are lacking in the parable, and hence the man emerges as a sluggard 'who will seek in vain for a harvest'. When the harvest does arrive the reader is left with the question of how this could be, given the proverbial wisdom that one reaps what one sows. The answer lies in the allusion to Joel. Just as 'Joel reversed the beating of plowshares into swords, so this parable reverses the quotation from Joel. In the parable the harvest is no longer the apocalyptic war but a harvest of sabbatical aftergrowth planted by an ignorant farmer.'[1]

In responding to Scott's ingenious attempt to interpret the story in light of current literary theory that parables should subvert conventional wisdom, I argue that his principles do not stand up under close examination. Far from showing the farmer to be a sluggard, the Isaiah parallel shows that his action is entirely prudent:

> Do those who plow for sowing plow continually? Do they continually open and harrow their ground? When they have levelled its surface, do they not scatter dill, sow cummin, and plant wheat in rows and barley in its proper place, and spelt as the border. For they are well instructed; their God teaches them (Isa. 28.24-26).

The rhetorical questions indicate that one does not continuously engage in one stage of the agricultural process. After suitable ploughing, one moves on to sowing, just as the farmer does in this parable. Scott has misread v. 27; the farmer does not sleep night and day as a sluggard. Rather, he sets about the common pattern of nature's cycle: sleeping at night and rising in the day. The farmer's willingness to work is made clear at the conclusion; when the harvest arrives, he immediately goes forth with a sickle to bring in the crop. Despite the human inability to comprehend the mysterious way in which God (or nature) brings a crop to maturity, the parable promises full assurance that the harvest will come. Far from reversing conventional wisdom, the invitation to trust in God's power entirely accords with biblical wisdom: not by might, nor by power, but by my

---

1. Scott, *Hear then the Parable*, p. 370. Discussion, pp. 366-70.

Spirit declares the LORD.[1] In this sense, the parable fits well thematically with the Sower. The introduction at v. 26 shares characteristics with the introduction to the Mustard Seed (the third parable in the chapter), providing further evidence for the thematic and linguistic unity of the three parables.

e. *The Parable and Orality*

The results of the above discussion are clear. We have reached the same impasse in recovering an oral form of this parable that was encountered with the Sower. First of all, Thomas offers no help in this process. Certainly the variations between Thomas and Mark are such that an independent oral transmission cannot be ruled out. Nevertheless one cannot tell what such an original structure might have been. Nor can one exclude the possibility of a literary relationship. The context in Thomas provides strong redactional grounds for abbreviation: logion 21 focuses on the theme of the moment of arrival. This theme is sufficient to explain the absence of the earlier elements of the narrative and the paraphrase of the allusion to Joel. Mark, or his source, could ultimately be the tradition behind Thomas. The Markan version likewise evidences strong ties linguistically with the Septuagint. A pre-Markan literary origin by an author with a more Semitic literary style than Mark seems to be the most reasonable hypothesis for the earliest recoverable version of the story. But these strong thematic and linguistic ties make it all but impossible to infer back from this to an earlier oral stage. Indeed, the similarity in image and theme with the Sower and Mustard Seed, the close parallel to the analogy in 1 Clement, and the difficulty in establishing a 'distinctive' meaning for the unit all suggest that Mack may be correct. This parable may represent an original composition created for the pre-Gospel tract.

3. *The Mustard Seed (Mark 4.30-32; Q 13.18-19;*
Gospel of Thomas 20)

The Mustard Seed introduces a new category of sayings: those with double attestation in Mark and Q. It is also found in Thomas (logion

---

1. Scott's interpretation of Joel is also novel: it is unlikely that normal practice was to forge a plowshare into a sword. Joel is, strictly speaking, not a reversal of usual practice but a powerful metaphor of juxtaposition.

20), and thus one is dealing with potentially three independent versions. But before I can consider the possibility of the unit's 'oral history' I must first reconstruct its form in Q and note any redactional additions in the Markan version.

a. The Parable's Original Form

The Mustard Seed is found at Lk. 13.18-19 in a different context from his parallel to Mark's parable sermon. Matthew follows Mark's order at this point and includes it in ch. 13. Since both Matthew and Luke twin the parable with the Leaven, its inclusion in Q is certain. The two versions are:

Mt. 13.31-32	Lk. 13.18-19
Ἄλλην παραβολὴν παρέθηκεν αὐτοῖς λέγων,	Ἔλεγεν οὖν·
Ὁμοία ἐστὶν ἡ βασιλεία τῶν	τίνι ὁμοία ἐστὶν ἡ βασιλεία τοῦ'
οὐρανῶν κόκκῳ σινάπεως, ὃν	θεοῦ καὶ τίνι ὁμοιώσω αὐτήν·
λαβὼν ἄνθρωπος ἔσπειρεν ἐν τῷ	ὁμοία ἐστὶν
ἀγρῷ αὐτοῦ· ὃ μικρότερον μέν	κόκκῳ σινάπεως, ὃν λαβὼν
ἐστιν πάντων τῶν σπερμάτων,	ἄνθρωπος
ὅταν δὲ αὐξηθῇ μεῖζον τῶν	
λαχάνων ἐστὶν καὶ γίνεται	ἔβαλεν εἰς κῆπον ἑαυτοῦ,
δένδρον, ὥστε ἐλθεῖν τὰ πετεινὰ	καὶ ηὔξησεν καὶ ἐγένετο εἰς
τοῦ οὐρανοῦ καὶ κατασκηνοῦν	δένδρον, καὶ τὰ πετεινὰ
ἐν τοῖς κλάδοις αὐτοῦ.	τοῦ οὐρανοῦ κατασκηνοῦν ἐν
	τοῖς κλάδοις αὐτοῦ.

Part of the disagreement in the introductions has been caused by Matthew's use of his stock formula Ἄλλην παραβολὴν παρέθηκεν αὐτοῖς (cp. Mt. 13.24, 31).[1] Luke also regularly introduces parables with εἶπεν/ἔλεγεν παραβολήν, so there is good reason to ascribe the introductory Ἔλεγεν οὖν to redaction.[2] Despite these

---

1. See H. Fleddermann, 'there can be little doubt that these introductions are all redactional', 'The Mustard Seed and the Leaven in Q, the Synoptics, and Thomas', in *SBL Seminar Papers* (ed. D.J. Lull; Atlanta: Scholars Press, 1989), p. 217. Also R. Laufen, *Die Doppelüberlieferungen der Logienquelle und des Markusevangeliums* (BBB, 54; Bonn: Peter Hanstein, 1980), p. 174: 'Die matthäische Einleitung 13,31a dürfte auf den Evangelisten aurückgehen.'

2. Fleddermann, 'Mustard Seed and the Leaven', p. 218. See Laufen, *Die Doppelüberlieferungen*, p. 174: 'Es ist zu vermuten, daß das Gleichnis in der Logienguelle mit einer kurzen Einleitungswendung begann, etwa mit ἔλεγεν (wie bei Lukas) oder εἶπεν ὁ Ἰησοῦς'. See also S. Schulz, *Q: Die Spruchquelle der*

introductory alterations, two points of agreement stand out. There is word-for-word agreement in ὁμοία ἐστὶν ἡ βασιλεία τοῦ θεοῦ (allowing for Matthew's preference for τῶν οὐρανῶν). Secondly, Luke's repetition of ὁμοία ἐστίν at the beginning of the parable places the phrase contextually in agreement with Matthew. Fleddermann observes that Matthew and Luke both tend to avoid Markan double questions, hence it is unlikely that Luke has conflated from Mark. Both ὁμοιόω and ὅμοιος appear in Luke almost exclusively in Q contexts.[1] These facts argue strongly that Luke has retained the Q original here.[2]

The major additions in Matthew (ὃ μικρότερον μέν ἐστιν πάντων τῶν σπερμάτων and μεῖζον τῶν λαχάνων ἐστίν) are due to conflation to Mark.[3] The phrases ἔσπειρεν ἐν τῷ ἀγρῷ αὐτοῦ (Matthew) and ἔβαλεν εἰς κῆπον ἑαυτοῦ (Luke) show close structural agreement, particularly in word order. Either author might have altered Q at this point. Since Luke's κῆπον is an unusual term it is likely redactional.[4] The Matthean phrase, however, finds close parallels at 13.36, 44; 24.18, 40.[5] This means that neither may

Evangelisten (Zurich: Theologischer Verlag, 1972), p. 299. Schulz believes Luke's ἔλεγεν represents the Q introduction.

1. Fleddermann, 'The Mustard Seed and the Leaven', p. 220.

2. A reconstruction supported by A. Polag, 'The Text of Q', in I. Havener, *Q: The Sayings of Jesus* (Good News Studies, 19; Wilmington, DE: Michael Glazier, 1987), p. 140. Marcus also sees ὁμοία...ὁμοιώσω as in Q, *Mystery of the Kingdom*, p. 206, n. 12. Crossan, 'Seed Parables', p. 254 believes Luke has retained the Q introduction. Also, Laufen, *Die Doppelüberlieferungen*, p. 176.

3. Both phrases are omitted from Polag's reconstruction of Q, 'The Text of Q', p. 140. Crossan likewise believes Matthew has conflated at these points from Mark, 'Seed Parables', p. 254.

4. See Scott, *Hear then the Parable*, p. 375. Crossan, 'Seed Parables', p. 254 believes Luke secondary in this element. Polag reconstructs 'sowed in his field', agreeing essentially with Matthew, 'The Text of Q', p. 140. See also H. McArthur,'The Parable of the Mustard Seed', *CBQ* 33 (1971), p. 201. Contra, Fleddermann, 'The Mustard Seed and the Leaven', p. 222; noting that Luke does not use βάλλω often while κῆπος appears only here in the synoptics. He stresses that Q is from a Greek/Hellenistic milieu, and hence that 'the Mustard Seed had already undergone Hellenistic influence before it reached Matthew and Luke' (p. 221). See also Schulz, *Die Spruchquelle*, p. 299, who believes that the rarity of κῆπον points to its inclusion in Q.

5. 'Auch ἐν τῷ ἀγρῷ αὐτοῦ geht auf matthäische Redaktion zurück', Laufen, *Die Doppelüberlieferungen*, p. 175.

represent the Q original. It is particularly difficult to decide with respect to the verb: Mark has σπαρῇ at this point, and hence Matthew may represent conflation. However, we have also seen βάλλω at Mark 4.26 (and *1 Clem.* 24), and this could account for Lukan alteration. Reconstruction of this particular phrase must remain tentative. Most likely, therefore, the Q original read:[1]

τίνι ὁμοία ἐστὶν ὁ βασιλεία τοῦ θεοῦ καὶ τίνι ὁμοιώσω αὐτήν· ὁμοία ἐστὶν κόκκῳ σινάπεως, ὃν λαβὼν ἄνθρωπος [ἔβαλεν ἐν τῷ ἀγρῷ αὐτου]'· καὶ ηὔξησε καὶ ἐγένετο εἰς δένδρον, καὶ τὰ πετεινὰ τοῦ οὐρανοῦ κατασκηνοῦν ἐν τοῖς κλάδοις αὐτοῦ.

The Markan parable has its own problems. As Crossan points out, the grammar is notoriously bad. This raises the possibility of Markan redaction. Attention is quickly focused on the repetitious and chiastic a) ὃς ὅταν σπαρῇ b) ἐπὶ τῆς γῆς. . . b') ἐπὶ τῆς γῆς a') καὶ ὅταν σπαρῇ. Mark's redactional technique often involves copying his source's phrase before and after an insertion.[2] This would indicate that the phrase μικρότερον ὂν πάντων τῶν σπερμάτων and the repetitions b' (ἐπὶ τῆς γῆς—v. 31c) and a' (καὶ ὅταν σπαρῇ— v. 32a) are redaction. The phrase finds its thematic parallel at v. 32b with μεῖζον πάντων τῶν λαχάνων, which argues for the latter's redactional character. As Crossan argues, 'the entire superlative contrast of smallest/largest is from Mark himself'.[3]

---

1. On the reconstruction of the Q form of the parable, see Crossan, 'Seed Parables', pp. 254-55; Polag, 'The Text of Q', p. 140; Marcus, *Mystery of the Kingdom*, pp. 204-06. The [bracket] represents uncertainty regarding the original. Laufen, *Die Doppelüberlieferungen*, p. 176, for example, has here ἔβαλεν εἰς κῆπον αὐτου. An overall scholarly consensus may be said to exist that Luke better preserves the Q original in this parable. See Schulz, *Q: Die Spruchquelle*, pp. 298-300; Kuhn, *Ältere Sammlungen*, p. 99 'daß der Text der Spruchquelle bei Lk besser erhalten ist'.

2. See Crossan, 'Seed Parables', p. 256. He lists as examples Mk 2.9b, 11 (framing v. 10) and 10.47b, 48b (framing 48a). On this technique, see J.R. Donahue's address 'Tradition and Redaction in the Markan Trial Narrative [Mk 14.53-65]' [CBA Convention; Sept. 1, 1970]; summarized in N. Perrin, 'The Christology of Mark: A Study in Methodology', *JR* 51 (1971), pp. 173-87. Perrin lists 47 instances of the technique in Mark! Also, Edwards, 'Markan Sandwiches', pp. 193-216.

3. Crossan, 'Seed Parables', p. 257. A conclusion supported by Marcus, *Mystery of the Kingdom*, p. 208. He holds vv. 31c-32a (μικρότερον ὂν πάντων τῶν σπερμάτων τῶν ἐπὶ τῆς γῆς, καὶ ὅταν σπαρῇ) Markan redaction. See also

Suspicious also is the phrase ὥστε δύνασθαι (v. 32c).[1] The repetition among ἀναβαίνει καὶ γίνεται ... καὶ ποιεῖ κλάδους μεγάλους, also causes difficulties. The first of these can be found in the Sower with respect to the thorns and the seed sown on good soil. Neither of the other terms can be identified as redactional. In view of the parallel at Mk 4.8, my reconstruction tentatively retains the first two verbs and assigns ποιεῖ as the necessary redactional addition due to the motif on the plant's largeness. When these redactional alterations are removed from consideration, we are left with the following pre-Markan text:

Καὶ ἔλεγεν, Πῶς ὁμοιώσωμεν τὴν βασιλείαν τοῦ θεοῦ ἢ ἐν τίνι αὐτὴν παραβολῇ θῶμεν, ὡς κόκκῳ σινάπεως, ὃς ὅταν σπαρῇ ἐπὶ τῆς γῆς, ἀναβαίνει καὶ γίνεται κλάδους μεγάλους, [καὶ] ὑπὸ τὴν σκιὰν αὐτοῦ τὰ πετεινὰ τοῦ οὐρανοῦ κατασκηνοῦν.

In his reconstruction of the earliest version, Crossan begins with the three versions Q, the pre-Markan text and Thomas. Thomas' independence is seen, in part, in that its concluding image is closer to that of birds seeking shade rather than building nests. A trajectory can be seen in the image moving gradually from shelter (Thomas) to shelter and nests (Mk 4.32b) and finally to nests alone (Q). The earliest version also started with the double question in Semitic parallelism (Mark and Q) which Thomas changes to emphasize the disciples.[2]

The parallel between the birds resting in the shade of a tree with such biblical texts as Ps. 104.12; Dan. 4.12, 21; and Ezek. 17.23; 31.6 is problematic for Crossan. 'Why begin', he asks, 'with a *mustard* seed if one intends to end with a tree (δένδρον in Q) rather than a bush (λάχανον in Mark 4.32)? Why use a mustard plant if one intends to have birds *nesting in* its branches?'[3]. Even in Mark one encounters the same problems with the biblical allusions: the context is not literal nor

---

Kuhn, *Ältere Sammlungen,* pp. 100-101; Laufen, *Die Doppelüberlieferungen,* p. 179; Pesch, *Markusevangelium,* I, p. 260.

1. The structure ὥστε + infinitive is identified by Pryke as redactional at Mk 1.27, 45; 2.2, 12; 3.10, 20; 4.1. He attributes 2.28; 4.32, 37; 9.26; 10.8; 15.5 to source material. See Pryke, *Redactional,* p. 115.

2. Crossan, 'Seed Parables', p. 258-59. The introduction in Thomas shows signs of being redactional. Compare at logions 8; 13; 21; 22; 76; 96; 98; 107; 109.

3. Crossan, 'Seed Parables', p. 255.

appropriate. In both instances, Crossan believes, the allusions are a secondary addition to the original parable.[1]

Four elements form the heart of the parable for Crossan; the initial sowing, the growth, the final size, and shade for the birds. All of these are present in Q and the pre-Markan tradition, although the latter's image of 'large branches' is more original than Q's tree.[2] The growth motif is lacking in Thomas. In its place we find an admonition regarding 'tilled earth', which 'no doubt represents the necessary preparation which the true gnostic must undergo'.[3] This aspect of Thomas, therefore, is redactional. The original version also contained some form of contrast regarding size, a contrast unavoidable once a mustard seed was chosen. This was present at least implicitly and probably as explicitly as in Thomas ('smaller than all seeds' and 'a large branch'). But this contrast is significantly different from the 'formally balanced contrast of Mark' (i.e., 'smallest/largest').[4] The earliest version, according to Crossan, probably contained no Hebrew Scripture allusions in the conclusion, or at most a vague recall of Ps. 102.12. But certainly the eschatological overtones of the other suggested parallels were not present.[5] Indeed, Crossan notes, the 'mustard plant would make a better burlesque than an image for eschatological plenitude in a tradition which usually invoked the mighty cedar of Lebanon for this function'.[6]

A number of problems may be noted with Crossan's reconstruction. The triple-stage trajectory of the final image (shelter; shelter and nests; nests) creates the illusion of unilinear development among the versions. But the differences between Q and Mark are slight in this regard. Q has καὶ τὰ πετεινὰ τοῦ οὐρανοῦ κατασκηνοῦν ἐν τοῖς κλάδοις αὐτοῦ while Mark reads ὥστε δύνασθαι ὑπὸ τὴν σκιὰν αὐτοῦ τὰ πετεινὰ τοῦ οὐρανοῦ κατασκηνοῦν. Since ὥστε δύνασθαι has close ties with favourite Markan vocabulary and

1. Crossan, 'Seed Parables', p. 257.
2. Scott likewise sees 'tree' as secondary. The change was made because 'the shrub is an inappropriate metaphor for the final state of the kingdom', *Hear then the Parable*, p. 377.
3. Crossan, 'Seed Parables', pp. 258-59. See Montefiore and Turner, *Thomas and the Evangelists*, p. 51.
4. Crossan, 'Seed Parables', p. 259.
5. These include Dan. 4.20-21; Ezek. 17.23; 31.3-6.
6. Crossan, 'Seed Parables', p. 259.

structure, and given the extensive word-for-word agreement of the central image, we are dealing with the difference between three words. Mark also mentions putting forth a large branch (ποιεῖ κλάδους μεγάλους), while Thomas mentions producing 'a large branch'. Such differences fit entirely within what is found in the redactional reworking of Mark by both Matthew and Luke. Since scholars seldom put these latter changes into a three-step trajectory, we may ask why Crossan is justified in doing so in this instance.

The contrast of small–large also raises a problem. This contrast is missing in the pre-Markan version of the parable. Yet Mark's redactional μικρότερον ὂν πάντων τῶν σπερμάτων τῶν ἐπὶ τῆς γῆς finds a parallel in Thomas' 'smaller than all seeds' while ἀναβαίνει καὶ γίνεται μεῖζον πάντων τῶν λαχάνων finds a parallel in Thomas' 'it puts forth a large branch'. If these are Markan redaction, the question of Thomas' knowledge of Mark becomes raised in a sharp form.[1]

Crossan's hypothesis of an earlier stage of the parable without the eschatological context, and possibly without the allusion to Ps. 104.12, raises another problem. The parallel to the Septuagint (Ps. 103.12) is particularly close within both Q and the pre-Markan tradition, while there are also possible echoes of Daniel. The appropriate texts can be set forth as follows:

LXX: ἐπ' <u>αὐτὰ</u> τὰ <u>πετεινὰ</u> <u>τοῦ</u> <u>οὐρανοῦ</u> <u>κατασκηνώσει</u>

pre-Mark: <u>ὑπὸ τὴν σκιὰν</u> <u>αὐτοῦ</u> <u>τὰ</u> <u>πετεινὰ</u> <u>τοῦ</u> <u>οὐρανοῦ</u>
            <u>κατασκηνοῦν</u>

Q: καὶ <u>τὰ</u> <u>πετεινὰ</u> <u>τοῦ</u> <u>οὐρανοῦ</u> <u>κατασκηνοῦν</u> <u>ἐν τοῖς</u>
            <u>κλάδοις</u> <u>αὐτου</u>

(Dan 4.21) καὶ <u>ἐν τοῖς κλάδοις</u> <u>αὐτοῦ</u> <u>κατεσκήνουν</u> τὰ ὄρνεα <u>τοῦ</u>
            <u>οὐρανοῦ.</u>[2]

---

1. See Marcus, *Mystery of the Kingdom*, p. 204, n. 9, who sees this as a sign of Thomas' dependence upon Mark.
2. The translation of Daniel is from Theodotion, as printed in J.S. Kloppenborg, *Q Parallels: Synopsis, Critical Notes and Concordance* (Sonoma, CA: Polebridge Press, 1988), S49.

Thomas offers the image of putting forth a large branch and giving the birds shelter. Crossan argues that the image contains no 'explicit allusion' to the Hebrew Scriptures, while H.K. McArthur believes Thomas 'has the least evidence of Old Testament phraseology'.[1] But even in Thomas the allusion is present and it is difficult to imagine the image of the birds without a parallel to either the Psalm or Daniel. A reconstruction of an original without the allusion involves the necessary corollary that this original has been entirely lost, and both the Markan and Q versions must descend from a common ancestor that has added the scriptural allusions. All three versions, in fact, must ultimately descend from this common (and secondary) stream of tradition in Crossan's reconstruction. It is difficult to see the advantage in such a cumbersome hypothesis over against viewing the scriptural allusion as integral to the original form of the parable.

The Markan and Q versions of the parable are actually closer than is often assumed, especially when allowance is made for the redactional additions to Mark. Particularly striking in this regard is the introduction. Mark's double question in synthetic parallelism recalls Isa. 40.18.[2] Q also begins with a double question:

LXX: τίνι ὡμοιώσατε Κύριον καὶ τίνι ὁμοιώματι .ὡμοιώσατε αὐτόν

Mark: Πῶς ὁμοιώσωμεν τὴν βασιλείαν τοῦ θεοῦ ἢ ἐν τίνι αὐτὴν παραβολῇ θῶμεν.

Q: τίνι ὁμοία ἐστὶν ἡ βασιλεία τοῦ θεοῦ καὶ τίνι ὁμοιώσω αὐτήν· ὁμοία ἐστίν.

When allowance is made for the obvious change to the 'reign of God' and Mark's thematic interest in 'parables', the similarities are striking. It is an especially significant agreement since the introduction is unique in Mark.[3] The closest parallel is with the Seed Growing Secretly which is the only other 'reign of God' parable in Mark. This

---

1. McArthur, 'The Parable of the Mustard Seed', p. 203. Crossan, 'Seed Parables', p. 258.

2. As noted by H.-W. Bartsch, 'Eine bisher übersehene Ziterung der LXX in Mark 4:30', *TZ* 15 (1959), pp. 126-28.

3. See Carlston, *The Parables of the Triple Tradition*, p. 157. He notes that there are biblical and rabbinic parallels. See M.-J. Lagrange, 'La parabole en dehors de l'évangile', *RB* 6 (1909), pp. 198-212, 342-67 (356). Compare Laufen, *Die Doppelüberlieferungen*, p. 177: 'Demgegenüber kann die Frage ἐν τίνι αὐτὴν παραβολῇ θῶμεν von der markinischen Redaktion her erklärt werden'.

raises the strong possibility that the introduction represents Mark's inherited written tradition, a tradition based upon Isaiah 40. That this particular introduction is also appended to the Mustard Seed in Q argues for a literary relationship between Q and the pre-Markan source. Independence here requires either an unusual degree of fidelity in preservation during oral transmission (particularly in light of orality's flexibility in order, context and introductions) or a highly unlikely coincidence of independent authors individually patterning their introductions on the same biblical model. When the reconstructed originals are compared, other agreements can be seen:

Q	Pre-Mark
Ἔλεγεν οὖν·	Καὶ ἔλεγεν,
τίνι ὁμοία ἐστὶν ἡ βασιλεία τοῦ θεοῦ	Πῶς ὁμοιώσωμεν τὴν βασιλείαν τοῦ θεοῦ
καὶ τίνι ὁμοιώσω αὐτήν·	ἢ ἐν τίνι αὐτὴν παραβολῇ θῶμεν;
ὁμοία ἐστὶν κόκκῳ σινάπεως,	ὡς κόκκῳ σινάπεως,
ὃν λαβὼν ἄνθρωπος ἔβαλεν	ὃς ὅταν σπαρῇ
ἐν τῷ ἀγρῷ αὐτοῦ·	ἐπὶ τῆς γῆς,
καὶ ηὔξησε καὶ ἐγένετο εἰς δένδρον,	ἀναβαίνει καὶ γίνεται κλάδους μεγάλους,
καὶ τὰ πετεινὰ τοῦ οὐρανοῦ κατασκηνοῦν ἐν τοῖς κλάδοις αὐτοῦ.	[καὶ] ὑπὸ τὴν σκιὰν αὐτοῦ τὰ πετεινὰ τοῦ οὐρανοῦ κατασκηνοῦν.

Admittedly, these agreements could be reduced by reassigning ἀναβαίνει καὶ γίνεται to Markan redaction. Mark might have substituted this for an original ποιεῖ. But this still leaves considerable agreement in overall structure and word order. In particular there is agreement regarding the image of the branch and birds seeking shade. The term κατασκηνοῦν is striking. As Hawkins remarks, the only other instance of the word in the New Testament is Acts 2.26. The term is frequent in the Septuagint, although other synonymous expressions could be found.[1]

The history of the tradition in Thomas is again complicated. As Schrage notes, Thomas' version is an eclectic mixture of all three synoptic texts. Evidence of dependence upon Matthew, he believes, is

---

1. See Hawkins, *Horae Synopticae*, p. 59. The term is found, for example in Theodotion's translation of Dan. 4.21 while the LXX has νοσσεύοντα. On the relationship between the Q and Markan forms of the parable see Lambrecht, 'Redaction and Theology', pp. 292-96. Lambrecht believes that all of these differences 'can be easily accounted for with a Q-text as starting point', p. 296.

seen in the agreement at 'Kingdom of Heaven', while the introductory 'it is like' (together with the agreements with Mark) point to conflation of the Markan and Q versions.[1] Sieber, in contrast, does not believe that 'Kingdom of Heaven' in itself proves Matthean dependence. He also argues that the lack of agreement with Matthew's introductory sentence and the combination of Q's 'tree' with Mark's 'bush' 'also shows that he was not dependent on Matthew'.[2] Instead, Sieber believes that the lack of synoptic editorial features in Thomas along with the independent secondary developments leads 'best to the conclusion that Thomas' source for this saying was not our Synoptic Gospels'.[3] This argument, however, fails to establish Thomas' independence since it does take account of the possibility that Thomas was influenced by the pre-Markan version of the parable. In fact, Thomas is strikingly close to the reconstructed pre-Markan text:

Pre-Mark	Gospel of Thomas
Καὶ ἔλεγεν,	The disciples said to Jesus,
Πῶς ὁμοιώσωμεν τὴν βασιλείαν	'Tell us what the Kingdom of
τοῦ θεοῦ	Heaven is like?' He said to them, 'It
ἢ ἐν τίνι αὐτὴν παραβολῇ θῶμεν	is like
ὡς κόκκῳ σινάπεως,	a mustard seed, smaller than all
ὃς ὅταν σπαρῇ ἐπὶ τῆς γῆς,	seeds.
ἀναβαίνει καὶ γίνεται κλάδους	But when it falls on plowed ground
μεγάλους,	it puts forth a large branch
[καὶ] ὑπὸ τὴν σκιὰν αὐτοῦ	and becomes a shelter
τὰ πετεινὰ τοῦ οὐρανοῦ	for the birds of heaven.'[4]
κατασκηνοῦν.	

There is striking similarity in the overall form and structure of the parable. The change in the introduction seems closely tied to the compositional level of Thomas, since such questions from the disciples

---

1. Schrage, *Das Verhältnis*, pp. 61-66. He again points to evidence of dependence on Sahidic Mark, although this may only prove that the Coptic translator was influenced by this version of the tradition rather than a dependence at the earliest level of Thomas.

2. Sieber, 'A Redactional Analysis', p. 174. It is difficult to see how this mixture of agreements must show total independence from Matthew rather than evidence of conflation of a variety of sources (at least at the final redactional stage of the Coptic translation).

3. Sieber, 'A Redactional Analysis', p. 174.

4. The translation of Thomas is from Davies, *The Gospel of Thomas*, p. 160.

are characteristic of this Gospel.[1] The major addition, 'smaller than all seeds' actually finds a close parallel in the Markan redaction of the parable. Other suggested redactional elements within Thomas include the 'tilled earth', which Crossan identifies with the gnostic's necessary preparation for salvation.[2] The parable's conclusion, as in Mark, still shows close thematic ties to the imagery of the Hebrew Scriptures. Marcus notes within Thomas a redactional tendency to decrease such Hebrew Scripture references.[3] The present form of the tradition in Thomas, in light of the inclusion of Markan redactional elements, shows some influence from the synoptic Gospels. Even eliminating this touch, the overall similarity between the pre-Markan version of the parable and Thomas strongly suggests a literary relationship between these two texts. If Thomas is not dependent upon Mark, it is likely that he has used Mark's literary source. In short, there is nothing here that demands an independent oral original for Thomas.

b. *Literary and Thematic Parallels*

Once again the parable has strong ties to the imagery of the Hebrew Scriptures. The introduction shows strong affinities to Isa. 40.18. The concluding image of birds resting (or nesting) in the shade of a tree can be found in such passages as Ps. 104.12; Dan. 4.12, 21; and Ezek. 17.23; 31.6.[4]

The smallness of the mustard seed is also proverbial. At Q 17.6, faith as small as a mustard seed can work miracles. The Rabbis also used the mustard seed as an image of smallness.[5] Specifically, the mustard seed was used as an analogy for Gentile proselytes brought into Israel.

Little, if anything, remains within the parable when these traditional elements are removed. These traditional parallels establish a strong 'burden of proof' against authenticity. I turn now to examine this problem in detail.

---

1. Marcus, *Mystery of the Kingdom*, p. 204, n. 9. Jeremias, *Parables*, p. 98.

2. Crossan, 'Seed Parables', pp. 258-59. See L. Cerfaux, 'Les paraboles du royaume dans l'évangile de Thomas', *Muséon* 70 (1957), pp. 318-19, 324.

3. Marcus, *Mystery of the Kingdom*, p. 204, n. 9.

4. The LXX texts are cited, for example, in Pesch, *Markusevangelium*, I, p. 262, n. 2.

5. Scott, *Hear then the Parable,* p. 381, citing *m. Nid.* 5.2. Carlston, *Parables of the Triple Tradition*, p. 158 also notes *Ber.* 31a; *m. Toh.* 8.8.

c. *Authenticity and the Ministry of Jesus*

Reconstructions within an appropriate setting in the ministry of Jesus are not wanting. For Jeremias, the parable (like the Leaven) responds to doubts regarding the 'wretched band' of disreputable characters that surrounded Jesus being the invited guests of God's Messianic era.[1] Cranfield believes the Mustard Seed is another parable of contrast, this time 'between the present veiledness of the kingdom of God and its future glorious manifestation in the Parousia'.[2]

Similarly, Carlston notes the problem of the conclusion, with the birds of the air signifying the Gentiles' inclusion into the reign of God. Although Jesus might have foreseen this, Carlston believes it more likely the conclusion represents an addition. In his apocalyptic interpretation, he sees a contrast between the proverbially small mustard seed and the great ending; i.e., the reign of God revealed on the Last Day, which 'does not depend upon men and women for its future: from a small band of the relatively insignificant, God, by his own act, will make a great Kingdom'.[3] Specifically, Jesus defends the presence of the reign of God in the small beginnings of his ministry and invites others to join his work.

All these interpretations rely on the assumption that the apocalyptic reign of God is central to the preaching of Jesus. Implicit is a great distance between Jesus and the Judaism of his day, and a christological awareness in Jesus of a distinctive mission. A circular argument has also been established to the degree that these reconstructions rely upon the authenticity of other Gospel texts.[4] Once such assumptions are questioned, however, there is no reason why the parable might not be in full accord with orthodox Jewish belief. Such an image might just as easily refer to the small beginnings of Israel and the great nation raised up from the seed of Abraham by Yahweh.

The appropriateness of the apocalyptic great cedar image has created a debate among more recent scholars. Funk and Scott see the change to a mustard plant as a light-hearted burlesque on the great

---

1. Jeremias, *Parables*, p. 149. This interpretation is taken up by Nineham, *The Gospel of St Mark*, p. 144.

2. Cranfield, *The Gospel According to Saint Mark*, p. 170.

3. Carlston, *Parables of the Triple Tradition*, p. 161.

4. This problem is acute in Jeremias' reliance upon a context of doubts regarding Jesus' disciples, and in Cranfield's contrast with the Parousia.

cedar as a metaphor for the reign of God.[1] Because there is no actual tree in the parable, Scott finds a tension and confusion created for the audience. Since the image of the great cedar's height is ambivalent (suggesting both strength and haughtiness), the parable of the Mustard Seed 'extends the logic of Ezekiel. All cedars and trees, even Israel, will be brought low. It is the mustard plant that will "bear Israel's true destiny." '[2] Scott also sees significance in the original planting in a garden: a violation of the law of diverse kinds, which would imply a scandal (illegitimate and tainted) in the planting and growth. It is a theme that coheres well with the other parables of Jesus which display a tendency to 'play in the minor key'. In the parable From Jerusalem to Jericho the hero is the unclean Samaritan; the Leaven begins its comparison with uncleanness (leaven, woman, hiding); while A Rich Man Had a Steward praises the action of a rogue.[3]

Crossan rejects this interpretation and believes the biblical allusions are secondary. The Mustard Seed is ill-suited to the purpose of birds nesting in the reign of God's branches. Instead, he believes that the Mustard Seed and the Sower 'articulate the gift of the kingdom's advent and the joyful surprise of its experience; despite all the problems of sowing there is the abundant harvest, and despite the smallness of the seed there is the shady peacefulness of the grown plant.'[4]

But postulating distinctiveness on the basis of the parable as burlesque, as with Funk and Scott, is a precarious endeavour. Although the hermeneutics have changed from the Dodd–Jeremias era, there remains an implicit distance between Jesus and the Judaism of his day. Distinctiveness, in this instance, relies upon a critique of Judaism as nationalistic in the extreme. The Mustard plant reverses the haughty image of Israel as a great nation. Yet biblical Judaism is a diverse tradition that was capable of showing a strong self-critique and an openness to the Gentiles (one thinks particularly of Jeremiah and Second Isaiah). Scott's thesis of the original planting in the garden extends a too-precise linguistic reading of the saying through the oral

1. See R.W. Funk, *Jesus as Precursor* (Semeia Studies; Philadelphia: Fortress Press 1975), p. 23. For B.B. Scott, see *Jesus, Symbol-Maker for the Kingdom* (Philadelphia: Fortress Press, 1981), pp. 70-71; and *Hear then the Parable*, p. 386.

2. Scott, *Hear then the Parable*, p. 386. Referring to Funk, *Jesus as Precursor*, p. 23, who stresses this point.

3. Scott, *Hear then the Parable*, p. 386.

4. Crossan, 'Seed Parables', pp. 265-66.

stage. Given orality's ability to exchange linguistically synonymous terms during transmission, the insistence on one specific term as authentic to the originating structure simply is not in accord with what we know about oral transmission.[1] Scott's scandal is remarkably similar to Jeremias' contention that Jesus reached out primarily to *am ha-aretz* (the 'people of the land') in distinction to the Pharisees.

Crossan promises to view the parables as aesthetic objects, yet despite this new emphasis his evaluation offers little that is new from Jeremias. Despite repeated failure and waste, God promises an abundant harvest; and despite the smallness of the seed there is the shady peacefulness of the grown plant. But promises of God's faithfulness despite failure and adversity were common in Judaism. One need only think of Israel's assurance of Yahweh's commitment to the chosen people despite the tragedy of their temple's destruction to find a parallel. The contrast of the smallness of beginnings in Abraham to a mighty nation more numerous than the stars in the sky is also thoroughly biblical.

Burton Mack has raised another cogent objection to the parable's setting in the ministry of Jesus. Each version of the parable assumes a social history: 'Someone took note of the small beginnings of a group that had become a movement with great expectations'.[2] Despite the parable's double attestation in Mark and Q, this provides a powerful case against the saying's authenticity.

d. *The Parable and Orality*
The oral history of this parable is elusive. Thomas shows strong dependence upon the synoptic tradition, while the pre-Markan and Q versions do not display independence. Given the extensive close

---

1. 'The change in Luke from "earth" or "field" to "garden" is an indication of Luke's familiarity with the Hellenistic world, and his unfamiliarity with Palestine; for in Palestine it was forbidden to sow mustard seed in a garden', F.W. Beare, *The Earliest Records of Jesus: A Companion to the Synopsis of the First Three Gospels by Albert Huck* (Oxford: Basil Blackwell, 1962), p. 115. Beare provides adequate redactional grounds for attributing the particular vocabulary item to Luke himself in this case. Scott's reasoning is also difficult to harmonize with his earlier insistence, 'It is futile to seek the original words of a parable. The efforts of those who preserved the parables should not be viewed as the efforts of librarians, archivists, or scribes preserving the past, but of storytellers performing a parable's structure', *Hear then the Parable*, p. 18.

2. Mack, *Myth of Innocence*, p. 152.

agreements between these two traditions some form of literary relationship must be in view. But even the reconstructed tradition common to Mark and Q is not directly transcribed orality. The extensive literary and cultural parallels for the parable were available to any number of authors prior to Mark. The act of writing the parable implies a sociological context to which the parable responds. One cannot, in this case, discount these redactional concerns and get behind the tradition into an earlier oral phase. The earliest sociological situation in view, in light of Mack's observations, is post-resurrectional. The attempted reconstructions within the ministry of Jesus have repeatedly failed to meet the burden of proof. In other words, the tradition cannot be traced back to an earlier form than the post-resurrectional pre-Gospel literary tradition common to Mark and Q. Orality has eluded us.

4. *Summary of Results*

We are in a position now to evaluate the ability to trace back into the oral phase with respect to the three seed parables in Mark. In each instance, despite the literary parallels in the *Gospel of Thomas* and/or Q, orality has proven elusive. The immediate source for Mark has proved to be literary rather than oral. This pre-Gospel source has shown strong characteristics of Semitic Greek and has drawn upon the imagery and language of the Hebrew Scriptures for its composition. Biblical allusions have been found in all three parables. These allusions have proved consistent throughout the other extant parallels to these sayings. When one takes into account the variations that inevitably accompany the independent use of sources by diverse authors one cannot demonstrate a degree of syntactic and thematic divergence that would preclude a literary relationship.

'Distinctiveness' too fails to establish these parables' oral history. Jeremias' reconstructions have been shown to be over-confident in terms of reconstructing a precise context for each of the stories. Crossan's attempt to treat the parables as metaphor brings to mind Perrin's assessment of Dan O. Via:

> Via's literary-critical discussion of the parables is of real interest and of obvious importance, but there is a surprising element of banality about his conclusions. There is something very incongruous about beginning with texts as powerful as the parables obviously are, going on to analyze them with critical tools as keen as those which Via uses, and then ending up

with neat little existentialist insights. There has to be more to the parables than that![1]

Perhaps the greatest fault, however, is in expectations. Conditioned to expect something 'earth shattering' in every parable, it is little wonder that few critics can consistently deliver such a reading of these stories. Distinctiveness for the parables, therefore, must be rethought. The continuing popularity of the form both in non-canonical Christian writings and the rabbinic documents attests to its vitality in a wide range of cultures and settings.[2] The widespread attestation of 'seed analogies' shows the problem in ascertaining a 'distinctive' character to these similitudes. The comparison can be said to be such a stock feature of culture, both literary and oral, that is impossible to determine the precise antecedents for the setting in the pre-Gospel source.

As evidence of the enduring nature of the seed analogy, I close with the following parable collected by the eighteenth-century Rabbi Jacob Krantz (the Preacher of Dubno). The tale's major misfortune is in failing to find its way into the canonical Gospels. Had it done so gospel critics undoubtedly would have demonstrated the story's coherence with the three seed parables and established a further connection with the Prodigal Son. In short, it would be proved a thoroughly distinctive composition demonstrating Jesus' radical reformulation of his first-century Jewish heritage.

Man Understands But Little

All their lives the two young brothers had lived in the city behind great stone walls and never saw field nor meadow. But one day they decided to pay a visit to the country.

As they went walking along the road they saw a farmer at his plowing. They watched and were puzzled.

'What on earth is he doing that for!' they wondered. 'He turns up the earth and leaves deep furrows in it. Why should someone take a smooth piece of land covered with nice green grass and dig it up?'

Later they watched the farmer sowing grains of wheat along the furrows. 'That man must be crazy!' they exclaimed. ''He takes good wheat and throws it into the dirt.'

---

1. Perrin, *Jesus and the Language of the Kingdom*, p. 154.
2. See *Apoc. Jas* 8.2; 6.8, 11.

'I don't like the country!' said one in disgust. 'Only queer people live here.'

So he returned to the city.

His brother who remained in the country saw a change take place only several weeks later. The plowed field began to sprout tender green shoots, even more beautiful and fresher than before. This discovery excited him very much. So he wrote to his brother in the city to come at once and see for himself the wonderful change [undoubtedly a secondary addition reflecting the ministry of Paul].

His brother came and was delighted with what he saw. As time passed they watched the sproutings grow into golden heads of wheat. Now they both understood the purpose of the farmer's work.

When the wheat became ripe the farmer brought out his scythe and began to cut it down. At this the impatient one of the two brothers exclaimed:

'The farmer is crazy! How hard he worked all these months to produce this lovely wheat, and now with his own hands he is cutting it down! I'm disgusted with such an idiot and I'm going back to the city!'

His brother, the patient one, held his peace and remained in the country. He watched the farmer gather the wheat into his granary. He saw him skillfully separate the grain from the chaff. He was filled with wonder when he found that the farmer had harvested a hundred-fold of the seed he had sowed. Then he understood that there was logic in everything that the farmer had done.[1]

1. N. Ausubel (ed.), *A Treasury of Jewish Folklore: Stories, Traditions, Legends, Humor, Wisdom and Folk Songs of the Jewish People* (New York: Bantam, abridged edn, 1980 [1948]), pp. 55-56.

Chapter 6

APHORISMS AND ORALITY: MARK 4.21-25

The aphorisms are another important data-base for an examination of orality. In literary terms they are a distinct category from parables, the miracle narratives or pronouncement stories. Their connection with the universal phenomenon of proverbs (both oral and literary) has long been recognized. Bultmann provides extensive parallels taken from a wide range of cultures to numerous synoptic aphorisms. He enumerates a range of possibilities for this material's 'authenticity', from the possibility of Jesus taking over or even coining secular proverbs to the appropriation of this material by the early church.[1] Crossan's evaluation of the aphorisms acknowledges this problem and aims at establishing a hermeneutical distinction between proverb and aphorism. The greatest difference is in voice: proverb uses collective voice while aphorism uses individual voice. Both may involve metaphor; both are non-narrative; both may be paradoxical. The aphorist may choose either to support or attack the content of community wisdom. The difference may even amount to the following subtle distinction:

> Proverb: A stitch in time saves nine.
> Aphorism: Jesus said, 'A stitch in time saves nine.'

Yet, Crossan also argues, aphorism has contradiction at its core; in distinction to the proverb its passion for contradiction leads inevitably to paradox.[2]

For Kelber, the distinction between parable and aphorism is particularly important, especially since none of the 52 texts of the Nag Hammadi library comes close to the narrative structure of the canoni-

---

1. Bultmann, *History*, pp. 101-104 and at various points in the exegesis of individual sayings.
2. Crossan, *In Fragments*, pp. 5-6, 20-26.

cal Gospels. The aphoristic genre is extensively represented in these so-called cluster, or dialogue, Gospels, while the parables are overwhelmingly represented in the canonical narrative Gospels. 'It is tempting to speculate that each of the two basic speech forms of the historical Jesus, the aphorism and the parable, created its own gospel!'[1]

The aphorisms raise the issue of double and multiple attestation in an acute form. Aphorisms constitute the majority of the 'double attestation' sayings in Mark and Q. Significantly, all five of the aphorisms in Mk 4.21-25 are in this data-base, while at least four of them have parallels in Thomas. If parables may fairly be said to represent the data-base usually claimed for the historical Jesus on the basis of 'distinctiveness', aphorisms probably constitute the most significant material claimed by the criterion of multiple attestation.[2] These sayings' widespread attestation, combined with their connection to the universal phenomenon of proverbial wisdom, merits a close examination for orality.

As with the parables, any examination needs to consider whether independence can be established among the various forms of these sayings. Failure to establish independence with the parables might represent an isolated case, particularly since Mark's source might have found its way to Thomas. I again begin with the text, seeking to understand the particular form of each saying in the overall context. Only when account is taken of the redactional shaping of the aphorisms can I proceed to evaluate the question of independence and orality. It is useful, therefore, before proceeding to an examination of the aphorisms themselves to outline Mark's redactional purpose with these logia.

Structurally, the aphorisms form two pairs, which we may call Markan 'parables'.[3] In each 'parable', the second aphorism serves as

1. W. Kelber, 'From Aphorism to Sayings Gospel and from Parable to Narrative Gospel', *Foundations and Facets Forum* 1.1 (March 1985), p. 29.

2. On the four criteria for authenticity see Perrin and Duling, *The New Testament*, p. 405.

3. There is scholarly debate whether Mark intends his readers to understand the sayings as 'parables'. Pesch asserts that he does, *Markusevangelium*, I, p. 248. J. Dupont, in contrast, believes Mark has alternated seed parables with general statements on the purpose of parables, 'La transmission des paroles de Jésus sur la lampe et la mesure dans Marc 4,21-25 et dans la tradition Q', in *Logia: les paroles de Jésus—The Sayings of Jesus* (ed. J. Delobel; BETL, 59; Leuven: Leuven

an explanation (and reinforcement) of the first, as made clear by the connective γάρ. Thus, the saying on Hiddenness (v. 22) explains the image of the Lamp (v. 21) while the statement on the One Who Has (v. 25) explains the Measure (v. 24c). These two Markan parables are linked by a double exhortation to hear (v. 23 and v. 24b).[1]

These sayings are related to Mk 4.10-13. This connection is made plain by the chapter's chiastic structure, the similarity in theme, and the word link ἵνα (four times in vv. 21-22).[2] The sayings thus have an intimate connection with Mark's secrecy motif and the hiddenness of Jesus' teaching. Mark's distinctive use of these sayings must be considered, particularly when one determines his tradition's relationship to Q and Thomas (i.e., independent, secondary or earlier) and the meaning and form that these sayings might have had during the oral phase. In what sense, then, do these aphorisms in their present literary form represent the direct deposit of oral tradition and how do they illuminate an ability to trace back through the oral phase of early Christianity?

1. *The Lamp (Mark 4.21; Q 11.33; Gospel of Thomas 33)*

a. *Mark and Q*

The saying on the lamp, Mk 4.21, is found at Mt. 5.15 and Lk. 11.33 in extensive 'double tradition' material. The agreement in the literary

---

University Press, 1982), pp. 201-36. I have outlined my own reconstruction of Mark's distinctive use of 'parables' above, Chapter 3, section 3, c; section 4, c.

1. Because of the Markan structure, I have chosen to examine the aphorisms within these two 'parables' first and then deal with the exhortation to hear at v. 23. On the redactional character of v. 24b, see above, Chapter 3, section 5, b. Best, 'Mark's Preservation', p. 126 discusses the problem of whether Mark inherited the four aphorisms as one unit or joined two units together for the first time: 'we appear to have a sequence of sayings of which the first were important for Mark but the others inappropriate yet were retained in order not to destroy the existing unity. It is, however, just possible that Mark himself added vv. 24, 25 which already existed as a unit to vv. 21, 22 which also was already a unit. He will then have joined them because he wished to use v. 25a.' I think the view of Lambrecht, 'Redaction and Theology', p. 286-87, that Mark himself arranged vv. 21-25 more likely. Lambrecht notes, for example, the symmetrical patterning of vv. 21-22 and vv. 24cd-25.

2. See above, Chapter 3, section 4, c. Fay, 'Introduction to Incomprehension', p. 81; Marcus, *Mystery of the Kingdom,* pp. 126-27; Dupont, 'La transmission', p. 206.

expression between them is extensive enough to strain the probability of independent alteration of the Markan original. All these factors demonstrate the saying's inclusion in Q. The three synoptic texts of this aphorism are:

Mk 4.21	Mt. 5.15	Lk. 11.33
μήτι ἔρχεται ὁ λύχνος ἵνα	οὐδὲ καίουσιν λύχνον	οὐδεὶς λύχνον ἅψας
ὑπὸ τὸν μόδιον τεθῇ	καὶ τιθέασιν αὐτὸν	εἰς κρύπτην τίθησιν
	ὑπὸ τὸν μόδιον,	οὐδὲ ὑπὸ τὸν μόδιον,
ἢ ὑπὸ τὴν κλίνην;		
οὐχ ἵνα ἐπὶ τὴν λυχνίαν	ἀλλ᾽ ἐπὶ τὴν λυχνίαν,	ἀλλ᾽ ἐπὶ τὴν λυχνίαν,
τεθῇ.	καὶ λάμπει πᾶσιν τοῖς ἐν	ἵνα οἱ εἰσπορευόμενοι
	τῇ οἰκίᾳ.	τὸ φῶς βλέπωσιν.

The following elements of Mark and Q are in agreement. The key term is ὁ λύχνος, which is not too significant until one remembers Bultmann's Oriental parallel 'You don't beat a drum under a rug'.[1] The main verb in both is a form of τίθημι despite the availability of other synonymous terms. Finally, the phrases ὑπὸ τὸν μόδιον and ἐπὶ τὴν λυχνίαν are repeated word for word. In terms of structure there is the order of lamp, false option, and correct location. If Matthew's word order at καίουσιν λύχνον is original to Q, we would have agreement of order (verb–subject—Mt., καίουσιν λύχνον; Mk, ἔρχεται ὁ λύχνος).[2]

How many of the differences in the two forms may be attributed to authorial redaction (Markan or Q)? Mark's choice of initial verb (ἔρχεται) has caused problems with some copyists. Bezae essentially conflates Mark into agreement with Luke (Μήτι ἅπτεται ὁ λύχνος;

1. Bultmann, 'Study', p. 54. In oral tradition there is greater possibility of the central image, that of the lamp, being interchanged for another appropriate one. For example the following Russian proverb, 'When the priest's away the Devil will play', is probably better known in our culture with the central image of a cat. The English proverb 'No cross, no crown' is now more familiar as 'No pain, no gain.' Again, consider the following two forms of the same essential proverb: 'Steal the hog, and give the feet for alms', George Herbert, *Jacula Prudentum*; 'Steal the goose and give the giblets in alms', John Ray: *English Proverbs*. Quotes from Mead, *Encyclopedia*, pp. 171, 143, 13, 14.

2. Marcus concludes that 'Matthew probably preserves the Q form almost intact' at this point, *Mystery of the Kingdom,* p. 131. Noting Dupont, 'La transmission', pp. 210-11 and G. Schneider, 'Das Bildwort von der Lampe', *ZNW* 61 (1961), pp. 184-86. For another reconstruction of Q 11.33, see Lambrecht, 'Redaction and Theology', p. 287.

cp. Luke, οὐδεὶς λύχνον ἅψας). Although some scholars have pointed out that 'the lamp comes' is popular speech, suspicions are raised.[1] The solemn proclamation of Jesus at 2.17 (οὐκ ἦλθον καλέσαι δικαίους ἀλλὰ ἁμαρτωλούς) and the christological overtones of Mark's parable sermon provide grounds for attributing this precise term to the evangelist.[2] Whether the lamp symbolizes Jesus himself, or the revelation of his true identity to the community, Mark's intention is clear. Jesus has come in order to be revealed: despite the temporary injunctions to silence, his true identity will eventually 'come to light'. The Markan community, living on the other side of the resurrection, lives in the light of the revelation of Jesus to the world.

The inclusion of ἵνα and οὐχ ἵνα gives the saying a strong sense of purpose in Mark, and in light of 4.11-12, can be said to be tied to the context. Marcus notes that ἵνα is a preferred Markan conjunction which plays a prominent role in ch. 4.[3] The question form seems redactional: Mark has a 'predilection for rhetorical questions and double questions' and the form fits well in the specific context of ch. 4.[4] A problem for a literary relationship would appear to be the οὐκ . . . ἀλλ' construction in Q. Since this is a Markan favourite, why would he change it if he found it in his source? Neirynck suggests that Mark transferred this construction to v. 22 when he turned v. 21 into a question.[5] The other unique element of Mark's text ἢ ὑπὸ τὴν κλίνην is more ambiguous: is it to be attributed to Mark or his source? Schneider and Jeremias hold it to be a secondary addition to the central image.[6] In an oral context either form would be equally

1. Carlston, *Parables of the Triple Tradition*, p. 150. Cp. Bar. 3.33 and Heliodorus viii.12.
2. On ἔρχεται as Markan, see Marcus, *Mystery of the Kingdom*, p. 131; Klauck, *Allegorie*, p. 228, n. 206 (pointing to 1.7, 9, 14, 29, 39; 2.17; 3.20).
3. Marcus, *Mystery of the Kingdom*, p. 131. See also Klauck, *Allegorie*, p. 228, n. 206.
4. See Marcus, *Mystery of the Kingdom*, pp. 131-33; Schneider, 'Das Bildwort von der Lampe', pp. 197-99
5. Neirynck, *Duality in Mark*, p. 136; Marcus, *Mystery of the Kingdom*, p. 136 supports the argument. Neirynck makes a plausible case, but it must be admitted that a difficulty remains here.
6. Schneider, 'Das Bildwort von der Lampe', pp. 197-99; Jeremias, 'Die Lampe unter dem Scheffel', in *Abba* (Göttingen: Vandenhoeck & Ruprecht, 1966), pp. 99-102. Schweizer sees the image as secondary also, *The Good News According to*

possible. The triadic form of Mark would fit the performance style of many traditionalists while the dual antithesis of Q would equally have its advocates.[1] Fluctuation between these two structural forms could well be expected during a period of oral transmission. But either form is equally at home in literary texts and either Mark or Q could redact the saying to its present structure. Finally, the agreement in the conclusions of Matthew and Luke indicates that the Q saying has a final statement of purpose. While it is possible that Matthew and Luke have independently added their own purposes here, inclusion in Q seems likely.[2] In Mark, such a phrase is unnecessary because v. 22 serves as the concluding purpose for the logion. This provides sufficient explanation for the absence in Mark; even if it was in his source deletion would be likely in view of v. 22.

The Markan and Q forms, therefore, linguistically show a pattern of agreement and disagreement consistent with either independent oral tradition or textuality. In the latter case, the 'percentage' of agreement is similar to that often found in 'sibling texts' (i.e., Matthew compared directly to Luke). Discounting the hypothesis of a direct literary relationship (Mark's knowledge of Q),[3] we are still faced with the possibility of an underlying pre-Gospel logia tract that was the source for both Mark and Q. The reason for not invoking such a hypothesis is clear: in one instance, such a procedure could (if consistently applied) lead *ad infinitum* to innumerable pre-Gospel sources. An explanation of independent 'oral tradition' initially would seem

Mark, p. 100. Carlston would appear less certain that the image is an addition, *Parables of the Triple Tradition*, p. 150, n. 5.

1. The Q form is seen in Bultmann's parallel 'You don't beat a drum under a rug'. But the triadic structure would appear to be in Q also, given the conclusion to Matthew and Luke. For the traidic structure compare Mt. 6.26 and 6.31.

2. Polag's reconstruction follows Matthew at this point, 'The Text of Q', p. 134. The Lukan image of welcoming those who come is more likely redactional, indicating Gentile inclusion in the reign of God through Jesus.

3. I have deliberately restricted the possibilities in this manner since hardly any critical scholar considers it likely that Q used Mark. Lambrecht, 'Redaction and Theology', p. 287 makes an important observation regarding all four of these doubly attested aphorisms, 'Now, if the line of thought in IV, 21-25 is consistent with that developed by Mark in the rest of his chapter *and if most of the verbal and stylistic differences from the Q-text can be explained by Mark's redaction*, then the assembling, composing, and structuring if IV, 21-25 by Mark are as good as proved' [emphasis added].

justified on the basis of 'common sense'. But orality on this basis is still an explanation of convenience rather than a proof. And the procedure of 'common sense' orality must be re-evaluated in light of a more extended evaluation of the relevant data. A literary relationship between Mark and Q (in the doubly attested logia) might appear far more likely after a close inspection of all the relevant sayings. This, in fact, will appear to be the case as the subsequent analysis will make clear.

b. *The Version in Thomas*
The parallel in Thomas (saying 33) needs to be examined. It has a strong fourfold structure and is in a significant context:

Gospel of Thomas 31–33

31. Jesus said, 'A prophet is not acceptable in his own village; a physician does not heal those who know him'.

32. Jesus said, 'A city they build and fortify upon a high mountain cannot fall, nor can it be hidden'.

33. Jesus said, 'What you hear in your ear, preach in [others'] ear[s from] your housetops. For no one kindles a lamp and puts it under a basket, nor does he put it in a hidden place, but he sets it on a lampstand so everyone who comes in and goes out will see its light.'[1]

We again find the themes of hiddenness, secrecy and eventual disclosure. The sequence of fortified mountain city and lamp (32, 33) is duplicated at Mt. 5.14-15 (minus Thomas' intervening 33a). Although Thomas demonstrates an overall distinctive order from the synoptics, the parallel here to Matthew is striking enough to warrant the conclusion of dependence of order in this instance.[2] It is significant that the intervening aphorism on open proclamation contains the key word 'ear' given in Mk 4.23, 24a. Thomas' distinctive 'nor does he put it in

---

1. The translation is by D.R. Cartlidge, in Davies (ed.), *The Gospel of Thomas*, p. 162. Unless otherwise noted, all translations from Thomas in this chapter are from Cartlidge and Davies.

2. See Marcus, who concludes that Thomas' order at logia 32-33 'seems to follow Matt 5.14-15 and Matt 10.26-27 par. Luke 12:2-3', *Mystery of the Kingdom*, p. 130, n. 28. Mt. 10.26-27 contains the sequence 'Nothing Hidden' and 'Housetop Proclamation'. Also J.S. Kloppenborg *et al.*, *Q Thomas Reader* (Sonoma, CA: Polebridge Press, 1990), pp. 86, 122. For a contrary conclusion, see Sieber, 'A Redactional Analysis', p. 47.

a hidden place' structurally parallels Mark's ἢ ὑπὸ τὴν κλίνην; and linguistically echoes Luke's εἰς κρύπτην.[1] The Lukan phrase is almost certainly redactional.[2] Finally, Thomas' conclusion parallels the Q version. But Matthew and Luke are not in word-for-word agreement. The three conclusions are:

Matthew:	...and it gives light to all in the house.
Luke:	...that those *who enter* may *see its light.*
Thomas:	...so everyone *who comes in* and goes out will *see its light.*

Luke and Thomas are just as close linguistically (if not closer) than Matthew and Luke (which share an underlying textuality). Some scholars have seen in Thomas' addition of 'going out' a reference to the gnostic's soul which comes into the world and then leaves ('goes out').[3] These verbal parallels, given the dependence in order, clearly show Thomas' dependence upon the canonical Gospels.[4] It is hypothetically possible that the aphorism belongs to the earliest stratum of Thomas (where it was deposited by an independent oral transmission) and has subsequently been modified in conformity with the canonical Gospels during the textual transmission. But this hypothesis does nothing to enhance the ability to use Thomas' version of the saying in retracing its oral history. Whatever original form it might have had in Thomas is now lost to us, and Thomas cannot be used as an independent witness to the oral phase.

1. 'Hiddenness' is a literary theme of Thomas; cf. Logions 5, 6, 83, 84, 96, 109.
2. Most English translations give 'in a cellar' for Luke at this point. I think it more likely that the meaning here is 'in a secret place' or 'in secret', and has christological connotations.
3. See Marcus, *Mystery of the Kingdom*, p. 131, n. 28. F. Hahn, 'Die Worte vom Lichte Lk 11, 33-36', in *Orientierung an Jesus: Zur Theologie der Synoptiker, Für J. Schmid* (ed. P. Hoffmann; Freiburg: Herder, 1973), pp. 113-14.
4. On the secondary character of Thomas, Marcus, *Mystery of the Kingdom*, pp. 130-31. Less certain is Kloppenborg, *The Formation of Q*, p. 135, n. 144. He notes that the agreements with Luke might suggest dependence, but goes on to argue that not all the features are clearly Lukan. Some may derive from Q. Sieber argues that Thomas is actually closest to Luke but does not see this as evidence of Lukan dependence. His case for Thomas' independence from the synoptics, however, quickly runs into the barrier of Thomas' potential use of Q or the pre-Markan tradition: 'Thomas' agreement with οὐδείς, for example, could represent an agreement with Q or an independent correction of the Marcan source as well as the text of Luke.' See 'A Redactional Analysis', p. 47.

c. *Double Attestation, Orality and Authenticity*

The use of light as a symbol of purity or the lamp as a method of 'illumination' is universal. The most significant biblical parallels include Ps. 119.105, Prov. 6.23 and Isa. 62.1. The use of the lamp as a symbol of Torah is maintained in apocalyptic literature (cf. *2 Bar.* 17.4-18.2; 59.2; 77.15-16). But the synoptic saying is most closely paralleled in the rabbinic documents. 'Antoninus asked Rabbi [Judah the Prince], "If a man has a dwelling which is ten cubits square, where does he set his lamp?" He answered, "In the middle of the dining room." '[1]

The synoptic tradition consistently applies the image christologically. In Mark the lamp has become a part of the secrecy theme. It stands in for Jesus: his current hidden identity is not intended to be a permanent reality. After the resurrection, Jesus' identity will be proclaimed openly.[2] In Q the aphorism follows closely upon the demand for a sign, true blessedness and the Beelzebul controversy. It is soon followed by the denunciation of the Pharisees. The Q context is thus within its theme of the rejection of wisdom's envoys and the resulting divine rejection of Judaism. If, for Q, the lamp does not directly signify Jesus it is implicitly christological in representing the community's witness to him.

Can one move behind the literary contexts and into the oral phase? The post-resurrectional applications of the logion in Mark and Q versus the general cultural image of the lamp as a symbol of illumination represent a 'gap'. Most scholars acknowledge that whatever meaning the logion originally had in the oral phase (or preaching of Jesus) is now lost. Taylor notes that the saying insists that a lamp's purpose is to give light, and concludes 'In what connection it was uttered is impossible to say.'[3] Earlier reconstructions of a setting in the life of Jesus were generally highly dependent upon now outdated assumptions of Jesus' self-awareness of a distinctive mission, a ministry in conflict with his Jewish contemporaries, and the overall

---

1. Midrash Hallel to Psalm 113. In S.T. Lachs, *A Rabbinic Commentary on the New Testament: The Gospels of Matthew, Mark, and Luke* (New York: Ktav, 1987), p. 84. From the Buddhist *Dhammapada*, compare 58-59, and 87-88.

2. One of the possible applications noted by Nineham, *The Gospel of St Mark*, p. 141. Taylor, *The Gospel According to St Mark*, p. 263 also notes the connection with the secrecy motif. See Schweizer, *The Good News According to Mark*, p. 100.

3. Taylor, *The Gospel According to St Mark*, p. 263.

theological motifs of the Markan context.[1] The difficulties in tracing behind the present Q form of the saying into the previous oral tradition is well illustrated by the following discussion by J. Kloppenborg:

> *On the assumption* that 'light' served as a metaphor for the kerygma, 11.33 *may have been employed* as encouragement to preach the kingdom openly. But this is not the original *Sitz* for Q 11.34-36 which focuses not on the light itself, but on its subjective appropriation. *If* it had an independent existence, this Q saying *may have functioned* as a post-baptismal parenetic word stressing the importance of unclouded moral vision.[2]

The aphorism's credentials for orality are as follows. The variation between the Markan and Q versions is entirely consistent with oral tradition. Indeed, in the context of such a pithy saying, even word-for-word agreement would not rule out oral independence.[3] The form of the saying in either Q or Mark would be at home in the oral milieu, and the central antithesis and parallelism would be well suited for an oral saying. The literary parallels attest that the lamp has widely entered ancient culture as a symbol of 'illumination'. The rabbinic parallel in particular provides a strong case in support of Bultmann's assessment that the aphorism was originally a proverb of secular wisdom which has been taken over by the church.[4]

For most scholars these considerations will assure orality. My reserve to this reconstruction arises from the following considerations. The core agreement between Mark and Q warns us that a

---

1. Cranfield, 'It seems likely then that for Mark the parable had reference to the ministry of Jesus. And it is intrinsically probable [not merely possible!] that this was also the original reference', *The Gospel According to Saint Mark*, p. 164. Carlston believes the logion could have been used either positively or negatively. 'Positively, it would then refer it not so much to the fate of the Word as to Jesus himself and his mission; it might have meant that Jesus did not intend to hide himself (Mk.) but to be a light to all Israel (Matt., Q)', *Parables of the Triple Tradition*, p. 151.

2. Kloppenborg, *Formation of Q*, p. 135 [emphasis added]. In n. 146, Kloppenborg attributes the second reconstruction to J. Wanke, 'Kommentarworte, Älteste Kommentierung von Herrenworten', *BZ* ns 24 (1980), p. 222.

3. Lord admits that full fixed textual stability is possible in the oral medium within short forms such as incantations, riddles, proverbs or sayings, 'Gospels as Oral Traditional Literature', p. 37. See above, Chapter 2, section 4, a.

4. Bultmann, *History*, p. 98. Bultmann quickly adds, 'It is plain that neither the evangelists' explanation nor the place that the sayings [Mk 4.21; 9.50] have in their context give us any information as to their original meaning.'

literary relationship is possible. And, even granting independence, the double attestation of the saying does not allow for tracing its previous oral history. Nor does it allow for 'authenticity' or a context in the life of Jesus. The applications of the image are infinite, and there is no reason to suppose that if Jesus or the early church used this proverb it did not originally have a positive application to Torah and Israel. God did not give Israel Torah to hide it under a bed; rather Torah was given to be a light to the gentiles. Only the critic's presuppositions can give a concrete meaning to the saying in the oral phase. Furthermore, the breadth of parallels puts us in exactly the situation as the 'Golden Rule'. We have a widely attested image taken over by the church and attributed to Jesus. This might just as easily have happened at the literary phase of transmission as during the oral tradition.

2. *The Hidden Revealed (Mark 4.22; Q 12.2; Gospel of Thomas 5, 6b)*

a. *Mark and Q*

The case for the inclusion in Q of the saying the Hidden Revealed is the same as with the Lamp: location in double tradition contexts and verbal agreement of Matthew and Luke against Mark. The three forms of the saying are:

Mk 4.22	Lk. 12.2	Mt. 10.26
οὐ <u>γάρ ἐστιν</u> κρυπτὸν	<u>οὐδὲν</u> δὲ	<u>οὐδὲν γάρ ἐστιν</u>
	συγκεκαλυμμένον	<u>κεκαλυμμένον</u>
ἐὰν μὴ ἵνα φανερωθῇ,	<u>ἐστιν</u>	
οὐδὲ ἐγένετο	<u>ὃ οὐκ</u>	<u>ὃ οὐκ</u>
ἀπό<u>κρυφον</u>	<u>ἀποκαλυφθήσεται</u>	<u>ἀποκαλυφθήσεται</u>
ἀλλ' ἵνα ἔλθῃ εἰς	<u>καὶ κρυπτὸν</u>	<u>καὶ κρυπτὸν</u>
φανερόν.	<u>ὃ οὐ γνωσθήσεται.</u>	<u>ὃ οὐ γνωσθήσεται.</u>

Aside from a minor variation in the opening, the Matthean and Lukan forms of the saying are in word-for-word agreement. This assures one of the saying's inclusion in Q and enables recovery of most of its exact wording.

Of the four aphorisms under investigation, the Hidden Revealed displays the greatest variation from its Q parallel. Significantly the sayings agree structurally in comprising two phrases of antithetical parallelism which are in turn in synthetic parallelism. It is striking that all four authors (the three synoptic evangelists and Q) have given the full saying and resisted any temptation to abbreviation, despite the repetition. Exactly this kind of abbreviation has taken place in *Gospel of Thomas* 108. It is likely that some of the differences are due to Markan redaction. Markan redaction lies behind the oft-repeated scholarly judgement that the Q form is 'primary' while the Markan 'secondary'.[1] Specifically, the οὐκ... ἀλλά pattern and the use of ἵνα are Markan favourites (the latter is particularly tied to the context).[2] Mark's ἐγένετο is also likely due to harmonization with v. 11, and used with ἵνα to link the two sayings together.[3] Marcus argues that the phrase ἔλθῃ εἰς φανερόν is reminiscent of ἔρχεται at the Lamp (v. 21) and the redactional use of words with the stem φανερ is seen in other 'secrecy' passages.[4] These redactional features explain the saying's form in Mark. However, the verbal dissimilarity would nonetheless fit well into a context of independent tradition.

b. *The Version in Thomas*
Thomas has three versions of the saying (logions 5-6; 108). The first two are:

5.   Jesus said, 'Know what is in front of your face, and what is concealed from you will be revealed to you. For there is nothing concealed which will not be manifest.'

6.   His disciples asked him, 'Do you want us to fast, and how shall we pray, and shall we give alms, and what food regulations shall we keep?' Jesus said, 'Do not lie, and do not do what you hate, because all is revealed before Heaven. For nothing is hidden that shall not be revealed, and nothing is covered that shall remain without being revealed.'

1. The assessment of Carlston, *Parables of the Triple Tradition*, p. 153; Marcus, *Mystery of the Kingdom*, p. 133; Klauck, *Allegorie*, pp. 235-36; contra, Taylor, *The Gospel According to St Mark*, who finds the roughness of Mark's Greek a sign of originalness, p. 264. For another reconstruction of the Q form, see Lambrecht, 'Redaction and Theology', p. 289.

2. Note Neirynck, *Duality in Mark*, pp. 90-94. He also suggests that Mark has transferred the οὐκ... ἀλλά pattern from his source's version of Mk 4.2, pp. 60-61.

3. Marcus believes this verb takes up loose ends from the chapter, *Mystery of the Kingdom*, p. 135.

4. See Mk 1.45; 3.12; 6.14; Marcus, *Mystery of the Kingdom*, pp. 135-36. Also Klauck, *Allegorie*, pp. 235-36.

Why does Thomas have two versions of the saying in such close proximity with variation in phraseology? The aphorism also concludes logion 108 (which has a distinctive Johannine ring): 'Jesus said, "He who drinks from my mouth will be as I am, and I will be he, and the things that are hidden will be revealed to him."' Again the wording varies, probably having been conformed to the context of 108a. We are in a similar situation as with the free-floating saying on Hearing (Mk 4.9, 23). Why has Thomas not 'harmonized' the three sayings? Did he inherit more than one literary version of the text? Is one form based closely on a literary model while the others are freer renderings of his tradition? Or are all three based upon the same memorized (and flexible) oral structure?

The context of the saying in logion 6 (= P. Oxy. 654.36-40) is ethical exhortation, as seen by the Golden Rule. Such a context would be in harmony with other literary parallels for the saying (see below, section c). The list of questions prefacing the logion shows a general *Sitz im Leben* of the church establishing its own moral code and religious practice. This establishes a post-resurrectional origin for the unit as a whole. The Greek version, as reconstructed from P. Oxy. 654, reads: [οὐδεν γάρ ἐστι]ν ἀ[π]οκεκρ[υμμένον ὅ οὐ φανερόν ἔσται].[1] The saying has been 'halved' (i.e., the second part of the synonymous parallelism is missing) and contains only one couplet in antithetic parallelism. The pivotal 'for all things are plain in the sight of truth' would provide the necessary explanation: after such a linking phrase, the full synthetic parallelism would be excessively redundant. Exact comparisons with the synoptics are, of course, based on conjecture since one is dealing with a partially reconstructed text. The fact that the Coptic version again cites the full double couplet of antitheses argues that the Coptic translation has been influenced by the synoptics at this point.

The context in logion 5 (= P. Oxy. 654.27-31) is more interesting. The emphasis on knowing what is concealed has 'gnostic' and 'christological' overtones. The 'secret knowledge' provided by Jesus and the revelation of his 'true identity' are promised the disciples. The parallel to Mark is striking: Mark's context stresses Jesus revealing secret teachings to the disciples, the hiddenness of the mystery of the reign of God as well as Jesus' identity being hidden to the outside

---

1. Kloppenborg, *Q Parallels*, p. 117.

world. This 'gnosticizing' and christological stamp on the logion is reinforced when it is viewed in the context of the entire Gospel. Certainly logion 108, quoted above, confirms this interpretation. Logions 83 and 91 provide further reinforcement. The post-resurrectional character of the unit, surprisingly, is even clearer in the Greek version preserved in the P. Oxy. 654:

λέγει Ἰη(σοῦ)ς· γ[νῶθι τὸ ὂν ἔμπροσ]θεν τῆς ὄψεώς σου, καὶ τὸ κεκαλυμμένον ἀπό σου ἀποκαλυφ (θ)ήσετ[σοι· οὐ γάρ ἐσ]τιν κρυπτὸν ὅ οὐ φανε[ρὸν γενήσεται], καὶ θεθαμμένον ὃ ο[ὐκ ἐγερθήσεται].[1]

The concluding promise of resurrection stamps this version of the saying as post-resurrectional. This secondary feature in the logion argues that it is unlikely to be from an earlier tradition from what we find in Q. The Coptic translation has removed this concluding promise of resurrection and 'conflated' the saying into greater conformity to the synoptics. In this case the evidence supports the conclusion that the Thomas tradition is secondary and dependent upon the synoptics.[2]

1. 'Jesus said, "[Recognize what is in] your sight, and [that which is hidden] from you will become plain to you. For there is nothing] hidden which [will] not [become] manifest, nor buried that [will not be raised]".' Text and translation from Kloppenborg, *Q Parallels*, p. 117.
2. Marcus, *Mystery of the Kingdom*, p. 133; H. Schürmann, *Lukasevangelium* (HTKNT, 3.1; Freiburg: Herder, 1969), 1.468; J. Fitzmyer, 'The Oxyrhynchus Logoi of Jesus and the Coptic Gospel According to Thomas', in *Essays on the Semitic Background of the New Testament* (SBS, 5; Missoula, MT: Scholars Press, 1974), pp. 381-84. Thomas appears to be, in their view, an amalgamation of Lk. 8.17 and the Q form of the saying. See also Schrage, 'Das Verhältnis', pp. 34-37, and 'Evangelienzitate in Oxyrhynchus-Logien und im koptischen Thomas-Evangelium', in *Apophoreta: Festschrift für Ernst Haenchen zu seinem siebzigsten Geburtstag* (BZNW, 30; Berlin: Töpelmann, 1964), pp. 259-60. In contrast, Sieber, 'A Redactional Analysis', pp. 108-10 argues for Thomas' independence at this point. Against Schrage, he points out that although the Coptic versions agree with Lk. 8.17, the Greek version at Pap. Ox. 654, 32-39 does not and thus cannot be so dependent. His analysis suffers, however, from the unproved argument that Lk. 8.17 is not simply a Lukan rewrite of Mark but proof of another source. 'Therefore, the agreement between Saying 5b (Pap. Ox. 654, 29-31) does not prove Thomas' use of Luke as his source. Thomas could have obtained it from Luke's source or from one similar to it.' But this still does not get us to independent oral tradition, nor does it explain why the assumption that Luke is slavishly copying yet another hypothetical source at 8.17 (which might lie behind Thomas) is superior to the conclusion that Luke is here rewriting Mark.

c. *Multiple Attestation, Orality and Authenticity*
Bitterness over the 'secret' conspiracies of others, and the desire for such acts to 'come to light' is a common experience. Conversely, the fear of disclosure is widespread. Three Jewish parallels attest to these common sentiments:

> Do not curse the king, even in your thoughts, or curse the rich, even in your bedroom, for a bird of the air may carry your voice, or some winged creature tell the matter (Eccl. 10.20).

> In the end every thing in this world which is done in secret will be publicized and made known to mankind, and for this reason, fear the Lord (*Targ. Koh.* 12.13).

> R. Johanan b Beroqa says 'Anyone who profanes the name of Heaven in secret, they exact the penalty from him openly' (*M. Avot.* 4.4).[1]

Parallels from Greek culture are easy to find. Pindar warns 'If any man hopes, in whatever he does, to escape the eye of God, he is grievously wrong', while Titus Maccius Palutus confidently asserts 'There is indeed a God that hears and sees whate'er we do'.[2]

The wide breadth of parallels warns against making dogmatic assertions about any one cultural background for the logion. The continued popularity of such parallels over an extended time almost guarantees that the aphorism was a part of the general cultural heritage of the first century. The overall structure of two clauses in synthetic parallelism which are in turn in antithetic parallelism (A, B; A', B') fits well into an oral context.[3] Just as such contemporary proverbs as 'Look before you leap' and 'The one who hesitates is lost' are extensively reproduced in the daily life of oral speech, so too one may reasonably infer such a life for the present aphorism. Thus almost certainly before us is a secular proverb taken over by the church during the transmission of the Jesus tradition.

---

1. As quoted by Lachs, *A Rabbinic Commentary,* p. 185.

2. Pindar, *Olympian Odes,* Titus Maccius Palutus: Captivi, II, 2, 63, in Mead, *Encyclopedia,* pp. 275-76. From the *Dhammapada,* compare 119-20, and 133.

3. This form cannot be limited to such a context and cannot be taken as direct proof. During the oral phase, transmission might also 'fluctuate' back and forth between this full form and a more streamlined version similar to Thomas 5b. Much would depend on the specific context, the performance style and the audience response.

Beyond the general conclusion, can the logion's transmission during the oral phase be constructed in greater detail? Here again we reach an impasse in the evidence. The use at Thomas 6b is entirely in accord with the widespread cultural application of this sentiment. Its setting as illumination for the Golden Rule may actually be Thomas' compositional redaction placing two well-known adages together for the 'first' time. Furthermore, I have already shown that Thomas displays dependence upon the synoptics.

A similar case would appear to be in view with Q. The context includes the sign of Jonah (Q 11.29-32), woes against the Pharisees (Q 11.37–12.1), and the exhortation to fearless confession (Q 12.2-12). The following warning not to fear those without the power to cast into hell would suggest an application similar to the warnings of Ecclesiastes and Pindar. The wider context of woes applies the logion in a more christological fashion: Jesus is the one 'hidden' to this sinful generation, temporarily rejected but soon to be vindicated even by the people of Nineveh and the queen of the South (Q 11.31-32).

This christological application is found in Mark and Thomas with respect to secret knowledge and Jesus' identity. Since the saying appears in Thomas and Mark in different clusters, the 'oral tradition' has not transmitted an aphorism cluster that actualized the connection between this common sentiment and certain gnostic and christological speculations. It is, of course, possible that this indicates an independent application of an obvious connection by Mark, Q, and Thomas. This kind of 'multiple attestation' might allow one to infer the existence of pre-Markan and pre-Thomastic 'gnosticized' christological sentiments in the early church. But beyond this one could infer little more about the precise relationship between the two texts and the relative dating of these speculations. Although set in the pre-literary phase, one simply could not deduce just how early, and certainly could not get beyond the post-resurrectional era. But, given the triple repetition in Thomas, it cannot be ruled out that this application of the saying is not part of the latest stream of Thomas and influenced by Q or Mark! Mark, on the other hand, gives few clues regarding his inherited tradition. He has so deeply integrated the saying into his parables chapter and redacted its form that one cannot even rule out a literary relationship with Q. The history of this logion's transmission during the oral phase, therefore, is lost.

3. *Measure for Measure (Mark 4.24b and Q 6.38)*

a. *Mark and Q*

Mark's second 'twin parable' is introduced by the saying 'Measure for Measure', which also expresses an universal desire. Here is an expression of the desire for proportionate retributive justice, either positively or negatively (reward or punishment). In modern terms, the adage 'You gave as good as you got' comes close to expressing the sentiment of this Markan proverb.

The argument for inclusion in Q includes the saying's location in Matthew and Luke in the context of 'double tradition'. As well, both Matthew and Luke preface the saying with an injunction against judging. Such a coincidence cannot reasonably be attributed to independent redaction.[1] The three versions are:

Mk 4.24	Lk. 6.38	Mt. 7.2
ἐν ᾧ μέτρῳ μετρεῖτε μετρηθήσεται ὑμῖν καὶ προστεθήσεται ὑμῖν.	ᾧ γὰρ μέτρῳ μετρεῖτε ἀντιμετρηθήσεται ὑμῖν.	καὶ ἐν ᾧ μέτρῳ μετρεῖτε μετρηθήσεται ὑμῖν.

The major difference between the Markan and Q forms is Mark's additional clause, καὶ προστεθήσεται ὑμῖν. But such a difference could easily be accounted for in a literary relationship by the simple alteration by either author. Discounting a direct relationship between Mark and Q, we are still left with the possibility of either Mark having added the phrase to his source or the Q community deleting it from theirs. Mark might have added the clause to bring the saying into closer harmony with what follows in v. 25.[2]

---

1. The Q saying is found at Mt. 7.2; Lk. 6.38.
2. Compare Pesch, *Markusevangelium*, I, p. 252. Marcus, *Mystery of the Kingdom*, pp. 137-38, notes a tension between the two sayings. In v. 24, one receives according to the measure one has; in v. 25, those who do not have do not receive according to the little they have. The conclusion to v. 24 decreases this tension, and is thus likely Mark's redaction. The contradictory nature of the saying is asserted also by Carlston, *Parables of the Triple Tradition*, p 156. But this contradiction needs to be limited. The sayings are contradictory, but so too are The Golden Rule and The Measure, or 'Look before you leap', and 'The one who hesitates is lost'. These proverbs are not so much contradictory as designed for different contexts and applications.

The first two clauses are in near-perfect word-for-word agreement, exactly as found in texts sharing a literary relationship. Matthew and Mark are arguably closer than Matthew and Luke in the opening, so the verbal agreements are entirely consistent with a literary relationship. Such near-perfect reproduction in independent oral versions occurs usually only due to formulaic language or in rare cases of memorized short sayings. Since the former explanation can be discounted, are we dealing here with the latter? In order to answer this question, it is necessary to examine the other relevant literary parallels.

b. *Multiple Attestation, Orality and Authenticity*

1 Clem. 13.2-3 and Polycarp's letter to the Philippians (2.3) provide the most relevant parallels from early Christianity for the aphorism. The context is exactly as in Q, although Clement has an expanded series of injunctions preceding the logion. Clement's form of the series compares favourably with Luke:

Lk. 6.37-38	*1 Clem.* 13.2-3
Καὶ μὴ <u>κρίνετε</u>, καὶ οὐ μὴ <u>κριθῆτε·</u>	Ἐλεᾶτε, ἵνα ἐλεηθῆτε·
καὶ μὴ καταδικάζετε,	ἀφίετε, ἵνα ἀφεθῇ ὑμῖν·
καὶ οὐ μὴ καταδικασθῆτε.	ὡς ποιεῖτε, οὕτω ποιηθήσεται ὑμῖν·
ἀπολύετε, καὶ ἀπολυθήσεσθε·	ὡς <u>δίδοτε</u>, οὕτω <u>δοθήσεται ὑμῖν·</u>
<u>δίδοτε</u>, καὶ <u>δοθήσεται ὑμῖν·</u>	ὡς <u>κρίνετε</u>, οὕτως <u>κριθήσεσθε·</u>
	ὡς χρηστεύεσθε, οὕτως χρηστευθήσεται ὑμῖν·
μέτρον καλὸν πεπιεσμένον	
σεσαλευμένον	
ὑπερεκχυννόμενον δώσουσιν	
εἰς τὸν κόλπον ὑμῶν·	
<u>ᾧ γὰρ μέτρῳ μετρεῖτε</u>	<u>ᾧ μέτρῳ μετρεῖτε</u>,
[ἀντι]<u>μετρηθήσεται ὑμῖν.</u>	ἐν αὐτῷ <u>μετρηθήσεται ὑμῖν.</u>[1]

The context in Clement leads us to expect a form of the saying beginning with ὡς. The change in form is jarring. If Clement is citing oral

---

1. 'Be merciful, that ye may obtain mercy. Forgive, that ye may be forgiven. As ye do, so shall it be done unto you. As ye give, so shall it be given unto you. As ye judged, so shall ye be judged. As ye are kind, so shall kindness be shewn you. With what measure ye mete, it shall be measured to you', translation Lake, *Apostolic Fathers*, I, p. 31.

tradition here, why has he not harmonized the logion more fully to the context? The near-perfect word-for-word agreement with the Markan and Q forms seems better explained by the influence of a written source: Clement has taken over the source's wording and not fully harmonized it to his new context. The addition of ἐν αὐτῷ needs no further explanation than Clement's literary addition to a written source.

Polycarp's series shares elements with both Q and *1 Clement*: μὴ κρίνετε, ἵνα μὴ κριθῆτε· ἀφίετε, καὶ ἀφεθήσεται ὑμῖν· Ἐλεᾶτε, ἵνα ἐλεηθῆτε· ᾧ μέτρῳ μετρεῖτε, ἀντιμετρηθήσεται ὑμῖν.[1] The introductory injunction, 'Judge not. . .' is exactly as in Q. This is surprising given that μὴ κρίνετε is hardly necessary or fixed. Independent oral versions could well be expected to show variation at this point.[2] The second element, the injunction to forgive, is Clement's second exhortation and found as the second and third elements in Luke under synonymous verbs. Polycarp's third element, on mercy, is Clement's first injunction and found at Q 6.36 (again, with a synonymous change of verbs). Both of these motifs are found in combination with the principle of measure in other contexts. Forgiveness is found at the Lord's Prayer (Q 11.2-4; Mt. 6.9-13), Mt. 6.14-15 and Mk 11.25. Mercy is found in Matthew's version of the beatitudes (Mt. 5.7) and Q 6.36 ('Be merciful, just as your Father is merciful'). Thus Q, Clement and Polycarp all include the theme measure for measure together with the motifs of judgement, mercy, and forgiveness. The order varies but this core agreement remains. Such overall agreement suggests a literary relationship: orality could be expected to show much greater variability. And most significantly, we again find in Polycarp near-perfect word-for-word reproduction of the aphorism as it is found in Mark and Q. Polycarp also shares Luke's redactional prefix upon the concluding verb.[3]

---

1. 'Do not judge, in order that you not be judged; forgive, and you shall be forgiven; be merciful, in order that mercy be shown to you; in the measure you measure, it shall be measured to you.' My translation.

2. This point is not decisive in itself, but has to be given weight in the context of overall agreements.

3. Polycarp must share a literary relationship with the synoptics, as is especially evident from the agreement with Luke at ἀντιμετρηθήσεται. He may, in fact, have both Matthew and Luke before him at this point. See Koester, *Synoptische Überlieferung*, '1st dieses Urteil richtig, so muß Polykarp das 1. und das 3.

The following agreements among Q, Clement and Polycarp argue for a literary relationship. Both Q and Polycarp begin the series with the injunction against judging (an injunction shared by Clement). Clement shows that there is no necessity in this order. If oral transmission is responsible for the three forms of the saying, how do we account for this agreement in the opening injunction between Q and Polycarp (Καὶ μὴ κρίνετε, ἵνα μὴ κριθῆτε)? All three authors agree on concluding the series with the measure aphorism. Yet there is no logical necessity for this logion to be the conclusion of the series. Mark uses it to begin a new series at 4.24, showing how easy it is to begin such a series with the aphorism. Similarly, the saying could just as readily be fitted into the middle of a series. If orality lies behind the three versions of the series, how do we account for the agreement in concluding order? Finally, there is the near-perfect word-for-word agreement in the logion among four supposedly 'independent' authors; Mark, Q, Clement and Polycarp. An oral context, spread across so many authors, would almost certainly demand some variation.

Cultural parallels to measure for measure are abundant. It is found in the Persian proverb, 'What I kept, I lost, What I spent, I had, What I gave, I have'. Confucius tells us that 'Good and evil do not befall men without reason. Heaven sends them happiness or misery according to their conduct.' It is implicit in Aeschylus' observation, 'God loves to help him who strives to help himself'.[1] In the Jewish tradition, the sentiment is expressed at Prov. 11.25, 'A generous person will be enriched, and one who gives water will get water'. But the saying finds its closest parallel in the common rabbinic axiom of divine mercy and justice:

Evangelium gekannt haben,' p. 118. Koester believes *1 Clement* to be independent, (pp. 12-16).

1. Taken from Mead, *Encyclopedia*, Persian proverb, p. 243; Confucius, *The Book of History* IV (Mead, *Encyclopedia*, p. 291); Aeschylus, *Fragments,* frag. 223 (Mead, *Encyclopedia*, p. 247). The continuing popularity of the final aphorism can be seen in 'Try first thyself, and after call in God; For to the worker God himself lends aid', Euripides, Hippolytus, frag. 435 (Mead, *Encyclopedia*, p. 259); 'Help yourself and Heaven will help you', Jean de La Fontaine, *Fables*, Bk. VI, 18 (Mead, *Encyclopedia*, p. 265).

במדה שאדם מדד בה מודדין לו.[1]

The rabbinic documents regularly use the impersonal plural in distinction to the consistent use of the passive, although Jewish sources with the passive can also be found.[2] The conformity of the Christian versions of this aphorism in light of the possibility of translational variation is highly significant. Orality or independent translation could be expected to show greater variation.

The rabbinic parallels show that the church has appropriated a proverb from the common heritage. Just as it ascribed the Golden Rule to Jesus, so too this logion. Exactly when this was done one cannot say. The forms in Clement and Polycarp, despite their differences, demand some literary explanation (either Q or one or both of Matthew and Luke). The agreements between Mark and Q likewise argue for a common literary form of the saying having found its way to both authors. This is probably the archetype for all the versions I have discussed. Its use has consistently been in total accord with the saying's application throughout antiquity, and nothing distinctive can be found in the church's use of this motif. Whatever history the logion had in the oral tradition is essentially lost.[3]

4. *To the One Who Has (Mark 4.25; Q 19.26; Gospel of Thomas 41)*

a. *Mark and Q*
'The rich get richer; the poor get poorer.' The principle in Mark's concluding aphorism would seem self-evident. One finds the saying earlier in Matthew's parable sermon (Mt. 13.12) and repeated as the conclusion to the parable of the Talents (Mt. 25.29). Luke includes it in his parables chapter (Lk. 8.18) and with the Talents (Lk. 19.26). Hence, inclusion in Q is assured. The following parallels set forth the

---

1. 'With what measure a man measures, in that same they (i.e., God) measure to him.' As quoted and translated in M. McNamara, *The New Testament and the Palestinian Targum to the Pentateuch* (Rome: Pontifical Biblical Institute, 1966), p. 139.

2. As for example at TJII Gn 38.26 in PTG, MS D. See McNamara, *New Testament and Palestinian Targum*, p. 140.

3. See Carlston, on vv. 24-25, 'We do not know, of course, what the sayings might have meant in their original context, now lost, since the possible applications are almost limitless', *Parables of the Triple Tradition*, p. 156.

five synoptic versions. By noting the minor agreements of Matthew and Luke and taking account of distinctively redactional elements, one can arrive at a reasonable reconstruction of the saying's form in Q.

Mark	Luke (Mk)	Luke (Q)
ὃς γὰρ ἔχει,	ὃς ἂν γὰρ ἔχῃ,	παντὶ τῷ ἔχοντι
δοθήσεται αὐτῷ·	δοθήσεται αὐτῷ,	δοθήσεται
καὶ ὃς οὐκ ἔχει,	καὶ ὃς ἂν μὴ ἔχῃ,	ἀπὸ δὲ τοῦ μὴ ἔχοντος
καὶ ὃ ἔχει	καὶ ὃ δοκεῖ ἔχειν	καὶ ὃ ἔχει
ἀρθήσεται ἀπ' αὐτοῦ.	ἀρθήσεται ἀπ' αὐτοῦ.	ἀρθήσεται.

Mark	Matthew (Mk)	Matthew (Q)
ὃς γὰρ ἔχει,	ὅστις γὰρ ἔχει,	τῷ γὰρ ἔχοντι παντι;
δοθήσεται αὐτῷ·	δοθήσεται αὐτῷ,	δοθήσεται
	καὶ περισσευθήσεται·	καὶ περισσευθήσεται,
καὶ ὃς οὐκ ἔχει,	ὅστις δὲ οὐκ ἔχει	τοῦ δὲ μὴ ἔχοντος
καὶ ὃ ἔχει	καὶ ὃ ἔχειν	καὶ ὃ ἔχει
ἀρθήσεται ἀπ' αὐτοῦ.	ἀρθήσεται ἀπ' αὐτοῦ.	ἀρθήσεται ἀπ' αὐτου.[1]

In reconstructing the Q original, it is more likely that Matthew's introductory γὰρ is due to conflation with Mark. The Matthean καὶ περισσευθήσεται is added to the Markan and Q forms and is thus redactional. Luke's ἀπό smooths out the Greek and is likely his own touch. Finally, it is difficult to judge regarding the final ἀπ' αὐτοῦ, only in Matthew. Matthew may be again conflating from Mark, while Luke could be omitting it from Q. Marcus favours the second explanation.[2] On the basis of this examination Mark and Q may be set out as follows:

Mark	Q
ὃς γὰρ ἔχει, δοθήσεται αὐτῷ·	παντὶ τῷ ἔχοντι δοθήσεται
καὶ ὃς οὐκ ἔχει, καὶ ὃ ἔχει	τοῦ δὲ μὴ ἔχοντος καὶ ὃ ἔχει
ἀρθήσεται ἀπ' αὐτοῦ.	ἀρθήσεται [ἀπ' αὐτου Matt.]

The sayings are remarkably close. Markan redaction explains certain differences, most notably the inclusion of γὰρ and ὃς.[3] On the other

---

1. Minor agreements between Matthew and Luke (and hence taken over from Q) will appear with the double underline.

2. Marcus, *Mystery of the Kingdom*, p. 139, see n. 57.

3. Marcus argues that Q's participial construction is more polished Greek and thus secondary. However, sayings cast with ὃς (esp. ὃς ἂν) are frequent in Mark, see 3.35; 8.35, 38; 9.37, 40-41, 42; 10.11, 29, 44. If Mark's source is responsible for this consistency, it must be held to be a written source, since this kind of stylistic consistency is impossible over a wider variety of independent oral traditions. If the

hand, παντὶ in Q is likely secondary.[1] The variations between the two are no different from the clear variations that are found in Matthew and Luke's rewriting of the Markan version in their respective parables chapters. A literary relationship between Mark and Q cannot be ruled out. I turn now the examine the saying's inclusion in Thomas.

b. *The Version in Thomas*
Thomas' version of the saying is found in a third context. It is preceded by the logion on the plant, not of the Father, and followed by the exhortation to 'be wanderers' and the comparison of the fruit and the tree. The saying displays one major stylistic variation from the synoptic versions:

> He who has in his hand, it shall be given to him; and he who does not
> have, even the little he has shall be taken away from him.

The addition of 'in his hand' is similar to Thomas' introduction to the parable of the Sower (logion 9) and the parable of the reaper (logion 21). This phrase, therefore, can hardly be ascribed to the oral tradition.[2] The remaining logion is so close to either Mark or Q that a literary relationship is highly likely. A thesis of oral independence would be based only on convenience.[3] And further, one again finds that oral tradition has not transmitted the logion independently in a consistent chain of aphorisms.

c. *Multiple Attestation, Orality and Authenticity*
Literary parallels from antiquity to the principle expounded at Mk 4.25 are easy to find. 'Give instruction to the wise, and they will become wiser still; teach the righteous and they will gain in learning' (Prov. 9.9—Cp. *4 Ezra* 7.24-25). In rabbinic literature a close parallel is found in the statement of R. Issi and R. Hoshaya regarding

---

form is traditional, Mark has found this particular form agreeable enough to retain in all these instances.

1. Marcus, *Mystery of the Kingdom*, p. 139; Dupont, 'La transmission', p. 226.

2. On the secondary character of the phrase, see Marcus, *Mystery of the Kingdom*, p. 139; Koester, 'Test Case', p. 79.

3. See Schrage, *Das Verältnis*, pp. 96-98, who argues that since this is a well-known mashal, Thomas' dependence upon Mark cannot be conclusively maintained. For Sieber, Thomas' lack of synoptic editorial features and the distinctive context show that 'Thomas did not use the Synoptic Gospels as his sources', 'A Redactional Analysis', pp. 164-65.

the serpent, 'Thus what he desired was not given to him, and what he possessed was taken from him'.[1] A parable of R. Zera further illustrates this principle:

> Observe how the character of the Holy One, blessed be He, differs from that of flesh and blood. A mortal can put something into an empty vessel but not into a full one, but the Holy One, blessed be He, is not so, He puts more into a full vessel but not into an empty one (*b. Ber.* 40a; *b. Suk* 46a).[2]

Finally, the exposition given to Dan. 2.21 by R. Jose b Ḥalafta:

> 'If two persons came to borrow money from you, one rich and the other poor, to whom would you lend, the richer or the poor?' She replied: 'To the rich man!' 'Why?' he asked; to which she answered: 'Because he has the wherewithal to repay me; but if the poor man loses my money from where can he repay me?' 'Do your ears hear what you have uttered with your mouth? If the Holy One, blessed be he, gave wisdom to fools, they would sit and meditate upon it [the Torah] in privies, theaters, and bathhouses; but the Holy One, blessed be He, gave wisdom to the wise, who sit and meditate upon it in Synagogues and Houses of Study, hence He giveth wisdom to the wise and knowledge to them that know understanding' (*Koh. R.* 1.7).[3]

The biblical and rabbinic parallels are entirely consistent with the application found in the synoptics and Thomas. God's sacred gifts of wisdom and knowledge are reserved for those who already have. Like the Golden Rule, the church has taken over a proverb from the cultural heritage and attributed it to Jesus.[4] In Mark and Thomas is this principle is set into a distinctive theology of 'secret' or 'hidden' knowledge but the basic similarity remains. But even granting that this occurred during the oral phase, what can be reconstructed about this phase of the saying's transmission?

1. *Gen. R.* 20.5; cf. *t. Sot.* 4.17-19.
2. Klauck, *Allegorie*, pp. 239-40 notes the parallel and emphasis upon hearing.
3. Rabbinic texts quoted by Lachs, *A Rabbinic Commentary*, pp. 219-20. To these may be added *Ab.* 1.13; *Ber.* 40a; and from the *Dhammapada*, 15-16; 131-32.
4. Nineham, 'This too was very likely a current proverb based on the conditions of oriental society, in which the rich man, being powerful, constantly receives presents, whereas the poor and uninfluential are constantly fleeced', *The Gospel of St Mark*, p. 142; Taylor, 'The saying may be a popular proverb suggested by social conditions in oriental society', *The Gospel According to St Mark*, p. 265; see Bultmann, *History*, p. 112. Best, 'Mark's Preservation', p. 126 also sees here a popular proverb akin to 'The rich grow richer, the poor poorer'.

What is notable in the Christian tradition (Mark, Q, Thomas) is the narrow range of linguistic expression. The phraseology shows such little variation that one can speak of an aphoristic core. Is this due to an oral memorized structure or to a literary relationship between Mark, Q, and Thomas? If the former, it is not possible to ascertain just how early in the pre-literary phase the saying was appropriated by the church, just as it is impossible to establish an evolutionary trajectory of the various forms (i.e., such as 'first Q, then Thomas and finally the Markan form' or some variation on this theme). Multiple attestation in this case, even if based on orality, cannot get one back further than the post-resurrectional church. The overall consistency of the saying likewise raises suspicion: if orality were responsible, would one not expect to find greater variation in the linguistic expression of this truism?

5. *Ears to Hear (Mark 4.9, 23; Q 14.35; Gospel of Thomas 8)*

Exhortations to hear are posted more frequently than speed limits, and usually with the same effect. The numerous cultural parallels, beginning with Ezek. 3.27 ('Ο ἀκούων ἀκουέτω—LXX) and continuing with the rabbinic documents (cf. 'Do your ears hear what you have uttered with your mouth?' *Koh. R.* 1.7; cited above) show that the early church has again taken over a contemporary proverb.[1]

But the particular linguistic expressions given the injunction by Mark raise an important question. The saying is also given twice by Luke and three times by Matthew. Let us compare the various versions:

Mk 4.9	Ὃς ἔχει ὦτα ἀκούειν ἀκουέτω.
Mk 4.23	εἴ τις ἔχει ὦτα ἀκούειν ἀκουέτω.
Lk. 8.8	Ὁ ἔχων ὦτα ἀκούειν ἀκουέτω.
Lk. 14.35	Ὁ ἔχων ὦτα ἀκούειν ἀκουέτω.
Mt. 13.9, 43	Ὁ ἔχων ὦτα ἀκουέτω.
Mt. 11.15	Ὁ ἔχων ὦτα ἀκουέτω.

The consistent agreement between Matthew and Luke ('Ο ἔχων) is significant because, offered two choices by Mark, both have chosen

---

1. Schrage argues that the saying is a widely travelled and much-loved 'wake-up formula'. In light of this, he believes its inclusion in Thomas cannot be proved to be evidence of dependence upon the synoptics. See *Das Verhältnis*, p. 42. Also, Sieber, 'A Redactional Analysis', pp. 177-78.

option three: 'none of the above'. This could arise from one of two possibilities. Either independent redactional change for stylistic reasons (perhaps based on Ezekiel); or adoption of a reading from Q. But if this latter possibility is the case, it would have to be admitted that Matthew's location of the logion in ch. 11 is redactional. Agreement in location of the doublet would strengthen the case.

The Markan variation in wording is curious in another respect. Matthew and Luke have consistently provided the reader with one form of the logion. Why has Mark not done the same? It raises the possibility that, in at least one instance, Mark is copying a written source very closely. The second version may thus differ due to freer stylistic expression by the evangelist.

This possibility is strengthened when one considers Thomas. Steven Davies has divided this document into four main 'chapters'. These chapters are logions: A) 2-37; B) 38-58; C) 59-91; and D) 92-113. Towards the end of each cycle Davies finds the following sequence of themes: making the two one; being chosen, solitary, standing; parables about finding; light; renunciation of the world or power; knowledge of which the world is not worthy; sayings on body and soul and spirit. Curiously, Davies makes the following observation:

> *Only* in Thomas chapter A is the expression 'he who has ears *to hear,* let him hear' used and it is used three times, 8, 21, 24. In all other places, throughout chapters B, C and D the expression is 'he who has ears, let him hear'.[1]

The form in Thomas chapter A agrees with Mark in the duplication of the infinitive. The other forms of the saying agree essentially with what we find in Matthew. Why? Since Thomas has this 'Markan' form of the logion appended before the Sower and immediately after the Seed Growing Secretly, Thomas must be basing this formulation upon written tradition. This written tradition already set the logion in the context of seed parables. If that source was not the Gospel of Mark it must have been some form of Mark's parables tract. In this instance 'orality' must be viewed as at least one further stage of literary tradition behind the written Gospel. The oral tradition did not directly reach Mark and Thomas; rather, each of them was dependent upon written tradition. Any ability to trace back into the oral phase is again frustrated by the mass of cultural parallels to the saying which robs it

---

1. S. Davies, *The Gospel of Thomas*, p. 153; discussion, pp. 149-53.

of any 'distinctiveness' and opens up an endless number of hypothetical settings for its use. Secondly, one is faced with tracing through no less than two literary phases of the tradition before reaching the oral phase. Orality may be assumed on the basis of common sense, but it cannot be reconstructed by the evidence available to us.

6. *Summary of Results; Signs of Orality in Mark 4.21-25*

The results of the above discussion are clear. All five of the aphorisms in Mk 4.21-25 show extensive parallels in the general cultural heritage of antiquity. 'Distinctiveness', and beyond that, a setting in the life of Jesus, are impossible to establish. If the sayings circulated within the oral tradition of the early church it is impossible to reconstruct with any certitude just what this process was like or its historical development. Furthermore, an hypothesis of independent citation of oral tradition is based, in most cases, on the basis of common-sense convenience. Free-floating sayings are common in the oral heritage of every culture and authors may invoke the same saying independently. This explanation, however, has become strained for all five of the logia under discussion. Some sort of literary relationship among the various citations of these sayings seems demanded by the evidence. This is particularly true with respect to the three aphorisms represented at Mk 4.23-25. And some form of literary relationship between Mark and Q cannot be ruled out: the linguistic similarities between the two versions of these sayings (Mark and Q) are entirely consistent with a literary relationship. The implications of these observations will be discussed in this book's conclusion.

Conclusion

ORAL TRADITION:
THE IRRECOVERABLE BARRIER TO JESUS

> Whoever prefers to put the name 'Jesus' always in quotation marks and
> let it stand as an abbreviation for the historical phenomenon with which
> we are concerned, is free to do so.
>
> Rudolf Bultmann[1]

The Oral phase of the Jesus tradition is now forever lost. The spoken
word is transitory by nature and exists for but a moment. It lives on
only in the memory of the audience and its recovery is entirely
dependent upon the accuracy of that memory to bring it back into
being. The present study has underscored the lack of critical tools to
reconstruct the oral phase of Christian tradition in any meaningful
fashion—particularly with regard to the teaching of Jesus. The
problems encountered—working back from the textual medium to the
oral phase itself—may be summarized as follows.

First there is the problem of writing itself, which may be termed
the existential moment. Words must be chosen and the author becomes
bound to one particular expression for the ideas to be conveyed to the
audience. Innovation is highly prized, and hence it need not surprise
us that over 40 written versions of the Golden Rule can easily be
found. Formulaic oral expression contains its own set of problems,
but the formula itself often binds the author to a certain linguistic
expression. As Parry demonstrates, most of the formulae in Homer
contain nothing in thought or style that sets them apart as particularly
effective—the particular linguistic expression is bound to the formula
and the poet must use it.[2] Only in textuality can thoughts be distilled
from their particular expression and recast in an endless variety of

---

1. R. Bultmann, *Jesus and the Word* (trans. L.P. Smith and E.H. Lantero; New
York: Charles Scribner's Sons, 1934), p. 14.
2. See above, Chapter 2, section 1, d; Parry, 'Epic I', p. 99.

possibilities. It is here that the first barrier to recovery of the oral phase is encountered. The Gospels are textuality—every last word has been chosen carefully by the evangelist and any previous tradition (written or oral) is now given as part of the overall theological message of the new literary Gospel. To be sure, redaction criticism allows one to identify a great many of the unique concerns of each author so that one need not identify them with prior tradition, but this does not resolve this fundamental problem. The two-source theory has given us a false sense of security and encouraged an unwarranted confidence. Since Mark exists, the 'correct' answer is immediately obvious in triple tradition while the reconstruction of Q at least has the control of two independent texts. But this simply represents the reconstruction of prior written tradition: the reconstruction of prior oral tradition often must proceed on the basis of only one text! One may discount the particular redactional concerns of the author in question and note the elements of stylistic expression that seem to be habitual, but then what? Reconstructing the inherited oral tradition is by no means simple; the language and form of the oral tradition may not be appropriate to the new textual medium. Parry demonstrates how literate poets increasingly turned away from the language of orality to give their works better linguistic expression.[1] There is no guarantee, as Kelber assumed, that textuality would freeze the inherited oral tradition resulting in a fossilized testimony to the prior tradition.[2] Indeed, the opposite possibility, acknowledged by Kelber, is more likely the case: the inherited oral tradition may have been textualized beyond recognition.[3]

The textual medium itself is not fully stable. The scribes' willingness at numerous points to alter their inherited tradition testifies that even the canonical text is by no means sacrosanct. Similarly, Matthew and Luke have not hesitated to adapt Mark and Q to their new context. Mark and Q themselves, it is well known, have their own distinctive theologies and literary styles. All of this gives abundant proof of the continuing 'existential' aspect of writing. Even the written tradition continues to be edited and improved. This warns us against assuming that the Gospels offer a directly transcribed orality: the inherited tradition may have been thoroughly textualized and altered in the

1. See above, Chapter 2, section 1, d; Parry, 'Epic I', p. 104.
2. See above, Chapter 1, section 3, c; Kelber, *Oral*, p. 46.
3. See above, Chapter 1, section 3, c; Kelber, *Oral*, p. 44.

transmission process, a process of alteration that did not end with the synoptic evangelists! Secondly, although there is an adequate manuscript data-base to reconstruct the 'original' of the canonical Gospels with a reasonable degree of accuracy, the same cannot be said of other essential points in the reconstruction of oral tradition. Manuscript testimony for the *Gospel of Thomas*, for example, is inadequate to guarantee that one has the Coptic autograph in view.

The manuscript testimony to Thomas is but the first in a number of factors that restrict its use as a direct testimony to the oral phase. There is also the problem of translation: not only has the document been translated into Coptic, the translator has often conflated the new text to conform to that of the Coptic canonical Gospels! Nor does this exhaust the alterations within Thomas at this stage. Comparison with even the few remaining fragments of the Greek text shows alteration of order and reworking of the text itself. The agreement in order, noted above, particularly at logia 31-33 with Mt. 5.14-15 shows that the Coptic version of Thomas has been influenced by the canonical texts. In every case (for the three parables and five aphorisms) it has proven impossible to assert Thomas' independence from the synoptic tradition, while some form of textual relationship has often proved likely. Even scholars who support an early date for this Gospel admit that additions have been made in its transmission. An interesting example of this is the following exchange by Ménard and Robinson. The former points out that logion 53 'picks up the debate between Tineius Rufus and Rabbi Akiba, in which the former emphasized that if circumcision were necessary children would be born circumcised'. Since Tineius was governor of Judea in 132 CE, and since Rabbi Akiba died in 135, this would give, for Ménard, a *terminus a quo* (starting date) for Thomas of about 135 CE.[1] Robinson responds:

> Even if it were clear, however, that the *Gospel of Thomas* were dependent on this incident, one must consider here as elsewhere the option of late interpolations. The latest trait in a sayings collection is far from being an assured indication of the date when the basic collection was made.[2]

---

1. Quoted in Robinson, 'On Bridging the Gulf from Q to Thomas', p. 160; J.E. Ménard, 'La datation des manuscrits', *Histoire et archéologie* 70 (1983), p. 12.
2. Robinson, 'On Bridging the Gulf from Q to Thomas', p. 160.

Nor does Koester posit complete independence of Thomas from the synoptics. Instead, he postulates at least two stages to Q and believes some form of literary relationship between the first edition of Q and Thomas to be likely. Thomas and Q overlap most in the so-called wisdom materials rather than in the apocalyptic passages. The sermon on the plain (Q 6) particularly shows a great number of parallels between these two documents. He comments:

> It is exactly with respect to the material that belongs to the earlier stage of Q, written probably within ten or twenty years of Jesus' death, that we find parallels in the *Gospel of Thomas*. Of the seventy-nine sayings of Thomas with Synoptic Gospel parallels, forty-six have parallels in Q, but the typical apocalyptic perspective of the later redaction of Q does not appear in any of these sayings. Rather, they are non-apocalyptic wisdom sayings, proverbs, prophetic sayings, parables, and community rules.[1]

Since Thomas, according to Koester, often preserves an earlier form of the saying than either Matthew or Luke, he argues that 'the *Gospel of Thomas* is either dependent upon the earliest version of Q or, more likely, shares with the author of Q one or several very early collections of Jesus' sayings'.[2] But this again brings one not into direct contact with the oral phase but only to an 'earlier' form of literary tradition. Postulating an early stratum in Thomas that is closer to the oral tradition than that found in the synoptic Gospels still does not get one back to the oral phase. My examination of Thomas' versions of the Mustard Seed (logion 20), the Lamp (logion 33), the Hidden Revealed (logions 5, 6, 108) and the One Who Has (logion 41) has clearly shown that even if these units were present in the earliest version of Thomas, their present form in the Coptic translation shows conflation with the synoptics. With three versions in Thomas of the Hidden Revealed, for example, how can one tell its 'earliest' form in this Gospel? The version of P. Oxy. 654, with its secondary promise of resurrection, has even been conflated into greater conformity with the synoptics. Clearly, the translator has not co-operated with modern biblical critics' desire to reconstruct the 'earliest tradition' and has not hesitated to alter the material from this earliest stratum of Thomas! Since Thomas' history of transmission is so complex, it must be admitted that its testimony as an independent witness to the oral

---

1. Koester, *Ancient Christian Gospels*, p. 87.
2. Koester, *Ancient Christian Gospels*, p. 95.

tradition is severely limited and often dependent upon form- and redactional-critical considerations to establish Thomas' version as the 'earliest'.

The independence of order within Thomas, Q and Mark points to another problem in the ability to reconstruct the oral phase. It has not been possible to establish even one instance where a chain of oral sayings has reached two literary authors independently. The similarity of context at the Measure among Q, Clement and Polycarp most likely has resulted from a literary relationship based upon Q. This is in strong contrast to Bultmann's model of organic growth within the oral phase wherein each logion circulates separately and then is joined with others in a chain. While it is true that Lord talks about blocks of tradition, and the rabbinic tradition often strung together sayings based upon an association with the biblical text, no such chains of tradition have been demonstrated in the synoptic–Thomas tradition. This implies an oral phase much more in keeping with contemporary culture where proverbs are often 'free-floating' and circulate individually, only to be joined with similar material in its textualization by association by the author. The difficulty in establishing oral chains of tradition underscores the inability to determine oral context for most (if not all) of the sayings in the synoptic–Thomas tradition.

The relationship between Mark and Q, on the other hand, is also complicated. In adopting the two-source reconstruction scholars are often content to ask whether Mark knew Q, answer in the negative, and leave it at that. Since there is so much in Q that does not appear in Mark it seems unlikely that he had a copy of this document. But this should not rule out some form of literary relationship, either that Mark knew an earlier edition of Q or that Mark and Q shared common sources. Our examination, particularly, of the Mustard Seed, the Measure, and the One Who Has demonstrates that a literary relationship between these two documents is likely. The above discussion has highlighted the fact that independence between the versions of sayings in these two documents is often based on 'common sense'. The hypothesis of a shared document is intuitively believed to be unnecessarily complicated. If one's view is based only on one or two sayings, 'oral tradition' and independence can be asserted without straining probability. It is the contention of this study that, just as with the double tradition of Matthew and Luke (i.e., Q), a thesis of independence breaks under the weight of evidence from a wider variety of sayings from the doubly attested traditions. I have already noted the linguistic evidence of similarity between the versions of the Mustard Seed, the Measure, and the One Who Has. Further evidence, cumulative in nature, can also be found. The Beelzebul controversy unit, as I noted in my discussion of Bultmann, contains up to five logions that share a common order in Mark and Q. To this may be added the agreement in wording of Mal. 3.1 in Mark and Q against the Septuagint:

Mk 1.2   Ἰδοὺ ἀποστέλλω τὸν ἄγγελόν μου πρὸ προσώπου σου,
            ὃς κατασκευάσει τὴν ὁδόν σου.

Q 7.27   Ἰδοὺ ἀποστέλλω τὸν ἄγγελόν μου πρὸ προσώπου σου,
            ὃς κατασκευάσει τὴν ὁδόν σου ἔμπροσθέν σου.

Mal. 3.1   Ἰδοὺ ἐγὼ ἐξαποστέλλω τὸν ἄγγελόν μου, καὶ ἐπιβλέψεται
            ὁδόν πρὸ προσώπου μου.

Exod. 23.20   καὶ ἰδοὺ ἐγὼ ἀποστέλλω τὸν ἄγγελόν μου πρὸ προσώπου
            σου, ἵνα φυλάξῃ σε ἐν τῇ ὁδῷ.

While a complete examination of the doubly attested sayings is beyond the scope of the present study, I would like simply to draw to the reader's attention other instances of significant agreement between these two sources for consideration.

The Demand for a Sign

Mk 8.12	Q 11.29
Τί <u>ἡ γενεὰ αὕτη ζητει'</u> <u>σημεῖον</u>;	<u>ἡ γενεὰ αὕτη</u> γενεὰ πονηρά ἐστιν
ἀμὴν λέγω ὑμῖν εἰ <u>δοθήσεται</u> τῇ	<u>σημεῖον ζητεῖ</u>, καὶ σημεῖον οὐ
γενεᾷ ταύτῃ σημεῖον.	<u>δοθήσεται</u> αὐτῇ εἰ μὴ τὸ σημεῖον
	Ἰωνᾶ.

Receives You, Receives Me

Mk 9.37	Mt. 10.40 (Q 10.16)
ὃ ἄν ἓν τῶν τοιούτων παιδίων	ὁ <u>δεχόμενος</u> ὑμᾶς
<u>δέξηται</u> ἐπὶ τῷ ὀνόματί μου,	
<u>ἐμὲ δέχεται</u>	<u>ἐμὲ δέχεται</u>
<u>καὶ ὃς ἄν ἐμὲ δέχεται</u>	<u>καὶ ὁ ἐμὲ δεχόμενος</u>
οὐκ ἐμὲ <u>δέχεται</u> ἀλλὰ	<u>δέχεται</u>
<u>τὸν ἀποστείλαντά με</u>.	<u>τὸν ἀποστείλαντά με</u>.

Save Soul, Lose It

Mk 8.35	Q 17.33
ὃς γὰρ <u>ἐὰν θέλῃ τὴν ψυχὴν αὐτοῦ</u>	<u>ὃς ἐὰν</u> <u>ζητήσῃ τὴν ψυχὴν αὐτοῦ</u>
<u>σῶσαι</u> <u>ἀπολέσει αὐτήν·</u>	<u>περιποιήσασθαι</u> <u>ἀπολέσει αὐτήν</u>
<u>ὃς δ'ἂν ἀπολέσει</u> τὴν ψυχὴν αὐτοῦ	<u>ὃς δ' ἂν ἀπολέσῃ</u>
ἕνεκεν ἐμοῦ καὶ τοῦ εὐαγγελίου	
<u>σωσει</u> <u>αὐτην.</u>	<u>ζωογονήσει</u> αὐτήν.

Ashamed of Me

Mk 8.38	Q 12.8-9
<u>ὃς</u> γὰρ <u>ἐὰν</u> <u>ἐπαισυνθῇ με</u> καὶ	πᾶς <u>ὃς ἂν</u> <u>ὁμολογησῃ ἐν ἐμοὶ</u>
τοὺς ἐμοὺς λόγους	ἔμπροσθεν τῶν ἀνθρώπων
ἐν τῇ γενεᾷ ταύτῃ τῇ μοιχαλίδι	
καὶ ἁμαρτωλῷ <u>καὶ ὁ υἱὸς τοῦ</u>	<u>καὶ ὁ υἱὸς τοῦ ἀνθρώπου</u>
<u>ἀνθρώπου</u>	
<u>ἐπαισυνθήσεται αὐτον</u> ὅταν	<u>ὁμολογήσει ἐν αὐτῷ</u>
<u>ἔλθῃ ἐν</u>	
τῇ δόξῃ τοῦ πατρὸς αὐτοῦ μετὰ	ἔμπροσθεν
<u>τῶν ἀγγέλων τῶν ἁγίων.</u>	<u>τῶν ἀγγέλων τοῦ θεοῦ.</u>

The evidence for a literary relationship between Q and Mark in these doubly attested logions is cumulative in nature. The evidence necessary to determine precisely what form this relationship was (one source or a series of logia tracts) may forever be lost due to the difficulty of historical reconstruction. And while a common order cannot be demonstrated for these units it is useful to remember that they all appear in Q after the Sermon on the Plain, and that some agreements of relative order can be demonstrated (i.e., the Malachi application and the Beelzebul controversy are early in both Mark and Q; the Mission of the Twelve is quickly followed by the Demand for a Sign in each and appears in the middle of the two documents while the Divorce unit is late in each). All of this suggests to me that the often-claimed independence of Mark and Q is an unproven assertion. The double attestation of sayings in these two documents by no means guarantees independence, nor does it grant direct entry into the oral tradition.

The conflation in Thomas to the synoptics, the influence of Q upon Clement and Polycarp's use of the Measure logion and the likelihood of a literary relationship between Q and Mark points to another problem in reconstructing the oral tradition underlying written Gospel texts. Too often Gospel critics have had an evolutionary and sequential model of the relationship between oral and written traditions. The material, in this view, is transmitted orally first and then is deposited into literary documents to start a second and distinct phase of transmission. Ruth Finnegan particularly has challenged this overall view of oral tradition, pointing to numerous instances of interaction between the written and oral word. Vansina also underscores this interaction, and the influence that written traditions can in turn have on contemporary oral life:

> When writing came to be practiced in a society, oral traditions did not die out as long as literacy was not general. Rather, people incorporated traditions into writings. The transmission became mixed and could remain so for centuries. D. Henige who has most forcefully drawn attention to the input of written material into oral traditions reserves the term 'feedback' for this process. After reviewing evidence from around the world he concluded that 'Uncontaminated oral tradition simply does not exist any more, except possibly in the most remote areas of Amazonia, the Philippines or New Guinea'. Historians should be aware of possible mixed transmissions and loans from written sources, and it behooves them to carefully examine all the writings that were available to the communities studied and especially those that concerned them.[1]

When it is remembered that anyone at Corinth who had access to Paul's letters would have received written versions of a number of prior traditions, the notion of 'feedback' becomes particularly relevant for early Christian tradition. The literary relationship among various traditions may be difficult—even impossible—to determine now, but this does not mean that such a relationship does not exist. The high probability of such pre-Gospel literary sources such as the Gospel of Signs, Mark's seed parables, Mark's apocalypse and a cycle of pronouncement stories warns that the present textual expression of tradition may often reflect a multi-layered textuality. Nor can these pre-synoptic sources simply be assumed to represent directly transcribed orality: each of them responds to a particular sociological situation and contains its own literary and theological perspective. The necessary evidence may be lacking to document these concerns and discount such redactional elements from the material in order to reconstruct the prior tradition. The reconstruction of an earlier literary form of the tradition may not necessarily point to a directly tran-

---

1. Vansina, *Oral Tradition*, pp. 156-57; quoting D. Henige, *Oral Historiography* (London: Longman, Green, 1982), pp. 80-87.

scribed orality. 'Feedback' and the interaction between the written and oral word as elements of a model of orality are particularly important given the urban Hellenistic milieu for the synoptic–Thomas tradition. The unconscious—and uncritical—evolutionary model of sequential tradition (oral then written) must give way to a more sophisticated acknowledgement that these two 'phases' of tradition are far more interrelated than is often acknowledged. And without the evolutionary and sequential assumption, it is by no means clear how exactly to push back behind the literary text into the oral phase to reconstruct the 'primitive' and 'authentic' tradition.

The tradition history of units within the oral phase is also lost because of the flexibility and instability of this medium. My examination of the aphorisms, for example, has shown that any clues whatsoever to their context or use within the oral phase of tradition are lacking. Since in the oral medium each performance is ever new and intimately connected with the audience, this lack of concrete evidence renders any reconstruction of the aphorisms' use in the oral tradition speculative in the extreme. Proverbs such as 'The one who hesitates is lost', for example, have limitless applications in the everyday life of oral speech. Implicit usually is an exhortation to the audience to take action in a concrete situation. A day later and the same person may say 'Look before you leap'. It is not that these proverbs are contradictory but rather that they are designed for different contexts. The aphorisms of the Jesus tradition, as Bultmann correctly noted, have an intimate relationship with the common proverbial tradition of antiquity. Determining precisely when these sayings entered into the synoptic–Thomas tradition (whether at a literary or oral stage) and how they 'originally' were used is a hopelessly complicated task. These materials in particular, like the Golden Rule, show an intimate connection with the literature of antiquity and may have been appropriated by any number of people involved in the traditions' transmission. In order to ascribe any such materials to Jesus one would have to demonstrate either a unique sentiment or application for a saying and postulate a continuity of such uniqueness during the entire course of the saying's transmission. Given the flexibility inherent in oral tradition it seems impossible to ascribe any of this material to Jesus.

The parables involve their own set of problems. Two main models of comparison may be invoked, each of which brings one quickly into a blind alley. To think of the parables as 'folk tales' is immediately to see the difficulty in ascribing distinctiveness and authenticity to these units. Folk tales have no original form and no one authentic structure. Precisely how could one determine that exactly *this* version of Cinderella, as opposed to *that* one, was more original? Certain oral versions or written renditions may be felt to be more dramatic or aesthetically pleasing, but it would be impossible to ascribe such distinctiveness back four or five 'versions' to a previous bard. It is precisely this kind of assertion that is needed to establish authenticity with the parables. Alternatively, one may think of the parables as a sort of 'thesaurus' of stereotypical plot-lines and characterizations, invoking Parry's formulae as the basis for the comparison. I have noted the invocation of this model by Stern and Scott. But here again, Jesus cannot be equated with 'Homer', nor can he be deemed the one original fountain source for the parabolic tradition. He stands in the midst of a long line of tradition. This thesaurus was also available, like the proverbial tradition, to everyone involved in the traditions' transmission. The stereotypical characterizations and plot-lines within the parables involve the constant generation of the old in new garb: material formulation is changed and one image creates two or three new ones. This can quickly be seen in the double and triple parables: Mustard and Leaven; Treasure, Pearl, Dragnet; Lost Sheep, Lost Coin, Lost Son; Leaven, Jar and Broken Handle; Tower Builder, King Going to War, Assassin; Serving Two Masters, Drawing Two Bows, Riding Two Horses. Precisely just which one 'originated' with Jesus, and how does it differ from his inherited tradition from the thesaurus? Parabolic stories in an oral medium derive their precise form and meaning from the immediate performance: any authentic Jesus parables have come to us removed from their context! The scholarly reconstructions of the distinctiveness of these units in the life of Jesus, as we have seen, almost always rely in strong measure upon the historical imagination and theological presuppositions of the critic. Attributing any such unit to Jesus again requires the presupposition of continuity of distinctiveness throughout the entire oral transmission, and requires an assumption of 'passivity' among all the intervening traditionalists as to be entirely at odds with everything known about the oral medium!

Even granting the possibility of recovering some authentic sayings on the basis of distinctiveness and double attestation, would this get one back to the historical Jesus? Again, the answer must be an emphatic no! Assuming a core material of a number of parables and aphorisms, it would be unlikely that the entirety would amount to more than an hour's speech. Extrapolating about the distinctive personality, the historical circumstances and development of such a person based on such a tiny slice of life must be viewed as speculative in the extreme! What would the view of Shakespeare be if only *Timon of Athens* remained extant? The entire process is so uncertain that one could not guarantee a sufficient degree of accuracy to be confident in an analysis. Even assuming a very generous margin of error of only 20 per cent one would be left with one in five erroneous sayings in the data-base distorting the 'authentic' and 'distinctive' voice of Jesus. These sayings all would have to be interpreted without their original context, and hence the precise meaning that any of these units had for Jesus is now a matter of the speculative imagination of the critic. In the scholarly reconstructions of the parables' original meaning it is as if one has broken into a psychiatrist's office and started reading the patients' descriptions of various ink blots. The vividness of these descriptions and the confidence related that the patient has in fact 'seen' the events therein should not confuse one into thinking that the ink blots can be reconstructed from the notes.

None of this, of course, will deter scholars from taking up Schweitzer's challenge and continuing to write monographs on the historical Jesus. By the nature of the case, it will always be impossible to prove that a form of 'oral tradition' does not lie behind at least some of the written text. What the present study has shown, however, is that it is far more difficult to prove the positive—i.e., that oral tradition does lie behind this particular text—than has been commonly acknowledged. And historical reconstruction must always be based upon what can be said, rather than upon what cannot be disproved. V. Harvey calls this the 'Morality of Historical Knowledge', noting that historical reconstruction is always a varying degree of probability. In light of these considerations, it is perhaps time to rewrite Bultmann's famous permissive into an imperative.

Appendixes

1. Markan Infrequent Redactional Vocabulary[1]

ἀγανακτέω 10.41; 14.4; 3-7

ἄγριος 1.6; 1-3

ἀκρίς 1.6; 1-4

ἀναγκάζω 6.45; 1-9

ἀναστενάζω 8.12?; 1-1

ἀποκαθίστημι 9.12; 3-8

ἄρρωστος; 6.5?, 13; 3-5

ἀφρίζω 9.20; 2-2

ἄσνετος 7.18; 1-5

γναφεύς 9.3; 1-1

διανοίγω 7.34; 1-8

διηγέομαι 9.9; 2-8

δύω, δύνω 1.32; 1-2

ἔθω 10.1; 1-4

ἔκστασις 5.42; 16.8 (?); 2-7

ἐμβριμάομαι 1.43; 2-5

ἀγέλη 5.11; 2-7

ἀγρυπνέω 13.33; 1-4

ἄλαλος; 7.37; 3-3

ἀναθεματίζω 14.71; 1-4

ἀποβάλλω 10.50; 1-2

ἀποκεφαλίζω 6.16; 2-4

ἀφεδρών 7.19; 1-2

ἀφσπαράσσω 9.26; 2-3

γαζοφυλακεῖον 12.41; 3-5

δαπανάω 5.26; 1-5

διαπεράω 5.21; 6.53; 2-6

δυσκόλος 10.24; 1-1

ἐκθαμβέω 9.15; 14.33; 4-4

ἐκπένω 15.39; 2-3

ἔκφοβος; 9.6; 1-2

ἐμπτύω 10.34?; 14.65; 3-6

ἀγρεύω 12.13; 1-1

ἀδημονέω 14.33; 1-3

ἀλλαχοῦ 1.38; 1-1

ἀναπηδάω 10.50; 1-2

ἀπόδημος; 13.34; 1-1

ἀποφέπω 15.1; 1-6

ἀφιβάλλω 1.16; 1-1

ἀχειροποίητος; 14.58; 1-3

γενέσια 6.21; 1-2

δερμάτινος 1.6; 1-2

διαφημίζω 1.45; 1-3

δυσκόλως 10.23; 1-3

ἐκθαυμάζω 12.17; 1-1

ἐκπερισσῶς 14.31; 1-1

ἐμβάπτω 14.20; 1-2

ἐναγκαλίζομαι 9.36; 10.16; 2-2

---

1. Table lists the Greek word followed by its redactional location(s) in Mark. Occurrences followed by a question mark (?) indicate that Pryke does not list the clause in question as redaction. They have been included because there are still strong grounds for believing the clause redactional. Finally, the total number of occurrences in Mark is given followed by the total number of times in the New Testament. These statistics have been taken from S. Kubo, *A Reader's Greek-English Lexicon of the New Testament and a Beginner's Guide for the Translation of New Testament Greek* (Andrews University Monographs IV; Grand Rapids: Zondervan, 1975). Thus, ἀγανακτέω is found three times in Mark, of which 10.41, and 14.4 Pryke believes to be redactional. It occurs seven times within the New Testament (i.e., four non-Markan occurences).

Appendixes 307

στάχυς 2.23?; 3-5	στίλβω 9.3; 1-1	συλλυπέω 3.5; 1-1
συμβαίνω 10.32; 1-8	συμβούλιον 15.1; 2-8	συμπορεύομαι 10.1; 1-4
συνακολουθέω 14.51;	συνανάκειμαι 2.15?;	συναποθνήσκω 14.31?;
2-3	6.22; 2-7	1-3
συνθλίβω 5.24, 31; 2-2	συντηρέω 6.20?; 1-3	συντρέχω 6.33; 1-3
συσπαράσσω 9.20; 1-2	συσταυρόω 15.32; 1-5	συντελέω 13.4; 1-6
σωφρονέω 5.15; 1-6	τελώνιον 2.14; 1-3	τίλλω 2.23?; 1-3
τρέμω 5.33; 1-3	τρόμος; 16.8?; 1-5	τρύβλιον 14.20; 1-2
ὑμνέω 14.26; 1-4	φανερῶς 1.45 1-3	φόνος 15.7; 2-9
χαλκίον 7.4; 1-1	χαλκός 12.41; 2-5	χειροποίητος 14.58; 1-6
ὠδίν 13.8; 1-4	ὠτάριον 14.47?; 1-2	

2. Mark 4.1-34 and Manuscript Variants

The UBS Third Edition text. Readings in **bold** have at least one variant listed in the Nestle-Aland apparatus; Underlined readings show variants in Alford's critical apparatus. Manuscripts listed in the [brackets] show a secondary variant from the UBS text at this point. The text thus shows the cummulative effect of the variants and allows the reader a greater sense of the frequency with which Mark's text has been altered. Textuality, at least before the printing press, is by no means a totally inflexible and stable medium!

4.1 Καὶ πάλιν ἤρξατο [D] διδάσκειν παρὰ [D] τὴν θάλασσαν. καὶ συνάγεται [D, A] πρὸς αὐτὸν ὄχλος [D] πλεῖστος [A, D], ὥστε αὐτὸν **εἰς πλοῖον ἐμβάντα** [B², D, W, Δ; A] καθῆσθαι ἐν τῇ θαλάσσῃ [D], καὶ πᾶς ὁ ὄχλος πρὸς τὴν **θάλασσαν ἐπὶ τῆς γῆς** [D, W] **ἦσαν** [A, D, W, Θ]. 2 καὶ ἐδίδασκεν αὐτοὺς ἐν παραβολαῖς πολλα [א, D], καὶ ἔλεγεν αὐτοῖς ἐν τῇ διδαχῇ αὐτοῦ, 3 Ἀκούετε [C]. Ἰδοὺ ἐξῆλθεν ὁ σπείρων [A, אᶜ] **σπεῖραι** [D]. 4 καὶ **ἐγένετο** [D, W] ἐν τῷ **σπείρειν** [W, D] ὃ μὲν ἔπεσεν παρὰ τὴν ὁδόν, καὶ ἦλθεν [D, H, K, Δ] τὰ πετεινὰ [D, G, M] καὶ κατέφαγεν αὐτό [D]. 5 καὶ ἄλλο [A, D] ἔπεσεν [D] ἐπὶ τὸ πετρῶδες [D] [καὶ — B, D] **ὅπου** [B, D, W] οὐκ εἶχεν γῆν πολλήν, καὶ εὐθὺς [A] **ἐξανέτειλεν** [W, D¹] διὰ τὸ μὴ ἔξειν βάθος [B] γῆς [D]· 6 καὶ ὅτε ἀνέτειλεν ὁ ἥλιος [A] **ἐκαυματίσθη** [B, D], καὶ διὰ τὸ μὴ ἔξειν ῥίζαν ἐξηράνθη [D]. 7 καὶ ἄλλο [א¹] ἔπεσεν εἰς [C, D] τὰς ἀκάνθας, καὶ ἀνέβησαν αἱ ἄκανθαι καὶ συνέπιξαν αὐτό, καὶ καρπὸν οὐκ ἔδωκεν. 8 **καὶ ἄλλα** [א*, A, D, 𝔐] ἔπεσεν εἰς [C] τὴν γῆν τὴν καλήν, καὶ ἐδίδου [C] καρπὸν ἀναβαίνοντα καὶ **αὐξανόμενα** [A, D, L, W, Δ, C, Θ, 𝔐], καὶ ἔφερεν [C, א, D] ἓν τριάκοντα καὶ ἓν ἑξήκοντα καὶ ἓν [B², א, C*, Δ] ἑκατόν. 9 καὶ ἔλεγεν [S], Ὃς ἔξει [A, C²] ὦτα ἀκούειν ἀκουέτω [D].

10 Καὶ ὅτε [A] ἐγένετο κατὰ μόνας, ἠρώτων [E, D] αὐτὸν οἱ περὶ αὐτὸν σὺν τοῖς δώδεκα τὰς παραβολάς [D, W, Θ; A, ℜ].
11 καὶ ἔλεγεν [D] αὐτοῖς, Ὑμῖν [D, A] τὸ μυστήριον δέδοται τῆς βασιλείας τοῦ θεοῦ· ἐκείνοις δὲ τοῖς ἔξω [B] ἐν παραβολαῖς τὰ [ℵ, D, W, Θ] πάντα γίνεται [D, Θ], 12 ἵνα [F, G, H, Δ] βλέποντες βλέπωσιν καὶ μὴ ἴδωσιν, καὶ ἀκούοντες ἀκούωσιν [C, M] καὶ μὴ συνιῶσιν [D¹], μήποτε ἐπιστρέψωσιν καὶ ἀφεθῇ [A, K, D] αὐτοῖς [A, D, Θ, ℜ].
13 Καὶ λέγει αὐτοῖς Οὐκ οἴδατε τὴν παραβολὴν ταύτην, καὶ πῶς πάσας τὰς παραβολὰς γνώσεσθε; 14 ὁ σπείρων τὸν λόγον σπείρει [ℵ]. 15 οἷτοι δέ εἰσιν οἱ παρὰ τὴν ὁδὸν ὅπου [D] σπείρεται ὁ λόγος, καὶ [B] ὅταν ἀκούσωσιν [D¹, G] εὐθὺς [A, D] ἔρχεται ὁ Σατανᾶς καὶ αἴρει [D; C, Δ, ℵ] τὸν λόγον τὸν ἐσπαρμένον εἰς αὐτούς [D, Θ, ℜ, ℵ, C, L, Δ]. 16 καὶ οἷτοι [ℵ, C, L, Δ] εἰσιν [A, B, K] οἱ ἐπὶ τὰ πετρώδη σπειρόμενοι, οἳ ὅταν ἀκούσωσιν τὸν λόγον εὐθὺς [A, D] μετὰ χαρᾶς λαμβάνουσιν αὐτόν [Θ], 17 καὶ οὐκ ἔχουσιν ῥίζαν ἐν ἑαυτοῖς ἀλλὰ πρόσκαιροί εἰσιν· εἶτα γενομένης θλίψεως ἢ [D] διωγμοῦ διὰ τὸν λόγον εὐθὺς [A, D] σκανδαλίζονται [D]. 18 καὶ ἄλλοι εἰσὶν [A; W, Θ, ℜ] οἱ εἰς [ℵ, C, Δ] τὰς ἀκάνθας σπειρόμενοι· οὗτοί εἰσιν [A, ℜ] οἱ [ℵ] τὸν λόγον ἀκούσαντες [A], 19 καὶ αἱ μέριμναι τοῦ αἰῶνος [D, W, Θ A] καὶ ἡ ἀπάτη τοῦ πλούτου [W, D, Θ; ℵ¹] καὶ αἱ περὶ τὰ λοιπὰ ἐπιθυμίαι [ℵ¹, D, W, Θ] εἰσπορευόμεναι συμπνίγουσιν τὸν λόγον, καὶ ἄκαρπος γίνεται [D]. 20 καὶ ἐκεῖνοί [A, D] εἰσιν οἱ ἐπὶ τὴν γῆν τὴν καλὴν [ℵ, C] σπαρέντες, οἵτινες ἀκούουσιν τὸν λόγον καὶ παραδέχονται καὶ καρποφοροῦσιν ἒν τριάκοντα καὶ ἒν ἑξήκοντα καὶ ἒν [W, B*, C*, ℜ] ἑκατόν.
21 Καὶ ἔλεγεν αὐτοῖς [B, L], Μήτι ἔρχεται [D, W] ὁ λύχνος [cp A] ἵνα ὑπὸ τὸν μόδιον τεθῇ ἢ ὑπὸ τὴν κλίνην; [D] οὐχ ἵνα ἐπὶ [ℵ, B*] τὴν λυχνίαν τεθῇ [A, K]; 22 οὐ γάρ ἐστιν [ℵ, A, C, L, Δ] κρυπτὸν [E] ἐὰν μὴ ἵνα [D] φανερωθῇ, οὐδὲ ἐγένετο ἀπόκρυφον ἀλλ' ἵνα ἔλθῃ εἰς φανερόν [A, B]. 23 εἴ τις ἔχει ὦτα ἀκούειν ἀκουέτω.
24 Καὶ ἔλεγεν αὐτοῖς, Βλέπετε τί [D] ἀκούετε. ἐν ᾧ μέτρῳ μετρεῖτε μετρηθήσεται ὑμῖν καὶ προστεθήσεται ὑμῖν [D, A, Θ]. 25 ὃς γὰρ [A, D] ἔχει [A], δοθήσεται [D] αὐτῷ· καὶ ὃς οὐκ ἔχει, καὶ ὃ ἔχει ἀρθήσεται ἀπ' αὐτοῦ.
26 Καὶ ἔλεγεν, Οὕτως ἐστὶν ἡ βασιλεία τοῦ θεοῦ ὡς ἄνθρωπος [W, A, C, Θ] βάλῃ τὸν σπόρον ἐπὶ τῆς γῆς 27 καὶ καθεύδῃ καὶ ἐγείρηται [E, F, ℵ, D] νύκτα καὶ ἡμέραν, καὶ ὁ σπόρος βλαστᾷ [A, ℵ] καὶ μηκύνηται [D] ὡς οὐκ οἶδεν αὐτός. 28 αὐτομάτη [D, W, Θ, ℜ] ἡ γῆ καρποφορεῖ, πρῶτον [Δ] χόρτον, εἶτα στάχυν [D], εἶτα [ℵ*, B*, L] πλήρη σῖτον [A, C, B, D, W] ἐν τῷ στάχυϊ. 29 [D] ὅταν δὲ παραδοῖ [A, C] ὁ καρπός, εὐθὺς [A, D] ἀποστέλλει τὸ δρέπανον, ὅτι παρέστηκεν ὁ θερισμός.

30 Καὶ ἔλεγεν [א], Πῶς [A, D] ὁμοιώσωμεν [C, K] τὴν βασιλείαν τοῦ θεοῦ, ἢ ἐν τίνι [A, D] αὐτὴν   παραβολῇ θῶμεν [W, A, D, Θ, 𝔐]; 31 ὡς [D] κόκκῳ [A, L, W, D, Θ, 𝔐] σινάπεως, ὃς ὅταν [D¹, א¹] σπαρῇ ἐπὶ τῆς γῆς [D, L], μικρότερον ὂν πάντων τῶν σπερμάτων [A, C, D] τῶν ἐπὶ τῆς γῆς, 32 καὶ ὅταν σπαρῇ, ἀναβαίνει [D] καὶ γίνεται μεῖζον πάντων τῶν λαχάνων [D, A] καὶ ποιεῖ κλάδους μεγάλους, ὥστε δύνασθαι ὑπὸ τὴν σκιὰν αὐτοῦ τὰ πετεινὰ τοῦ οὐρανοῦ κατασκηνοῦν [B].

33 Καὶ τοιαύταις παραβολαῖς   πολλαῖς [D, L, Δ] ἐλάλει αὐτοῖς [D] τὸν λόγον, καθὼς ἠδύναντο [A, D] ἀκούειν· 34 [B] χωρὶς δὲ παραβολῆς οὐκ ἐλάλει αὐτοῖς, κατ' ἰδίαν δὲ τοῖς ἰδίοις μαθηταῖς [A, D] ἐπέλυεν [Θᵇ] πάντα [D, W].

BIBLIOGRAPHY

Abel, E.L., 'The Psychology of Memory and Rumor Transmission and their Bearing on Theories of Oral Transmission in Early Christianity', *JR* 51 (1971), pp. 270-81.

Abrahams, I., *Studies in Pharisaism and the Gospels* (Library of Biblical Studies; New York: Ktav, 3rd edn, 1967 [1917, 1924]).

Achtemeier, P., *Mark* (Proclamation Commentaries; Philadelphia: Fortress Press, 1975).

Alford, H., *Alford's Greek Testament: An Exegetical and Critical Commentary* (repr. Grand Rapids: Guardian, 1976 [1844–77]).

Allport, G., and L. Postman, *The Psychology of Rumor* (New York: Henry Holt, 1947).

Alter, R., *The Art of Biblical Narrative* (New York: Basic Books, 1981).

Anderson, H., *The Gospel of Mark* (NCB; London: Oliphants, 1976).

Andrzejewski, B.W., and I.M. Lewis, *Somali Poetry: An Introduction* (Oxford: Clarendon Press, 1964).

Aune, D.E., 'The Problem of the Messianic Secret', *NovT* 11 (1969), pp. 1-31.

Ausubel, N. (ed.), *A Treasury of Jewish Folklore: Stories, Traditions, Legends, Humor, Wisdom and Folk Songs of the Jewish People* (New York: Bantam, abridged edn, 1980 [1948]).

Baird, J.A., 'A Pragmatic Approach to Parable Exegesis: Some New Evidence on Mark 4:11, 33-34', *JBL* 76 (1957), pp. 201-207.

Ballou, R.O. (ed.), *The Portable World Bible* (New York: Penguin Books, 1957).

Bartsch, H.-W. 'Eine bisher übersehene Ziterung der LXX in Mark 4.30', *TZ* 15 (1959), pp. 126-28.

Bassler, J.M., 'The Parable of the Loaves', *JR* 66 (1986), pp. 157-72.

Bauer, J., 'Synoptic Tradition in the Gospel of Thomas', in *Studia Evangelica*, III (Texte und Untersuchungen, 88; Berlin: Akademie Verlag, 1964), pp. 314-17.

Beare, F.W., *The Earliest Records of Jesus: A Companion to the Synopsis of the First Three Gospels by Albert Huck* (Oxford: Basil Blackwell, 1962).

Benson, L.D., 'The Literary Character of Anglo-Saxon Formulaic Poetry', *PMLA* 81 (1966), pp. 334-41.

Best, E., *Following Jesus: Discipleship in the Gospel of Mark* (JSNTSup, 4; Sheffield: JSOT Press, 1981).

—'Mark's Preservation of the Tradition', in *The Interpretation of Mark* (ed. W. Telford; Philadelphia: Fortress; London: SPCK, 1985), pp. 119-33.

—'Mark's Use of the Twelve', *ZNW* 69 (1978), pp. 11-35.

—*The Temptation and the Passion: The Marcan Soteriology* (SNTSMS, 2; Cambridge: Cambridge University Press, 1965).

Birkeland, H., *The Language of Jesus* (Oslo: Jacob Dybwad, 1954).

Black, M., *An Aramaic Approach to the Gospels and Acts* (Oxford: Clarendon Press, 1946).

Blaylock, J.P., *The Disappearing Dwarf* (New York: Ballantine Books, 1983).

Boas, F., 'Stylistic Aspects of Primitive Literature', *JAF* 38 (1925), pp. 329-39.

Boobyer, G.H., 'The Redaction of Mark iv.1-34', *NTS* 8 (1961–62), pp. 59-70.

Boomershine, T.E., 'Oral Tradition and Mark', (Unpublished manuscript, 1979).

Boring, M.E., 'Criteria of Authenticity: The Lucan Beatitudes as a Test Case', *Foundations & Facets Forum* 1.4 (December, 1985), pp. 3-38.

Bornkamm, G., *Jesus of Nazareth* (trans. I. and F. McLuskey with J.M. Robinson; New York: Harper & Row, 1960).

—*Paul* (trans. D.M.G. Stalker; New York: Harper & Row, 1971).

Bornkamm, G., G. Barth and H.J. Held, *Tradition and Interpretation in Matthew* (Philadelphia: Fortress Press, 1963).

Boucher, M.I., *The Mysterious Parable: A Literary Study* (CBQMS, 6; Washington, DC: Catholic Biblical Association, 1977).

Bowker, J.W., 'Mystery and Parable: Mark iv. 1-20', *JTS* 25 (1974), pp. 300-17.

Breech, J.E., *The Silence of Jesus: The Authentic Voice of the Historical Man* (Philadelphia: Fortress Press, 1983).

Brown, F., S.R. Driver and C.A. Briggs, *Hebrew and English Lexicon of the Old Testament* (Oxford: Clarendon Press, 1907).

Brown, S., '"The Secret of the Kingdom of God" (Mark 4.11)', *JBL* 92 (1973), pp. 60-74.

Buchan, D., *The Ballad and the Folk* (London: Routledge & Kegan Paul, 1972).

Bultmann, R., *History of the Synoptic Tradition* (trans. J. Marsh; New York: Harper & Row, 1963).

—*Jesus and the Word* (trans. L.P. Smith and E.H. Lantero; New York: Charles Scribner's Sons, 1934).

—'The Study of the Synoptic Gospels', in *Form Criticism: A New Method of New Testament Research* (ed. and trans. F.C. Grant; repr. New York: Harper, 1962 [New York: Willett, Clark & Company, 1934]), pp. 7-75.

Burkill, T.A., 'Concerning St Mark's Conception of Secrecy', *HibJ* 55 (1956–57), pp. 150-58.

—'The Cryptology of Parables in St Mark's Gospel', *NovT* 1 (1956), pp. 246-62.

—*Mysterious Revelation: An Examination of the Philosophy of St Mark's Gospel*, (Ithaca, NY: Cornell University Press, 1963).

—*New Light on the Earliest Gospel: Seven Markan Studies* (Ithaca, NY: Cornell University Press 1972).

Burney, C.F., *The Poetry of Our Lord: An Examination of the Formal Elements of Hebrew Poetry in the Discourses of Jesus Christ* (Oxford: Clarendon Press, 1925).

Cameron, R., 'Parable and Interpretation in the Gospel of Thomas', *Foundations and Facets Forum* 2.2 (1986), pp. 3-40.

Carlston, C.E., *The Parables of the Triple Tradition* (Philadelphia: Fortress Press, 1975).

Cave, C.H., 'The Parables and the Scriptures', *NTS* 11 (1964–65), pp. 374-87.

Cerfaux, L., 'Les paraboles du royaume dans l'évangile de Thomas', *Muséon* 70 (1957), pp. 307-27.

Charlesworth, J.H., (ed.), *The Old Testament Pseudepigrapha* (2 vols.; Garden City, NY: Doubleday, 1985).

Chilton, B., *A Galilean Rabbi and his Bible* (Wilmington, DE: Michael Glazier, 1984).

Collingwood, R.G., *An Autobiography* (Oxford: Oxford University Press, 1939).

Conzelmann, H., *1 Corinthians* (Hermeneia; trans. G.W. MacRae; Philadelphia: Fortress Press, 1975).

—*Jesus* (trans. J.R. Lord; Philadelphia: Fortress Press, 1973).

—*The Theology of St Luke* (trans. G. Buswell; New York: Harper & Row, 1961).

Cranfield, C.E.B., *The Gospel According to Saint Mark* (Cambridge: Cambridge University Press, 1959).

—'St Mark 4:1-34 Part I', *SJT* 4 (1951), pp. 398-414.

—'St Mark 4:1-34 Part II', *SJT* 5 (1952), pp. 49-66.

Crosby, R., 'Oral Delivery in the Middle Ages', *Speculum* 11 (1936), pp. 88-110.

Crossan, J.D., *Cliffs of Fall: Paradox and Polyvalence in the Parables of Jesus* (New York: Seabury, 1980).

—*The Dark Interval: Towards a Theology of Story* (Niles, IL: Argus Communications, 1975).

—*Finding is the First Act: Trove Folktales and Jesus' Treasure Parable* (Semeia Supplements, 9; Missoula, MT: Scholars Press; Philadelphia: Fortress Press, 1979).

—*In Fragments: The Aphorisms of Jesus* (San Francisco: Harper & Row, 1983).

—*In Parables: The Challenge of the Historical Jesus* (New York: Harper & Row, 1973).

—'The Seed Parables of Jesus', *JBL* 92 (1973), pp. 244-66.

Dahl, N., 'Parables of Growth', *ST* 5 (1951), pp. 132-66; reprinted in Dahl's *Jesus in the Memory of the Early Church* (Minneapolis: Augsburg-Fortress, 1976), pp. 141-66.

Danby, H., *The Mishnah* (Oxford: Clarendon Press, 1954).

Daube, D., 'Public Pronouncement and Private Explanation in the Gospels', *ExpTim* 57 (1945–46), pp. 175-77.

Davies, S., *The Gospel of Thomas and Christian Wisdom* (New York: Seabury, 1983).

Dawsey, J.M, 'Characteristics of Folk–Epic in Acts', *SBL Seminar Papers, 1989* (Atlanta: Scholars Press, 1989).

Dehandshutter, B., 'The Gospel of Thomas and the Synoptics: The Status Quaestionis', *Studia Evangelica*, VII (Texte und Untersuchungen, 162; Berlin: Akademie Verlag, 1982), pp. 157-60.

Delobel, J. (ed.), *Logia, les paroles de Jésus—The Sayings of Jesus* (BETL, 59; Leuven: Leuven University Press, 1982).

Dewey, J., 'The Literary Structure of the Controversy Stories in Mark 2.1–3.6', *JBL* 92 (1973), pp. 394-401; reprinted in *The Interpretation of Mark* (ed. W. Telford; Philadelphia: Fortress Press; London: SPCK, 1985), pp. 109-18,

—*Markan Public Debate: Literary Technique, Concentric Structure and Theology in Mark 2.1-3.6* (SBLDS, 48; Chico, CA: Scholars Press, 1980).

—'Oral Methods of Structuring Narrative in Mark', *Int* 43 (1989), pp. 32-44.

Dibelius, M., *From Tradition to Gospel* (trans. B.L. Woolf; New York: Charles Scribner's Sons, 1935).

—*Jesus* (trans. C.B. Hendrick and F.C. Grant; Philadelphia: Westminster, 1949).

Diels, H. (ed.), *Die Fragmente der Vorsokratiker*, II (ed. W. Kranz; Berlin: Weidmann, 9th edn, 1959).

Dodd, C.H., *The Parables of the Kingdom* (London: Collins, rev. edn, 1961 [1936]).

Donahue, J.R., *The Gospel in Parable: Metaphor, Narrative, and Theology in the Synoptic Gospels* (Philadelphia: Fortress Press, 1988).

—*The Theology and Setting of Discipleship in the Gospel of Mark* (Milwaukee, WI: Marquette University, 1983).

Dorson, R.M. (ed.), *Folklore and Folklife: An Introduction* (Chicago: University of Chicago, 1972).

Doty, W.G., *Letters in Primitive Christianity* (Guides to Biblical Scholarship; Philadelphia: Fortress Press, 1973).

Drury J., *The Parables in the Gospels: History and Allegory* (New York: Crossroad, 1985).

—'The Sower, the Vineyard, and the Place of Allegory in the Interpretation of Mark's Parables', *JTS* ns 24 (1973), pp. 367-79.

Dschulnigg, P., *Sprache, Redaktion und Intention des Markus-Evangeliums: Eigentümlichkeiten der Sprache des Markus-Evangeliums und ihre Bedeutung für die Redaktionskritik* (Stuttgarter Biblische Beiträge, 11; Stuttgart: KBW, 1984).

Dundes, A., *The Study of Folklore* (Englewood Cliffs, NJ.: Prentice-Hall, 1965).

Dupont, J., 'La transmission des paroles de Jésus sur la lampe et la mesure dans Marc 4,21-25 et dans la tradition Q', in *Logia: les paroles de Jésus—The Sayings of Jesus* (ed. J. Delobel; BETL, 59; Leuven: Leuven University Press, 1982), pp. 201-36.

Easton, B.S., *The Gospel Before the Gospels* (New York: Charles Scribner's Sons, 1928).

Eddings, D., *Magician's Gambit: Book Three of the Belgariad* (New York: Ballantine, 1983).

Edmonds, J.M. (trans.), *The Greek Bucolic Poets* (The Loeb Classical Library; Cambridge, MA: Harvard University Press, 1912).

Edwards, J.R., 'Markan Sandwiches: The Significance of Interpolations in Markan Narratives', *NovT* 31 (1989), pp. 193-216.

Edwards, R.A., *A Theology of Q: Eschatology, Prophecy, and Wisdom* (Philadelphia: Fortress Press, 1976).

Essame, W.G, 'καὶ ἔλεγεν in Mark iv. 21, 24, 26, 30', *ExpTim* 77 (1965–66), pp. 21.

Eusebius, *The History of the Church from Christ to Constantine* (trans. G.A. Williamson; Harmondsworth: Penguin Books, 1965).

Evans, C.A., 'On the Isaianic Background of the Sower Parable', *CBQ* 47 (1985), pp. 464-68.

—*To See and not Perceive: Isaiah 6.9-10 in Early Jewish and Christian Interpretation* (JSOTSup, 64; Sheffield: JSOT Press, 1989).

Farmer, W.R., *The Synoptic Problem: A Critical Analysis* (New York: Macmillan; London: Colier-Macmillan, 1964).

Fay, G., 'Introduction to Incomprehension: The Literary Structure of Mark 4.1-34', *CBQ* 51 (1989), pp. 65-81.

Feldman, A., *The Parables and Similes of the Rabbis: Agricultural and Pastoral* (Cambridge: Cambridge University Press, 1927).

Finnegan, R., *Oral Poetry: Its Nature, Significance and Social Context* (Cambridge: Cambridge University Press, 1977).

Fischel, H. (ed.), *Essays in Greco-Roman and Related Talmudic Literature* (New York: Ktav, 1977).

Fitzmyer, J., 'The Oxyrhynchus Logoi of Jesus and the Coptic Gospel According to Thomas', in *Essays on the Semitic Background of the New Testament* (SBS, 5; Missoula, MT: Scholars Press, 1974), pp. 355-433.

Fleddermann, H., 'The Mustard Seed and the Leaven in Q, the Synoptics, and Thomas' *SBL Seminar Papers, 1989* (ed. D.J. Lull; Atlanta: Scholars Press, 1989), pp. 216-36.

Fortna, R.T., *The Gospel of Signs: A Reconstruction of the Narrative Underlying The Fourth Gospel* (Cambridge: Cambridge University Press, 1970).

Frazer, J.G., *Folklore in the Old Testament* (London: Macmillan, 1918).

Friedrich, M., 'Tabellen zur markinischen Vorzugsvokabeln', in *Der Dreuzigungsbericht des Markusevangeluums: Mk 15, 20b-41* (ed. J. Schreiber; BZNW, 8; Berlin: de Gruyter, 1986).

Funk, R.W., *Jesus as Precursor* (Semeia Studies; Philadelphia: Fortress Press, 1975).

—*Language, Hermeneutic and the Word of God* (New York: Harper & Row, 1966).

—*Parables and Presence* (Philadelphia: Fortress Press, 1982).

Gaston, L., *Horae Synopticae Electronicae: Word Statistics of the Synoptic Gospels* (SBL Sources for Biblical Study, 3; Missoula, MT: Scholars Press, 1973).

Gealy, F.D., 'The Composition of Mark iv', *ExpTim* 48 (1936–37), pp. 40-43.

Gerhardsson, B., *Memory and Manuscript: Oral Tradition and Written Transmission in Rabbinic Judaism and Early Christianity* (trans. E.J. Sharpe; Lund: Gleerup, 1961).

—'The Parable of the Sower and its Interpretation', *NTS* 14 (1967–68), pp. 165-93.

Gnilka, J., *Das Evangium nach Markus* (EKK, 2.1-2; 2 vols.; Zurich: Benzinger Verlag; Neukirchen–Vluyn: Neukirchener Verlag, 1978–79).

—*Die Verstockung Israels* (Munich: Kösel, 1961).

Goehring, J.E. *et al.* (eds.), *Gnosticism and the Early Christian World: In Honor of James M. Robinson* (Sonoma, CA: Polebridge Press, 1990).

Goetchius, E. Van Ness, *The Language of the New Testament* (New York: Charles Scribner's Sons, 1965).

Gonda, J., *Stylistic Repetition in the Veda* (Amsterdam: Noord-hollandsche Uitgevers-Maatschappij, 1959).

Goodenough, E.R., 'The Perspective of Acts', in *Studies in Luke–Acts* (ed. L.E. Kech and J.L. Martyn; Nashville: Abingdon Press, 1966).

Goody, J., and I. Watts, 'The Consequences of Literacy', in *Literacy in Traditional Societies* (ed. J. Goody; Cambridge: Cambridge University Press, 1968).

Grant, M., *Jesus: An Historian's Review of the Gospels* (New York: Charles Scribner's Sons, 1977).

Grant, R., and D. Freedman, *The Secret Sayings of Jesus according to the Gospel of Thomas* (Garden City, NY: Doubleday, 1960).

Grasknou, D.M, *Preaching on the Parables* (Philadelphia: Fortress Press, 1972).

Gray, B., 'Repetition in Oral Literature', *JAF* 84 (1971), pp. 289-303.

Greenspoon, L., 'The Pronouncement Story in Philo and Josephus', *Semeia* 20 (1981), pp. 73-80.

Grobel, K., *The Gospel of Truth* (London: A. & C. Black, 1960).

Guenther, H.O., 'Greek: Home of Primitive Christianity', *TJT* 5 (1989), pp. 247-79.

Hadas, M., *Ancilla to Classical Reading* (New York: Columbia University Press, 1954).

Haenchen, E., *The Acts of the Apostles: A Commentary* (trans. B. Noble and G. Shinn; rev. R.McL. Wilson; Philadelphia: Westminster Press, 1971).

Hahn, F., 'Die Worte vom Lichte Lk 11,33-36', in *Orientierung an Jesus: Zur Theologie der Synoptiker, Für J. Schmid* (ed. P. Hoffmann; Freiburg: Herder, 1973), pp. 107-38.

Hainsworth, J.B., 'Structure and Content in Epic Formulae: The Question of the Unique Expression', *Classical Quarterly* ns 14 (1964), pp. 155-64.

Hargreaves, J., *A Guide to St Mark's Gospel* (London: SPCK, 1965).

Harries, L., *Swahili Poetry* (Oxford: Clarendon Press, 1962).

Harrington, W.J., *Key to the Parables* (New York: Paulist Press, 1964).

—*Parables Told by Jesus* (New York: Alba House, 1974).

Harris, W.V., *Ancient Literacy* (Cambridge, MA: Harvard University Press, 1989).

Harvey, V.A., *The Historian and the Believer: The Morality of Historical Knowledge and Christian Belief* (Philadelphia: Westminister Press, 1966).

Havelock, E.A., *Preface to Plato* (Cambridge, MA: Belknap Press, 1963).

Havener, I., *Q: The Sayings of Jesus* (Good News Studies, 19; Wilmington, DE: Michael Glazier, 1987).

Hawkin, D.J., 'The Incomprehension of the Disciples in the Marcan Redaction', *JBL* 91 (1972), pp. 491-500.

Hawkins, J.C., *Horae Synopticae: Contributions to the Study of the Synoptic Problem* (Oxford: Clarendon Press, 2nd edn, 1909).

Henaut, B.W., 'Anthropomorphism and Josephus: An Examination of *Against Apion and Jewish Antiquities* Book I', *JRC* 3 (1988), pp. 31-54.

— 'Empty Tomb or Empty Argument: A Failure of Nerve in Recent Studies of Mark 16?', *SR* 15 (1986), pp. 177-90.

—'Is Q but the Invention of Luke and Mark? Method and Argument in the Griesbach Hypothesis', *RST* 8.3 (Sept. 1988), pp. 15-32.

—'John 4:43-54 and the Ambivalent Narrator: A Response to Culpepper's *Anatomy of the Fourth Gospel*', *SR* 19 (1990), pp. 287-304.

—'Matthew 11.27: The Thunderbolt in Corinth?', *TJT* 3 (1987), pp. 282-300.

—Review of *Sociology and the Jesus Movement*, by Richard A. Horsley, *RST* 10.1 (Jan. 1990), pp. 59-61.

Hendrick, C.W., 'Kingdom Sayings and Parables of Jesus in *The Apocryphon of James*: Tradition and Redaction', *NTS* 29 (1983), pp. 1-24.

Henige, D., *Oral Historiography* (London: Longman, Green, 1982).

Herder, J.G., *Christliche Schriften* (Riga, 1797).

Hiskett, M., 'The "Song of Bagauda": A Hausa King List and Homily in Verse', *BSO(A)S* 27 (1964), pp. 540-67; 28 (1965), pp. 112-35; 363-85.

Horman, J., 'The Source of the Version of the Parable of the Sower in the Gospel of Thomas', *NovT* 21 (1979), pp. 326-43.

Horsley, R.A., *Sociology and the Jesus Movement* (New York: Crossroad, 1989).

Hunter, A.M., *Interpreting the Parables* (London: SCM Press; Philadelphia: Westminster Press, 1960).

Hurtado, L.W., *Mark: A Good News Commentary* (San Francisco: Harper & Row, 1983).

Innes, G., 'Stability and Change in Griots' Narrations', *ALS* 14 (1973), pp. 105-18.

—*Sunjata: Three Mandinka Versions* (London: School of Oriental and African Studies, 1974).

Jacobson, A.D., 'Proverbs and Social Control: A New Paradigm for Wisdom Studies', in *Gnosticism and the Early Christian World: In Honor of James M. Robinson* (ed. J.E. Goehring *et al.*; Sonoma, CA: Polebridge Press, 1990), pp. 75-88

—'Wisdom Christology in Q' (dissertation, Claremont Graduate School, 1978).

Jason, H., *The Narrative Structure of Swindler Tales* (Rand paper, Santa Monica, CA, 1968).

Jeremias, J., 'Die Lampe unter dem Scheffel', in *Abba* (Göttingen: Vandenhoeck & Ruprecht, 1966), pp. 99-102.

—*New Testament Theology*. I. *The Proclamation of Jesus* (trans. J. Bowden; London: SCM Press, 1971).

—'Palästinakundliches zum Gleichnis vom Säsemann, Mark IV.3-8 par', *NTS* 13 (1966–67), pp. 53.

—*The Parables of Jesus* (trans. S.H. Hooke; New York: Charles Scribner's Sons, 2nd rev. edn, 1972 [1954]).

Johnson, J.W., 'The Development of the Genre *Heello* in Modern Somali Poetry' (MPhil thesis, University of London, 1971).

Johnston, R.M., 'The Study of Rabbinic Parables: Some Preliminary Observations', in *SBL Seminar Papers* (Missoula, MT: Scholars Press, 1976), pp. 337-57.

Jones, G.V., *The Art and Truth of the Parables* (London: SPCK, 1964).

Jousse, M.S.J., *Etudes de psychologie linguistique: Le style oral rythmique et mnémotechnique che les verbo-moteurs* (Paris: Beauchesne, 1925).

—*Le Parlant, la parole et le souffle* (Paris: Gallimard, 1978).

Jülicher, A., *Die Gleichnisreden Jesu* (Leipzig: Mohr [Paul Siebeck], 2nd edn, 1910 [1888, 1899]).

Keck, L.E., and J.L. Martyn, *Studies in Luke–Acts* (Philadelphia: Fortress Press, 1966).

Kee, H.C., *Community of the New Age: Studies in Mark's Gospel* (Philadelphia: Westminster Press, 1977).

—*Good News to the Ends of the Earth* (London: SCM Press; Philadelphia: Trinity, 1990).

Kelber, W.H., 'From Aphorism to Sayings Gospel and from Parable to Narrative Gospel', *Foundations and Facets Forum* 1.1 (March 1985), pp. 23-29.

—*The Kingdom in Mark: A New Place and a New Time* (Philadelphia: Fortress Press, 1974).

—'Mark and Oral Tradition', *Semeia* 16 (1979), pp. 7-55.

—*The Oral and the Written Gospel: The Hermeneutics of Speaking and Writing in the Synoptic Tradition, Mark, Paul, and Q* (Philadelphia: Fortress Press, 1983).

—(ed.), *The Passion in Mark: Studies on Mark 14-16* (Philadelphia: Fortress Press, 1976).

Kilgallen, J.J., 'The Messianic Secret and Mark's Purpose', *BTB* 7 (1977), pp. 60-65.

Kingsbury, J.D., *The Parables of Jesus in Matthew 13* (Richmond, VA: John Knox, 1969; repr., St. Louis: Clayton; London: SPCK, 1977).

Kirkland, J.R, 'The Earliest Understanding of Jesus' Use of Parables: Mark IV 10-12 in Context', *NovT*, 19 (1977), pp. 1-21.

Kissinger, W.S., *The Parables of Jesus: A History of Interpretation and Bibliography* (Metuchen, NJ: Scarecrow Press and American Theological Library Association, 1979).

Kittle, G., *The Problems of Palestinian Judaism and Primitive Christianity* (1926).

Klauck, H.-J., *Allegorie und Allegorese in synoptischen Gleichnistexten* (NTAbh, 13; Münster: Aschendorff, 1978).

Kloppenborg, J.S., *The Formation of Q: Trajectories in Ancient Wisdom Collections: Studies in Antiquity and Christianity* (Philadelphia: Fortress Press, 1987).

318 *Oral Tradition and the Gospels: The Problem of Mark 4*

Malherbe, A.J., *The Cynic Epistles: A Study Edition* (SBLSBSD, 12; Atlanta: Scholars Press, 1977).

Maloney, E.C., *Semitic Interference in Marcan Syntax* (SBLDS, 51; Chico CA: Scholars Press, 1981).

Manson, T.W., *The Teaching of Jesus* (Cambridge: Cambridge University Press, 2nd edn, 1935).

Marcus, J., 'Mark 4:10-12 and Marcan Epistemology', *JBL* 103 (1984), pp. 557-74.

—*The Mystery of the Kingdom of God* (SBLDS, 90 Atlanta: Scholars Press, 1986).

Marshall, C.D., *Faith as a Theme in Mark's Narrative* (SNTSMS, 64; Cambridge: Cambridge University Press, 1989).

Martin, R., 'Semitic Tradition in Some Synoptic Accounts', *SBL Seminar Papers, 1987* (Atlanta: Scholars Press), pp. 295-335.

Marxsen, W., *Mark the Evangelist: Studies on the Redaction History of the Gospel* (trans. J. Boyece *et al.*; Nashville: Abingdon Press, 1969).

—'Redaktionsgeschichtliche Erklärung der sogenannten Parabeltheorie des Markus', *ZTK* 52 (1955), pp. 255-71.

Mascaró, J. (trans.), *The Dhammapada: The Path of Perfection* (Harmondsworth: Penguin Books, 1973).

McArthur, H., 'The Parable of the Mustard Seed', *CBQ* 33 (1971), pp. 198-210.

McKnight, E.V., *What is Form Criticism?* (Guides to Biblical Scholarship; Philadelphia: Fortress Press, 1969).

Mead, F.S. (ed.), *The Encyclopedia of Religious Quotations* (Old Tappan, NJ: Spire, 1965).

Meagher, J.C., *Clumsy Construction in Mark's Gospel: A Critique of Form- and Redaktionsgeschichte* (Lewiston, NY: Edwin Mellen, 1979).

Meyers, E., and J. Strange, *Archaeology, the Rabbis and Early Christianity* (Nashville: Abingdon Press; London: SCM Press, 1981).

Ménard, J., 'La datation des manuscrits', *Histoire et archéologie* 70 (1983), pp. 12-13.

—*L'évangile selon Thomas* (Nag Hammadi Studies, 5; Leiden: Brill, 1975).

Miller, W.J. (trans.), *Homer: the Odyssey* (New York: Simon & Schuster, 1969).

Minton, W.W., 'The Fallacy of the Structural Formula', *TAPA* 96 (1965), pp. 241-53.

Montefiore, C.G., *Rabbinic Literature and Gospel Teachings* (New York: Ktav, 1970).

Montefiore, C., and A. Loewe, *A Rabbinic Anthology* (London: Macmillan, 1938).

Montefiore, H., and H. Turner, *Thomas and the Evangelists* (Studies in Biblical Theology, 35; Naperville, IL: Allenson, 1962).

Moore, W.E., '"Outside" and "Inside": A Markan Motif', *ExpTim* 98 (1986–87), pp. 39-43.

Morgenthaler, R., *Statistik des neutestamentlichen Wortschatzes* (Zürich–Frankfurt: Gotthelf-Verlag, 1958).

Moule, C.F.D., 'Mark 4.1-20 Yet Once More', in *Neotestamentica et Semitica: Studies in Honour of Matthew Black* (ed. E.E. Ellis and M. Wilcox; Edinburgh: T. & T. Clark, 1969), pp. 95-113.

Murray, A.T. (trans.), *Homer, The Odyssey* (The Loeb Classical Library; Cambridge, MA: Harvard University Press, 1919).

Neirynck, F., *Duality in Mark: Contributions to the Study of the Markan Redaction* (BETL, 31; Leuven: Leuven University Press, 1972).

—'Hawkins's Additional Notes to His "Horae Synopticae"', *ETL* 46 (1970), pp. 78-111.

—'The Redactional Text of Mark', *ETL* 57 (1981), pp. 146-49

—'Words Characteristic of Mark: A New List', *ETL* 63 (1987), pp. 367-74.

Neusner, J., *Early Rabbinic Judaism* (SJLA, 13; Leiden: Brill, 1975).

—'The Formation of Rabbinic Judaism: Yabneh (Jamnia) from AD 70–100', *ANRW* II.19.2, pp. 3-42.

—*Judaism in the Beginning of Christianity* (Philadelphia: Fortress Press, 1984).

—'The Rabbinic Traditions About the Pharisees Before 70 AD: The Problem of Oral Tradition', *Kairos* 14 (1972), pp. 57-70.

—*Rabbinic Traditions about the Pharisees before 70* (3 vols.; Leiden: Brill, 1971).

Newman, B.M. Jr, *A Concise Greek–English Dictionary of the New Testament* (London: United Bible Societies, 1971).

Nineham, D.E., *The Gospel of St Mark* (Harmondsworth: Penguin Books, 1963).

Nordheim, E. von, 'Das Zitat des Paulus in 1 Kor 2:9 und seine Beziehung zum koptischen Testament Jakobs', *ZNW* 65 (1974), pp. 112-20.

Oesterley, W.O.E., *The Gospel Parables in the Light of their Jewish Background* (London: SPCK, 1938).

Olrik, A., 'Epic Laws of Folk Narrative', in *The Study of Folklore* (ed. A. Dundes; Englewood Cliffs, NJ: Prentice-Hall, 1965), pp. 129-41.

Ong, W.J., *Orality and Literacy: The Technologizing of the Word* (London: Methuen, 1982).

—*Interfaces of the Word: Studies in the Evolution of Consciousness and Culture* (Ithaca, NY: Cornell University Press, 1977).

—*The Presence of the Word: Some Prolegomena for Cultural and Religious History* (New Haven: Yale University Press, 1967).

O'Nolan, K., 'Homer and Irish Heroic Narrative', *Classical Quarterly* 19 (1969), pp. 1-19.

Opland, J., '"Scop" and "Imbongi"—Anglo-Saxon and Bantu Oral Poets', *ESA* 14 (1971), pp. 161-78.

Parry, M., *L'épithète traditionnelle dans Homère* (Paris: Société d'éditions Belles Lettres, 1928).

—'Studies in the Epic Technique of Oral Verse-Making, I: Homer and Homeric Style', *HSCP* 41 (1930), pp. 73-147.

—'Studies in the Epic Technique of Oral Verse-Making, II: The Homeric Language as the Language of Oral Poetry', *HSCP* 43 (1932), pp. 1-50.

Patten, P., 'The Form and Function of Parable in Select Apocalyptic Literature and their Significance for Parables in the Gospel of Mark', *NTS* 29 (1983), pp. 246-58.

Pavur, C.M., 'The Grain is Ripe: Parabolic Meaning in Mark 4.26-29', *BTB* 17 (1987), pp. 21-23.

Payne, P.B., 'The Order of Sowing and Ploughing in the Parable of the Sower', *NTS* 25 (1978–79), pp. 123-29.

Perkins, P., *Hearing the Parables of Jesus* (New York: Paulist Press, 1981).

Perrin, N., 'The Christology of Mark: A Study in Methodology', *JR* 51 (1971), pp. 173-87; reprinted in *The Interpretation of Mark* (ed. W. Telford; Philadelphia: Fortress Press; London: SPCK, 1985), pp. 95-108,

—*Jesus and the Language of the Kingdom: Symbol and Metaphor in New Testament Interpretation* (Philadelphia: Fortress Press, 1976).

Perrin, N., and D.C. Duling, *The New Testament: An Introduction* (New York: Harcourt Brace Jovanovich, 2nd edn 1982).

Pesch, R., *Das Markusevangelium* (HTKNT, 2; 2 vols.; Freiburg: Herder, 1976).

Polkow, D., 'Method and Criteria for Historical Jesus Research', *SBL Seminar Papers, 1987* (Atlanta: Scholars Press), pp. 287-355.

Porton, G.G., 'The Pronouncement Story in Tannaitic Literature: A Review of Bultmann's Theory', *Semeia* 20 (1981), pp. 81-99.

Pryke J., *Redactional Style in the Marcan Gospel: A Study of Syntax and Vocabulary as Guides to Redaction in Mark* (Cambridge: Cambridge University Press, 1978).

Räisänen, H., *The 'Messianic Secret' in Mark* (trans. C. Tuckett; Edinburgh: T. & T. Clark, 1990).

—*Die Parabeltheorie im Markusevangelium* (Schriften der Finnischen exegetischen Gesellschaft, 26; Helsinki: Lansi-Suomi, 1973).

Reddish, M.G. (ed.), *Apocalyptic Literature: A Reader* (Nashville: Abingdon Press, 1990).

Redlich, E.B., *Form Criticism: Its Value and Limitations* (New York: Charles Scribner's Sons, 1939).

Richardson, P., with D. Granskou (eds.), *Anti-Judaism in Early Christianity.* I. *Paul and the Gospels* (Studies in Christianity and Judaism, 2; Waterloo, Ont.: Wilfred Laurier Press, 1986).

Ricoeur, P., 'Biblical Hermeneutics', *Semeia* 4 (1975), pp. 27-148.

Riddle, D.W., 'Mark 4.1-34; The Evolution of a Gospel Source', *JBL* 56 (1937), pp. 77-90.

Riesenfeld, H., *The Gospel Tradition* (trans. E.M. Rowley and R.A. Kraft; Philadelphia: Fortress Press, 1970).

Rieu, E.V. (trans.), *Homer: The Iliad* (Harmondsworth: Penguin Books, 1950).

—(trans.), *Homer: The Odyssey* (Harmondsworth: Penguin Books, 1946).

Robinson, J.M, 'On Bridging the Gulf from Q to the Gospel of Thomas (or Vice Versa)', in *Nag Hammadi, Gnosticism, and Early Christianity* (ed. C.W. Hedrick and R. Hodgson, Jr; Peabody, MA: Hendrickson, 1986), pp. 127-75.

Roth, W.M., 'The Secret of the Kingdom', *The Christian Century* 100 (1983), pp. 179-82.

Russo, J.A., 'Is "Oral" or "Aural" Composition the Cause of Homer's Formulaic Style?', in *Oral Literature and the Formula* (ed. B.A. Stola and R.S. Shannon, III; Ann Arbor: Center for the Co-ordination of Ancient and Modern Studies, The University of Michigan, 1976), pp. 31-54.

Sabbe, M. (ed.), *L'évangile selon Marc* (BETL, 24; Leuven: Leuven University Press, 1971).

Safrai, S. (ed.), 'Oral Tora', in *The Literature of the Sages; First Part: Oral Tora, Halakha, Mishna, Tosefta, Talmud, External Tractates* (ed. S. Safrai; Assen: Van Gorcum; Philadelphia: Fortress Press, 1987).

St. John Thackeray, H., *Josephus: The Man and the Historian* (New York: Jewish Institute of Religion, 1929; repr. New York: Ktav, 1967).

Sanders, E.P., *Jesus and Judaism* (London: SCM Press, 1985).

—*The Tendencies of the Synoptic Problem* (SNTSMS, 9; Cambridge: Cambridge University Press, 1969).

Schmidt, K.L., *Der Rahmen der Geschichte Jesu: Literarkritische Untersuchungen zur Ältesten Jesusüberlieferung* (Berlin: Trowitzsch & Sohn, 1919).

Schmithals, W., *Das Evangelium nach Markus: Kapitel 1-9,1; Kapitel 9,2-16,18* (OTKNT, 2.1-2; 2 vols.; Gütersloh: Gerd Mohn; Würzburg: Echter Verlag, 1979).

Schnackenburg, R., *The Gospel According to St John*. I. *Introduction and Commentary on Chapters 1-4* (trans. K. Smyth; New York: Herder & Herder; London: Burns & Oates, 1968).

Schneider, G., 'Das Bildwort von der Lampe', *ZNW* 61 (1961), pp. 183-209.

Schoedel, W., 'Parables in the Gospel of Thomas: Oral Tradition or Gnostic Exegesis?', *Concordia Theological Monthly* 43 (1972), pp. 548-60.

Schrage, W., 'Evangelienzitate in den Oxrhynchus-Logien und im koptischen Thomas-Evangelium', in *Apophoreta: Festschrift für Ernst Haenchen zu seinem siebzigsten Geburtstag* (BZNW, 30; Berlin: Töpelmann, 1964), pp. 251-68.

—*Das Verhältnis des Thomas-Evangeliums zur synoptischen Tradition und zu den koptischen Evangelienübersetzungen: zugleich ein Betrag zur gnostischen Synoptikerdeutung* (BZNW, 29; Berlin: Alfred Töpelmann, 1964).

Schreiber, J. (ed.), *Der Dreuzigungsbericht des Markusevangeliums: Mk 15,20b-41* (BZNW, 8; Berlin: de Gruyter, 1986).

Schulz, S., 'Mark's Significance for the Theology of Early Christianity', in *The Interpretation of Mark* (ed. W. Telford; Philadelphia: Fortress Press; London: SPCK, 1985), pp. 158-66.

—*Q: Die Spruchquelle der Evangelisten* (Zurich: Theologischer Verlag, 1972).

Schürmann, H., *Lukasevangelium* (HTKNT, 3.1; Freiburg: Herder, 1969).

Schweizer, E., *The Good News According to Mark* (trans. D.H. Madvi; Richmond, VA: John Knox, 1970).

—'Zur Frage des Messiasgeheimnisses bei Markus', *ZNW* 56 (1965), pp. 1-8.

Scott, B.B., *Hear then the Parable: A Commentary on the Parables of Jesus* (Minneapolis: Fortress Press, 1989).

—*Jesus, Symbol-Maker for the Kingdom* (Philadelphia: Fortress Press, 1981).

Segal, A.F., *Two Powers in Heaven: Early Rabbinic Reports about Christianity and Gnosticism* (Leiden: Brill, 1979).

Segal, R.A. (ed.), *In Quest of the Hero: The Myth of the Birth of the Hero* (Princeton, NJ: Princeton University Press, 1990).

Sellew, P., 'Early Collection of Jesus' Words: The Development of Dominical Discourses' (ThD dissertation, Harvard Divinity School, 1986).

—'Oral and Written Sources in Mark 4.1-34', *NTS* 36 (1990), pp. 234-67.

Sider, J.W., 'The Meaning of *Parabole* in the Usage of the Synoptic Evangelists', *Bib* 62 (1981), pp. 453-70.

Sieber, J.H., 'A Redactional Analysis of the Synoptic Gospels with Regard to the Question of the Sources of the Gospel According to Thomas' (PhD dissertation, Claremont Graduate School, 1966).

Smith, M., 'A Comparison of Early Christian and Early Rabbinic Traditions', *JBL* 82 (1963), p. 169

Sparks, H.F.D. (ed.), *The Apocryphal Old Testament* (Oxford: Clarendon Press, 1984).

Spencer, B.J., 'Doctor shortage taking toll', *The Regina Leader Post* (Monday, December 19, 1988), p. A3.

Stein, R.H., 'The Proper Methodology for ascertaining a Marcan Redaktions-geschichte' (ThD dissertation, Princeton University, 1968).

Stern, D., 'The Rabbinic Parable: From Rhetoric to Poetics', in *SBL Seminar Papers, 1986* (Atlanta: Scholars Press; 1986), pp. 631-43.

—'Rhetoric and Midrash: The Case of Mashal,' *Prooftexts* 1 (1981), pp. 261-77.

Stock, B., *The Implications of Literacy: Written Language and Models of Interpretation in the Eleventh and Twelfth Centuries* (Princeton: Princeton University Press, 1983).

Streeter, B.H., *The Four Gospels: A Study of Origins* (London: Macmillan, 1924).

Sykes, J.B. (ed.), *The Concise Oxford Dictionary of Current English* (Oxford: Clarendon Press, 6th edn, 1964).

Synge, F.C., 'Intruded Middles', *ExpTim* 92 (1980–81), pp. 329-33.

Talbert, C.H., *Literary Patterns, Theological Themes, and the Genre of Luke–Acts* (SBLMS, 20; Missoula, MT: Scholars Press, 1974).

—'Oral and Independent or Literary and Interdependent? A Response to Albert B. Lord', in *The Relationships Among the Gospels: An Interdisciplinary Dialogue* (ed. W.O. Walker, Jr; San Antonio, TX: Trinity University Press, 1978), pp. 93-102.

—*What Is a Gospel? The Genre of the Canonical Gospels* (Philadelphia: Fortress Press, 1977).

Tannehill, R.C., 'The Disciples in Mark: The Function of a Narrative Role', in *The Interpretation of Mark* (ed. W. Telford; Philadelphia: Fortress Press; London: SPCK, 1985), pp. 134-57.

—*The Sword of his Mouth* (Semeia Studies, 1; Philadelphia: Fortress Press; Missoula, MT: Scholars Press, 1975).

Taylor, V., *The Gospel According to St Mark* (London: Macmillan, 2nd edn, 1966).

Telford, W. (ed.), *The Interpretation of Mark* (Philadelphia: Fortress Press; London: SPCK, 1985).

Theissen, G., *Sociology of Early Palestinian Christianity* (trans. J. Bowden; Philadelphia: Fortress Press, 1977).

Tolbert, M.A., *Perspectives on the Parables: An Approach to Multiple Interpretations* (Philadelphia: Fortress Press, 1979).

—*Sowing the Gospel: Mark's World in Literary-Historical Perspective* (Minneapolis: Fortress, 1989).

Tolkien, J.R.R., *The Fellowship of the Ring, Being the First Part of The Lord of the Rings* (London: Methuen, 2nd edn, 1966).

Trocmé, E., 'Why Parables? A Study of Mark IV', *BJRL* 59 (1976–77), pp. 458-71.

Tucker, G.M, *Form Criticism of the Old Testament* (Guides to Biblical Scholarship; Philadelphia: Fortress Press, 1971).

Turner, C.H., 'Marcan Usage: Notes, Critical and Exegetical, on the Second Gospel', *JTS* 25 (1923–24), pp. 378-86; 26 (1924–25), pp. 12-20; 145-56; 225-40; 337-46; 27 (1925–26), pp. 58-62; 28 (1926–27), pp. 9-30; 349-62; 29 (1927–28), pp. 275-89; 346-61.

Tyson, J.B., 'The Blindness of the Disciples in Mark', *JBL* 80 (1961), pp. 261-68.

—*The New Testament and Early Christianity* (New York: Macmillan, 1984).

—'Sequential Parallelism in the Synoptic Gospels', *NTS* 22 (1976), pp. 276-308.

Vaage, L.E, 'Q^1 and the Historical Jesus: Some Peculiar Sayings (7.33-34; 9.57-58, 59-60; 14.26-27)', *Foundations and Facets Forum* 5.2 (June 1989), pp. 159-76.

Vansina, J., *Oral Tradition as History* (Madison, WI: University of Wisconsin, 1985).

Vermes, G., *The Dead Sea Scrolls in English* (Baltimore: Penguin Books, 2nd edn, 1975).

—*Jesus and the World of Judaism* (Philadelphia: Fortress Press, 1984).

—*Jesus the Jew: A Historian's Reading of the Gospels* (Philadelphia: Fortress Press; London: William Collins, 1973).

Via, D.O. Jr, 'Editor's Foreword', in *What is Redaction Criticism?* (ed. N. Perrin; Philadelphia: Fortress Press, 1969), pp. v-viii.

—*The Parables: Their Literary and Existential Dimension* (Philadelphia: Fortress Press, 1967).

Wanke, J., 'Kommentarworte, Älteste Kommentierung von Herrenworten', *BZ* ns 24 (1980), pp. 208-33.

Weeden, T.J. Sr, *Mark—Traditions in Conflict* (Philadelphia: Fortress Press, 1971).

—'Recovering the Parabolic Intent in the Parable of the Sower', *JAAR* 47 (1979), pp. 97-120.

Weiss, B., *The Life of Christ* (trans. J.W. Hope; Edinburgh: T. & T. Clark, 1883).

Whallon, W., *Formula, Character, and Context: Studies in Homeric, Old English, and Old Testament Poetry* (Cambridge, MA: Harvard University Press, 1969).

White, K.D., 'The Parable of the Sower', *JTS* ns 15 (1964), pp. 300-07.

Wilder, A., *Jesus' Parables and the War of Myths: Essays on Imagination in the Scriptures* (Philadelphia: Fortress Press, 1982).

Wiles, M.F., 'Early Exegesis of the Parables', *SJT* 11 (1958), pp. 287-301.

Wilkens, W., 'Zur Frage der literarischen Beziehung Zwischen Matthäus und Lukas', *NovT* 8 (1966), pp. 48-57.

Williams, J.G., *Gospel Against Parable: Mark's Language of Mystery* (Sheffield: Almond Press, 1985).

Williamson, L. Jr, *Mark, Interpretation: A Bible Commentary for Teaching and Preaching* (Atlanta: John Knox, 1983).

Wilson, S.G. (ed.); *Anti-Judaism in Early Christianity. II. Separation and Polemic* (Studies in Christianity and Judaism, 2; Waterloo, Ont.: Wilfrid Laurier Press, 1986).

Wrede, W., *The Messianic Secret* (trans. J.C.G. Grieg; London: James Clarke, 1972 [1901]).

Zeitlin, I., *Jesus and the Judaism of his Time* (New York: Polity Press, 1988).

Zerwick, M., *Untersuchungen zum Markus-Sil: Ein Beitrag zur stilistischen Durcharbeitung des Neuen Testaments* (Rome: Pontifical Biblical Institute, 1937).

INDEXES

INDEX OF REFERENCES

OLD TESTAMENT

NEW TESTAMENT

POST-BIBLICAL JEWISH WRITINGS

INDEX OF AUTHORS